The Politics of Inclusive Pluralism

The Politics of Inclusive Pluralism

*A Proposed Foundation for Religious Freedom
in a Post-Communist, Democratic China*

Bob Fu

FOREWORD BY
Tom Farr

☙PICKWICK *Publications* · Eugene, Oregon

THE POLITICS OF INCLUSIVE PLURALISM
A Proposed Foundation for Religious Freedom in a Post-Communist,
Democratic China

Pickwick Publications
An Imprint of Wipf and Stock Publishers
199 W. 8th Ave., Suite 3
Eugene, OR 97401

www.wipfandstock.com

PAPERBACK ISBN: 978-1-7252-6753-4
HARDCOVER ISBN: 978-1-7252-6751-0
EBOOK ISBN: 978-1-7252-6754-1

Cataloguing-in-Publication data:

Names: Fu, Bob, author. | Farr, Tom, foreword.

Title: The politics of inclusive pluralism : a proposed foundation for religious
freedom in a post-communist, democratic China / by Bob Fu ; foreword by
Tom Farr.

Description: Eugene, OR: Pickwick Publications, 2021 | Includes bibliographical
references.

Identifiers: ISBN 978-1-7252-6753-4 (paperback) | ISBN 978-1-7252-6751-0
(hardcover) | ISBN 978-1-7252-6754-1 (ebook)

Subjects: LCSH: Religion and politics | Religious pluralism—China | China—
Politics and government | China—History | Christianity and culture—China

Classification: BL1803 F8 2021 (print) | BL1803 (ebook)

My heart fills with love and gratitude
as I dedicate this book to:

Heidi, my wife, and our three children,
Daniel, Tracy, and Melissa.

Everyone has the right to freedom of thought, conscience and religion;
this right includes freedom to change his religion or belief, and freedom,
either alone or in community with others and in public or private,
to manifest his religion or belief in teaching, practice, worship and observance.

～Article 18 of The Universal Declaration
of Human Rights

Contents

Figures

Tables

Foreword

DR. THOMAS F. FARR

"Long live the red terror!"

"Strike the enemy down on the floor and step on him with a foot."

"Those who are against Chairman Mao will have their dog skulls smashed into pieces."[1] These and other political slogans which China's communist rulers used as leverage for conflict and conflict management during 1949 China's Cultural Revolution movement fueled anger, fear and terror among Chinese citizens.

Even though the Cultural Revolution failed, China, a perennial source of human rights violations, continues to include anger, fear and terror in systematic assaults on the dignity of its own citizens. The Great Leap Forward (1958–62) and the Cultural Revolution under Mao Zedong (1966–76) have assumed a rightful place high in the catalogue of human barbarism, their depredations designed to impose the will of the communist state by torture, starvation, and murder. The destruction of those Chinese religions perceived as a threat ranked high among its goals Under the most brutal circumstances imaginable, China's communist officials killed or maimed tens of millions of Chinese citizens.

---

1. Shaorong Huang, "The power of Words: Political Slogans as Leverage in Conflict and Conflict Management during China's Cultural Revolution Movement," in Guo-Ming Chen and Ringo Ma (eds.), *Chinese Conflict Management and Resolution* (Westport, CT: Greenwood, 2001), 182.

During following decades, China's communist rulers have sought to adapt its lessons to the realities of modernity. One critical lesson evolved that still stands, no one—neither the state nor any other human agency—can kill the religious impulse built into the DNA of humankind.

Mao, like all totalitarians of the 20th century, sought to eliminate religion because by its nature it limits the power of the state by positing an authority greater than the state. His successors have fully understood that threat, but, recognizing religion's staying power, they have experimented with more realistic ways of suppressing and controlling it. China's current president, Xi Jinping, has decided to consolidate the lessons from those decades of experiment into a more sophisticated policy of religious repression so draconian that some have dubbed the endeavor as "a Second Cultural Revolution."

Bob Fu, a son of China born in the throes of the Cultural Revolution to parents devastated by the Great Leap Forward, experienced first-hand the savagery of Mao's policies. He has recounted his early life in a 2013 book, *God's Double Agent: The True Story of a Chinese Christian's Fight for Freedom.* Xiqiu, Bob's non-religious mother, gave the name, 傅希秋; pinyin: Fù Xīqiū, to Bob." Notwithstanding her suffering, Xiqiu, which means "Hopeful Autumn, name serves as the key to Bob's book.

I have known Bob for more than 20 years. During those two decades, he has become the preeminent Chinese American advocate for persecuted Christians and other religious minorities in China. He has in countless venues around the world urged the United States and other nations to work for freedom in China. But, like other distinguished sons of liberty, he has yearned to explain to those who rule the country of his birth how freedom can benefit them.

The result is *Baorong Duoyuan,* the product of a decade's scholarly immersion in Chinese history, culture, and politics. In English, the phrase means "inclusive pluralism," the book's proposed constitutional framework for a China whose own demographic projections show a dramatic increase in its religious population, especially, but not only, its Christians.

Bob's careful diagnosis of the ways religious freedom might evolve in China will challenge readers who believe that "realism" requires us to set aside the Western experience in thinking about the orient, especially in matters concerning the relationship between religion and state. His explorations of Kuyper and Rawls, however, lead him to a church-State model that, he believes, the Chinese can and should adopt.

Given the book's author, Chinese authorities will certainly read it. As his moderate tone and beguiling conviction enhance his balanced argument, one critical lesson continues to command attention: no entity—neither the

State nor any other human agency—can kill the religious impulse built into the DNA of humankind. One can only hope—indeed one must hope—that Chinese authorities will see this book as Bob intended, a scholarly *cri de Coeur*, from a son of China. Despite China's flaws, Bob loves the nation of his birth and hopes that *Baorong Duoyuan,* a labor of love, will contribute to the demise of the anger, fear and terror that the reign of "the red terror" fuels and help usher in religious freedom for all Chinese citizens.

Preface

Listen . . .

"The Chinese Communist Party (CCP) must hear the cries of its own people for religious freedom and act to correct its wrongs," Sam Brownback, United States (US) ambassador for religious freedom, stressed, calling to end religious persecution of its citizens. The CCP not only actually imprisons thousands of Chinese citizens who practice their religious beliefs, in a sense it "imprisons" all religions in China as it routinely subjects registered religions to exploitive measures and threats of annihilation. The Chinese Constitution carefully codifies the right of public officials to sternly monitor registered as well as unregistered groups to prevent events that reportedly disturb public order, harm the health of citizens or adversely affect the State's educational system. In addition, constitutional government surveillance frequently targets peaceful religious activities protected by international law.

By nature, the CCP refuses to permit the perception of an individual, group or institution as independent of the party's complete control. Even as China undergoes a religious revival, Believers, under the rule of President Xi Jinping, China's most powerful leader since Mao Zedong, experience a dramatic shrinking of their freedoms. Both activists and experts note that although the CCP wrote religious freedom into the Chinese Constitution in 1982, Xi fortifies his power to wage a severe systematic suppression of Christianity and other religions in the country.[1]

1. "China Clamps Down on Religious Freedom," *Daily Herald (Arlington Heights, IL)*, August 8, 2018, http://www.questia.com/read/1G1-550212110/china-clamps-down-on-religious-freedom.

Xi envisions the control of the CCP to encompass every aspect of the lives of Chinese citizens; from poor farmers to white collar workers; from students to soldiers. The party predicts that it will embed its atheistic philosophy in each facet of Chinese society. Nevertheless, because it has not derived public trust and recognition democratically, to legitimize and maintain its authority, the regime must continuously resort to using repressive instruments and tools of propaganda. For religious freedom to truly exist in China, its political system must shift toward more democratic reforms.

Contrary to the Chinese Communist Party's authoritarian rule in China, *Baorong Duoyuan*, the amenable theory I developed, encapsulates the potential to facilitate religious freedom in China's future. *Baorong Duoyuan*, which in English translates as "inclusive pluralism," correlates with the theme of letting each religion (or school of thought) not only resonate or speak freely in the public square, but likewise permits adherents to freely practice their religious beliefs. *Baorong Duoyuan*, also harmonizes with the Golden Rule. Versions of this maxim to treat others as one desires to be treated can be found in all major contemporary cultures and worldviews.

The time I invested developing *Baorong Duoyuan* led me to recount critical life challenges and numerous soul-searing struggles I experienced during my childhood, youth, and early adulthood prior to my life in the United States (US). Ultimately, this time transformed me from a compassionate, biased activist, ready to take a stance of "us [Christians] against them [political liberals and CCP officials]" to an even more passionate, compassionate, objective brother in the faith of Jesus Christ. Now, I prayerfully seek to offer hope and help to those persecuted for their faith, furthering the quest of religious freedom for all.

My quest to further the reality of religious freedom for all began years ago, when, as a student attending Westminster Theological Seminary, I helped organize a retreat for numerous, prominent political dissidents. The conference, 'Christianity and the Future of China', focused on the concept of the Christian faith and explored the potential role of Christianity for the democratization of the anticipated new China. During the conference, the CCP arrested 58 leaders and sentenced five of the top leaders within the South China Church to death. Those of us attending the conference joined in prayer for these imprisoned, persecuted believers and explored how we might help them.

Later, however, I and others at the conference discovered that the circumstances were more complicated than we initially thought. We had originally considered this case to be another example of the State persecuting the Christian church due to its animosity toward unregistered religious groups. Then, we discovered that the founder of the South China

Church, Gong Shengliang, had been engaging in numerous extramarital sexual relationships with other believers in his church network. Although we could not confirm the CCP rape charges against Gong, we realized that the State had a legitimate concern for their investigation. This revelation forced me to rethink the State–religion relationship in China. Prior to this time, I had envisaged aspects of this connection as 100 percent black and white, with the State totally at fault when targeting believers for their religious beliefs and legitimate practices. Now, I had to reconsider problems relating to both sides of the issue.

Ultimately, the CCP freed most of the jailed South China Church leaders after they had served their prison sentences. This experience prompted me to launch China Aid, a ministry with the mission to expose religious persecution, to encourage those brothers and sisters in the faith of Jesus Christ, particularly those the State persecutes, and to equip leaders to help strengthen the persecuted church in China. The more involved I became in the work of China Aid and the more I learned of the ongoing, inhumane torture the CCP inflicted on the South China Church, the more concerned I became. Even though, I knew that torture regularly occurred, I did not realize the magnitude of the cruelty the church suffered—that the cruelty extended beyond my imagination.

As I regard myself as part of "the Church,"[2] I began to prayerfully and physically dedicate myself to helping persecuted believers, preachers, and their families in China. In 2002, China Aid helped overturn the death sentences of the five South China Church leaders. My work with China Aid encouraged me to explore the potential for a healthier, biblical model for the State–religion relationship. Research I conducted at Boston University Library helped me recognize that a myriad of complex legal, theoretical, and other components contributes to the State–religion relationship. This revelation led me to expand my concentration beyond the purely theological form.

Due to being diagnosed with kidney cancer and undergoing treatments necessary for my recovery. I took a medical sabbatical until my cancer went into remission. Under the direction of Dr. Robert Song, I completed this study and in 2018 I obtained my PhD. Today, I continue to work to contribute to the development of a better State–religion relationship in China that will hopefully help ensure religious freedom for all.

Baorong Duoyuan, the theory which evolved from my study, proves culturally compatible as well as mutually beneficial to Chinese government officials, Chinese Christians and those who choose to practice or

2. The "Body of Christ."

refrain from practicing diverse religions. It also reflects my heart for China, that the country of my birth will listen to . . . will hear the cries of its people; stop the CCP's reign of persecution, and procure, permit and practice—religious freedom for all its citizens.

Acknowledgments

Thank you:

PICKWICK Publications and Dr. Robin Parry, editor managing this book project. This opportunity to present *Baorong Duoyuan*, my theory for religious freedom for all, to a myriad of readers throughout the world strengthens my hope for the realization of that freedom in China.

Shelah Sandefur, my sister in Christ, who not only helped me with the original editing, but continues to encourage me to persevere in sharing my hope for China. With English as my second and her only language, the process sometimes tested each of us. Nevertheless, the result: *Baorong Duoyuan* proved worth the challenge.

Others I thank God for and say "Thank you" to include those who support China Aid, who have committed to helping our persecuted Chinese brothers and sisters. As I remember each of the precious people who have encouraged me, I am thankful for God's provisions and for permitting me to be part of their lives.

God, our Heavenly Father, most of all. Without His work in my life, my work would have no life.

Abbreviations

BD	*Baorong Duoyuan*
CCP	Chinese Communist Party
DRR	Doctrine of religious restraint
DNA	Deoxyribonucleic Acid
ECHR	European Convention on Human Rights
IRFA	International Religious Freedom Act
PRC	People's Republic of China
PL	Political Liberalism
PP	Principled Pluralism
PRSR	Principle of religious self-restraint
RE	Religious Education
RF	Religious Freedom
UK	United Kingdom
UN	United Nations
US	United States
USCIRF	*U.S. Commission on International Religious Freedom*

Chapter 1

Introduction

In a globalizing world, linked in so many ways
by economic, political, and security concerns,
it is important to recognize the local impact of the global and
the global impact of the local.[1]

∼ K. S. NATHAN

"Help [. . .]. Help? Help!"

ON 14 APRIL 2016 in the Chinese jurisdiction of Guanjin sub-district, Zhumadian City, Henan Province, Pastor Li Jiangong repeatedly shouted, "Help!" as he frantically dug in the dirt to free his wife, Ding Cuimei, from beneath a massive mound of freshly bulldozed soil where he and Cuimei had been buried alive.[2] On this particularly dark day when Jiangong attempted to save Cuimei, the dozer operator ignored the couple's cries for help as he continued demolishing Beitou Church, the house church Jiangong pastored. Others ran to help Pastor Jiangong free Cuimei, but by the time they uncovered her, she had stopped breathing. As calling for police protection would have proved futile, none of those present phoned local authorities for help.

Earlier that morning, when Pastor Jiangong and Cuimei had tried to stop the demolition of Beitou Church, a man supervising the demolition

1. Nathan, *Religious Pluralism*, 204.
2. Lodge, "Church Wins."

1

crew abruptly shouted out, "Bury them alive for me! I am responsible for their deaths."[3] Initially, following Cuimei's death by suffocation after being buried alive, the local government did not respond. Authorities did not begin investigating Cuimei's tragic death until after critical, international outcries and pressure.

Several sources confirm that CCP authorities reportedly ordered that the church be demolished. Li Jiangong, in charge of the church, and his wife, Ding Cuimei, refused to turn the church grounds over to a local developer. This incident seriously violates the rights to life, religious freedom, and rule of law. Chinese authorities should hold those murderers accountable and take concrete measures to protect the religious freedom of these house church's members. Bulldozing and burying Ding Cuimei, a peaceful and devout Christian woman, alive was a cruel, murderous act. This and other horrific examples of the unbalanced State–religion relationship in China reflect the failure of the State to protect the religious freedom of its citizens.

CCP authorities have heavily targeted Christians in China through-out the past few years due to their rapidly increasing numbers. Although Chinese officials claim that church demolitions and the forced removal of church rooftop crosses relate to building code violations, human rights activists and other Christian leaders perceive these acts as clear persecu-tion against religious groups.

Contrary to the positive façade that China projects regarding human rights under the control of the CCP, a much darker reality reveals a brutal authoritarian State with no concern for religious freedom.[4] China's blatant disregard for religious freedom fueled the critical, hypothetical question launching my study: What guiding philosophy could best help procure, provide, and protect religious freedom for all in a post-communist, Chris-tianized, democratic China? Researching to find "the" answer/answers for this question coupled with concerns for religious freedom in China founded this study which led to developing my theory, *Baorong Duoyuan*.

Baorong Duoyuan asserts:[5]

> If Chinese citizens consent to protect religious freedom, then
> *Baorong Duoyuan*, a contextualization of principled pluralism,
> which closely aligns with international norms under a liberal

---

3. Nong, "Church leader's," para. 3.

4. Peerenboom, *China Modernizes*.

5. Political liberalism, based on a secular worldview, is not adequately inclusive while principled pluralism, albeit with Judeo-Christian orientation and minor favorit-ism toward Christianity, is perceived less pluralistic. In a post-communist democratic China, *Baorong Duoyan*, later further defined and developed, will prove sufficiently pluralistic and inclusive to protect religious freedom for all.

constitutional framework, offers the most reasonable, consistent, and coherent guiding theory to help ensure that consensus.

Since 2013, the CCP has removed approximately 1,700 crosses from Catholic and Protestant churches in Zhejiang Province.[6] The *World Watch Monitor* reports that in Zhejiang Province (known as the "Jerusalem of the East" for its strong Christian presence) the Chinese government formulates reasons to claim churches are illegal constructions and, therefore, demolishes them.[7] The demolition campaign continues as the CCP regularly imprisons pastors and human rights lawyers in this area for reasons that conflict with international guidelines for freedom, particularly religious freedom. Activists claim that the CCP has targeted Zhejiang Province for religious persecution and that anti-Christian measures may soon increase in other provinces.

In China, as the CCP officials misapply the unsound policy regarding religious freedom, the relationship between the CCP and organized religion continues to prove challenging to religious freedom for all. Eleanor Albert reports that in 2014, contrary to a number of pro-government voices proposing that the CCP demonstrate more tolerance of Christian groups, a spike occurred "in state repression against house churches and state-sanctioned Christian organizations alike, including a campaign to remove hundreds of rooftop crosses from churches."[8] In July 2014, Chinese officials sentenced Zhang Shaojie, a prominent Christian pastor, to twelve years in prison for "gathering crowds to disturb public order. The 2014 annual report from China Aid, a Texas-based Christian nonprofit organization (NGO), said that religious persecution, primarily against Christians, was on the rise."[9] This account confirmed 572 cases of religious persecution, with more than 2,994 people detained, and an additional 1,274 Chinese citizens sentenced in relation to charges connected with their demonstrations of their religious beliefs.

In another example of religious persecution and China's unbalanced State–religion relationship, Pastor Yang Hua, founder of Yang's Huoshi Church in Guiyang, China, has been imprisoned by the CCP since December 2015 for resisting State attempts to seize church property. According to Joyce Huang, in October 2015, government authorities issued fraudulent notices claiming that the buildings Huoshi Church owned had not been

6. Lee, "Pastor of China's."

7. *World Watch Monitor,* "China: Woman Buried."

8. Albert, "Christianity in China."

9. Albert, "Christianity in China."

officially sanctioned for church use.[10] Subsequently, the State imposed fines of 12,960 Yuan (US $2,030) per day. On 9 December 2015, when Pastor Yang attempted to stop officials from destroying a hard drive belonging to the church, officials arrested him. Later, CCP officials charged Pastor Yang with illegally holding State secrets.

Pastor Yang represents one of the latest cases among more than 19,426 of Chinese Christians being detained for their faith and opposing the Chinese government's religious oppression. To restrict religious practices, the Chinese government frequently fabricates charges (including "divulging State secrets") against pastors who publicly oppose government attempts to restrict their activities.[11] The 2016 *Annual Report of the U.S. Commission on International Religious Freedom* confirms an increasingly alarming surge in the ongoing, methodical, and egregious abuses of Chinese citizens by the CCP.

The following two figures depict data analyses of instances of persecution during 2014 in China by region and province.[12] Figure 1 portrays religious persecution and severe abuse cases in China by region.

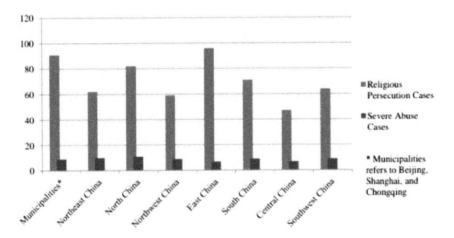

Religious Persecution and Severe Abuse Cases by Region

10. Huang, "Church Crackdown."

11. Huang, "Church Crackdown."

12. China Aid, *2014 Annual Report.*

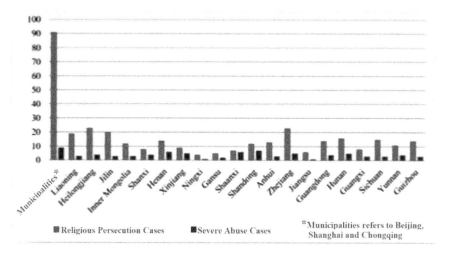

Religious Persecution and Severe Abuse Cases by Province

Figure 2 reflects religious persecution and severe abuse cases in China by province while

Table 1 reports persecution that occurred in China during 2015 and 2016 in six categories.

Table 1: Comparison of Persecution during 2015 and 2016 by Categories[13]

Year	2015	2016
Number of persecution cases	634	762
Number detained	> 19,426 (church leaders > 1,728)	> 48,100 (church leaders > 1,800)
Number arrested	> 3,178 (church leaders > 521)	> 3,526 (church leaders > 600)
Number sentenced	232	303
Number of abuse cases	195	278
Number of people abused	463	785

As Table 1 reveals, China Aid notes that the 762 documented persecution cases in 2016 indicate an 11 percent increase in the number of individuals arrested during the previous year. This number includes more than 600

13. China Aid, *2016 Annual Report*.

church leaders, a 15.2 percent increase from 2015. The 303 individuals who received prison terms in 2016 represent a 30 percent increase from 2015. During 2016, 278 abuse cases, which included physical, verbal, mental abuse, and torture, depict a 42.6 percent increase from 2015. The 785 individuals abused constitute a 69.5 percent increase from 2015.

The 2016 *Annual Report of the U.S. Commission on International Religious Freedom* (USCIRF) confirms an increasingly alarming surge in the ongoing, systematic, and egregious abuses of religious freedom (RF) of Chinese citizens by the CCP. USCIRF has recommended that China be designated a "country of particular concern" under the International Religious Freedom Act (IRFA). The CCP's current campaigns reflect "unprecedented violations against Uighur Muslims, Tibetan Buddhists, Catholics, Protestants, and Falun Gong practitioners. People of faith continue to face arrests, fines, denials of justice, [and] lengthy prison sentences."[14] Julia A. Seymour reports that the CCP interferes with religious affairs in the name of "the rule of law."[15] According to Seymour, "Chinese officials are defending their human rights record and lashing out at a US commission that accused the country's communist government of continuing to commit 'severe religious freedom violations.'"[16] Nevertheless, the CCP maintains dictatorial monopoly of power over almost all aspects of Chinese citizens' lives, including their religious freedom.[17]

Contrary to the CCP's current campaigns to stifle religious freedom, the Constitution of the People's Republic of China (PRC)[18] decrees freedom of religious belief for its citizens.[19] The State[20] claims to defend normal religious activities and affirms that there may not be any discrimination against citizens because of their religious beliefs or affiliations. Article 36 specifically states: "No state organ, public organization or individual may compel citizens to believe in, or not believe in, any religion; nor may they discriminate against citizens who believe in, or do not believe in, any religion."[21] Historical and contemporary accounts, however, challenge China's claims

---

14. USCIRF, "*Annual Report 2015.*"

15. Seymour, "China Denies."

16. Seymour, "China Denies," para. 1.

17. USCIRF, "*Annual Report 2015.*"

18. *Constitution of the People's Republic*, Article 36.

19. Lum and Fischer, *Human Rights in China.*

20. References to the word "State" indicate any form of political governmental authority to which an individual or group may be subject.

21. *The Constitution*, Religious Freedom section.

and confirm that the State's stance appears convoluted regarding People's Republic of China human rights legislation.[22]

In the light of growing concerns regarding China's human rights' practices, especially in the areas of religious freedom, I investigated the potential for a contextualized model of principled pluralism to help foster and maintain religious freedom for all in China.

In recent years, as the CCP continues to carry out an extensive crackdown on all religious institutions, Xi ordered all religions to "sinicize" to forcibly secure loyalty to the officially atheistic party. Sinicize means to make or remake something so that it and/or its character become Chinese.[23] The efforts include removing crosses from churches and bulldozing large numbers of churches and mosques, excluding Tibetan children from Buddhist religious studies, and imprisoning more than a million Islamic ethnic minorities in reported "re-education centers."[24]

News reports in 2019 reveal that due to Muslim's practice of Islam, CCP authorities arrested and imprisoned from approximately one to three million Muslims in internment camps (re-education), also perceived as concentration camp in China's Xinjiang region. In efforts to ensure Uighur and other Muslim groups adapt their culture to traditional Chinese, CCP authorities order them to disregard their religious principles. For example, officials order them to eat pork and/or drink alcoholic beverages.

To include individuals in a surveillance database, China offers "free health checks" and uses the data to obtain deoxyribonucleic acid (DNA), fingerprints, and photos. Although China has not established camps for Christians, authorities regularly harass members of church congregations. Officials also routinely close or demolish churches, and in some areas, regulations bar children under eighteen from attending services. In 2018, research, which China Aid secured, reveals that the CCP detained Christians approximately 100,000 times.

Xi's intensified religious persecution affects religious groups other than the Uighur Muslims. CCP authorities routinely destroy houses of worship and increasingly bulldoze churches, mosques as well as Tibetan Buddhist schools and temples. Officials have begun escalating their Internet monitoring, particularly that with religious references. The CCP closely monitors and controls contributions to religious groups. They have outlawed public proselytism and unjustly imprison pastors, priests, nuns, monks, and religious lay persons.

22. Lum and Fischer, *Human Rights in China.*

23. China Passes Law.

24. Yun, "Christian family details."

In addition to Uighur and other Muslims being enslaved and forced to perform labor, individuals of other faiths lose their freedom because of their beliefs. The CCP also forces them to manually produce products under intolerable circumstances. One Christian described the time he spent in a Chinese prison as "hell on Earth." In 1957, the Chinese regime instituted re-education through labor camps, known as *laojiao*. Authorities generally used these to control protesters, followers of banned religions, and real or alleged "counter-revolutionaries." Although China officially abolished these "camps" in 2013, the government initiated a revival of forced labor practices in China, reaping profits from the prisoners.

As they struggle to survive the deplorable prison living conditions, religious prisoners frequently eat vegetable-leaf soup, seasoned with floating insects. Due to malnutrition, they habitually experience dizziness as they force their weakened bodies to work. When sick and/or physically exhausted prisoners fail to complete their quotas or work, prison guards use torture to ensure they complete their tasks.

At times, prison authorities employ brutal prisoners to control other inmates. When a prisoner fails to complete the assigned task, one of the prison bullies often beat them. Sometimes, prison guards tie prisoners' hands and feet to an iron fence when they cannot complete their tasks. Often, authorities force prisoners to continually stand except during meals. No matter the season, prisoners being disciplined are not permitted to sleep as they remain tied up for three or four days.

Guards routinely subject prisoners to abuse and severe beatings which result in death or crippling for many. After his arrest, one member of The Church of Almighty God (CAG), imprisoned seven years ago, survived prison's persecution. Nevertheless, beatings cost him sight in his left eye. This thirty-year-old "young" man said:

> On December 19, 2012, more than 30 CAG members, including myself, were arrested while sharing the gospel. We were dragged to a police station.
>
> In the interrogation room, two police officers fastened me to a torture device called "tiger bench." One of them viciously kicked me three times in my chest, while pressuring me to give up information about the Church. Because I said nothing, he threatened me: "All the torture instruments in this room are for dealing with prisoners on death row. I don't know how many leather belts have been broken by beatings. Tell us everything you know. If you don't, we'll beat you to death—you deserve to be killed!" He then grabbed my hair and slapped me in the face. I suddenly felt hot pain in my face, which immediately became

swollen. They were unable to extract any information from me. That evening, they sent me to a detention house.

> ... To escape persecution, my family was forced to embark on a life in exile. Later, I learned that the police had issued a warrant for our arrest. They often come to my home to investigate, hoping to track us down. To this day, we do not dare to return home.[25]

Since 1995, CCP officials have listed the Church of Almighty God, reportedly one of the largest new religious movement in China, in the *xie jiao*. Because of its rapid growth, the CCP considers this group a threat to its power. Consequently, government authorities regularly arrest and severely persecute CAG members.

In another persecuted prisoner's account, one house church Christian reported that once during the winter when he failed to complete his quota, guards escorted him outside and ordered him to remove his pants. Outside, they repeatedly poured cold water over his head. During another disciplinary session, a prison guard gathered prisoners together who failed to complete their tasks and severely beat them with his baton. The house church Christian reported that he continued to experience pain with breathing for two months after the beating. As prisoners seldom receive medical treatment, the excessive labor and corporal punishment inescapably contribute to excruciating pain, illnesses, disabilities and premature deaths.[26] The United States and some other countries have launched investigations to determine if goods which inmates produces in internment camps reach their markets. Another former, religious prisoner from CAG, Zhu Jianyu (pseudonym), released in August 2018, incarcerated in Henan Province, reported that initially, his quota for making small electrical transformers totaled 3,000 units per day. Later, he made 3,500 toys per day. Even when his fingernails wore off several times, and the skin on his fingertips peeled off layer by layer, he had to meet his quota. When Zhu and other prisoners were able to reach their quotas, the guards would increase their required number. Without exception, those who failed to reach the designated quota had to work overtime. Reports regarding persecution of religious prisoners include:

> Peeling cloves of garlic is another job that religious prisoners frequently encounter. Every day, they must peel 60 to 80 *jin* (30 to 40 kilograms). Often prisoners' fingernails fall off, but they must continue peeling in intense pain.

25. Young Believer Loses Sight.
26. Lu, "Profiting from Persecution."

The high expectations of output are met by similarly long working hours. Among the interviewed, the shortest daily work shift was 12 hours, while some worked 20 hours per day.[27]

The Chinese government has immensely invested in facial recognition technology as well as coercive DNA collection. They use information retrieved from these tactics to track anyone who appears to be a challenge to Communist control—religious or not. Under Xi, the fear of religion, a fear inherent to all totalitarian systems, produces an extensive, meticulously planned national anti-religion strategy with a myriad of moving parts.[28]

My early years in China birthed a barrage of firsthand experiences which overtly contributed to my decision to share concerns regarding those who currently live there. As a survivor of persecution and imprisonment in China,[29] and personal interactions with many who have experienced persecution for their religious beliefs, I empathize with those experiencing horrific repercussions from the State-sponsored activities of the CCP. Interactions between the motives and rights of the church (religion) as opposed to the motives and rights of the State not only create appalling ramifications but also critical contemporary concerns that challenge citizens in China not only locally but also globally. Both arenas correlate with each other economically and politically, as well as in the areas contributing to the security of and in relation to concerns about freedom of religion.

Along with recent reports of increasing religious persecution in China, ongoing attacks on the economic and social freedoms of the citizens occur, and increased governmental controls are imposed on many aspects of individuals' lives.[30] Such developments have produced occasional, mild 'people power' outbursts in China. Variables, such as local government actions, central government policies, civil and social activism, or short-term versus long-term trends, frequently stimulate disagreements as to whether progress has been realized in the realm of China's human rights. Stories of increasing government restrictions often follow reports on the same citizens experiencing extensions of civil rights.[31]

In the light of China's repeated disregard for religious freedom, a universal, critical contemporary concern, I present *Baorong Duoyuan*, my contextualized model of principled pluralism in this book. I pray that one day, China,

27. Lu, "Profiting from Persecution."

28. Farr, "Diplomacy and Persecution."

29. Fu and French, *God's Double Agent.*

30. Li, *Civil Liberties in China.*

31. Lum and Fischer, *Human Rights in China,* 1.

my beloved birth country, not only considers this theory but implements its inherent ideas to facilitate and help ensure religious freedom for all.

Standing for religious freedom not only reflects a legal or moral obligation, but a practical imperative.[32] Freedom of religion envelopes individual freedom but even more so, a dearth of religious freedom for all jeopardizes the well-being societies throughout the world. Religious freedom links to robust democracies, diminished violence, as well as greater prosperity and stability. Nations that abuse religious liberty often incubate intolerance, extremism, poverty, insecurity, violence and repression. In our increasingly global world, connected by economic, political, and security interactions as well as concerns for human rights and religious freedom, it becomes critical to recognize that as the local impacts the global—the global impacts the local.[33] It also becomes vital to help eradicate persecutions inflicted because of one's beliefs—locally and globally.

Without freedom of as well as freedom from religion, a fundamental foundation for human rights—no other liberty can flourish.[34] For the sake of our local and global worlds, instead of burying reports of persecution in China, we need to acknowledge them. We must not only recognize cries for help from those being persecuted for their religious faiths, however—we must respond with compassion . . . with help . . . .

32. "No Human Rights without."
33. Nathan, *Religious Pluralism in Democratic,* 204.
34. "Corbyn Could be a Massive."

Chapter 2

Principled Pluralism Expounded in Relation to Religious Freedom

Genuine freedom implies pluralism;
pluralism demands equality; and equality cannot be
maintained under an ecclesiastical establishment.[1]

∽ RONALD THIEMANN

2.1 Introduction

IN CHAPTER 1, I presented the premise for this study, which focuses on contextualizing a constitutional, democratic, and pluralist theory appropriate to a presumed post-communist China, in which religions, particularly Christianity, will have substantially expanded in presence and influence. This study explicates the place of religious freedom in such an order. Also, in Chapter 1, in addition to noting a prominent facet of the area of study for this study, principled pluralism, I disclosed my aim—to design and develop my theory, *Baorong Duoyuan*, a contextualization of principled pluralism.

In this chapter, which outlines the model of principled pluralism, I initially define religious freedom, recounting the historical origins of principled pluralism—in the thought of Abraham Kuyper (1837–1920) and its further development by Herman Dooyeweerd (1894–1977). Kuyper,[2] a "theologian, minister, politician, newspaper editor, educational innovator, neo-Calvinist

---

1. Thiemann, *Religion in Public Life*, 21.
2. Kuipers, *Abraham Kuyper: An Annotated*.

reformer, and prime minister of the Netherlands from 1901 to 1905,"[3] developed the theory of sphere sovereignty,[4] which provides the foundation for the type of Christian pluralism later recognized as principled pluralism. Dooyeweerd, a Dutch philosopher[5] and legal theorist, fleshed out Kuyper's theory of sphere sovereignty, especially regarding the role of the State.[6]

From the historical roots of principled pluralism, I then move on to discuss several key contemporary neo-Calvinist authors, including Mouw and Griffioen as well as Skillen and Schmidt. Before I expound principled pluralism and argue why it provides the most reasonable, consistent, and coherent foundation for ensuring religious freedom for all in a pluralistic society, I introduce a full definition of the meaning and scope of religious freedom, primarily within the context of the international code of human rights.

2.2 Religious Freedom

Although religious freedom may be defined in multifaceted ways and interpreted from the perspective of history, culture, ethnicity, nationality, and political and legal connotations, I choose to present the definition of religious freedom or Freedom of Religion or Belief (FoRB) from the legal and political standpoint. In 1948, the UN General Assembly unanimously approved and adopted the most accepted definition of religious freedom, known as Article 18 in the Universal Declaration of Human Rights. Article 18 stipulates:

> Everyone has the right to freedom of thought, and religion; this right includes freedom to change his religion or belief, and freedom, either alone or in community with others and in public or private, to manifest his religion or belief in teaching, practice, worship and observance.[7]

Subsequently, in a similar spirit, the UN further reaffirmed and expounded these principles of religious freedom in both the International Covenant on Civil and Political Rights (ICCPR) in 1966[8] and the Declaration on the Elimination of all Forms of Intolerance and of Discrimination

---

3. Bratt, *Abraham Kuyper: Modern Calvinist.*

4. Chaplin, "Dooyeweerd's Theory of Public Justice," 10. Dooyeweerd elaborated and extended the principle of sphere sovereignty (*soevereiniteit in eigen kring*, literally "sovereignty in one's sphere"), which Guillaume Groen van Prinsterer (1801–76), the nineteenth-century Dutch Calvinist, first conveyed.

5. Chaplin, *"Herman Dooyeweerd: Christian Philosopher."*

6. Schmidt, "Principled Pluralist," 127–68.

7. "Article 18," *Universal Declaration of Human Rights.*

8. *International Covenant on Civil.*

Based on Religion or Belief in 1981.[9] The latter two are now accepted as internationally recognized, legally binding human rights treaties. The most recent U.N. update in February 2017 reports that 169 countries have signed and ratified the ICCPR. Six countries, however, including China, have signed but not ratified this international law.[10] Religious freedom, as the previously specified, international agreements and laws prescribe, can only be actualized or achieved when the State fully guarantees the following two principles. Certain limitations may apply only when the stated laws, as noted by the ICCPR, are violated.[11]

1. Everyone has the freedom to adhere to any religion or belief as well as the right to change his/her religion or belief, or non-belief.

2. Each person possesses the right to practice/manifest/observe his/her religious belief alone or in a group, in private or in public and to express that belief in public discourse.

The scope of religious freedom that international norms dictate encompasses private as well as public dimensions and, in Timothy Shah's judgment, includes:

> the freedom to pray, to worship, to commune with one's fellows of like mind and heart in the private practice of faith. But it is also the freedom to bear witness to one's beliefs and commitments, to be visibly religious in public life, to associate freely based on religion, and peacefully to encounter others with differing views on a basis of equality. It is the freedom to organize and act politically, to vote, to make arguments about public policy, and to legislate, based on one's religious beliefs, consistent with principles of universal justice toward others.[12]

The above principles imply several key parameters by which the degree or dearth of religious freedom may be measured. These parameters include not only the right for citizens to believe or to change their beliefs or non-beliefs in any religion, in private and in public, but also to practice their beliefs or religions in any peaceful way. In addition, the State should neither show preference towards nor discriminate against one religion or worldview

9. Passed by the U.N. General Assembly Resolution 36/55.

10. Status of Ratification.

11. According to the ICCPR, Article 18, no. 3, freedom to manifest one's religion or beliefs may be subject only to such limitations as are prescribed by law and are necessary to protect public safety, order, health, or morals or the fundamental rights and freedoms of others.

12. Shah, *Religious Freedom, Why*, vi–vii.

over another, particularly in its education system, but should offer teachings about diverse religions, making these equally accessible to all children in public schools.[13] Furthermore, as part of religious freedom relating to children's religious education, international laws stipulate that parents and legal guardians have the right to ensure their children receive an education that conforms with their own religious convictions.[14] This right applies to both private and public education.

Heiner Bielefeldt asserts that regarding the freedom of religious practices, a civil government should ensure citizens have the right to proclaim their religion's messages, convert others using non-coercive means, and present public policy proposals directly based on their religious convictions.[15] Full religious freedom can only be realized when a country or State guarantees rights to its citizens in a pluralistic, democratic society, and protects those freedoms indicated in a constitutional mechanism—noted earlier—equally and fairly.

2.3 Principled Pluralism Delineated

Kuyper and Dooyeweerd, two prominent Dutch thinkers, created the terms "sphere sovereignty" and "sphere universality," which in time became known as principled (or structural) pluralism,[16] one of numerous classifications of pluralism. Michael Barnes Norton explains that depending on the context of the term "pluralism" or the authors' intended use of the word, the term can indicate something ranging from the fact of religious diversity to a specific kind of philosophical or theological approach to such diversity. Typically, the approach would be "characterized by humility regarding the level of truth and effectiveness of one's personal religion, as well as the goals of deferential dialogue and mutual understanding with other traditions."[17] In this context, the term "diversity" denotes different religious beliefs, practices, and traditions, while "pluralism" refers to a certain form of response to that diversity.

13. "Article 18," *Universal Declaration of Human Rights.*

14. United Nations Human Rights, "International Covenant on Economic," 98–118. The States parties to the present Covenant undertake to have respect for the liberty of parents and, when applicable, legal guardians to ensure the religious and moral education of their children in conformity with their own convictions."

15. Bielefeldt, *Freedom of Religion or Belief.*

16. Ahdar and Leigh, *Religious Freedom in Liberal,* 110.

17. Norton, "Religious Pluralism," para. 1.

Jeffrey Wattles defines pluralism to portray an attitude that responds to the element of "diverse traditions of thought, faith, and practice"[18] by: (1) appreciating each person's shared humanity and their inordinate, inimitable individuality while examining the explicit differences of class, gender, race, religious belief, or other category deemed relevant for a certain purpose; (2) investing time to explore the course that "leads from understanding to tolerance, friendship, and love."[19] Principled pluralism should be perceived as one way of interpreting pluralism as understood in this general sense.

Sphere sovereignty provides the foundational framework for principled pluralism as the main principle of operation between religion and State within a pluralistic society. During his inaugural address, entitled "Sphere Sovereignty," at the founding of the Free University of Amsterdam in 1880, Kuyper compares concepts of *soevereiniteit in eigen kring*,[20] which means the sovereignty of each sphere,[21] to State sovereignty, a condition which, according to Kuyper, "led to an idolatrous worship of nation."[22] Kuyper argued that because God allocated governing powers to diverse spheres within human society, it stood to reason that civil government could only make claims to limited authority.[23] He simultaneously stressed that because spheres interrelate and originate in God, the sovereignty of those spheres only exists under God's infinite sovereignty.[24]

As Dooyeweerd perceives sphere sovereignty as a creation-wide principle more than a societal principle, he develops "sphere universality," which asserts that although spheres are mutually irreducible, they are reciprocally interconnected and not hermetically sealed off from each other. Chaplin explains that the distinctiveness of each aspect is expressed within the internal structure of all the others. There is an "intermodal coherence binding them all together in a unified diversity."[25] Consequently, the ubiquity or "universality" of the spheres contributes to Dooyeweerd's term, "sphere universality."

To be sovereign, an authority structure such as the State maintains the right to issue directives on matters that a certain sphere (domain, sector) encompasses. Authorities in one sphere may issue directives for those

18. Wattles, "What is Pluralism?" para. 1.

19. Wattles, "What is Pluralism?"

20. Kuyper, *Soevereiniteit in Eigen Kring*, 13.

21. Petrin and Visscher, "Revisiting Sphere Sovereignty," 99–122.

22. Van Til, "Abraham Kuyper and Michael Walzer," 267.

23. Bratt, Abraham *Kuyper, Centennial Reader*, 241.

24. Bratt, Abraham *Kuyper, Centennial Reader*, 241.

25. Chaplin, *Herman Dooyeweerd*.

in that sphere—for example, higher education—but may not maintain authority for the entirety of life within that sphere. Kuyper explains that just as "the president of Yale has no right to issue directives to the students and staff of Harvard University,"[26] neither the State nor any other authoritative body maintains the right to issue directives for the totality of life within a sphere. Corwin E. Schmidt notes the following regarding Kuyper's perception of the roles of the diverse spheres:

> First, the state is to maintain parity between the different spheres. Thus it has anobligation to enforce mutual respect for the boundary lines separating the different spheres of authority whenever a conflict arises between areas or when one sphere steps over its boundary of authority into the domain of another.
>
> Second, the state is to prevent authorities within a particular sphere from abusing their power by acting unjustly toward those who are relatively powerless within that sphere.
>
> Finally, the state has the right to impose taxes to support the apparatus of government and to facilitate its task of maintaining the health and vitality of the commonwealth. Thus, while the state is merely one among various social spheres, it does not enjoy supremacy and sovereignty over those other spheres; in turn, the state is to be regulated by means of both constitutional law and representative government.[27]

Kuyper challenges the homogeneity that the increasingly commercialized and industrialized world he lived in promoted. Instead of uniformity at each level of society, his theory of sphere sovereignty emphasizes diversity[28] and embraces the idea that authority structures in society possess only a limited scope. Although all spheres are still perceived as an organic unity under God the Creator, who exercises sovereignty over all, each sphere of society—the State, church, family, and others—enjoys its own autonomy. According to Kuyper, as only God retains the right to issue decrees to every individual on all matters, the State's right does not include issuing directives to every citizen—only to specific people on certain matters.[29]

As he promotes Christian involvement in the political sphere, Kuyper embraces pluralism as God's creation norm. He argues that rather than the

26. Wolterstorff, *Teachings of Modern Christianity*, 315.
27. Schmidt, "Principled Pluralist," 136–37.
28. Kuperus, *State, Civil Society and Apartheid*, 1967.
29. Kuyper, *Abraham Kuyper*, 468.

State utilizing coercive power to defeat idols and false teachings, it would fare better to support a crowded, public square. This would permit truth to prevail through peaceful discussion, an essential element for ensuring religious freedom. Kuyper prefers pluralism structured on strong Christian principles with the role of the State including the protection of societal structures to enable them to function freely. Kuyper perceived the State's role to also include overseeing structural balances. He insists that the span of the State's sphere should otherwise encourage society to operate freely without coercive constraints.[30]

Kuyper stresses that the State should use its power to maintain order when necessary as well as maintain structural balance between different societal spheres. He typically proclaims that the State should basically permit other societal spheres, including that of the church (religion), to operate without State interference. He calls for equal rights for all, whatever the individual's religion or situation. Kuyper maintains that he and others in agreement with his stance will defend freedom of conscience, a free press, freedom of assembly, and freedom of opinion with all their might.[31]

According to Kuyper, the sphere sovereignty of numerous distinct social institutions entitles each organization to express "a certain facet of a dynamic order of divinely created possibilities and each fitted to make a unique contribution to the realization of justice and the public good."[32] Sphere sovereignty provides the foundation for principled pluralism as the main principle of operation between religion and State within a pluralistic society. Kuyper's body of work, especially proposals relating to sphere sovereignty, which constitutes the foundation for principled pluralism, continues to influence contemporary supporters of religious freedom throughout the world.[33]Sphere sovereignty, the groundwork

30. Kuyper, *Abraham Kuyper*, 468.

31. Kuyper, *Abraham Kuyper*, 315.

32. Chaplin, *Herman Dooyeweerd*, 1.

33. Bratt, *Abraham Kuyper, Modern*, 1. Kuyper's influence on Bratt, a professor from Calvin College and supporter of religious freedom, may be seen in the introduction of this book. Bratt notes that Kuyper proposed believers utilize their religious freedom by expressing "the full weight of their convictions into public life while fully respecting the rights of others in a pluralistic society under a constitutional government," xiii. Kuyper also influenced James W. Skillen, the former executive director and president of the Center for Public Justice as well as a strong, contemporary advocate for religious freedom in "The point of Kuyperian pluralism." Jonathan Chaplin notes that Skillen advocates not only religious freedom for religious entities such as churches and mosques but that the State should treat all faith-based bodies justly. In "Contested religious space in Jakarta," Chang-Yau Hoon notes that Dr. Stephen Tong, a renowned Chinese Indonesian, Christian theologian, philosopher, and founder of the International Reformed Evangelical Seminary (IRES), avidly supports religious freedom. In personal

Kuyper cultivated for principled pluralism, maintains that as a feature of the created order, God ordained distinct spheres of authority with each retaining a purpose for existence as well as its unique right to exist. Figure 3 portrays the vertical interrelationships between God and His creations in human society as well as the societal relationships existing between the horizontally portrayed spheres.

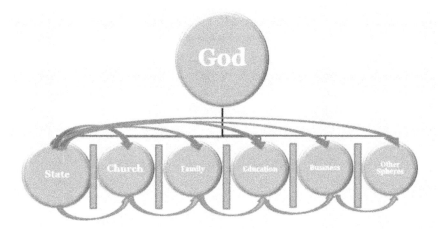

Interrelationships Kuyper Noted between Spheres

The vertical alignment of each sphere reflects its sovereignty and independence as a part of God's created order under His sovereignty. Simultaneously, each sphere also interrelates to each of the others as it functions in society within the designated boundaries that separate them.[34] Gordon J. Spykman stresses that Kuyper's sphere sovereignty captures the concept: "No sphere may exercise its authority at the expense of another. Each has its own rightful area of jurisdiction. Each is entitled to full and equal standing before the law."[35] In the next section, I examine both the philosophical and theological foundations of principled pluralism and then highlight the State–religion relationship under the framework of principled pluralism. Principled pluralism correlates with Kuyper's sphere sovereignty in that both maintain that as the State performs specific tasks in its sphere, its primary task is to promote justice equally for its citizens.

---

communication with Dr. Tong, I learned that he considers his theological beliefs supporting religious freedom rooted in Kuyperian teachings.

34. Schmidt, "Principled Pluralist," 136.

35. Spykman, "Principled Pluralist Position," 98.

In addition to Kuyper's sphere sovereignty providing a base for principled pluralism, his ideas reflect the philosophical foundation of this theory. Kuyper asserts that God has given each sphere, including the State as well as the church (religion), family, education, businesses, and other spheres, specific tasks to perform and that as each sphere remains subservient in its relationship to God, no sphere is ultimately sovereign. Nevertheless, each sphere possesses a level of sovereignty not only in its own domain but also in its interrelationships with each of the other spheres. According to Kuyper, "Each sphere has its own identity, its own unique task, its own God-given prerogatives."[36] Each authority structure within these different areas qualifies as "sovereign," in that "each sphere in society has its own independent authority; no one sphere should dominate or usurp the role of the others."[37] Although Kuyper insists that the various social spheres retain their autonomy, he reserves a restricted, yet simultaneously "elevated" role for the government regarding certain social settings. Robert K. Vischer contends that as Kuyper's sphere sovereignty limits the State's authority to the political sphere, it carves out analogous spheres of authority for other areas of social life, including education, family, business, the arts, and science.[38] I agree with Vischer that Kuyper's writings not only offer a detailed blueprint to appropriate power among the spheres but also argue that the framing Kuyper designates for sovereignty provides the image of a social order in which voluntary associations do not depend on the State for their legitimacy or authority.

Vischer argues that the significance of sphere sovereignty relates to its emphasis on the link between the preservation of various sources of authority in society and the common good of citizens.[39] Principled pluralists assert that due to the social nature of humans, associations and communities constitute a fundamental feature of society. Instead of society being constructed by autonomous individuals, independent from each other, social groups, organically related, create a society. As they experience their lives, human beings commonly form social groups that include associations and communities. Within the social structures of these groups, human beings establish their identities and form their values.[40] These social groups and structures exist independently of and prior to the initiation of the State. In creating a healthy polity, principled pluralists confirm the critical role of associations and communities, a stance between the extremes of the individualism that laissez-faire reflects

36. Schmidt, "Principled Pluralist," 136.

37. Schmidt, "Principled Pluralist."

38. Vischer, *Conscience and the Common Good*, 106.

39. Vischer, *Conscience and the Common Good*, 106.

40. Schmidt, "Principled Pluralist."

and the collectivism that utilizes socialist and nationalist ideologies. "This assertion of the social nature of human beings compels principled pluralists to oppose individualism (at least in its extreme forms)."[41] Principled pluralists contend that, fundamentally, human beings are social beings. Kuyper argues, "Human life [. . .] is so constituted that the individual can exist only within the group and can come to full expression only in community."[42] Like those advocating at least some other pluralisms, principled pluralists accentuate the social nature of human beings and the inherent existence of associations and communities in society as well as the critical contributions society receives from these entities. I concur with Kuyper that, under a pluralistic but organic societal order, the worth of an individual in the community can be more fully and distinctly manifested and valued.

Kuyper argues that neither the individual as an officeholder nor the magistrate is immune from fallen nature or the consequences of the ensuing human state of total depravity. God chose to allocate the authority to administer public justice to the magistrate, not to the individual person or to any societal institution or organization. Kuyper also passionately argues that a Christian should "meddle in politics."[43] As the following recounts, Kuyper rebukes what he deems the "pious" concept of isolating oneself from the affairs of the world, a practice he considers "leaving the reins of government in the hands of the world."[44]

> And moreover, they [those who feel that a Christian should not meddle in politics] protest that there is too much filth and crookedness about politics, so that no child of God can meddle in political affairs without becoming contaminated and suffering spiritual loss.
> But this is not the Christian view. [. . .] A life of pious isolation and meditation was not their [the Reformers] idea of obedience to God. They militated against such inactivity and passivity.[45]

Kuyper views the notion of a citizen being passive and not participating in politics as both unattainable and a misinterpretation of the Word of God. It muddles the difference between two kinds of duties in the Scriptures: (1) the duty of a private person or individual; and (2) the obligation of the official or magistrate. Kuyper not only argues for his concepts regarding

41. Schmidt, "Principled Pluralist," 163.

42. Schmidt, "Principled Pluralist," 140.

43. Kuyper, *Practice of Godliness*, 40.

44. Kuyper, *Practice of Godliness*, 41.

45. Kuyper, *Practice of Godliness*, 40–41.

sphere sovereignty, he also promotes an epistemology and a doctrine of common grace. Kuyper's doctrine of common grace asserts that God does not discriminate between Christians and non-Christians regarding gifts of knowledge and cultural blessings. He gives both to all so they may share.[46] Kuyper's antithesis doctrine declares that when the Scriptures provide guidance contrary to that of the world, including that which the State promotes, Christians are not to compromise Scriptural directives.

Kuyper notes that Reformers from France, the Netherlands, Scotland, and Switzerland militated against isolationism and extreme versions of separation of State and religion. Furthermore, according to Kuyper, Calvin, and Zwingli, who were essentially theocratic in their mirrored views of the relationship between the two authorities, affirmed a more robust, forceful role for religion over the State's authority, especially in the prevention of heresy. In a sense, Kuyper argues for the not yet named concept of "principled pluralism," which I illustrate in the next section, contending that each sphere, including education, church (religion), business, etc., has the right to be sovereign in its own domain. Kuyper derived his perception of the role of the State from the Christian worldview, particularly the doctrine of common grace.[47] He stresses, "The sovereignty of the state as the power that protects the individual and that defines the mutual relationships among the visible spheres, rises high above them by its right to command and compel."[48] Nevertheless, Kuyper insists, another, much higher authority, namely that authority which descends directly from God separate from the State, overshadows the rule of the State. "Only God is Sovereign; [. . .] He is sovereign and gives that authority to whomever He will—sometimes to kings and princes, other times to nobles and patricians, but sometimes also to the people as a whole."[49] Although the State can acknowledge that sovereign authority, Kuyper stresses, it cannot confer it. Kuyper perceives the State to possess a limited role to exercise its "power of the sword"[50] when it is required to maintain public order.[51]

Principled pluralism draws numerous concepts from the foundation of Kuyper's notion of sphere sovereignty, particularly the fact that the social

46. Kuyper, *Practice of Godliness.*

47. "For he makes his sun rise on the evil and on the good, and sends rain on the just and on the unjust." Matthew 5:45b (NKJV).

48. Kuyper, *Abraham Kuyper*, 468.

49. Kuyper, *Abraham Kuyper*, 307.

50. Kuyper, *Abraham Kuyper*, 23.

51. Boyd, *Myth of a Christian Nation*, 18, "The power of the sword is the ability to coerce behavior by threats and to make good on those threats when necessary: if a law is broken."

nature of humans, associations, and communities constitutes a fundamental feature of society. Instead of society being constructed by autonomous individuals, independent from each other, social groups, organically related, create a society. As they experience their lives, human beings commonly form social groups that include associations and communities. Within the social structures of these groups, they establish their identities and form their values. These social groups and structures exist independently of and prior to the initiation of the State. According to the designs Kuyper and Dooyeweerd[52] developed, the State, as one of the sphere authorities, should hold a rather crucial role to advance and protect justice and the common good, which includes religious freedom—for all.

Dooyeweerd argues that the State could amicably explain the convoluted "right and might" nature of its role. He defines the State as a legal institution of government grounded on the historical foundation of a monopolistic organization of power inside a specific geographical area.[53]

As Dooyeweerd systematically fleshes out Kuyper's theory,[54] his work, like that of Kuyper, helps develop the theory of principled pluralism.

Dooyeweerd broadened his concepts regarding the nature and role of the State with his contribution of establishing a key component of PP based on his unique articulation of God's two modes of revelation and the respective responses by individuals, both regenerated and unregenerated through various spheres of society. Figure 4 shows that Dooyeweerd advanced Kuyper's construction of a social order from God's creation perspective on two fronts: (1) Instead of only considering the biblical account of the creation order, he also took the 'fall and redemption' narrative into account; and (2) Dooyeweerd constructed his social order by including both sphere sovereignty and sphere universality, which I explained earlier. In this sense, Kuyper falls short by a long way, perhaps by being too "creation-based," thus risking a baptism of factually existing institutions after the fall and foreclosing a critique of the spheres in the light of the redemption.

---

52. Dooyeweerd, *A New Critique of Theoretical*, 32.

53. Dooyeweerd, *A New Critique of Theoretical*, 215.

54. Schmidt, "Principled Pluralist."

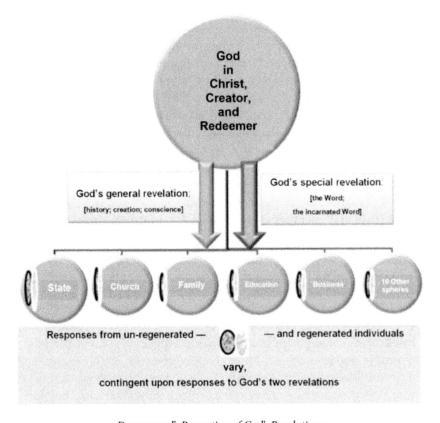

Dooyeweerd's Perception of God's Revelations

Dooyeweerd further developed the foundation for principled plural-ism regarding legitimate authority, especially the sphere of the State. He also comprehensively and systematically expounded the task of each sphere, the norms or principles governing them, and how each sphere should relate to the other spheres.[55] These proclamations evolved as an ongoing develop-ment under the scheme of Kuyper's sphere sovereignty.[56]

Although principled pluralism is primarily oriented from a Christian worldview, Kuyper and Dooyeweerd do not consider an explicit Christian social structure necessary for the State to perform its duties and protect the freedom of its citizens.[57] Their work provides support for my proposal of *Baorong Duoyuan*, my contextualization of principled pluralism in Chapter

---

55. Dooyeweerd, *A New Critique of Theoretical*, 102–5.

56. Smith, *Introducing Radical Orthodoxy*, 33.

57. Chaplin, *Herman Dooyeweerd*, 197.

5. Instead of insufficient pluralisms shared by Christian nation/reconstructionist/theonomist perspectives and secularist understandings, principled pluralism should be adopted in a manner that permits the State to function as one authority, advancing and protecting justice and common good for each of its citizens, despite their different comprehensive ideas.

Kuyper and Dooyeweerd concur on the concept of a limited, public-interest State.[58] Jeong Kii Min also stresses the State should facilitate and nurture respect of people as unique individuals; distinct from their roles within their families and organizations.[59] Thus, the relationships between the State and religious institutions should be both distinctive and interwoven. On the one hand, the State is neither capable of making nor assigned to make a judgment on any internal religious matter such as moral discipline or doctrine, or of taking part in ecclesiastical deliberation, and vice versa. On the other hand, the two must also partner together in fair cooperation in distribution of public justice, including the protection of religious freedom. Kuyper, as noted earlier, perceives the State to possess a limited role regarding exercising its "power of the sword." In the next section, I examine Dooyeweerd's stance, emphasizing that, first and foremost, the State constitutes a legal institution with the primary purpose of establishing public justice through the manifestation of its coercive nature.

In exceptional scenarios, the role of the State encompasses some degree of higher allowance for conditional interference in other spheres. The State maintains the right to safeguard harmony between different spheres and protect justice for all, especially for vulnerable groups and minorities in society. In addition, according to Dooyeweerd, when conflicts arise between spheres due to injustice, the State can legally utilize coercive measures in order to intervene to secure order and justice according to different principles under each sphere.[60] The State's identity encompasses a distinct combination of justice and power or, alternatively, it is an identity where power proves to be foundational for the State but only in the sense that the promotion of justice serves as the destination.[61] This constitutes the State's unique, irreducible role compared to that of other social institutions.

Jonathan Chaplin explains that Dooyeweerd further developed Kuyper's initial theory of sphere sovereignty by expounding the unique qualifying function of the State with a justice-promoting role, applicable to all societal

---

58. Chaplin, *Herman Dooyeweerd*, 197.

59. Min, *Sin and Politics*, 112.

60. Chaplin, "Dooyeweerd's Theory of Public," 64–65.

61. Chaplin, "Dooyeweerd's Theory of Public," 9.

sectors including church, family, industry, and nation.[62] Dooyeweerd accomplished this by characterizing the State with identifications of power and law, which he distinguished as its founding and qualifying functions respectively. Chaplin considers Dooyeweerd's terms regarding the State as meaning that the State holds the following two functions:

1. founding function, to maintain a territorial monopoly of power;

2. founding function, to establish just laws.

Under Dooyeweerd's structure of the dual function of the State listed above, Chaplin notes that the State holds intrinsically designed, essential coercive power as its founding principled function. This inseparable qualifying function does not merely encompass physical force but is a composite of resources through which public justice can be equally distributed. Chaplin further points out that Dooyeweerd's understanding between law (the founding function to maintain a territorial monopoly of power) and public justice through law (qualifying function, to promote public justice by means of law) assists in mapping the ways in which the State and other differentiated sectors of civil society should, under structural pluralism, pair together to achieve justice and public good.[63] I endorse this solid, genuine view of the State's role as public-legal, the leading function, because it implies that the norm of public justice directs the State in all its activities.

From his examination of Dooyeweerd, Chaplin also surmises that the rightly formulated concept of public justice can serve to guide the State through significant public policy matters that confront a complex, modern society. His examination of Dooyeweerd's thought reveals that Dooyeweerd perceives the State as an organized, segregated, public-legal community, yet distinguished by a juridically qualified, structural principle. The State's public-legal leading function, the norm of public justice, according to Dooyeweerd, implies that this standard should direct the State's actions in all its doings. Chaplin additionally notes that for Dooyeweerd "the founding function of the State is subservient to, and can only be analyzed adequately in relation to, its leading function."[64] The distinctive "legal sphere sovereignty" of the State depicts its irreducible identity: the specific relationship between law and the power that the State possesses. "The coercive power at the foundation of the State exists not for its own sake but only to sustain the State in realizing its definitive destination, which is the discharge of its

---

62. Chaplin, *Herman Dooyeweerd*.

63. Chaplin, "Dooyeweerd's Theory of Public."

64. Chaplin, *Herman Dooyeweerd*, 187.

distinctive task of advancing public justice."[65] According to Dooyeweerd, Chaplin explains that the State not only reflects a "juridically qualified community" but also constitutes "a territorial public legal community."[66] The State's essential responsibility in this reasoning is actualizing an amicable juridical balance in the public realm.

Chaplin asserts that:

> Various interlocking concepts make their appearance in Dooyeweerd's discussion of public justice. In addition to juridical harmonization, the most important of these are the distinction between internal functions and external relations; the principle of sphere sovereignty; the idea of the public interest; the distinctions between "structure" and "purpose" or "task" and "typical" and "atypical" tasks.[67]

Chaplin stresses that the realization of Dooyeweerd's view regarding the relationship between the State and society involving retribution, or harmoniously balancing diverse juridical interests, thereby precisely illuminating the interrelations of the diverse concepts, proves challenging. Nevertheless, in contrast with Kuyper, Dooyeweerd did not consider society to be an entity with an inherent internal infrastructure but as a system of multifaceted enkaptic interrelationships between structures like families, schools, and political parties. D. F. M. Strauss explains that the enkaptic which Dooyeweerd "developed (as) a specific theory in terms of which he accounts for the interconnections between different kinds of entities—where each entity maintains its sphere sovereignty—designated as the theory of enkaptic interlacements."[68] A straight-forward whole-parts relation differs from enkaptic intertwinements because in their being-a-part, all parts in the whole-parts relation share a structure which the whole determines. In other words, in contrast to the ordinary part-whole relation where the parts are dependent by their roles in the whole, enkaptic relations emphasize independence among diverse parts within the whole.

Unlike part–whole relationships in which the part has no meaning apart from its whole (as with a person's arm), Dooyeweerd stresses that in these enkaptic relationships, a degree of meaningful independence exists. In contrast to Kuyper, who focused more on each sphere's independence and sovereignty from the State's intrusiveness under God's creation order, in fighting an increasingly dictatorial State demanding uniformity,

65. Chaplin, *Herman Dooyeweerd*, 186.

66. Chaplin, *Herman Dooyeweerd*.

67. Chaplin, *Herman Dooyeweerd*, 219.

68. Strauss, "Best Known but Least Understood," 2.

Dooyeweerd's applies his enkaptic theory, with emphasis on dependence in these relationships among different structures of society. He perceives this as Correlative Enkapsis (community–person).

As explained earlier in this chapter, Kuyper notes that distinct types of social institutions exist, each possessing a divinely ordained nature and purpose. Each of these institutions, which qualify as associational structural pluralisms, have responsibilities and rights that are not to be consumed or consolidated by those of the other spheres. Chaplin asserts that although Dooyeweerd did not present a detailed statement regarding the principle of societal sphere sovereignty that Kuyper himself stressed, he captures concepts contributing to principled pluralism in the central principle of "legal sphere sovereignty."[69] G. J. Spykman, like Chaplin and Schmidt, notes that as Dooyeweerd expanded Kuyper's concepts regarding sphere sovereignty, he developed his sphere universality concepts. Both sets of concepts are central to principled pluralism.[70]

While Dooyeweerd stresses that God's normative order of creation proclaims not only the differentiation of society and the State but also the distinct realm of individual freedom,[71] he argues that a person's interactions in diverse societal spheres manifests a plurality of worldviews.[72] Later in this chapter, I not only expand on concepts regarding pluralism, I also present alternatives that Christian nonpluralists propose in relation to principled pluralism. Principled pluralism, I will argue, not only constitutes a credible antithesis to other types of pluralism, it surpasses them because, despite its limitations (historical, cultural, social and religious under Dutch context), this theory best fits the foundational commitment to ensuring religious freedom for all.

James W. Skillen, who initially employed the term "principled pluralism," also developed and expanded this concept at length.[73] Jonathan Chaplin notes, "James Skillen has given the name 'principled pluralism' to [. . .] Kuyper's pluralist legacy."[74] Skillen explains that, among several other things, principled pluralism indicates that the State's responsibility includes recognizing and protecting every individual as well as each valid human vocation, institution, and organization. Skillen terms this "structural pluralism." As most of a citizen's social life is not characteristically political,

69. Chaplin, *Herman Dooyeweerd*, 186.

70. Spykman, "Principled Pluralist Position," 75.

71. Chaplin, *Herman Dooyeweerd*, 186.

72. Harris, *Fundamentalism and Evangelicals*, 238.

73. Skillen, *Recharging the American Experiment*.

74. Chaplin, "Point of Kuyperian."

neither the government nor the political community created many of the institutions and organized activities that citizens are involved in. Therefore, the reality of human associations and relationships that do not form subdivisions of the political community depicts part of the limit of the State's jurisdiction.[75] Several strong Christian principles contribute to the foundation of principled pluralism. These include the following:

1. Principled pluralism, rooted in Christian pluralism, expounds criteria promoting a specific stance regarding the ethical attitude the State should employ concerning the various religious affiliations of its citizens. Principled pluralism holds that in a religiously diverse society, instead of the State overtly promoting a belief system, its primary role includes demonstrating impartiality, and maintaining a public square equally open to contributions from its plural citizenry, which consists of diverse faiths. As noted earlier, Skillen perceives this as confessional pluralism. Based on the account of God's creation and design recorded in Genesis, principled pluralism holds that all people live within a system of divinely designed life relationships.[76] Kuyper refers to 1 Corinthians 15:23 regarding the diverse systems he identifies in sphere sovereignty.[77]

2. Another Christian belief, also noted throughout the Bible, contributes to principled pluralism in that people do not acquire meaning and/or purpose in their individual identities but achieve it through associational pluralism or by being a part of a collective whole. This occurs within a plurality of communal associations that include spheres of activity ordained by God, such as family, schools, and the State.[78]

3. The Christian concept of God-ordained spheres which, conjoined, constitute community life serves as yet another contribution to the foundation for principled pluralism. This principle also correlates with Mouw's associational pluralism.[79]

75. Skillen, *Good of Politics*, 124.

76. Spykman, "Principled Pluralist Position," 79.

77 Kuyper, *Abraham Kuyper: A Centennial*, 467: "[T]here are in life as many spheres as there are constellations in the sky and that the circumference of each has been drawn on a fixed radius from the center of a unique principle, namely the apostolic injunction 'each in its own order' from 1 Corinthians 15:23 [. . . .] Just as we speak of a 'moral world,' a 'scientific world,' a 'business world,' the 'world of art,' so we can more properly speak of a 'sphere' of morality, or the family, or social life, each with its domain. And because each comprises its own domain, each has its own Sovereign within its bounds."

78. Spykman, "Principled Pluralist Position," 79.

79. Spykman, "Principled Pluralist Position."

4. Another primary Christian principle that contributes to the foundation of principled pluralism holds that each person possesses the right to adhere to his/her beliefs and conscience.

William Edgar explains:

> Principled pluralism demands and guarantees for everyone the right to follow the dictates of his/her conscience and belief. Moreover, it encourages people to advocate public policy positions shaped and influenced by those beliefs.[80]

As these four principles demonstrate, the stance of principled pluralism expounds criteria promoting a specific stance regarding the ethical attitude the State should employ concerning the various religious affiliations of its citizens. Mouw and Griffioen, who have also contributed to establishing principled pluralism, credit Dooyeweerd with not only bringing clarity to Kuyper's neo-Calvinist perspective but also for contributing to the understanding of the theme of associational pluralism.[81] Following this section, I examine associational pluralism with two more of the three primary facets of pluralism that Mouw and Griffioen identify: contextual and directional pluralism. I also note two additional qualifiers that characterize each of these three types of pluralism: the terms "descriptive" and "normative."

As Mouw and Griffioen set out to clarify societal structures, they identify the following types of pluralism: three distinctive classifications of pluralism which confirm that as Kuyper and Dooyeweerd note, no vacuum or absolute separation exists between the various societal spheres.

1. Associational pluralism. This depicts the diversity of organizations and institutions that make up human society: associations such as families, churches, businesses, etc.

2. Directional pluralism. This refers to the various visions of the appropriate life to which people adhere, for example, being Christian, an atheist, or a hedonist. In a sense, because the directions individuals take or the ideas to which they follow (worldviews/religions) are not autonomous, directional pluralism usually presupposes associational pluralism.[82]

3. Contextual pluralism. This distinguishes general cultural contexts that reflect the lives of large groups or communities of people. These contexts, for example, being Hispanic, French, or South African, male or

---

80. Edgar, *God and Politics: Four Views*, 176–99, 283.

81. Mouw and Griffioen, *Pluralisms & Horizons*, 170.

82. Mouw and Griffioen, *Pluralisms and Horizons*..

female,[83] are much larger and more encompassing than a distinct association and may manifest contrary directional pluralisms within them.

Whether a person adheres to being an atheist, a Christian or a hedonist is almost always demonstrated in certain associational contexts, such as the family, the church, or other religious belief or non-belief organizations or institutions, such as the school, the political party, and the State. Conversely, contextual pluralism refers to whether a person is identified as male or female, what race he/she is or what country he/she comes from. However, being American, French, Hispanic, Italian, or South African does not always necessarily assume associational or directional pluralism because these pluralisms are not contingent upon individual reasoning or choices.[84]

The presence of contextual pluralism does not of itself guarantee that associational or directional pluralism will be in fact respected by the state or other bodies. Culturally plural countries such as China, Iran,[85] and even Israel, where one monolithic directional ideology or religion or a belief such as Communism, Islam, or Judaism is legally enshrined or promoted by the State as its national identity,[86] can often be found guilty of violating the universal principles of religious freedom and human rights. Some exceptions can be noted, for example, in a monolithic theocratic situation, as in Israel during Old Testament times, where ethnic Jews (contextual pluralism) were perceived as almost identical to religious Jews (directional pluralism) and associated with the relevant institutions, such as Jewish temples (associational pluralism).

In addition to classifying pluralisms as associational, contextual, and directional, Mouw introduces two sets of distinctions for these that he terms "descriptive" and "normative."

Descriptive pluralism aims to emphasize a specific pluralism's significance; there is no accompanying action. According to Mouw and Griffioen,

---

83. Mouw and Griffioen, *Pluralisms and Horizons*, 157..

84. In contemporary times, when a nation, State or ethnicity (contextual pluralism) comparatively, exclusively identifies itself with one monistic social structure (associational pluralism) under a solitary worldview (directional pluralism), this endangers basic human rights and religious freedom of the minority group/s. These concerns exist where the State imposes one uniform, national ideological or religious identity for all its citizens, including in some Communist, Islamic, Buddhist, and even Jewish countries/ states.

85. *2017 Annual Report Overview*. The U.S. Commission on International Religious Freedom (USCIRF), as it has done since 1998, listed China as well as Iran as a CPC (country of particular concern), due to the State engaging in or tolerating serious violations of religious freedom.

86. Harkov, "Israeli Ministers Approve Controversial."

descriptive pluralism serves to acknowledge a diversity, "a way of acknowledging [a pluralism's] existence as a fact that is worth noting."[87] It simply indicates the mode of existence of the three noted types of pluralism. By contrast, the normative label of "pluralism" can also be used to indicate a way to advocate for diversity.[88] "Normative pluralism aims to act and argue for this pluralism as a good state of affairs."[89] It entails a preferred action or reaction, either defending or challenging a given type of pluralism.

Mouw and Griffioen label and explain the following three types of pluralism:

1. Associational plurality is the plurality of human associations of many kinds naturally emerging in many societies.

2. Directional plurality is the plurality of "spiritual directions" or comprehensive doctrines present in contemporary societies.

3. Contextual plurality is the plurality of cultural contexts in which associational and directional plurality appear.[90]

One concept from Kuyper's work that Skillen refers to is called "confessional pluralism" and matches the directional pluralism that Mouw and Griffioen identify. It refers to the principal spiritual orientation an association or institution maintains: the basic convictional structure which guides a group or sphere. Readily recognizable contemporary examples could include "a Christian trade union, a Buddhist environmental group, a Jewish school, an Islamic bank, a Catholic family."[91] The practices of some institutions or associations, even if not stated, for example, reflect their bond or commitment to secular liberal beliefs, their founding faith base, or their commitment to science and technology. In addition, even though Kuyper did not clearly distinguish "confessional pluralism," which I note as comparable to directional pluralism, and although he did not identify another sector in civil society that Skillen later labeled 'structural pluralism,' this being comparable to the associational pluralism that Mouw and Griffioen designate, both evolved from Kuyper's work.

Skillen explains that the State's jurisdiction is not unlimited but originates in the reality of associations and human relationships that do not epitomize sectors of the political community. He asserts that: "Doing justice to the

87. Mouw and Griffioen, *Pluralisms and Horizons*, 14.

88. Mouw and Griffioen, *Pluralisms and Horizons*.

89. Mouw and Griffioen, *Pluralisms and Horizons*, 18.

90. Mouw and Griffioen, *Pluralisms and Horizons*, 13–19.

91. Mouw and Griffioen, *Pluralisms and Horizons*, 19.

multiple rights and responsibilities of persons and non-governmental institutions is what we might say is government's responsibility to uphold 'structural pluralism.'"[92] Additionally, Skillen refers to a subsequent kind of pluralism, which holds that the State should uphold what he refers to as "confessional pluralism." He draws from a reference in the Scriptures, as did Kuyper, who noted common grace in support of his sphere sovereignty, correlating with God sending rain and sunshine equally to those considered just and unjust. Skillen argues that the State should treat all citizens equally, not negatively discriminating against or providing superior privileges to anyone in relation to his/her religious beliefs. Skillen infers that confessional or directional pluralism should be a critical component of the State's constitution.[93]

Each of the three types of pluralities or pluralisms, which Skillen identifies, referring to Mouw and Griffioen, may be further classified into the following six distinct categories. Mouw and Griffioen accordingly designated:

1. descriptive contextual pluralism,

2. normative contextual pluralism,

3. descriptive directional pluralism,

4. normative directional pluralism,

5. descriptive associational pluralism, and

6. normative associational pluralism.[94]

Implementing this scheme, Mouw and Griffioen emphasize the differences between the indication of each type of pluralism and the normative action (for or against) for each. Of the six categories of pluralism, they conclude that Christians should endorse and affirm five, excluding "normative directional pluralism," a position they charge with causing danger regarding ultimate relativism.[95] Table 2 illustrates the six categories Mouw and Griffioen classify as well as related indications and their correlating stances.

---

92. Skillen, *Good of Politics*, 128.

93. Mouw and Griffioen, *Pluralisms and Horizons*, 135.

94. Mouw and Griffioen, *Pluralisms and Horizons*, 17–18.

95. Mouw and Griffioen, *Pluralisms and Horizons*, 19.

Table 2: Six Pluralisms and Approaches[96]

Pluralism	Indication	Mouw's & Griffion's Stance
Descriptive associational pluralism	Identifies a plurality of associations within which people live	Endorses and affirms
Normative associational pluralism	Argues for a plurality of associations within which people live	Endorses and affirms
Descriptive contextual pluralism	Classifies contexts and cultures within which people live	Endorses and affirms
Normative contextual pluralism	Argues for a plurality of contexts and cultures within which people live	Endorses and affirms
Descriptive directional pluralism	Denotes different views of life and values that people hold	Endorses and affirms
Normative directional pluralism	Argues for different views of life and values that people hold	Does not endorse or affirm because this causes danger regarding ultimate relativism

Mouw and Griffioen also note that the six facets of pluralism illustrated above not only depict diversity within a society but also denote six distinct approaches to its multiplicity. In addition, Mouw and Griffioen offer several questions to cultivate understandings relating to their characterizations of pluralisms and the relationships between contexts and directions. Questions they consider include:

- In what sense is the notion of a cultural context distinct from that of a directional vision?

- And what role, furthermore, does associational diversity play in a proper understanding of differences within diversity?[97]

According to Mouw and Griffioen, when contemplating a plurality of cultural contexts, some individuals may perceive that the situation is characterized by a diversity of directional perspectives. Diana L. Eck gives

96. Author's original table created from information by Mouw and Griffioen, *Pluralisms and Horizons*, 17–18.

97. Mouw and Griffioen, *Pluralisms and Horizons*, 151.

a further important insight in relation to directional pluralism. As pluralism dynamically seeks to cultivate understanding across differences, it represents more than tolerance. Eck notes that tolerance, "a critical public virtue, does not mandate that Christians and Muslims, Hindus, Jews, and ardent secularists know anything about each other,"[98] only that they [may] stereotype other groups. On the other hand, pluralism involves an understanding of different beliefs/philosophies and encompasses the differences in beliefs/philosophies between people, even those which diverse religions demonstrate. Pluralism, also based on dialogue, not only involves speaking but also listening to reveal differences and common understandings regarding a person's beliefs/philosophies.[99]

Eck perceives religious pluralism or directional pluralism to be a means of bringing individuals together and asserts that she believes a society increases its strength as citizens exercise their religious freedom.[100] She stresses the need for one generation of free individuals to continue fighting to protect and ensure religious freedom and defend normative contextual pluralism. The war against religious freedom, or what Mouw and Griffioen would call "normative directional pluralism," will never end, Eck asserts.[101] Eck stresses that in its diverse relationships, pluralism simultaneously creates challenges and enhances life as it compels individuals to choose between contending goals, obligations, principles, and virtues.

This raises the question whether one should endorse a normative directional pluralism. In response to this, Mouw and Griffioen endorse a "dialogical theocentrism," which draws on the thought that despite the fall, Christians can and should learn a number of things from non-believers.[102] To do this, Christians engage in dialogues with non-believers within the ontological common ground that, under one creation, the same sun shines its light on, and the same rain falls on, all. God shares his common grace in one human world, with both the "righteousness and the unrighteousness."[103] Based on this rationale, in addition to the four types of pluralism, associational and contextual in both descriptive and normative forms, Mouw and Griffioen, although with legitimate reservation on normative directional pluralism, endorse descriptive directional pluralism. In other words, their

---

98. Eck, "Pluralism Project."

99. Eck, "Pluralism Project."

100. Eck, *New Religious America.*

101. Eck, *New Religious America,* 14–19.

102. Mouw and Griffioen, *Pluralisms and Horizons,* 104–7.

103. Matthew 5:45 (NIV).

position is to endorse all but "normative directional pluralism" which they charge increases the danger toward ultimate relativism.[104]

Ultimate relativism is not only the primary concern of advocates of Christian pluralism but also, to a great extent, of principled pluralism supporters. Mouw and Griffioen propose a key question: "Where /what is the common ground/standard for evaluating competing worldviews (diversity) without sinking into relativistic pluralism or normless pluralism?"[105] Rick Simpson argues that Christian belief is not incompatible with pluralities in public life.[106] I assert that followers of Christianity and other religious adherents do not have to abandon their exclusive truth proclamation for meaningful peaceful co-existence in the public square.

In order to accommodate the spirit of toleration, Tom Driver suggests the abandonment of strong religious truth-claims. He argues that unless Christians divest theological requirements (salvation and liberation) of conforming public behavior, Christians will fail to have hope of ridding the world of the remnants of formal political alliance between Church and State.[107] If Driver's point is true, however, then in restraining the full public expression of the core conviction of religions or no religions and its adherents, how can a democratic society effectively protect freedom of religion or belief for all in accordance with the international norms?

Baorong Duoyuan does not duplicate Driver's exclusive approach but shares some of his legitimate concerns. On the one hand, there might be a risk of religious intolerance and conflict if the State endorses or establishes one religion, or belief, or non-belief over the other. On the other hand, there could be religious relativism if truth-claim religions are censuring themselves because of institutional and societal humiliation. Nevertheless, by the same reasoning, in order to guarantee religious freedom for all, *Baorong Duoyuan* endorses and affirms the need for the protection of normative directional pluralism by the State. By agreeing and adopting the rationale for dialogical theocentrism, not only for descriptive but normative pluralism, the State, under a constitutional structure, provides both the guarantee for religious freedom, as well as the highest level of fair mechanism for constitutional appeal if violations occur. Under *Baorong Duoyuan*, the State will treat every religion, or belief, or non-belief system with impartiality. *Baorong Duoyuan* also guarantees that in a post-communist

---

104 , *Pluralisms and Horizons*, 10.

105. Mouw and Griffioen, *Pluralisms and Horizons*, 12.

106. Simpson, "Can a Faithful."

107. Driver, *Liberating Rites*.

democratic pluralistic society, the freedom for each of these can be manifested in public and private, equally and fairly.

I assert that even Christians should agree, at least in principle, to engage in humble dialogue with others without compromising the truth-claims as a crucial means to facilitate a covenant partnership with God and each other. Not doing so limits the ability of citizens with diverse beliefs to understand and communicate with each other. Under God's common grace, at least as members of the free and equal citizenry in a democratic pluralistic civil society, the State, for the sake of protection of religious freedom for all citizens who are associated in different contexts or structures, should encourage each association under every context, religious or non-religious, to contribute to our pluralistic society's common good. I endorse Mouw and Griffieon's "dialogical theocentrism" approach in both descriptive and normative directional pluralism by which they choose not to constrain those who do not share their views from expressing his/her other ideas but, instead, to deliberately engage them in dialogue in order to learn from non-believers. Talking with and learning from others about different beliefs opens the door for a person to share his/her beliefs and increases understanding for both.

As noted earlier, Eck rightly asserts that pluralism depicts more than a tolerance which is ignorant of the other. As pluralism permeates more societies worldwide, states become increasingly heterogeneous and, in turn, citizens face pluralism and frequently incompatible identities, ideals, and interests.[108] Inherent tensions within societies often increase tensions relating to contrasting claims of ethnicity, gender, locality, and ideology as well as diverse religions, moral codes, and social spheres subject citizens to competing values and commitments. Consequently, public as well as private life spheres experience challenges correlating to increasing pluralism. As Bielefeldt emphasizes, states should facilitate an open arena where citizens can draw from their beliefs to formulate and express their political concerns and ideas in public discourses. In the next section, I examine ways in which those preferring theories of Christian nonpluralism would likely address tensions amid the diverse spheres of society, especially those between the State and religion.

108. Bellamy, *Liberalism and Pluralism*, 1.

2.4 Critique of Christian Non-Pluralism
under Religion–State Relationship

During the lifetimes of Kuyper[109] and Dooyeweerd as well as in the following century, numerous theologians and philosophers explored the issue of how best to address tensions amid the diverse spheres of society, especially those between the State and religion. On the one hand, under the influence of secularization and globalization, the State's role increasingly expanded, while on the other, the role of religion shrank significantly under the banner of religious privatization. Consequently, ensuing changes confronted religious freedom and endangered it in both democratic and non-democratic societies.

While secularists have instigated attempts to exclude religious worldviews from any public discourse in the public square, some religious supporters have challenged religious freedom from the opposite direction through attempts to theocratize society under a solitary religious confession. Under the latter scheme, some groups, such as Islamic extremists, have implemented violent measures, including acts of terrorism, to achieve goals for their group's version of theocracy. Concurrently, several Christian-based views, including Christian Nation thought, Christian Reconstructionism, and theonomy argue for a theocratic structural design for society.[110]

Contrary to Kuyper's assertion that the unrelenting goal of the people ought to be the demand of justice for all (justice for each life-expression), these contemporary combatant entities seek privileged "justice for us." Rather than complementing society's pluralistic nature, these views tend toward a "monolithic" orthodox rule of society, constraining freedom for diverse groups. In the context of a post-Christian age within Western countries that have a Christian heritage but are facing increasing directional pluralism in society as well as growing secularization, Christian philosophers and theologians have offered multiple proposals. According to Bogue, "While theonomists believe that structural [associational and contextual] pluralism is biblical, we [theonomists] contend that confessional [directional] pluralism is not." Identifying these groups as Christian nonpluralists does not mean that they are all against any form of pluralism.

---

109. Skillen, "Reformed . . . and Always Reforming," 53–72. In many countries, including the US, due to their discomfort with State-established churches, Reformed Christians have complied with or actively promoted secularization of State and society. In turn, Reformed and Presbyterian Christians have too readily accepted the Enlightenment's arguments for privatizing religion to develop an ostensibly tolerant, rational, secular public square.

110. Spykman, "Principled Pluralist Position."

For example, even theonomists would allow for both associational and contextual pluralisms. While some support a liberal line of thought, or the principled pluralism which this study supports, there are also Christian nonpluralist positions.[111] These include:

1. the Theonomic position (Greg L. Bahnsen),[112]
2. the Christian American position (Joseph N. Kickasola) and[113]
3. the National Confessional position (William Edgar).[114]

Despite minor differences between the three groups, the theonomic position, the Christian American position, and the National Confessional position oppose the normative directional pluralistic approach by the State. As noted earlier in this chapter, Mouw and Griffioen do not endorse normative directional pluralism due to the danger of ultimate truth relativism, a legitimate concern for any adherents of the absolute truth in the sphere of confessional religions. On pages [***], I reference why I endorse the need for the protection of normative directional pluralism; nevertheless, I limit my endorsement in this study to the sphere of the State, without extending it to other spheres of society. In addition, contrary to principled pluralism, these groups choose to embrace a more theocratic society led by Christian worldviews. For the purposes of this study, I choose the theonomic position as representative of all three Christian nonpluralist positions, including the Christian American position and the National Confessional position. I believe that among their shared commitments to bring the State to conform with God's laws as revealed in the totality of the Scriptures, theonomy has articulated the most systematic formula to support its position.[115] Theonomism, also known as "dominion theology", denotes rule by God's law.[116] This movement, which often replicates the theology that early New England Puritans observed, literally represents the law of God and maintains the State should continue to apply the social and judicial laws that God gave to biblical Israel. Theocracy differs from democracy, which literally represents "rule by the people," and contrasts with the U.S. constitutional separation of State and religion.[117]

111. Bogue, "Theonomic Response," 100–106.
112. Bahnsen, "Theonomic Position," 21–53.
113. Kickasola, "Theonomic Response to Christian, 150–57.
114. Edgar, "National Confessional Position."
115. Bahnsen, "Theonomic Position," 17.
116. *Encyclopedia of Religion*, Schultz et al., 244.
117. Bahnsen, "Theonomic Position." Some mistakenly claim that if the State implemented the social and judicial laws God gave to biblical Israel, citizens who failed

Bahnsen explains that theonomists reason that God's laws—the Law of Moses—epitomize the supreme standard for contemporary civil affairs, except for considerations that the New Testament disavows.[118]

Theonomy alleges that God's laws, revealed to Israel, the Old Testament nation, are still applicable. In a contemporary theonomic State, the legal system would subject adulterers, blasphemers, and rebellious children to the death penalty. The post-millennialism principle proclaims that even though it may not occur for centuries, Christians will ultimately govern society.[119]

Rather than agreeing with theonomy, which regards the role of civil government to be under the authority of the rule of God, principled pluralism proposes that the State operates as a constitutional democracy, embracing most forms of pluralism. If one religion only were to rule, Kuyper reasons, religion could develop tyrannical traits.[120] By contrast, regarding the role of civil government being under the authority of the rule of God,[121] the theonomic perception maintains that the ruler's sphere of authority includes reproving evil, thus aligning the rule of the State with God's laws. This stance asserts that only one religion rules. Although principled pluralists agree with theonomists in some areas, including that Christians should obey and support biblical guidelines in the realm of political life, they disagree with the one-religion rule of the theonomic position.[122] Presumably, they also do not believe that all biblical moral guidelines, fornication being wrong, for example, should be criminalized.

Also, in contrast to theonomists, principled pluralists, along with most Reformed believers do not agree that Christians should observe the Old Testament civil laws as part of a continuing mandate. Instead, they are to follow the new covenant that Christ Jesus came to implement. Traditional Reformed theology accepts the division of Old Testament laws into three types:

1. civil

2. ceremonial (or ritual) and

---

to comply with the laws would be subject to Old Testament penal sanctions. Some mis understanding this sect allege theonomists support punishments for infractions to include but not limited to the execution of "blasphemers, adulterers, homosexuals, and rebellious children." Bahnsen disputes this charge as the New Testament rejects this harsh punishment for these infractions.

118. Schrotenboer, "Principled Pluralist Response," 54–60.

119. Bahnsen, "Theonomic Position," 48–49.

120. Brito, "An Analysis of Kuyper's Lecture."

121. Bahnsen, "Theonomic Position," 48–49.

122. Smith, "Principled Pluralist Response," 213–20.

3. moral laws.[123]

The transition from the covenant in the Old Testament to the new one following Christ has entailed discontinuity and continuity among these laws. As John Calvin puts it:

> We must attend to the well known division which distributes the whole law of God, as promulgated by Moses, into the moral, the ceremonial, and the judicial law, and we must attend to each of these parts, in order to understand how far they do, or do not, pertain to us. Meanwhile, let no one be moved by the thought that the judicial and ceremonial laws relate to morals. For the ancients who adopted this division, though they were not unaware that the two latter classes had to do with morals, did not give them the name of moral, because they might be changed and abrogated without affecting morals. They give this name specially to the first class, without which, true holiness of life and an immutable rule of conduct cannot exist.[124]

Calvin stresses the continuity of the moral law to believers in New Testament times:

> Now, as it is evident that the law of God which we call moral, is nothing else than the testimony of natural law, and of that conscience which God has engraven on the minds of men, the whole of this equity of which we now speak is prescribed in it. Hence it alone ought to be the aim, the rule, and the end of all laws. Wherever laws are formed after this rule, directed to this aim, and restricted to this end, there is no reason why they should be disapproved by us, however much they may differ from the Jewish law, or from each other.[125]

123. Some early church fathers, including Martyr, Irenaeus, and Augustine attempted to classify the laws in the Old Testament and their implications to the New Testament into two parts. They distinguished between that known as the moral law and the ceremonial/civil law and connected the moral law with the Ten Commandments. Aquinas, widely acknowledged as perhaps the first theologian distinctly defend a threefold division of the law, classified these as moral, ceremonial and civil law. His division portrays a development from the division Augustine and other church fathers maintained; distinguishing the moral law from parts of the law which passed away in the new covenant. Subsequently, many reformers like Calvin and the Westminster Divines also continued to adopt the viewpoint of the tripartite division of the law. Calvin calls the threefold distinction "well known" and attributes it to the "ancients." Although not offering an extensive biblical defense, Calvin provided an extensive deliberation on implications and applications of the three divisions of the OT laws to NT believers.

124. Calvin, *Institutes* IV, 14.

125. Calvin, *Institutes* IV, 15.

Oliver O'Donovan argues that individuals should not only respect the laws of the community, they should practice and uphold its moral laws as well. They should also honor God's moral authority.[126] Wayne Grudem stresses that Jesus taught that the realms of "God" and "Caesar" distinctly imply freedom of religion and, therefore, today as in the past, all civil governments should protect each citizen's freedom regarding the religious or any anti- or non-religious faith they follow. "Caesar" should not control the religious doctrines that individuals hold or how they do or do not worship God, for these belong to God, not the government.[127]

I suggest of believe that Christians in every State should support freedom of religion for all and oppose government attempts to have only one specific religion. Furthermore, (1) although principled pluralists and theonomists disagree regarding whether civil laws should be treated the same as moral laws, they agree that biblical moral laws are still valid. They maintain that as part of biblical continuity, Christians and Christian churches individually, as well as collectively, should observe and obey these moral laws; (2) in general, principled pluralists believe that Christians are called to obey moral laws in their faith and practices according to the New Testament.

While not disagreeing with theonomists that the moral laws should be obeyed and practiced by individual Christians and institutional churches, principled pluralists disagree with theonomist and even some Reformed teachers about the mechanism for implementing the moral laws. In the history of the church, major disputes have arisen regarding whether the civil magistrate or the ecclesiastical authority should have the responsibility to enforce the moral law, and, if so, which part to enforce. Perhaps the most controversial dilemma concerns how to enforce moral law. These disputes have been manifested in the civil authorities' treatment of doctrinal cult.[128]

Some schools of thought suggest that while the civil magistrate does not act as a purely "neutral" agent in a nonmoral or moral-less vacuum, neither should he/she act as a coercive enforcer of the moral law except for

---

126. O'Donovan, *Resurrection and Moral Order*, 190.

127. Grudem, "Why Christians Should."

128. A few schools of thought include: the full ecclesiastical enforcement approach, including use of coercive force by the Catholic Church's authority in the Middle Ages; the Anabaptists' belief that the church should involve non-coercive enforcement of any part of the moral law approach because they support total separation between church and civil magistrate, and believe that only the civil magistrate has no responsibility to involve doctrinal disputes; Calvin holds the view that both the church and the State have the responsibility to enforce all of the moral law codes, including cracking down on the doctrinal cults; modern Presbyterians and Baptists believe that as a matter of religious freedom, the State should have no role in doctrinal disputes, and the cult issue should be resolved within ecclesiastic authorities.

criminal activities such as stealing. As stated at the beginning of this chapter, true religious freedom will not be fully protected if the State prosecutes an individual or religious group for breaking a moral norm such as spiritual idolatry. If no public judicial statutes are violated, the State should stay away from interfering with the moral conduct of any religious or non-religious citizen, institution, or organization. The responsibility for disciplining someone who contravenes a moral norm solely belongs to the sphere of different associations: for example, church, family, club, or business. Principled pluralism asserts that the primary role and authority of the civil government spheres, under God's common grace, is not that of a moral law enforcement police officer. The principle of freedom of religion or belief is especially rooted in religious belief and conscience.

Paul Marshall rightly stresses that the State does not hold the right to do anything it desires. "If following the principled pluralist perspective, with the State as an agent of God's common grace, its authority, while limited, is charged with 'the responsibility for maintaining an overall order of justice in a territory.'"[129] Constitutional law aims to regulate the State's power and ensure that various spheres, including religious domains, retain their authority, do not encroach on the other's domain, and that the relationships between authorities (whether within one sphere or across different spheres) conform to a just order. Although the conflict between the State and religion is the focus of the discussion in my study, I assert that when the State commits to ensuring justice for all, it will conversely protect and safeguard religious freedom for all.[130]

I maintain that Christians in authority should protect the religious freedom of individuals with the same beliefs just as it should those with other religious beliefs and practices, including those adhering to different (denominational) interpretations. Christians in authority should also ensure religious freedom for those professing beliefs incompatible with biblical law and teachings. This religious freedom protection should even extend to those in conflict with or contrary to Christianity, including individuals believing and practicing cultic or pagan "religions."

In contextualizing principled pluralism, I expand on this posture and stress that no one religious or non- or anti-religious belief should supersede another in a State. In addition to defending religious freedom based on biblical guidelines and ascertaining that obedience to God's law supremely matters, I maintain that this freedom serves as a criterion to secure political and social freedoms as well as a deterrent to religious persecution.

---

129. Marshall, *God and the Constitution*, 61.

130. Skillen, *Recharging the American Experiment*.

As theonomy and other Christian nonpluralist theories essentially demonstrate bias against other religions and fail to protect the rights of all citizens, principled pluralists cannot support the theonomist perspective. I maintain that theonomists, subsequently, deny religious freedom for all. This fundamental difference between theonomy and principled pluralism, in that theonomy excludes other religious groups, reflects a primary reason why theonomy should not be adopted as a viable governance mechanism or theory in a pluralistic society. Theonomists who adopt and adhere to Old Testament laws deny religious freedom to other individuals practicing different religions.[131] Proponents for political liberalism, a popular theory with a secular worldview I explore in the next chapter, ironically share a commonality with theonomy to some extent and, in effect, may also fail to protect religious freedom for all. As we will see, those supporting political liberalism could also prevent some theonomists from contributing to the political decision-making process in the public square, particularly if they deemed those professing theonomy as unreasonable.

Principled pluralists agree with certain points inherent in the theonomists' religious convictions, and with the basic Christian doctrine. They acknowledge God's sovereignty and concur that, ultimately, God remains in control.[132] However, applying the theonomist viewpoint to society yields wrong conclusions. Not only does theonomy not support normative pluralism as part of the role of the State, in addition, unless instituted in a committed dictatorial environment, the theonomist view cannot be practicably implemented. Consequently, in a modern pluralistic society, theonomy, unlike principled pluralism, would fail to nurture religious freedom.

2.5 Conclusion

Contrary to theonomy, principled pluralism embraces social, cultural, and religious pluralism in most forms. In pursuit of religious freedom and "justice for all," the principled pluralist philosophy can most coherently and consistently offer relief for the often-overpowering tension occurring in different structures of society. Principled pluralism, unlike theonomy, can help achieve true harmony among the various spheres and ultimately strengthen society as diverse groups function to work together as a free and equal society.

131. Rawls supports this concept relating to political liberalism (expounded in Chapter 3).

132. Bahnsen, "Theonomic Position."

As principled pluralism nurtures harmony amid societal spheres, it maximizes the protection of freedom of religion and implements justice for all faiths. This practice reduces the potential for religious wars and neutralizes the dilemma facing monopolistic, exclusive attempts by both secularists and theonomists to dismiss views that differ from their own. Under principled pluralism, the arrangements afford "not only negative liberties for individual adherents to diverse worldviews (the classical liberal version of religious freedom) but also positive liberties for diverse worldview-based associations."[133] Principled pluralism, which complements religious freedom for all, promotes the objective of using the public square within constitutional democracies to facilitate rather than frustrate the representation of deep diversity.

Principled pluralism will not only ensure the same public defense and equal protection for any believer within one religion and to those who belong to diverse confessional beliefs but also to non-confessional individuals. Under the framework of principled pluralism, every citizen, no matter what his/her worldview, may manifest his/her faith freely and equally within different associations and in different contexts.

My argument in this study primarily focuses on how the State should carry out its relationship to religions in order to best protect religious freedom for all citizens. Thus, I conclude that the State should adopt the protection of the normative directional pluralism approach to demonstrate neither prejudice nor privilege for any type of religion or worldview. Although principled pluralism, a political theory closely compatible with normative directional pluralism, appears to best protect religious freedom for all, it still has limitations, mainly due to its overtly Christian orientation. In the next chapter, I point out that in contrast to principled pluralism, political liberalism, the most prevalent political philosophy practiced in nearly all contemporary Western democracies,[134] fails to impartially and coherently protect directional pluralism. Political liberalism, as represented by John Rawls, inadvertently contradicts its claim to protect the freedom and equality of all citizens by proposing constraints upon public discourse about religion and even excluding some religious groups if they fail to meet Rawlsian criterion for public reasoning.

In the following sections and chapters, I illustrate several points of contention relating to religious freedom that apply to principled pluralism as well as political liberalism, chiefly by examining the relationship between two types of "associational pluralism," the State and religion and, second, by

133. Chaplin, "Full Weight," para. 5.
134. Chaplin, "Full Weight."

considering the field of public education. I validate my argument by demonstrating the inadequacy and failure of the protection of religious freedom within two cases of "contextual pluralism": four Western liberal societies, and contemporary China. Thus, I later propose *Baorong Duoyuan*, a contextualization of principled pluralism, which is aligned with the intent of political liberalism to achieve civic harmony among diverse and sometimes conflicting comprehensive ideas to ultimately serve the wider common good.

Contrary to political liberalism, which fails to adequately meet the requirements of pluralism, as I surmise in Chapter 3, but according to principled pluralism that I assert in this chapter, the State is bound to guarantee that all citizens can express their political opinions in public discourses, whether directly or indirectly derived from their religious convictions. As James W. Skillen rightfully proclaims, the true nature of religious freedom requires that the State does not have the right to determine limits of nor predefine religion.[135]

---

135. Skillen, *Recharging the American Experiment*, 119.

Chapter 3

Public Reason in Light
of Religious Freedom

[E]very actual society . . . will normally contain numerous unreasonable doctrines that are not compatible with a democratic society—[this
includes] certain religious doctrines, such as fundamentalist religions.
. . . Unreasonable doctrines are a threat to democratic institutions.

∽JOHN RAWLS[1]

3.1 Introduction

IN CHAPTER 2, I defined principled pluralism, introduced Kuyper and
Dooyeweerd as early, primary proponents of this theory, and contrasted principled pluralism with various Christian non-directional pluralist approaches.
My research for the previous chapter led me to conclude that although with
a distinct Christian root and orientation, principled pluralism constitutes
the most coherent, systematic contemporary political theory to guarantee
religious freedom for all. In this chapter, I present and critique political liberalism, one of the popular, contemporary constitutional liberal approaches
among democratic countries, concentrating my study on public reason. My
rationale for choosing political liberalism to compare with principled pluralism relates to the main theme of my thesis: to formulate a theoretical model
for China, which I identify as *Baorong Duoyuan* in Chapter 5, guaranteeing
religious freedom for a post-communist China in a projected Christianized

---

1. Rawls, "Idea of Public Reason Revisited," 806.

and democratic future. The increasing influence of Rawls among younger Chinese liberal intellectuals today not only positions political liberalism as a conceivable way forward for China, it also makes Rawls's political liberalism a viable opponent of principled pluralism and, therefore, dictates that a model of *Baorong Duoyuan* must engage with him.[2]

Political liberalism, substantially articulated in recent times by the late John Rawls,[3] a contemporary American political philosopher. Unlike theonomist and programmatic secularist[4] approaches, this theory embraces directional pluralism only to the extent of toleration. I maintain that if strictly implemented, political liberalism, like Christian non-directional pluralisms, as I suggested in Chapter 2, will also fail to protect religious freedom coherently, sufficiently, and fully for all.

In Chapter 3, I initially examine the concept of liberalism, reviewing three distinct yet interrelated branches of this perception.[5] I analyze aspects of constitutional liberalism, the only form of liberalism which deals with issues related to my topic of concern, the State–religion relationship as it relates to religious freedom.[6] I also introduce political liberalism, which Rawls developed from constitutional liberalism.

Despite its professed commitment to religious freedom, in the context of reasonable pluralism, political liberalism: (1) subtly camouflages concepts that restrain comprehensive worldviews, particularly religious worldviews, as demonstrated by its demand for the principle of religious self-restraint (PRSR),[7] which places limits on religions being able to justify public policy; (2) further prescribes, under the filter of public reason,[8] disallowing certain religions deemed unreasonable or irrational from

2. He, *The Democratisation of China*, 2.

3. Gaus, "The Place of Autonomy . . . ."

4. Williams, "Secularism, Faith and Freedom," para. 1.

5. Song, *Christianity and Liberal Society*, 37. Song, a professor of theology and religion, identifies three branches of liberalism, "constitutional liberalism, classical economic liberalism, and welfare or revisionist liberalism."

6. McIlwain, *Constitutionalism: Ancient and Modern*, 24. "Constitutionalism [. . .] is a legal limitation on government; it is the antithesis of arbitrary rule; its opposite is despotic government, the government of will instead of law."

7. Eberle and Cuneo, "Religion and Political Theory," 574. I derive the principle of religious self-restraint (PRSR) from the doctrine of religious restraints (DRR), noted in Eberle and Cuneo (p.3) that restrains a citizen from supporting a coercive law if he/she does not believe a plausible secular rationale for that law exists.

8. Rawls, *Political Liberalism*. Public reason stipulates the basic moral and political values that determine a constitutional, democratic government's relationship to its citizens as well as their relationship to each other. It relates to how "the political relation [of free and equal citizens] is to be understood."

participating in political discourse; and (3) implies, although not explicitly, the potential infringement of parents' religious freedom by denying
preferred religious education for some children according to their parents'
religion-based social and political convictions.[9]

As I note throughout this study, restrictions and persecutions relating
to religious freedom in China prove much more serious and oppressive than
anything seen in Western liberal democracies. Nonetheless, in this chapter,
I have chosen to focus on the three specific concerns regarding religious
freedom expounded by Rawls's political liberalism, noted in the previous
paragraph. These include the PRSR, the filter of public reason, and the potential infringement of parents' religious freedom. Although not necessarily
implemented by the State's coercive power, each of these three problematic points shows either: (1) an inconsistency; (2) an insufficiency; or (3)
an infringement on religious freedom. In turn, these challenges to political
liberalism contradict its claims to protect religious freedom.

Ultimately, I conclude Chapter 3 by emphasizing that contrary to
political liberalism, which restrains comprehensive religiously based arguments from contributing to public policy—even going so far as to contain
certain religions and violate parental religious freedom regarding the choice
for their children's religious education—principled pluralism permits all
groups, religious as well as non-religious, to equally manifest their voices
in both political and nonpolitical discourses. Regarding matters of constitutional decisions, especially related to the State's coercive power, principled
pluralism agrees with political liberalism in that certain political officehold-
ers should exercise a proper degree of restraint when applying their comprehensive worldview-based convictions.[10] As noted in Chapter 2, principled
pluralism, under a constitutional framework, guarantees the full spectrum
of religious freedom not only for those who meet the criteria that Rawls's
proviso[11] and public reason stipulate—but for all.

3.2 Concepts of Liberalism and Constitutional Liberalism

Across and within scholarly discourses, the definition of liberalism draws on
diverse concepts as well as presumptions regarding its core, meaning, and

---

9. Pennanen, "Political Liberalism and the Preventive," 191–208.

10. Chaplin, *Talking God*, 58–76. Chaplin proposes a posture of confessional impartiality in the State's decision-making.

11. Chaplin, *Talking God*, 35. Rawls's proviso requires that citizens support any
religious reasons they present in public debate with arguments that every other citizen
will consider reasonable.

history.[12] Although liberalism has become increasingly visible during contemporary times, it did not merit significant discussion as an intellectual tradition until the early twentieth century. According to Duncan Ivison, the roots of liberalism, a nineteenth-century development, extend from "the seventeenth- and eighteenth-century European political discourse."[13] By the early 1960s, liberalism had become a dominant force in Western political and social arenas. Kenneth Minogue, a theorist from the London School of Economics, describes liberalism as a single, continuing, extensive entity that encompasses most guiding beliefs of modern Western opinion.[14] Ivison points out that despite liberalism's significant history, records for the seventeenth and eighteenth century did not expressly acknowledge John Locke (1632–1704),[15] a British philosopher now often regarded as the "founding father"[16] of liberalism. As the chief early liberal theorist of toleration, however, Locke serves as an example of liberalism relevant to religious freedom.

Locke's social contract theory of limited government and pioneering work promoting religious tolerance proved central to liberalism. Karen Murphy asserts that Locke recognizes that justice (as a facet of liberalism) requires respect for an individual's rights. These fundamental rights include life, liberty, and property; perceiving the State as guardian of an individual's right to pursue his/her choice of religion and not promoting a specific religion.[17] In 1689, Locke argued for religious freedom on behalf of all religious adherents:

> [I]f Solemn Assemblies, Observations of Festivals, publick Worship be permitted to any one sort of Professors [i.e. religious people], all these things ought to be permitted to the Presbyterians, Independents, Anabaptists, Arminians, Quakers, and others, with the same Liberty. Nay, if we may openly speak the Truth, and as becomes one Man to another, neither *Pagan*, nor

12. Shklar, *Political Thought and Political Thinkers*, 21. Shklar contends that throughout years of philosophical considerations and overuse, as humans have regularly shaped and then reshaped the meaning of liberalism to fit their purposes, the term appears to have become amorphous. Consequently, Shklar notes, liberalism currently depicts "an all-purpose word, whether of abuse or praise." She characterizes liberalism as a political doctrine with "only one overriding aim: to secure the political conditions necessary for the exercise of personal freedom." To avoid confusion throughout this section and the thesis, I, as Shklar does in her writing, consider liberalism to reflect a political doctrine, not a philosophy of life or partisan ideology.

13. Ivison, *Philosophy of John Locke*, 94.

14. Minogue, *Liberal Mind*.

15. Ivison, "Locke, Liberalism, and Empire," 94.

16. Minogue, *Liberal Mind*.

17. Murphy, *State Security Regimes*, 15.

Mahometan, nor *Jew* ought to be excluded from the Civil Rights of the Commonwealth because of his Religion.[18]

Approximately three centuries later, this right which Locke highlights, that no one "ought to be excluded," became integral to the fundamental elements of religious freedom. Other rights Locke supports include "the right to have or to adopt a religious belief, and the right to practice that religion without discrimination."[19] In the early formation of religious freedom, the State subjected freedom of religion to a method of legal oversight. In domestic law and policy, however, freedom of religion evolved gradually. "The human right to religious freedom is a relatively recent invention, enshrined in human rights declarations and conventions that are less than, or little more than, 50 years in existence."[20] In the past, religious tolerance proved to be a luxury delegated to one or only a few groups. In contemporary times, the majority of regional as well as international declarations and treaties, as I note in Chapter 2, include a provision to protect religious freedom.

Despite attempts by some contemporary liberals to eliminate any theological assumptions from the history of liberalism, more contemporary research, as noted earlier, including that by David Marquand and several others, such as J. G. A. Pocock,[21] Duncan Ivison,[22] and Larry Siedentop,[23] confirms that liberalism initially assumed a theological structure. Like Kuyper, Locke presumes the existence of an ordered cosmos where all of creation serves a purpose and all things must serve God's implicit created purposes. Here, based on what Rawls deems as comprehensive reasonable religious views,[24] Locke, as an example of constitutional liberalism relevant to religious freedom, delivers one of the earliest theories of justification for religious toleration.[25] Under the historical context of religious persecution by the State-sanctioned church in England, religious tolerance became a central outcry of liberalism in the United States. Liberalism initially set out to confront religious intolerance. It also served as a resistance to the displays of discretionary power, including ecclesiastical, by other

---

18. Locke, *Letter Concerning Toleration*, 53.
19. Murphy, *State Security Regimes*, 15.
20. Murphy, *State Security Regimes*, 16.
21. Pocock, *Political Thought and History*.
22. Ivison, "Locke, Liberalism, and Empire."
23. Siedentop, *Inventing the Individual*.
24. Rawls, *Political Liberalism, Expanded*, 438.
25. Fesser, *Locke*, 159.

institutional monopolies.[26] At times, that intolerance resulted in multiple religious conflicts and wars, a primary motivation for Rawls to propose political liberalism.

As William Dunning, a political theorist during the early 1900s, noted, nineteenth-century liberalism, which basically means a democratic, human-centered, political structure, emerged to balance the monopolistic, ecclesiastical-controlled powers.[27]

> Fundamentally, nineteenth-century liberalism['s . . .] ultimate aim was to break down the bars which excluded from political life the classes of people whose intellectual, social and economic significance was becoming unmistakably predominant. For its immediate aim, it demanded liberty and equality.

This nineteenth-century liberalism, which Dunning refers to—classical liberalism—contrasts with contemporary liberalism and relates to that which Locke supports. Ryan explains that classical liberalism focuses on the premise of limited government yet maintains the rule of law as it circumvents arbitrary and discretionary power.

Although the general secular worldview serves as the foundation for most contemporary versions of liberalism and its concepts, some liberal theorists disagree regarding the State's relationship to religion.[28] In the following section, I review three branches of liberalism with an ensuing focus on constitutional liberalism. As noted in this chapter's introduction, constitutional liberalism embraces issues related to my topic of concern—religious freedom.

3.2.1 Branches of Liberalism

Amid diverse complex and complicated concepts, the definition of liberalism remains elusive. Song explains that constitutional liberalism, which I focus on in the next section, purposes to secure theoretical justification for practices encompassing the precept of limited government.[29] Constitutional

26. Ivison, "Locke, Liberalism, and Empire."

27. Bell, "What Is Liberalism?"

28. Ryan, *Making of Modern Liberalism*, 21. Three areas of potential controversy include: (1) the appropriate boundaries of toleration; (2) the validity of the welfare state; and (3) the character (virtue) of democracy.

29. Song, *Christianity and Liberal Society*, 37. This would include many or all of "effective restraints on the arbitrary or tyrannical exercise of power, constitutional definition of government powers, the rule of law, government legitimized by consent of the people, [and] maintenance of the rights of individuals," 37.

liberalism, which represents the earliest kind of liberal philosophy, relates to the liberalism of the American and French revolutions with a viewpoint opposing "arbitrary, personal, or unlimited power, to the possession of privileges by the few, and to the cramping demands of the feudal order."[30] Tayob notes that the initial core elements of constitutional liberalism[31] included "government based on the rule of law, separation of powers, popular consent through representative assemblies, [. . .], protection of the rights of property, and guarantees of freedom of the press and other liberties."[32] This liberalism embraces the most conspicuous contemporary defense of limited government. Figure 5 portrays three variations of liberalism. With the root system representing liberalism, constitutional liberalism depicts the trunk. Laissez-faire or classical economic liberalism (to the left), and welfare or revisionist liberalism (represented by the branch on the right), share the same commitments of constitutional liberalism.

30. Song, *Christianity and Liberal Society*, 37.

31. Tayob, "Islam and Democracy in South Africa," 22. "Constitutional liberalism emerged in the late seventeenth and eighteenth centuries, expounded in the writing of, among others, John Locke, Montesquieu, and the framers of the U.S. Constitution (particularly James Madison), and later in the work of such figures as Benjamin Constant, Alexis de Tocqueville, and John Stuart Mill."

32. Tayob, "Islam and Democracy," 22.

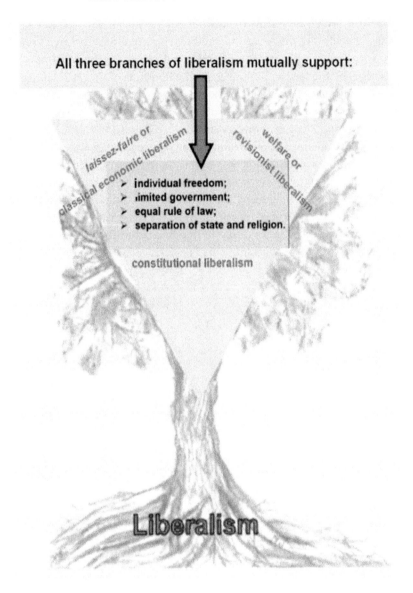

Three Branches of Liberalism

Even though disputes between economic liberals and welfare liberals constitute a regular feature of contemporary political life, those on both sides will invariably be committed to a limited government and, almost as frequently, support some form of constitutional liberalism. Moreover, it can be argued that an overlapping range of commitments exists among all three varieties of liberalism, which one may therefore interpret in terms of family resemblances.

Each of the three variations of liberalism noted in Figure 5 could conjoin a liberal worldview (characteristically anti-religious or secular). As some religious convictions prove compatible in principle with these three varieties of liberalism, they may also be aligned with theological commitments. Consequently, a certain amount of common ground enables some Christian pluralists, like Chaplin[33] and Skillen,[34] to embrace liberalism. Nevertheless, as their primary concern regards the role of the State relating to economic, welfare, and constitutional principles, in themselves, these facets of liberalism are not as such intrinsically either secular or religious.

Of the three variations of liberalism, only constitutional liberalism primarily deals with the authority of the State regarding its relationship to religion under a given constitutional frame.[35] Political liberalism and principled pluralism both presuppose constitutional liberalism and, in a sense, also develop diverse aspects of it with different orientations. Principled pluralism holds a Christian orientation while political liberalism takes a more secular liberal direction. As my primary concern for this study encompasses considerations of whether political liberalism or principled pluralism best serves to protect religious freedom, I narrow my focus to facets of constitutional liberalism within which the need for the protection of normative directional pluralism serves as a point of contention.

3.2.2 Constitutional Liberalism

As noted in this chapter's introduction, constitutional liberalism[36] depicts the one form of liberalism which correlates with my topic of concern, religious freedom. Bounded by constitutionalism or,[37] at a minimum, operating under

33. Chaplin, *Talking God*. Chaplin notes that he uses this term in his article "Rejecting Neutrality, Respecting Diversity."

34. Skillen, *Good of Politics*, 90–95.

35. Rawls, *Lectures on the History of Moral Philosophy*.

36. One of three branches of liberalism portrayed in the next section. Rawls partially derived political liberalism from procedural liberalism.

37. Waluchow, *Stanford Encyclopedia of Philosophy*, para. 1. "Constitutionalism [. . .] often associated with the political theories of John Locke and the founders of the American republic, [maintains that] government can and should be legally limited in its powers, and that its authority or legitimacy depends at on its observing these limitations." Despite the preeminence of constitutionalism, no agreed definition exists for this term. Similarly, no universally agreed rights or values explicitly identify the term "liberalism," nor do academic sources explicitly state what constitutes a liberal explanation of application of fundamental rights. To a considerable extent, liberalism

constitutionally guaranteed principles,[38] this branch of liberalism seeks to find reasons for basic human rights, including freedom of religion.[39] Nimer Sultany reports that various origins of constitutionalism emanate from three distinct societies, the United States, France, and the United Kingdom,[40] which I survey later in this chapter. These cultures not only recognize but also implement the concept of constitutional liberalism[41] in diverse ways.

Although the precise forms of government under a democratic constitutional liberalism structure may vary, the protection of essential liberties, including religious freedom by a limited government depicts a common feature of each. Song explains the difference between constitutional liberalism and limited government and notes that in general, constitutional liberalism:

> attempts to provide a theoretical justification for a set of practices clustered around the principle of limited government, including most or all of the following: effective restraints on the arbitrary or tyrannical exercise of power, constitutional definition of governmental powers, the rule of law, government legitimated plurality of religions and moral codes.[42]

According to Wen-Chen Chang et al., when a State and/or block of States implement(s) a secular liberal constitutional model, one may identify four pillars of constitutional liberalism regarding religion. Chang et al. explain that for a non-religious State which maintains a rationalist worldview "that strives to be 'neutral' toward towards religion."[43]

1. [T]here must be "a minimal threshold" of institutional, organizational, and role differentiation between state and (organized) religion.[44]

---

is marked less by a set of permanent attributes than by its effort against illiberalism. Therefore, fully assessing constitutional liberalism proves challenging. The explanation by Wen-Chen Chang and colleagues, coupled with observations that Song makes, however, enhances the understanding of the concept.

38. Philogène, *From Black to African American*, 118.

39. Slagstad, *Constitutionalism and Democracy*, 103–30.

40. Sultany, "The State of Progressive Constitutional Theory.

41. Hirschl, *Constitutional Theocracy*, 73. "Most modern constitutions, including those of most Middle Eastern, African, and Southeast Asian countries, contain some form of constitutional catalogue of rights, individual freedoms, formal equality, and procedural justice, including basic due-process rights, freedom of expression, freedom of religion, and in some cases the right to privacy." As an embedded piece of legislation, a constitution advances the rule of law, "often in lieu of and at times in tandem with the rule of God."

42. Song, *Christianity and Liberal Society*, 37.

43. Chang et al., *Constitutionalism in Asia*, 861.

44. Chang et al., *Constitutionalism in Asia*, 861.

In supreme constitutions or popular sovereignty, the state's role in guaranteeing democratic rights receives respect because religion's influence on state power is restrained. As a liberal state claims to be neutral regarding religions, it must ensure that it does not deliberately or extensively encourage or discourage belief or disbelief.

2. [T]he constitution must guarantee freedom of conscience and the right to have or to reject religious belief (freedom from religion).

3. [I]t must protect religious minorities from majorities.

4. [I]t must guarantee to treat religions equally, ensure mutual tolerance, and secure freedom for religious groups from state regulation.[45]

The diverse emphasis and interpretations of these four pillars of liberal constitutionalism have contributed to centuries of controversies and heated debates[46] as well as significant differences regarding the way the State relates to religion. Later in this chapter, I note several diverse expressions of constitutional liberalism regarding religious freedom, reflected in the United States, France, and the United Kingdom. Ideally, constitutional liberalism, under consensual, constitutionally decreed, legal guarantees, indiscriminately secures the individual's fundamental rights, including his/her religious freedom. As the constitution empowers the State to protect the individual's fundamental rights "in a well-ordered society,"[47] this in turn would ensure common good.

According to Rawls, for a democratic, pluralistic society with diverse and even irreconcilable, yet primarily reasonable, comprehensive doctrines or views, liberal or illiberal, dominant in public and political discourse, it is impossible to reach an overlapping consensus without conflicts.[48] Consequently, Rawls proposes political liberalism as a political theory by which competing reasonable worldviews can work together under justice as fairness, via public reason.

45. Chang et al., *Constitutionalism in Asia*, 861.

46. Supreme Court, "Court and Constitutional Interpretation." The Supreme Court serves as the final arbitrator regarding the interpretation of constitutional matters.

47. Rawls, *Political Liberalism*, 35.

48. Rawls, *Political Liberalism*, 35. Rawls asserts, "in an ideal overlapping consensus, each citizen affirms both a comprehensive doctrine and the focal political conception . . . ." In "Idea of Public Reason Visited," 801. Rawls further notes, "When political liberalism speaks of a reasonable overlapping consensus of comprehensive doctrines, . . . all of these doctrines, both religious and non-religious, support a political conception of justice underwriting a constitutional democratic society whose principles, ideals, and standards satisfy the criterion of reciprocity."

In its stance regarding basic political rights and liberties, Rawls's political liberalism reflects a narrower version of constitutional liberalism, demonstrated by his discussion of steps for building a political conception of justice and constitutional consensus. Rawls formulates what he deems as the constitutional consensus, to portray "a constitution satisfying certain basic principles [which] establishes democratic electoral procedures for moderating political rivalry within society."[49] Thus, Rawls's approach centers more on the political liberal conception of justice for the constitutional procedural system than a comprehensive social ideal.

As I introduce and examine political liberalism, particularly Rawls's concept of public reason, I commend his approach, which appears much more tolerant than that of his liberal predecessors regarding religious views in public discourse. His goal to explore the best liberal mechanism for a peaceful, democratic governing system which ensures freedom, or at least to the extent possible, a system not in opposition to any reasonable comprehensive doctrine, warrants recognition. Nevertheless, political liberalism may contribute to serious problems for religious freedom. I link these difficulties to three categories that I foreshadowed in this chapter's introduction: the PRSR, the filter of public reason, and the potential infringement on parents' religious freedom. These challenging concepts correlate with the way in which the practices of political liberalism restrain, contain, and potentially infringe on or violate religious freedom for all—concerns I address in the forthcoming sections.

3.3 Public Reason Related to Religious Freedom under Political Liberalism

Rawls works on the premise that the historical origins of political liberalism lie in and after the Reformation, with extended controversies over religious toleration occurring in the sixteenth and seventeenth centuries. Rawls explains that religious wars contributed to the need for political liberalism and therefore stimulated its introduction:

> During the wars of religion people were not in doubt about the nature of the highest good, or the basis of moral obligation in divine law [. . .]. The problem was rather: How is society even possible between those of different faiths? What can conceivably be the basis of religious toleration? For many there was none, for it meant the acquiescence in heresy about first things and the calamity of religious disunity. Even the earlier proponents of

49. Rawls, *Political Liberalism, Expanded*, 158.

toleration saw the division of Christendom as a disaster, though a disaster that had to be accepted in view of the alternative of unending religious civil war. Thus the historical origin of political liberalism (and of liberalism more generally) is the Reformation and its aftermath.[50]

Later, Rawls reiterates his point regarding the tensions between diverse religious truth claims and the role of the democratic State. He poses the question: "How is it possible for those holding religious doctrines, some based on religious authority, for example, the Church or the Bible, to hold at the same time a reasonable political conception that supports a reasonable constitutional democratic regime?"[51] Admittedly, in the history of the church (religion), injustices such as the conflicts and even bloody wars during the time of the Reformation regularly occurred in the name of one religion or denomination. Historically, from the Middle Ages to the Reformation, both theocratic and autocratic governments have applied their coercive powers to purely religious matters, such as peripheral doctrinal disputes and minor confessional differences. These have included, but have not been limited to, ways and means of baptism, infant baptism, liturgy, etc. Great religious reformers such as Luther and Calvin have sometimes failed miserably to match the standard of religious freedom. Rawls rightly points out that as Luther and Calvin appeared as dogmatic and intolerant as the church had been, those having to choose whether they would become Protestant or remain Catholic experienced trying times.

Chaplin recognizes Rawls's concerns regarding conflicts related to religion and emphasizes that most people understand that some public manifestations of religion are troublesome, and some may even incite violence. Nevertheless, Chaplin argues, religion can contribute in positive ways to public life. Religion that intentionally aims to impact the public square basically serves as a healthy response to a "sustained marginalisation of religious speech and identity in certain western democracies."[52] It may also reflect as well as remind religious communities of the need to engage in public struggles for justice and religious freedom for all in a world where these appear to be eroding away.

From examining Rawls's political liberalism, as well relevant reviews, reports,[53] and reflections, I have garnered ample academic evidence,

50. Rawls, *Political Liberalism, Expanded*, 797.

51. Rawls, *Law of Peoples*, 149.

52. Chaplin, *Talking God*, 20.

53. Rawls, "Idea of Public Reason," 437. For precision and clarity, I primarily draw from this source. Rawls considered this article as statement of his view on public reason

mirrored in the following three observations, to support my stance that political liberalism fails to coherently and sufficiently protect religious freedom
for all. I will argue that: (1) it includes inconsistencies that restrain reasonable comprehensive worldviews, particularly religious, demonstrated not
only by public reason but also by its demands for the PRSR and the proviso;
(2) under the filter of public reason, through the process of reciprocity,[54] it
further prescribes the containment of certain religions deemed unreasonable or irrational, prohibiting their adherents from participating in political discourse; and (3) it implies potential infringement of parents' religious
freedom relating to their children's education, especially religious education.
I address these critical concerns in the following three subsections, expressly
emphasizing public reason in light of religious freedom.

3.3.1 Inconsistencies in the PRSR,
the Proviso, and Self-Respect

Rawls initiates his design of political liberalism based on his fundamental
concern of what he perceives as inevitable social conflicts among different
reasonable, yet irreconcilable, comprehensive doctrines. He stresses that
"a basic feature of democracy is the fact of reasonable pluralism–the fact
that a plurality of conflicting reasonable comprehensive doctrines, religious, philosophical, and moral, is the normal result of its culture of free
institutions."[55] With reasonable yet conflicting pluralistic views as a normal
reality, Rawls does not propose removing any religious or non-religious
views as long he deems them reasonable. Instead, he seeks to answer the
question: "What kinds of reasons [may] they [those with diverse irreconcilable, comprehensive world views? . . .] reasonably give one another when
fundamental political questions are at stake?"[56] Rawls's solution in political
liberalism is to substitute the comprehensive doctrines of truth or right with
the idea of political justice deliberated not by individuals as associational
members drawing solely from their fundamental beliefs but through public
reason as equal and free citizens. Further analysis of political liberalism's

---

and political liberalism, especially regarding the compatibility of public reason with
religious views.

54. Rawls, *Political Liberalism, Expanded*, 52. Rawls explains reciprocity as "the
methodology of justifying political power with reference to principles acceptable to all
those affected. The methodology begins with what we already share—with the reasons
we are already presumed to find motivating—and uses what is shared to provide us
with reasons to support and defend principles of political justice."

55. Rawls, *Political Liberalism, Expanded*, 439.

56. Rawls, *Political Liberalism, Expanded*, 440.

mechanism of public reason, however, reveals inconsistencies that either fail to support or conflict with his stated goals.

Rawls contends that to secure agreement "between citizens on political questions of justice in a democracy, [. . . citizens] must avoid controversial philosophical, moral, and religious questions."[57] He admits, however, that this proves challenging: "[I]n a constitutional democracy, how can religious and secular doctrines of all kinds get on together and cooperate in running a reasonably just and effective government?"[58] Rawls argues that even though citizens, as well as legislators and proponents of public policy, are of diverse religious and secular doctrines, when they apply the limitation of argument to public reason, these citizens can, especially in relating religious reasons to secular ones, work together for common good.[59] Regarding public reason, I consider the following two questions worth exploring: (1) What is the nature and scope of Rawls's public reason? (2) What distinguishes public reason from non-public reasons?

Rawls stresses that a citizen's zeal to embody the whole truth in the political realm proves incompatible with public reason. He explains that the idea of public reason possesses a certain structure, and that for public reason to be plausible ["applied to the background culture"], none of its following five aspects can be ignored:[60]

1. the fundamental political questions to which it applies,

2. the persons to whom it applies (government officials and candidates for public office),

3. its content as given by a number of reasonable political conceptions of justice,

4. the application of these conceptions in discussions of coercive norms to be enacted in the form of legitimate law for a democratic people, and

5. citizens checking that the principles derived from their conceptions of justice satisfy the criterion of reciprocity.[61]

Rawls essentially equates public reason to a critical criterion necessary to bind public, politically related affairs in a democratic society, to various branches of government as well as political candidates and office holders.

---

57. Cline, *Confucius, Rawls*, 75.

58. Rawls, *Collected Papers*, 616.

59. Rawls, "Politics, Religion and Public Good."

60. Rawls, *Political Liberalism, Expanded*, 452.

61. Rawls, *Political Liberalism, Expanded*, 441.

He assumes that if he/she supports a democratic constitutional regime, any citizen with comprehensive worldviews, religious or non-religious, will endorse public reason. Rawls attempts to separate what he terms "public political reason" from "non-public" reasons.

> The nature of public reason will be clearer if we consider the differences between it and non-public reasons. First of all, there are many non-public reasons and but one public reason. Among the non-public reasons are those of associations of all kinds: churches and universities, scientific societies and professional groups. [. . .] Non-public reasons comprise the many reasons of civil society and belong to what I have called the "background culture," in contrast with the public political culture. These reasons are social, and certainly not private.[62]

Instead of contrasting public and private reasons, Rawls denies the existence of private reason. He categorizes reasons as public and non-public, with public reason belonging to political justice matters and non-public reasons including social and domestic reasons. In contrast to public reason that belongs to public political culture, social reasons concern different associations in a civil society that belong to the background culture. These may include religious institutions like churches, businesses, educational institutions, and other organizations.

Although it is noteworthy that Rawls's public reason would not exclude non-public reasons, particularly religious reasons, from participating in all public political affairs in the public sphere, his arbitrary separation between public reason and non-public reasons (social, religious, familial) leads to great inconsistencies, especially in relation to how he perceives the role of religious reasons when it comes to justifying coercive laws.[63] On the one hand, Rawls emphatically claims that political liberalism "does not aim to replace comprehensive doctrines, religious or non-religious, but intends to be equally distinct from both and, it hopes, acceptable to both."[64] He pointedly proclaims:

---

62. Rawls, *Political Liberalism, Expanded*, 220.

63. Bailey and Gentile, *Rawls and Religion*, 8. In their defenses on Rawls's behalf, Bailey and Gentile attempt to vindicate his barring religious and other comprehensive doctrines from the political arena. They argue that this exclusion "need not render political reasonings objectionably indeterminate or narrow in scope; insofar as citizens' shared conception of political authority provides a framework of considerations for reasoning."

64. Rawls, *Political Liberalism, Expanded*, xviii.

> We try, so far as we can, neither to assert nor to deny any par-
> ticular comprehensive religious, philosophical, or moral view,
> or its associated theory of truth and the status of values. Since
> we assume each citizen to affirm some such view, we hope to
> make it possible for all to accept the political conception as true
> or reasonable from the standpoint of their own comprehensive
> view, whatever it may be.[65]

Despite Rawls' repeated insistence, as shown above, regarding equal treatment for both secular and religious comprehensive views, I assert that Rawls'
scheme of public reason indicates a preference for secular reasons over religious ones. Historically, this biased practice is known as "the doctrine of
religious restraint" (DRR).[66] Rawls admits that in his past, he leaned toward
supporting a stringent version of the DRR which restrains citizens of a liberal democracy from appealing to religious reasons when deliberating about
matters of basic justice and constitutional essentials.[67] After he encountered
repeated criticisms, however, Rawls modified his position to assert that although a citizen may appeal to religious reasons to justify coercive law, he/she
may not base such an appeal solely on these reasons.

Although I created my original PRSR, by referencing the DRR, unlike
the DRR, which prevents any appeal to religious reasons in support of a
coercive law, the PRSR permits some religious reasoning and only restrains
a citizen from supporting a coercive law if he/she does not believe that
a plausible secular rationale for that law exists. The PRSR requires that a
citizen reasonably believes he/she will be prepared to provide reasonable
secular rationale for each coercive law he/she supports in political discussions. It also places fewer restrictions on the content of secular reasons
which citizens can appeal to when they deliberate or support coercive laws.
Nevertheless, Rawls reportedly reforms his position regarding the relation
between coercive law and religious reasons and continues to surmise that

65. Rawls, *Political Liberalism, Expanded,* 150.

66. Eberle and Cuneo, "Religion and Political." The DRR, a negative restraint, depicts a kind of reason that cannot justify a coercive law, a type of reason that citizens
may not entirely rely on to support a coercive law. This negative constraint usually goes
along with a permission. Citizens may not support coercive laws they believe to only
have a religious rationale; however, they may support coercive laws that they believe
have only a plausible secular rationale. Those advocating the DRR furnish reasons to
support the idea that religious and secular reasons have this asymmetrical justificatory
role (3).

67. Rawls, *Political Liberalism* (1993), (li–lii; 247, fn. 36). Rawls calls this "the proviso": reasonable comprehensive doctrines (and so religious reasons) may be offered "in
public reason at any time, provided that in due course public reasons [. . .] are presented
sufficient to support whatever the comprehensive doctrines are introduced to support."

despite an agent appealing to religious reasons to justify coercive law, he/ she cannot exclusively refer to religious motives. Rawls also attempts to distance himself from the charge that public reason will exclude only religious reasons and certain "irrational" sectarian doctrines to justify legislation in a democratic society and claims that political liberalism shows no preference for secular arguments over religious ones. He states, "these secular philosophical doctrines do not provide public reason. Secular concepts and reasoning of this kind belong to first philosophy and moral doctrine, and fall outside of the domain of the political."[68] However, Rawls's failure to address his public reason in the domain of political affairs through the lens of religious worldviews shows his inconsistency in his treatment of religious and secular reasons. After all, in the political arena, according to Rawls,[69] secular reasons must be paramount.

The PRSR puts an undue burden on citizens who seek to live an existence integrated with religion. Chaplin notes, that if "evangelical public reasoning" can't go out unchaperoned, Christian citizens will be compelled to veil it in the interests of consensus and acceptability. If they succumb to the obligation to offer justifying reasons in a secular public vernacular alongside any religious one,"[70] this will undermine the authenticity of their religious reasoning. In further justifying the PRSR, Rawls warns of the potential danger of oppressive use of State power if religious reasoning is being used to justify a coercive law. "[B]ontinuing shared understanding on one comprehensive religious, philosophical, or moral doctrine can be maintained only by the oppressive use of State power [. . .] Call this "the fact of oppression" [. . .] We may mistakenly think there are exceptions for other [reasonable] comprehensive views [. . .]. [T]here are no exceptions."[71] Rawls terms this "the fact of oppression.".

Nicholas Wolterstorff, an American Christian philosopher,[72] challenges Rawls's assumptions and insists that each person, including Christians and other believers, holds the right to utilize religious reasons to debate and decide political issues. Again. Wolterstorff states that "there is no prospect whatsoever [. . .] of all adherents of particular religions refraining from using the resources of their own religion in making political decisions."[73] He argues:

68. Rawls, *Political Liberalism, Expanded*, 458.

69. Rawls, *Political Liberalism, Expanded*, 458.

70. Chaplin, *Talking God*, 34.

71. Rawls, *Political Liberalism, Expanded*, 37.

72. Wolterstorff, "Why Can't We," 17–36.

73. Wolterstorff, and Audi, *Religion in the Public Square*, 11–12.

> I think it is appropriate in our liberal democracy for Christians, along with adherents of other religions, to make decisions about political issues on the basis of whatever considerations they find true and relevant. I also think it appropriate for them to cite those reasons in public discussions and debates about those political issues. [Al]though not always, these reasons will be distinctly religious reasons—Christian, Jewish, whatever.[74]

Furthermore, as noted in Chapter 2 when I defined religious freedom, a person's freedom to manifest his/her religion cannot be separated from his/her deliberation (based on religion) regarding public political policy. This principle is preserved by (1) the *Universal Declaration of Human Rights* (1948); (2) Article 18(1) of the ICCPR[75] (1966); and (3) the U.N. General Assembly Resolution 36/55 of 25 November 1981. The concept of freedom of practice of religion, as national and international agreements repeatedly confirm, constitutes the most critical component for true religious freedom. Thomas F. Farr stresses that the concept of religious freedom includes the expression of religious convictions in public activities, including the right to peacefully "manifest one's beliefs to others and the right to make religious and religiously based moral arguments in public policy debates."[76] In contrast with the PRSR, Rawls's public reason appears to conflict with the *Universal Declaration of Human Rights* and Article 18 of the ICCPR because it restrains significant aspects of religious freedom.

Chaplin argues, and I concur, that for the sake of public good and "candour in representation"[77] in civil society, it is absolutely legitimate for citizens who are religious to offer explicit religious reasons in both presenting public justifications for laws and voting for public policies. Nevertheless, instead of using the PRSR under Rawls's public reason in the deliberative process of legislation, I agree with Chaplin that those citizens who are religious and who are also political office holders involved in actual political policy decision-making that involves coercive powers, should exercise a certain amount of caution and constraint.[78]

Wolterstorff and Rawls disagree regarding the value of religion in the public sphere; nevertheless, they appear to agree with the need for certain restrictions regarding religions, particularly if those religious voices call for illegal activities, such as murder or violent actions. Rawls contends

---

74. Wolterstorff, "Rights and Wrongs," 63.

75. *International Covenant on Civil and Political Rights.*

76. Farr, *Future of Religious Freedom*, 347.

77. Chapin, *Talking God*, 58.

78. Chapin, *Talking God*, 58–70.

that the inclusion of religions in public conversations "must adhere to the values of the public sphere and, indeed, implicitly do so in the very act of conversing."[79] Restrictions on religions that disrupt or endanger citizens in the liberal State must not only be established but also enforced. Clause 3 of Article 18 of the ICCPR specifically identifies the few occasions when a person's freedom to manifest his/her religious beliefs may be limited: "Freedom to manifest one's religion or beliefs may be subject only to such limitations as are prescribed by law and are necessary to protect public safety, order, health, or morals or the fundamental rights and freedoms of others."[80] In those instances, the State must honor its obligation to the majority of its citizens to protect the "at risk" institutions and values.

Although the restraint on religious freedom under the PRSR comprises a moral limitation rather than a legal coercive one, the bottom line still encompasses a critical question: How can political liberalism draw a clear, distinctive line between an individual's public political participation and engagement based on the conception of political justice under public reason and his/her own or associations, for example, church or family religious and moral convictions, for non-public reasons? To a Catholic, either as a voter or a political officeholder or campaigner who believes in the teachings of both the Scriptures and the Pope on the issue of sanctity of life, the idea of this arbitrary separation (between political and deeply held religious convictions) will almost inevitably force an irreconcilable choice between a person's inalienable integrated life identity as an individual and his or her vocational calling to serve in the public political sphere.

In a sense, the proviso replicates a gag rule because it appears to openly discriminate in significantly stifling religious freedom of expression at a time when a person would present political views based on his/her religious convictions. While it seriously compromises a person's equality and freedom, this inconsistency in the proviso stands to accuse political liberalism of the very same "exclusivism" it implements.[81]

As I note in the introduction of this chapter, contrary to Wolterstorff's stance, in which he stresses an existence that is integrated with religion, Rawls stipulates that by means of its demand for the PRSR, public reason under political liberalism can restrain comprehensive views, particularly religious worldviews, from being able to justify public policy. Even though official powers do not police the PRSR in any way and it does not need enforcement by State coercion or social stigma, nevertheless, the

79. Flood, *Importance of Religion*, 204.

80. *International Covenant on Civil.*

81. Chaplin, *Talking God*, 34.

inconsistencies I note undeniably contradict Rawls's initial commitment to both the equal treatment of all reasonable comprehensive ideas and religious freedom. Nonetheless, as it conflicts with the scope of religious freedom under international law, this constraint on religious reasoning prevents it from being fully or even partially manifested in political discourse. In the next section, I note that even though political liberalism does not propose to totally silence the use of religious ideas in all public discourse, another of its primary mechanisms, the proviso, restricts religious voices by insisting that religious reason cannot serve as a public intellectual resource unless it conforms to its criteria.

Later in his life, Rawls accepted that religious believers are entitled to draw from and present religious reasons in political debate and that they may do this "at any time."[82] He explains that:

> I now believe and hereby revise *political liberalism* VI: 8, that reasonable such doctrines should be introduced in public reason at any time, provided that in due course public reasons, given by a reasonable political conception, are presented. I refer to this as the *proviso* and it specifies what I now call the wide view of public reason.[83]

Despite the fact that Rawls has revised his account to leave space for religious reasoning for public discourse, nevertheless the proviso is still fundamentally debilitating for religious believers. Rawls's proviso requires that "if citizens bring religious reasons into public debate, they must *also* find arguments which every other citizen will consider reasonable—'public reasons.'"[84] When the content of the debate falls into the category of political justice, the secular reason driven by the proviso, under Rawls's public reason, clearly enjoys preference over the religious reason. Furthermore, despite of Rawls' reluctance to agree with Audi, who specifically favors secular reason over religious one, in explaining Audio's definition of secular reason, Rawls found his proviso aligns with what Audi's view as it:

> is roughly one whose normative force does not evidentially depend on the existence of God or on theological considerations, or on the pronouncements of a person or institution qua religious authority.[85]

---

82. Chaplin, *Talking God*, 35.

83. Rawls, *Political Liberalism, Expanded*, Introduction.

84. Chaplin, *Talking God*, 35.

85. Audi, "Place of Religious Argument," 692.

[Rawls explains] This definition is ambiguous between secular reasons in the sense of a non-religious comprehensive doctrine and in the sense of a purely political conception within the content of public reason. Depending on which is meant, Audi's view that secular reasons must also be given along with religious reasons might have a role similar to what I call the proviso.[86]

Rawls asserts that the filter of the proviso depicts the only means by which reciprocal respect for citizens' equal rights may be achieved.[87] In due course, he insists, citizens will present reasons others can be expected to accept. Here, two questions arise that point out an additional inconsistency and problem: (1) Under Rawls's mechanism of public reason, will the proviso satisfy the public justification of political affairs as both necessary and sufficient enough? (2) If the proviso fails to satisfy the public justification of political affairs as both necessary and sufficient enough, confirming this as an inconsistency and this inconsistency proves true, how does this then impact religious freedom?

In addressing how the proviso needs to be satisfied by citizens with comprehensive doctrines, both religious and non-religious, Rawls states, "When these doctrines accept the proviso and only then come into political debate, the commitment to constitutional democracy is publicly manifested."[88] This statement reveals that prior to any political debate, citizens adhering to comprehensive doctrines must first accept the proviso before they manifest their commitment to constitutional democracy in public. In other words, when a citizen engages with any issue of constitutional essentials and matters of justice, the proviso process will be satisfied as both necessary and sufficient. However, in accepting three other forms of reasoning outside of public reason, namely declaration, conjecture, and witnessing,[89] Rawls seems to suggest that the proviso may not be sufficient or absolutely required if arguments based on religion subscribe to the support of basic constitutional values.

According to Weithman, Rawls permits citizens to draw from their comprehensive doctrines without citing public reasons to support their positions if this does not cause others to question that they respect the

---

86. Rawls, *Political Liberalism, Expanded*, 457.

87. Dreben, "On Rawls and Political."

88. Rawls, *Political Liberalism, Expanded*, 463.

89. Rawls, *Public Reason*, 465–66. Rawls concurs that an individual or group may present religious arguments in public debate to clarify the presenter's reason for a specific political view. However, he stipulates three instances in which political liberalism permits religious reasons to be included in public discourse: (1) declaration; (2) conjecture; (3) witnessing.

authority of the public conception of justice. If no doubts arise, then the proviso will not be incited, and no public reason will be required; however, Weithman notes Rawls in stating: "the details about how to satisfy [the] proviso must be worked out in practice and cannot feasibly be governed by a clear family of rules given in advance."[90] He stresses that Rawls's statement regarding the proviso presents challenges in interpretation: "provided that in due course public reasons, given by a reasonable political conception, are presented sufficient to support whatever the comprehensive doctrines are introduced to support."[91] Weithman notes Rawls's reference to the "provided that" clause as "the proviso" [and explains] "the difficulty with interpreting it lies in figuring out what he means by 'in due course.'"[92] Weithman also asserts that if Rawls had substituted the phrase "at the same time" with "in due course" in the proviso, it would require citizens to adopt and deliberate with public reason without exception. Instead, according to Weithman's interpretation, citizens must do so only when they have good reason to believe the need for assurance exists. If the proviso fails to satisfy the public justification of political affairs as both necessary and sufficient, confirming this as an inconsistency, and this inconsistency proves true, how does this impact religious freedom?

Weithman emphasizes, and I agree, that Rawls does not totally prohibit arguments based on religion from public or political discussion. Citizens *can* draw from their religion as an intellectual resource in political argument. Yet, in the name of "civic friendship and citizens" mutual reassurance,"[93] the proviso still requires religious citizens to provide additional public justification to ultimately support their public policy. Rawls states that:

> [B]itizens of faith who cite the Gospel parable of the Good Samaritan do not stop there, but go on to give a public justification for this parable's conclusions in terms of political values.[94]

> Thus, instead of being eliminated or morally prohibited, the use of religiously-based reasons, nonetheless, is constrained.[95]

Weithman points that due to Rawls' primary assertions constraining political arguments based on religion, his conditional stipulations on using religious or conviction-based arguments in public debate deserve some praise.

90. Weithman, *Rawls, Political Liberalism*, 462.

91. Rawls, *Political Liberalism, Expanded*, 453.

92. Weithman, *Rawls, Political Liberalism*, 161.

93. Rawls, *Political Liberalism, Expanded*, 456.

94. Rawls, *Political Liberalism, Expanded*.

95. Weithman, *Rawls, Political Liberalism*, 58.

Nevertheless, political liberalism's insistence that a citizen who draws from his/her religion to offer support for a specific position regarding a particular issue must comply with the proviso proves particularly problematic for religions, particularly for ensuring religious freedom.[96] According to Rawls:

> What's important is that people give the kinds of reasons that can be understood and appraised apart from their particular comprehensive doctrines: for example, that they argue against physician-assisted suicide not just by speculating about God's wrath or the afterlife, but by talking about what they see as assisted suicide's potential injustices.[97]

In explaining the proviso, Rawls notes the role a reasonable comprehensive doctrine may hold in public reason, something I examine further later in this chapter:

> the content of public reason is given by the principles and values of the family of liberal political conceptions of justice [. . .] To engage in public reason is to appeal to one of these political conceptions—to their ideals and principles, standards and values—when debating fundamental political questions. This [. . .] still allows us to introduce into political discussion at any time our comprehensive doctrine—[religious or non-religious], provided that, in due course, we give properly public reasons to support the principles and policies our comprehensive doctrine is said to support.[98]

Rawls public reason's stance on the filter of political liberalism's proviso regarding religion reveals yet another inconsistency in his reasoning regarding freedom of religion. As it contradicts the scope of international definitions of religious freedom,[99] which I noted earlier, the proviso's stipulations clearly conflict with this basic liberty and, simultaneously, place an undue, extra burden on religious expression in the public square. In general, from the perspective of religious freedom, although both the proviso and public reason portray more moral constraints than legal ones initiated more from societal persuasion than governmental coercive power, they still place an unreasonable qualifying burden on religions.[100]

---

96. As this stipulation does not equally apply to all rationales but singles out religious and certain comprehensive doctrines, this proves particularly problematic for individuals with strong religious beliefs and foundations.

97. Rawls, "Politics, Religion and Public Good," para. 23.

98. Rawls, *Political Liberalism*, 462.

99. Dreben, "On Rawls," 343.

100. Rawls, *Political Liberalism*.

Thus, I argue that in deliberating procedures and even in voting processes, unclear details regarding the proviso and other political liberalism restrictions regarding religious voices in the political realm, which I previously noted, demonstrate that no proviso should be imposed for any citizen. Nevertheless, I agree, as Chaplin deliberates,[101] that certain cautious restraints may be warranted during times of legislative decision-making and the execution of coercive laws by actual office holders, religious or non-religious alike. Later, I point out that, to a certain extent, principled pluralism agrees with political liberalism on this point.

As I note earlier in this thesis, Rawls's motives in developing political liberalism, with the aim of avoiding religious wars, reflect concerns for securing a safe, orderly society. I maintain, however, that on the merits of self-respect, as I relate in the next section, Rawlsian public reason and the proviso both fall short in protecting religious freedom for all. In the next section, I address inconsistencies from the perspective of self-respect (according to the concept of public reason under political liberalism) that infringe on religious freedom and demonstrate disrespect for citizens who, according to Rawls, are to be considered "free and equal persons."[102]

Rawls asserts that, despite diverse religious and philosophical commitments, political liberalism can serve as an ideal mechanism for reaching agreements on fundamental political matters among free and equal citizens. As I explained in the previous section, he also points out that when citizens in a well-ordered and pluralist society engage in public debate, they "must respect a duty of civility and offer reasons to one another in terms that all can reasonably be expected to endorse."[103] Referring to the word "respect" in another sense, Rawls explains that public reason, first, "identifies the fundamental role of political values in expressing the terms of fair social cooperation consistent with mutual respect between citizens regarded as free and equal."[104] In yet another instance, Rawls refers to a citizen's self-respect thus:

> Self-respect is rooted in our self-confidence as a fully cooperating member of society capable of pursuing a worthwhile conception of the good over a complete life. Thus self-respect presupposes the development and exercise of both moral powers and therefore an effective sense of justice. The importance of self-respect is that it provides a secure sense of our own value, a firm conviction that our determinate conception of the good

---

101. Chaplin, *Talking God*, 67–70.
102. Rawls, *Political Liberalism*, 5.
103. Patton, "Foucault and Rawls," 154.
104. Rawls, *Political Liberalism*, 158.

is worth carrying out. Without self-respect nothing may seem worth doing, and if some things have value for us, we lack the will to pursue them.[105]

Wolterstorff argues that Rawls's methodology for political liberalism implies that appealing to public reason does not nurture self-respect or foster mutual respect between citizens but correlates with treating others with subtle yet serious disrespect.[106] When Rawls establishes his form of public reason, for example, he claims to incorporate the idea that liberal democracy constitutes a system of fair cooperation over time. He fails to adequately identify such a system, however. According to Rawls's explanation, this requires setting those who are "unreasonable" aside. Those who are unreasonable, he asserts, are those "unwilling to honor, or even to propose [...] fair terms of cooperation."[107] This infers that when citizens engage in political discourse regarding an issue of basic justice, "reasonable" citizens can set reportedly "unreasonable" individuals off to the side and dismiss the views of their reportedly "unreasonable" compatriots. To Wolterstorff, this promotes a concern: Instead of encouraging a system where all citizens are respected as free and equal, Rawls's political liberalism presents the paradoxical implication that following "the duty of civility"[108] inevitably perpetrates injustice—and disrespect.

Chaplin states that respect warrants citizens listening to each another on an equal basis, despite their different worldviews. "If we respect our fellow-citizens, we won't ignore them, dismiss them as of no account, misrepresent them, slander them, or incite hatred against them (and there are laws against the latter two kinds of disrespect)."[109] Chaplin argues, and I concur, that when one citizen disrespects another's reasons, he/she does not disrespect him/her. Instead of dismissing or ruling another person's reasons "out of order" prior to hearing them, a person demonstrates greater respect to their fellow citizens when he/she critically engages with their preferred political reasons in public forums. Likewise, one citizen shows another more respect when he/she offers them his/her genuine reasons for a policy than he/she would by presenting reasons he/she cannot completely identify with. In both scenarios, citizens validate each other. This depicts genuine civic reciprocity among free and equal citizens.[110]

---

105. Rawls, *Political Liberalism*, 318.

106. Wolterstorff, *Understanding Liberal Democracy*, 121.

107. Rawls, *Political Liberalism* (1993), 51.

108. Wolterstorff, *Understanding Liberal Democracy*, 121.

109. Chaplin, *Talking God*, 34

110. Chaplin, *Talking God*, 37.

Similarly, Wolterstorff asserts that using pressure or coercion to force someone to do something or to make them refrain from doing something is wrong unless:

1. The agent respects the subject as free and equal.

2. [T]he agent respects the subject as free and equal only if he has a good and irrefutable reason for believing that the subject is openly justified in agreeing with him so much so that pressuring him is likely to prove to be a good thing overall.

3. [T]he agent, in applying the pressure, treats the person subjected to the pressure with due respect.[111]

Chaplin asserts that Rawls's argument for the proviso subtly suggests a simple, almost sinister message. He interprets Rawls to infer, "to respect me as an equal, you have to speak in my language; if you lobby for policies based on reasons I can't possibly agree with, you sweep my views aside and thereby diminish and disrespect me."[112] The underlying, disrespectful, assuming message appears to be, according to Chaplin, that "'my' language is also 'our' common language."[113] Chaplin unveils the inconsistency and exclusive nature of Rawls's argument in relation to reasons and respect as the following:

1. A liberal democracy is based on the principle of political equality.

2. Political equality means that citizens should adopt a duty of respect toward one another in political debate.

3. The duty of respect requires that citizens only offer reasons for the public policies they advocate that everyone equally can find intelligible and acceptable in principle.

4. Religious reasons can only be found intelligible and acceptable by some citizens, and indeed are repudiated by many.

5. Therefore, religious reasons should not be employed to justify public policies.

6. To employ religious reasons to justify a policy—to seek "justification by faith alone"—is disrespectful and inadmissible.[114]

---

111. Wolterstorff, *Understanding Liberal Democracy*, 71.

112. Chaplin, *Talking God*, 34.

113. Chaplin, *Talking God*.

114. Chaplin, *Talking God*, 34.

Catherine Audard contends that Rawls's proviso discounts the value of the distinctiveness of citizens and, in turn, negates the respect and equality he professes for them.[115] A person is not considered free and equal if an agent ignores his/her views because they draw on his/her religion. "Equal voice wins hands down over public reason in respecting one's fellows as free and equal."[116] Wolterstorff suggests calling "the principle that citizens should respect each other as free and equal, the respect principle,"[117] and labeling the maxim that citizens should "satisfy one or another version of the subject-doxa condition when functioning as political actors, the public reason imperative."[118] He then poses the dilemma of how a citizen can shift from the respect principle to the public reason imperative. Rawls's notion of a public reason imperative, that to fulfill the respect principle, a citizen must satisfy one or an alternative version of the public reason, raises significant questions. The connection between public reason and mandated respect is not self-evident. According to Wolterstorff, in the matter of the political arena, Rawls's political liberalism proves insufficient in self-respect because it does not encourage everyone to listen with an open mind to whatever reasons citizens offer for or against some political concern. Contrary to the disrespect perpetrated by political liberalism's restrictive filters, which exclude certain worldviews, each person's voice deserves equal weight and inclusion in matters that affect him/her.

As I point out in this section, despite its honorable aim, Rawls's principle of respect according to his imperative public reason, will either fail to be implemented consistently or even worse, by contradicting his stated goal, it will stimulate disrespect. Respect serves as the key when convincing someone to do something or to refrain from doing it. It is impermissible, Wolterstorff insists, for the pressuring agent to fail to employ respect. "Not only must the agent treat the subject with due respect; he must also not treat anyone at all with less than due respect."[119] Respecting a person involves giving proper value to his/her wellbeing; however, respecting someone also includes acknowledging that each person has worth, that one person's worth varies from that of another person, nor does it depend on the worth of another individual. Ignoring a citizen's voice and removing him/her from the legitimation pool, as public reason under political liberalism does, disrespects him/her. If citizens are deemed incompatible with public reason, according to Rawls,

---

115. Audard, *John Rawls*, 45.

116. Wolterstorff, *Understanding Liberal Democracy*, 89.

117. Wolterstorff, *Understanding Liberal Democracy*.

118. Wolterstorff, *Understanding Liberal Democracy*.

119. Wolterstorff, *Understanding Liberal Democracy*, 71.

they are subject to containment. As I show in the next two sections, the ensuing containment will inevitably either lead to insufficiently protecting or further eroding religious freedom.

3.3.2 Insufficiencies under Containment

In the previous section, I examined three primary inconsistencies relating to the concept of public reason under political liberalism. From the standpoints of the PRSR, the proviso, and self-respect, I pointed out that in a reasonable pluralistic society these inconsistencies will either conflict with Rawls's stated goals or fail to protect religious freedom for all. In this section, I explore the justification for Rawls's containment of those citizens or groups whom he deems as "incompatible with the essentials of public reason and a democratic polity."[120] I also examine the various approaches with regard to how to contain them. Rawls's political liberalism is designed to engage only with what he calls reasonable persons who affirm only reasonable comprehensive doctrines. According to Rawls, three primary features define a reasonable comprehensive doctrine: (1) it involves "an exercise of theoretical reason"; (2) it involves "an exercise of practical reason"; (3) it "normally belongs to, or draws upon tradition of thought and doctrine."[121] Based on the principle of justice as fairness, under a reasonable pluralistic society, only those reasonable persons holding reasonable comprehensive doctrines are able to reach an overlapping consensus. According to Rawls, the principle of justice as fairness entails two kinds of political values: political justice and public reason.

Public reason, a basic structure at the heart of Rawls's conception of legitimate democratic government, reflects the rationale of reasonable citizens about constitutional essentials and matters of basic justice. This includes society's basic structure as well as societal public policies.[122] Rawls "develops the ideal of public reason to explain how, despite being divided over various moral, religious, and philosophical comprehensive doctrines, liberal democratic citizens may nevertheless sustain themselves as a politically autonomous body politic capable of legitimately using coercion to enforce its legal order."[123] In other words, public reason can only be upheld by reasonable citizens who can support a constitutional regime that guarantees a stable democratic society.

120. Rawls, *Political Liberalism*, 441.
121. Rawls, *Political Liberalism*, 59.
122. Rawls, *Justice as Fairness*.
123. Reidy, "Rawls's Wide View," 55.

Reasonable citizens, according to Rawls, are those individuals who, when given assurance that others will likely do the same, are ready to propose principles and standards as fair terms of cooperation as well as being willing to abide by them. Those reasonable persons are prepared to discuss norms they perceive as reasonable for everyone to accept as well as ready to discuss the fair terms others propose. These norms, which Rawls summarizes as constitutional essentials and matters of justice, include:

1. a list of certain basic rights, liberties, and opportunities (such as those familiar from constitutional regimes);

2. assignment of special priority to those rights, liberties, and opportunities, especially with respect to the claims of the general good and perfectionist values; and

3. measures ensuring adequate all-purpose means for all citizens to make effective use of their freedoms.[124]

Reasonableness according to the capacity of public reason involves citizens desiring to control their lives in common, utilizing concepts each citizen can accept. Rawls stresses "that public reason provides the norms which citizens, judges, and public officials should follow when making claims about matters of justice."[125] Using the test of public reason, citizens can present political justifications to one another to solicit and provide support for laws and policies that affect them.

Rawls argues that, "reasonable persons will think it unreasonable to use political power, should they possess it, to repress comprehensive views that are not unreasonable, though different from their own."[126] Following this reasoning, the question arises: What characteristics do unreasonable persons holding unreasonable comprehensive doctrines display? Rawls seems to suggest that three distinct characteristics define unreasonable persons: (1) those who hold unreasonable comprehensive doctrines; (2) those who refuse to operate under public reason; and (3) those who, when they hold political power, would use that power to suppress views that differ from their own.[127] Thus, the unreasonable person or groups of people will most likely be found violating other citizens' freedom of religion or belief. Rawls states:

124. Rawls, *Political Liberalism, Expanded*, 450.

125. Mahoney, "Public Reason and Moral," 88.

126. Rawls, *Political Liberalism*, 5.

127. Rawls, *Political Liberalism*, 60–61.

[P]eople are unreasonable in the same basic aspect when they plan to engage in cooperative schemes but are unwilling to honor, or even to propose, except as a necessary public pretense, any general principles or standards for specifying fair terms of cooperation. They are ready to violate such terms as suits their interests when circumstances allow.[128]

In contrast, I note Rawls's reasoning regarding reasonable persons in what he asserts here:

[R]easonable persons see that the burdens of judgment set limits on what can be reasonably justified to others, and so they endorse some form of liberty of conscience and freedom of thought. It is unreasonable for us to use political power, should we possess it, or share it with others, to repress comprehensive views that are not unreasonable.[129]

Consequently, Rawls prescribes containment to deal with those who hold unreasonable, illiberal comprehensive views that are incompatible with public reason. Although only a few paragraphs exist in which Rawls discusses the containment of potentially harmful, unreasonable political views using the specific term "contain," the following explicitly reveals his rationale on both his scope and purpose of containment.

Of course, a society may also contain unreasonable and irrational, and even mad, comprehensive doctrines. In their case the problem is to contain them so that they do not undermine the unity and justice of society.

And:

That there are doctrines that reject one or more democratic freedoms is itself a permanent fact of life, or seems so. This gives us the practical task of containing them—like war and disease—so that they do not overturn political justice.[130]

In addition, Rawls explains:

Of course, every society also contains numerous unreasonable doctrines. Yet in this essay I am concerned with an ideal normative conception of democratic government, that is, with the conduct of its reasonable citizens and the principles they follow, assuming them to be dominant and controlling. How far

128. Rawls, *Political Liberalism*, 50.
129. Rawls, *Political Liberalism*, 61.
130. Rawls, *Political Liberalism*, 64.

unreasonable doctrines are active and tolerated is to be determined by the principles of justice and the kinds of actions they
permit.[131]

From Rawls's words, I conclude that the scope of containment covers
both public and private spheres,[132] while the purpose of containment includes
maintaining the unity and political justice in a democratic society.

Although Rawls does not present a scheme for implementing containment for "unreasonable and irrational, and even mad, comprehensive doctrines," and does not define or specify what he means by the term "contain,"
he notes several times that containing unreasonable views is necessary to
ensure the stability of a liberal society. In the next subsection, I examine
several approaches that political liberalism implements, mechanisms not
only to contain those unreasonable doctrines but also those who hold such
doctrines, barring their ideas from entering public discourse. Rawls appears
hesitant to restrict political speech for the sake of preserving democratic
institutions and other basic freedoms,[133] yet as I pointed out in the previous subsection, he still prescribes containment for certain individuals or
groups who are deemed to threaten his political justice. Rawls notes several
times that containing unreasonable views is necessary to ensure the stability
of a liberal society, yet he fails to specifically explain how the method he
envisages would be implemented to achieve this goal. In addition to Rawls
neglecting to relate his definition for the word "contain" or offer guidelines
to distinguish between reasonable and unreasonable—two critical terms in
political liberalism—he also fails to propose explicit ways for advocates of
political liberalism to engage with "unreasonable" people. Joonas Pennanen
identifies three basic approaches which he derives from Rawls, regarding
containment available through the framework of political liberalism:

1. The non-engagement approach. In this approach, "voicing of illiberal
   ideas (or actions taken on such bases) is dismissed without arguing
   against those ideas."[134] From Rawls, one may presume that because he

---

131. Rawls, *Political Liberalism*, 441.

132. Rawls, *Political Liberalism*, 53. "A further basic difference between the reasonable and the rational is that the reasonable is public in a way the rational is not. This
means that it is by the reasonable that we enter as equals the public world of others and
stand ready to propose, or to accept, as the case may be, fair terms of cooperation with
them. These terms, set out as principles, specify the reasons we are to share and publicly
recognize before one another as grounding our social relations."

133. Rawls, *Political Liberalism, Expanded*, 355.

134. Pennanen, "Political Liberalism and Preventive, 192.

perceives some conceptions of society as irrational and unreasonable, one need not invest time or energy in arguing against them.

2. The clear and imminent danger approach. This approach permits the suppression of illiberal doctrines and ideas that extend a clear and impending danger to security and/or stability.

3. The preventive approach. This approach permits specific measures to be utilized and allows the State to implement certain measures to protect the liberal character of society even before a dire need arises.[135]

Regarding non-engagement, the first approach for containment that Pennanen identifies, the primary point stipulates that apart from the justifications which political liberalism asserts, no other or further justification ought to be presented in political discourse. Any ideas presented that do not align with the terms of political values that all reasonable citizens can accept in principle, such as those Rawls considers illiberal, are to be ignored or dismissed without any consideration or argument to counter them.[136]

> Those who reject constitutional democracy with its criterion of reciprocity will of course reject the very idea of public reason. For them the political relation may be that of friend or foe, to those of a particular religious or secular community or those who are not; or it may be a relentless struggle to win the world for the whole truth. Political liberalism does not engage those who think this way. The zeal to embody the whole truth in politics is incompatible with an idea of public reason that belongs with democratic citizenship.[137]

Rawls asserts that in public reason, ideas of truth or right based on comprehensive doctrines are replaced by an idea of the politically reasonable addressed to citizens as citizens.[138] He insists that this step is essential for political liberalism to establish a political reasoning base that all citizens can share as free and equal. Burton Dreben maintains that Rawls's intent for this first containment approach relates to his perceptions of irrational and unreasonable doctrines in society and,[139] therefore, no need exists to invest time or energy in considering them.

Pennanen explains that the second available approach for containment, that of the clear and imminent danger, correlates with what Rawls's

135. Pennanen, "Political Liberalism," 193.
136. Pennanen, "Political Liberalism."
137. Rawls, *Political Liberalism, Expanded*, 442.
138. Rawls, *Political Liberalism, Expanded*, 480.
139. Dreben, *Cambridge Companion to Rawls*, 316–46.

political liberalism would confirm when involved in the process of State coercion and containing illiberal ideas. This approach implies that liberal states may suppress illiberal doctrines and ideas from spreading only when they indicate the potential for "a clear and imminent danger to security and/or stability."[140] Rawls does not offer much information regarding his thoughts on the containment method; nevertheless, Pennanen argues that Rawls's position parallels the clear and imminent danger approach. He explains that complications of insubordinate advocacy do not surface in a well-ordered society under ideal circumstances, and that Rawls perceives the right to free speech as being violated only during extreme circumstances of constitutional emergency. These include imminent danger of political justice being overturned, and as Rawls states:

> "the constitutional guarantees of free speech and press do not permit a State to forbid to proscribe advocacy of the use of force or of law violation except where such advocacy is directed to inciting or producing imminent lawless action and is likely to incite or produce such action." Observe that the proscribed kind of speech must be both intentional and directed to producing imminent lawless action as well as delivered in circumstances which make this result likely.[141]

The preventive approach, according to Pennanen, allows the most latitude regarding coercive actions of the State. This approach permits the State to take specific measures to protect the liberal character of society prior to any actual evidence of an urgent need for counter action. Pennanen argues that the reasoning behind this approach includes weeding out the plainly undesirable tendencies prior to them manifesting into a massive and potentially unresolvable dilemma.[142] Rawls reasons regarding this measure:

> Thus as a matter of constitutional doctrine the priority of liberty implies that free political speech cannot be restricted unless it can be reasonably argued from the specific nature of the present situation that there exists a constitutional crisis in which democratic institutions cannot work effectively and their procedures for dealing with emergencies cannot operate.[143]

Rawls's statement implies that the State may only justify introducing restrictive measures regarding freedom of political speech when two

140. Pennanen, "Political Liberalism," 193.

141. Rawls, *Political Liberalism, Expanded*, 344.

142. Pennanen, "Political Liberalism," 193.

143. Rawls, *Political Liberalism, Expanded*, 354.

conditions are met: (1) a liberal democratic institution becomes dysfunctional; and (2) the constitutional procedure to rectify the dilemma fails. A justification for preventive containment, according to Jonathan Quong, may be found in "the fundamental importance of normative stability in a well-ordered liberal society."[144] This basically means that when the liberal regime is threatened, the State can "permissibly restrict the actions of unreasonable citizens [as] it has a compelling moral reason to do so."[145] Quong further develops Rawls's notion of containment in this regard. He lists three extremely compelling public reasons according to which certain basic rights of those considered unreasonable, who pose a real threat to the liberal democratic order, may be restricted.

1. Politically active but unreasonable citizens "clearly pose more of stability threat, and so I think it is reasonable to suppose that the liberal state might need to apply a policy of containment more frequently to such groups."[146]

2. Restriction of basic rights may also accompany a threat to the realization of the capacity of justice, in which the inculcation of illiberal ideas impedes the formation of a moral and political identity in tune with the political conception of justice.

3. In addition, containment may be necessary where citizens have been promulgated/inculcated to pursue unreasonable objectives. Although "unreasonable persons have all the normal rights and liberties of citizenship, it turns out these rights do not protect them in the pursuit of unreasonable objectives"[147] rendering the rights claims of unreasonable citizens invalid.

Despite Rawls's claims to welcome every comprehensive idea into the political justification arena through public reason, he may not fully subscribe to all three containment approaches which Quong expands. Nevertheless, Rawls's ideas regarding containment may serve to silence religious voices in political discourse or exclude them. No matter whether containment measures consist of passive non-engagement means or active restrictions and preventions, those holding unreasonable doctrines will certainly insufficiently guarantee religious freedom for all citizens, whether reasonable or unreasonable. Moreover, Rawls's weak definition of unreasonable doctrines

144. Quong, *Liberalism without Perfection*, 300.
145. Quong, *Liberalism without Perfection*.
146. Rawls, *Political Liberalism, Expanded*, 304.
147. Rawls, *Political Liberalism, Expanded*, 291.

makes some major religions, such as evangelical Christianity, susceptible to containment such that they might very well accept the ethical content of political liberalism.[148] Furthermore, as Cass Sunstein argues, the danger of excluding dissenting voices from the discussion and decision-making may bring about group polarization through enclave deliberation[149]—that is, people with quite moderate initial beliefs end up assuming more extreme positions when deliberating only with like-minded persons.

Overall, Rawls's notion of containment of unreasonable views will prove to be counter-productive because it might intensify threats to the liberal democratic order and destabilize it, an outcome that political liberalism aims to avoid. As the risk of "excluding the unreasonable outside the society in a way that they would be no longer disposed in any way to see the benefits of political liberal society,"[150] the containment approach would delegitimize political liberalism's claim of inclusion. Consequently, this renders the liberal project of inclusion virtually impossible.

Although Bailey and Gentile assert that Rawls's guidelines regarding public reason do not show he is suspicious of all comprehensive doctrines, particularly religious ones, or that he perceives religious political arguments as inherently destabilizing, I assert that Rawls's containment of certain religious groups deemed unreasonable could also consequently infringe upon the group's as well as the individual's religious freedom –namely, the freedom of religious manifestation in public. Justice Kennedy clearly stresses that religious freedom implies more than the freedom of religious belief. More importantly, the term also means "to express religious beliefs and to establish one's religious (or no religious) self-definition in the *political* (emphasis mine), civil, and economic life of our larger community."[151] Contrary to Rawls's approach of containment, like Wolterstorff,[152] I stress that the voices of all groups or individuals or individuals from all groups, religious or non-religious, who adhere to a comprehensive doctrine, should be allowed to freely address issues of public concern.

Ronald Beiner surmises that under political liberalism, religious freedom is not as fully protected as Rawls proposes. "Rawls writes that 'equal liberty of conscience [. . .] takes religious truths off the political agenda.'"[153] According

---

148. Nussbaum, "Perfectionist Liberalism," 25–30.

149. Sunstein, *Why Societies Need Dissent*, 132.

150. Pennanen, "*Political Liberalism*," 201.

151. Sullivan, "Impossibility of Religious Freedom," para. 5.

152. Wolterstorff, "Why Can't We."

153. Beiner, *Civil Religion*, 292. Beiner asserts that it appears unfair to use the contemporary standard of religious liberty out of the context of their bygone eras to criticize historical figures such as Luther and Calvin.

to Beiner, one could construe the success of the seventeenth-century fight for liberty of conscience a major historical accomplishment.

Prior to conducting a pointed critique of political liberalism in the light of religious freedom to clarify several misunderstandings and criticisms that Tom Bailey and Valentina Gentile also challenge, I address several of their concerns. These include Rawls being criticized for his handling of the feasibility of religious beliefs and accused of being exclusivist, perhaps suggesting that religion or religion-based reasoning have no role in any public discourse.[154]

I agree with Bailey and Gentile that most of such criticisms that they note are not fully justified. As they state in *Rawls and Religion*, Rawls's "exclusion" of religions is extremely limited and qualified, such that he provides for an extensive accommodation of religions in political life, and the notions of "respect" and "consensus" on which he bases his "exclusion" are subtle, yet are also more open, and flexible than his critics presume.[155]

In my finding that Rawls's restrictions on citizens' reasoning could not fully alienate religion from public discourse, I note that Bailey and Gentile outline and rebut six considerations that critics regularly present to discredit Rawls. Bailey and Gentile are right that Rawls limits his restriction on the use of religion-based, public discourse to political constitutional matters, not primarily implemented through the State's direct coercive power. Nevertheless, I perceive that overall, as a narrow political philosophy, Rawls's political liberalism lacks the coherence, sufficiency, and inclusiveness necessary to protect religious freedom for all.[156] Rawls asserts that his principles of justice are of more substantial value than purely procedural ones.[157] Shane O'Neill explains that procedural liberalism, as a procedural framework of justice, responds to the fact that individuals in Western democratic societies do not share comprehensive conceptions of the good. According to Selma K. Sonntag:

> Procedural liberalism as a school of political thought does not prescribe culture or community for the individual—it merely prescribes institutions that facilitate the autonomy of the individual to determine for herself "the good life" and the acquisition of the necessary tools to achieve it. On the global level,

---

154. Gaus and Vallier, "Roles of Religious Conviction," 58–62.

155. Bailey and Gentile, *Rawls and Religion*, 24.

156. Shane O'Neill, *Impartiality in Context*, 71–72.

157. Rawls, *Political Liberalism, Expanded*, 192.

this translates into an advocacy for universal human rights to be upheld by democratic institutions.[158]

I concur with Chaplin as he argues that Rawls's political liberalism belongs to the family of procedural liberalism.[159] Gerhard Wegner also appears to equate procedural liberalism to political liberalism as he asserts that "political (procedural) liberalism"[160] represents liberalism. Sebastiano Maffettone alludes to the same equation with "procedural liberalism à la Rawls."[161]

Chaplin argues against Rawls's negative stance regarding religion and proposes that as societies change and become more morally and religiously plural, instead of, as Rawls purports, an increasing consensus occurring in the political realm with regard to justifying reasons, a growing dissensus will occur.[162] Instead of expecting a unanimously accepted set of secular political principles, Wolterstorff argues, "we must learn to live with a politics of multiple communities."[163] Whether motivated by religious or secular concerns, he stresses, citizens "need to reckon with, and indeed encourage, the practice of what might be termed "confessional candour" in political debate."[164] In a political culture defined by religious and secular world views, which often clash, rather than discouraging the verbalization of the deep convictions that lead individuals to take their stands on conflicting policies and stifling democratic debate, encouraging instead the confident declaration of competing justifying reasons, religious and secular, confessional candour opens the opportunity for critical, innovative, and perhaps even radical interventions that can challenge the tendency for liberal democracy to become complacent, conformist, or oppressed.

Chaplin explains that the objective of confessional candor, which he notes cannot be merely expressive, as the point of political debate does not entail a person indulging him/herself and publicly displaying his/her deepest convictions. Public debate should increase the level as well as expand the quality of political discourse. Although some perceive confessional candor to be disruptive, the willingness to face an adversarial stance within democratic debate contributes to mutual respect much better than adhering to political liberalism's constraints.[165] According to Chaplin, "the 'normal' stance in most

---

158. Sonntag, *Local Politics of Global English*, 24.

159. Chaplin, *Talking God*, 20–28.

160. Wegner, *Political Failure*, 6.

161. Maffettone, *Rawls: An Introduction*, 159.

162. Chaplin, *Talking God*, 46–47.

163. Audi and Wolterstorff, *Religion in Public Square*, 109.

164. Audi and Wolterstorff, *Religion in Public Square*, 99.

165. Chaplin, *Talking God*, 54.

contexts of political debate will be to exercise confessional self-restraint."[166] Decisions regarding if and when a speaker should exercise confessional restraint should not be dictated by a theory but determined by the one speaking, with some minimal agreement, nevertheless, on the principles which justify the representative democracy's structures. Chaplin asserts:

> [W]hatever policy consensus will emerge from such structures may sometimes only follow a protracted, vigorous, potentially turbulent, even temporarily destabilising, exchange of justifying reasons. In the absence of a universal common ground of shared political reasons, and in the presence of an ever-deeper diversity of public faiths, this seems inescapable.[167]

Rawls's aim to avoid religious wars, as noted earlier in this chapter, as well as his quest to contain unreasonable doctrines, which he asserts threaten democratic institutions, reflect reasonable concerns. Contrary to Rawls's reasoning and concerns for securing a well-ordered society, his public reason falls short in protecting religious freedom for all. What of political liberalism's containment ploys to silence the voices of those with reasons considered incompatible with the public reason filter?[168] I maintain that Rawlsian public reason falls short in protecting religious freedom for all in the following two major points: (1) the inequality (mentioned above) that contradicts political liberalism's commitment to equality; and (2) the numerous ways in which Rawls's "containment" policy against those whose doctrines are deemed incompatible with the public reason filter in the name of arbitrarily set "reciprocity" which Pennanen reveals. The doctrine of containment which Rawls proposed shows the exclusiveness and intolerance of the "intolerant" in the political liberalism system. Thus, I conclude that political liberalism clearly constrains religious freedom for all.

Additional research on political liberalism and examination of Rawls's ideas in relation to parents, their children, and education further raises questions regarding inconsistencies that infringe on religious freedom. Rawls's reported respect for the family appears conditional, and as in the case of educational choice, violates the capacity for justice—contingent on fulfilling the capacity for justice. If education, even family education, does not fulfill the capacity for justice which political liberalism proposes, this implies the State can take on the role to "reform" the family.

166. Chaplin, *Talking God.*
167. Chaplin, *Talking God.*
168. Pennanen, *"Political Liberalism."*

3.3.3 Implied Potential Infringement of Parents' Choice of Religious Education

Rawls recognizes that the family constitutes a vital part of society's basic structure, with its primary role serving as the foundation for the orderly creation and reproduction of society, securing the transfer of its culture to the next generation. He asserts that "citizens must have a sense of justice and of the political virtues that support political and social institutions [and that the] family must ensure the nurturing and development of such citizens in appropriate numbers to maintain an enduring society."[169] As the family raises and cares for its children, Rawls states, it must also ensure their children's moral development and education to help ensure they can later function in the wider culture.

As we shall see, additional examination of Rawls's concepts of political justice relating to parental choice regarding their children's education, raises questions regarding the implied potential infringement of parents' religious freedom. In the following two subsections, I explore Rawls's rationale regarding State intervention in educational choices and how such interventions potentially violate parental religious freedom.

Natasha Levinson asserts that Rawls does not impart much information on education, a dearth she perceives strange, because reasonable pluralism encompasses educational as well as political achievement.[170] Nevertheless, Rawls defines two moral powers critical to the education of children that he perceives as identifying individuals as "free and equal free persons."[171]

> A sense of justice is the capacity to understand, to apply, and to act from the public conception of justice which characterizes the fair terms of social cooperation. Given the nature of the political conception as specifying a public basis of justification, a sense of justice also expresses a willingness, if not the desire, to act in relation to others on terms that they also can publicly endorse.
>
> The capacity for a conception of the good is the capacity to form, to revise, and rationally to pursue a conception of one's rational advantage or good.[172]

Levinson recognizes that for Rawls, education's goal must not focus on training children to become philosophically liberal. Nevertheless, under

---

169. Rawls, *Political Liberalism*, 474.

170. Levinson, "Contemporary Political Theory," 71.

171. Rawls, *Political Liberalism, Expanded*, 19.

172. Rawls, *Political Liberalism, Expanded*.

the parameters of political liberalism, it is essential that children learn about their rights as individuals under a democratic constitutional regime. When Rawls addresses one aspect of education connected with developing citizen virtues, he explains what education "entirely within the political conception" means:

> Observe here that we try to answer the question of children's education entirely within the political conception. Society's concern with their education lies in their role as future citizens, and so in such essential things as their acquiring the capacity to understand the public culture and to participate in its institutions, in their being economically independent and self-supporting members of society over a complete life, and in their developing the political virtues, all this from within a political point of view.[173]

Regarding the State's role in relation to the family, Rawls explains that political principles enforce vital constraints on the family as an institution, along with providing opportunities for each of its members, to guarantee its/their fundamental rights and freedoms. Political principles, however, do not directly apply to the internal life of a family. Rawls points out the differences between the perception of an individual as a citizen and his/her viewpoint as a family member and as a member of other associations in the following:

> As citizens we have reasons to impose the constraints specified by the political principles of justice on associations, while as members of associations we have reasons for limiting those constraints so that they leave room for a free and flourishing internal life appropriate to the association in question. Here again we see the need for the division of labor between different kinds of principles. We wouldn't want political principles of justice—including principles of distributive justice—to apply directly to the internal life of the family.[174]

Rawls stresses that the principles of distributive justice do not inform parents how to raise their children, and that they are not required to relate to their children according to political principles because these do not fit the familial realm. Rawls ascertains that parents will, within certain limits, adhere to some "concept of justice (or fairness) and due respect regarding their children." He stipulates, "Citizens must have a sense of justice and of the political virtues that support political and social institutions."[175] To facilitate

---

173. Rawls, *Political Liberalism, Expanded*, 200.
174. Rawls, *Political Liberalism, Expanded*, 469.
175. Rawls, *Political Liberalism, Expanded*, 467.

this, the family must ensure their children's moral development, as well as their education, so they will develop into citizens who not only possess a sense of justice but are also conversant with political virtues which sustain political and social institutions. These political virtues consist of two kinds of powers: (1) "their two moral powers (a capacity for a sense of justice and for a conception of the good)"; and (2) "the powers of reason (of judgment, thought, and inference connected with these powers)."[176] Rawls surmises that these "requisite minimum" qualifications categorize fully cooperating members of society as free and equal citizens. Rawls and political liberalism embrace certain values, including religious freedom, the equality of children as future citizens, and the value of the family in orderly procreation.[177] In the following paragraphs, however, I challenge these claims as I critique the inconsistencies of and even contradictions inherent in them as they contribute to the potential infringement of parents' religious freedom.

Although Rawls specifies that the political virtues of political liberalism cannot be imposed on associational values or meshed with familial ones in a civil society, children are required to learn the political virtues to empower them to be "fully cooperating members of society."[178] Rawls asserts that these qualities not only reflect the virtues of "civility and tolerance," they mirror "reasonableness and the sense of fairness."[179] In turn, political liberalism stipulates that children's education should include knowledge of their constitutional and civic rights to ensure they realize the existence of liberty of conscience in their society. It also specifies that parents should nurture their children to develop the capacity for a sense of justice so that, as adults, they become fully cooperating members of society. According to Rawls, parental choice for their children's education should encourage political virtues so that as adult citizens they want to honor the fair terms of social cooperation with the principle of reciprocity.[180]

Even though Rawls appears intent on protecting the autonomy of the family and categorizes it under the term of non-public domestic reason with internal non-public reason constraints, he asserts that, at times, the State has grounds for interventions. As I noted earlier, when education, including family education, fails to fulfill the capacity for justice that political liberalism requires, this implies the State can assume the role of "reforming" the family. Alluding to this potential, Rawls explains:

176. Rawls, *Political Liberalism, Expanded*, 467.
177. Rawls, *Political Liberalism, Expanded*, 474.
178. Rawls, *Political Liberalism, Expanded*, 199.
179. Rawls, *Political Liberalism, Expanded*, 194.
180. Rawls, *Political Liberalism, Expanded*.

> Just as the principles of justice impose constraints on the family on behalf of children who as society's future citizens have basic rights as such [. . .] injustices bear harshly not only on women but also on their children; and they tend to undermine children's capacity to acquire the political virtues required of future citizens in a viable democratic society. [. . .] When the family [as in Mill's day] inculcates habits of thought and ways of feeling and conduct incompatible with democracy [. . .], principles of justice enjoining a reasonable constitutional democratic society can plainly be invoked to reform the family.[181]

Rawls advocates for such interventions to "reform" the family if parents' choice for their children's education undermines their children's development of the capacity for the moral powers required by the principles of political justice. In discussing education, Quong, using reasoning he developed from Rawls, suggests that as a result of parents asserting their right to educate and raise their children the way they perceive best, "even if the threat to normative stability is relatively low, there may still be good grounds for intervention."[182] Containment, a possible result of an intervention aimed at reform, may ensue if political liberalism perceives the parents' choice of education as a kind of illiberal one with the potential to harm their children's ability to grow and exercise either of their two moral powers or their capacity for justice.[183] I assert that this potential infringement on parental religious freedom, limiting and restricting the educational choices that parents may make for their children under the scheme of public reason, not only proves inconsistent with, but actively violates Rawls's own stated values, particularly the religious freedom that he professes to support.[184]

Rawls's infringement of his stated value of religious freedom, revealed in his prescription for parental "reform," concomitantly possesses the potential to violate parental religious freedom that international laws stipulate. As I note in Chapter 2, Article 18(4) of the ICCPR states: "The States Parties to the present Covenant undertake to have respect for the liberty of parents and, when applicable, legal guardians to ensure the religious and moral education of their children in conformity with their own convictions."[185] Bielefeldt[186] further confirms that actions repressing parental choices for

---

181. Rawls, *Political Liberalism, Expanded*, 470.

182. Quong, *Liberalism without Perfection*, 305.

183. Quong, *Liberalism without Perfection*.

184. Rawls, *Political Liberalism, Expanded*, 194.

185. *International Covenant on Civil and Political Rights*.

186. Bielefeldt, *Freedom of Religion or Belief*, 118.

their children's education may not only violate children's freedom of religion or belief but also "the parents" right to ensure an education for their
children in conformity with their own convictions and in a manner consistent with the evolving capacities of the child."[187] In addition, Bielefeldt
states other concerns relating to parents' exercising their right to choose
to educate their children in ways that conform with their own convictions,
which Article 18(4) of the ICCPR enshrines.

One concern involves school education, in which children "are exposed to religious instruction against their will or the will of their parents
or guardians."[188] Other possible concerns include exerting pressure on children to participate in rituals and ceremonies of other religions without the
consent of their parents, pressure which at times has extended to punishing
or assaulting students.[189]

Macedo argues that when parental choice for their children's education involves insulating their children from diversity, it impedes their children's level of awareness of alternative ways of life. Bielefeldt notes similar
concerns, such as parents withdrawing their children from learning about
other religions or children being forced to participate in religious practices
that conflict with their own. According to Macedo, however, knowledge
and awareness regarding diversity constitute a prerequisite of citizenship as well as a prerequisite for the ability to make basic life decisions.[190]
Macedo asserts that:

> The religious liberty of parents does not extend with full force
> to their children. [. . .] I would concede the right to opt out of
> public schooling, but that right should be understood to be
> conditioned by a public authority to regulate private schools to
> insure [sic] that civic basics are taught. True enough, in most
> states private schools and home schooling are only minimally
> regulated, especially with respect to civic education. That states
> do not fully exercise their rightful authority, however, does not
> mean they do not have it. So while there is a (moral and consti-
> tutional) right to opt out of public schooling, there is no right
> to opt selectively out of those basic civic exercises that the state
> may reasonably require for all children.[191]

---

187. Bielefeldt, *Freedom of Religion or Belief.*

188. Bielefeldt, *Freedom of Religion or Belief.*

189. Bielefeldt, *Freedom of Religion or Belief,* 138–39.

190. Macedo, "Liberal Civic Education," 486.

191. Macedo, "Liberal Civic Education," 486.

Macedo, like Rawls, appears to employ his words to suit his preferred intent. He states that diversity often indicates a great liberal resource, but then interjects a conflicting qualifier, "but not always." "There are religious and other forms of diversity," he emphasizes, "that we have no reason to embrace or even accommodate."[192] Macedo concedes, nevertheless, that children whose parents have religious beliefs need lessons in tolerance, but they are not alone. He asserts that children whose parents advocate totalistic versions of liberalism and those whose parents are "evangelical atheists,"[193] as well as children whose parents who hold other reasonable views, all need to learn political respect for fellow citizens.

Contrary to Macedo's assertion, Goodman proclaims that efforts to instill values are not always coercive, dogmatic, and narrowing as political liberalism may appear to indicate those of parents with religious world-views to be. Neither should parental choice regarding religious education nor a curriculum designed to foster the aims and means of creative and critical thinking and consisting of components that constitute a wholesome and fulfilling life for well-rounded human beings be discounted or excluded from a child's education.[194] Even the lesser goals of becoming a good citizen or cultivating marketable job skills may be subject to condemnation as these include assumptions about human potential and worth. Goodman stresses that good schools contribute to making good citizens or valuable employees and that, typically, a good citizen means a law-abiding one. He also notes that the goal in relation to Rawls's stipulations regarding education does not actually stipulate providing a good education.[195] Unlike Quong, I assert that parents should not be subject to containment or "reform" if they choose not to succumb to political liberalism's aim for education, which primarily targets the development of a sense of justice and political virtues to support political and social institutions. Instead of parents relinquishing their freedom of religion, which encompasses their preference for their children's education, a better goal for education would be to provide the best education possible for children. Such a goal would also embrace the unfettered freedom of parents to practice their internationally decreed right to choose an education for their children which complements their personal religious beliefs. I further address this issue relating to parents' choice for their children's education, especially religious education, in Chapter 4 as well as in Chapter 6.

---

192. Macedo, "Liberal Civic Education," 486–87.
193. Macedo, *Diversity and Distrust*, 204.
194. Rawls, *Political Liberalism, Expanded*, xxiii–xxiv.
195. Goodman, *Religious Pluralism and Values*, 71.

3.4 Public Reason and Religious Freedom under Political Liberalism

Although Western democracies broadly recognize the four pillars listed in Section 3.2.2, and basically agree on them, manifestations regarding State–religion relationships can sharply differ. Several diverse expressions can be noted in the following examples found in the United States, France, and the United Kingdom. The way the State should relate to religion has stimulated centuries of controversies and heated debates[196] as well as demonstrated significant differences in the way State–religion relationships have developed. Due to increasing pluralism in some countries, particularly in the United States, the once traditional connections between religion and the State[197] as well as the accepted basis of the State–religion relationship have essentially changed.[198] Jeroen Temperman notes that worldwide, State practices and perceptions of the apposite State–religion relationship range from some states being explicitly secular to others appearing clearly religious, with yet others somewhere in between. International human rights law does not explicitly stipulate the parameters for the State–religion relationship, nor does it offer guidance on the relationship the State and religion must observe for compliance with human rights norms.[199]

3.4.1 The United States

The U.S. Constitution (1787), arguably perceived as a liberal constitution,[200] embraces the four pillars of liberal constitutionalism regarding religion in its various amendments.[201] The First Amendment to the Constitution of the United States (1789), which guarantees freedoms relating to religion, also forbids Congress from either promoting one religion over another or restricting individuals from manifesting their religious practices. The amendment dictates: "Congress shall make no law respecting an establishment of religion, or prohibiting the free exercise thereof."[202] In addition, this constitutional amendment supports freedom of expression and pledges to protect the right both for citizens to freely verbalize their

---

196. "Court and Constitutional."
197. Haupt, *Religion–State Relations*, 163.
198. Temperman, *State-Religion Relationships*, 164.
199. Temperman, *State-Religion Relationships*, 1.
200. Seidman, "Should We Have."
201. Rosenfeld and Sajo, *The Migration of Constitutional Ideas*, 142–77.
202. Temperman, *State-Religion Relationships*, 1.

thoughts and to assemble in an amicable fashion. These rights cannot be "surrendered, or waived by the holder/bearer of the rights."[203] According to this amendment, human rights portray natural, inherent elements of the human personality; therefore, no entity (neither person nor government) can take these rights from another.

The U.S. constitution, which has provisions concerning the nonestablishment of a State church, does mandate a kind of separation or wall between the State and religion.[204] Consequently, tensions often arise between those holding different worldviews on the degree of separation or height of the wall between the two, especially in the public square, as I note in two much-discussed U.S. Supreme Court rulings relating to the First Amendment and concerning praying and reading the Bible in school. In 1962, the Supreme Court ruled in *Engel v. Vitale* "that a school policy of reciting a nonsectarian prayer written by the New York Board of Regents was unconstitutional."[205] The following year, 1963, the U.S. Supreme Court ruled in *Abington Township School District v. Schempp* and *Murray v. Curlett*, banning religious exercises, including prayers and Bible readings, in public schools."[206] The court's ruling evoked a huge nationwide protest, primarily from evangelical Protestants and Catholics. Cardinal Spellman called the decision "a tragic misreading of our Founding Fathers."[207] According to Billy Graham, the decision reflected "another step toward secularism."[208] Thousands of U.S. citizens concerned about religious freedom, as well as individuals from churches and civic and religious organizations, wrote to the then U.S. president, John F. Kennedy, protesting against the Supreme Court ruling. Justice Potter Stewart, who cast the only dissenting vote, surmised that regarding religion, the ruling did not represent true neutrality but rather contributed to establishing a religion of secularism in the United States.[209]

On 26 June 2017, Sam Hananel and Mark Sherman reported that the Supreme Court ruled in another controversial case which involved the Trinity Lutheran Church of Columbia, Missouri, appealing against the rejection of its 2012 application for a State grant for funds to cover the cost of applying a soft surface to its preschool playground. The justices overturned the State's decision with a 7–2 vote. "Chief Justice John Roberts said for the

203. Condé, *Handbook of International Human*, 154.

204. Haupt, *Religion–State Relations*, 178.

205. Gold, *Engel v. Vitale*, 135.

206. Gold, *Engel v. Vitale*, 135.

207. Smith, *Faith and the Presidency*, 135.

208. Smith, *Faith and the Presidency*, 138.

209. DelFattore, *The Fourth R.*

court that the State violated the U.S. Constitution's First Amendment by denying a public benefit to an otherwise eligible recipient solely on account of its religious status."[210] Justice Sonya Sotomayor, as well as several liberal civil liberties groups agreed, however, argued that the ruling contradicts the longstanding commitment of the US to separation of church and State. This dispute vividly reflects the distance that may exist between the church and State in a civil society, particularly in the United States.

As one of the many establishment clause litigations, the case in which Judge Roy Moore, of Etowah County, Alabama, determined to keep the Ten Commandments hanging on his courtroom wall similarly mirrors the distance between the church and State. Ronald Bruce Flowers reports that in 1980, prior to this incident, the court declared in *Stone v. Graham* it unconstitutional to post the Ten Commandments in public school classrooms. In 1998, Judge Roy Moore of Alabama countered legal challenges after he refused to remove the plaque presenting the Ten Commandments displayed in his courtroom. After running for and being elected to the position of Chief Justice of the Alabama Supreme Court, Judge Moore, who became known as the "Ten Commandments candidate," arranged for a stone monument weighing 5,200 pounds with the Ten Commandments etched on it to be crafted and then delivered and positioned in the lobby of the Alabama judicial building.[211] Ultimately, Flowers recounts:

> A federal district court, on Establishment Clause grounds, ordered him to remove the monument. He refused—and the story made national headlines. When the court had the monument removed, earnest believers (in both the Ten Commandments and Roy Moore) rallied on his behalf. Finally, Judge Moore was removed by Alabama legal authority from his position on the state Supreme Court. He asked the US Supreme Court to review his case. It did not.[212]

At times, fierce battles by the ideological right and left in the United States regarding decisions oscillating between the "Free Exercise Clause" and the "Establishment Clause" stimulated confusion, concerns, and controversies. The two noted U.S. Supreme Court rulings, the first relating to the First Amendment regarding prayer and reading the Bible in school, the second being the ruling regarding Ten Commandments, reflect a sample of the division between and the passion of both sides. Legal cases such as these also illustrate how public reason under political liberalism manifests

---

210. Hananel and Sherman, "Supreme Court rules for Missouri," para. 4.

211. Flowers, *That Godless Court*, 178.

212. Flowers, *That Godless Court*, 178.

insufficiencies, inconsistencies, and potential infringement of religious rights, revealing that political liberalism will fail to protect religious freedom for all.[213] Principled pluralism, as I argued in chapter 2, and contrast with political liberalism in the next section, mandates State impartiality toward all religions. Instead of ruling out all prayers or displays of religious symbols like statues of the Ten Commandments in any pubic-funded space, principled pluralism will accept and welcome prayers and symbols from all faiths or beliefs—if the State conducts these activities in a non-compulsory way and does not show favoritism toward one religion or belief. This practice will not only decrease religion-State tensions, it will also increase the level of religious freedom for all.

3.4.2 France

Like the United States, France does not establish, nor does it subsidize any religion (Article 2 of the 1905 law).[214] Article 2 of the 1958 French constitution reflects a perceived ideal of constitutional liberalism:

> France is a Republic, indivisible, secular, democratic and social.
> It shall ensure the equality of all citizens before the law, without
> distinction of origin, race or religion. It shall respect all beliefs.[215]

The understandings of the United States and France in relation to freedom of religion, however, differ dramatically, and during 1998 this gap expanded when both the U.S. Congress and the French government passed legislation that reflected conflicting goals for religious freedom. In the United States, the IRFA redefined the rule of the State at the international level and levied potential sanctions on countries convicted of violating religious freedom. The National Assembly in France, however, created a governmental task force, the Inter-Ministerial Mission against Sects (MILS), to monitor cults considered dangerous.[216] The role that France assumes regarding religion appears contradictory. On the one hand, the constitution

---

213. Hypothetically, regarding what *Baorong Duoyuan* adherents would decide for the Ten Commandments' case by the Supreme Court: I would argue, using a bottom-up approach,that the Supreme Court should allow biblical Ten Commandments, as well as other historical symbols from different religious traditions to exist in the court building. A level-down approach would argue to remove all symbols of religious nature from public spaces.

214. Decherf, "*French Views of Religious.*"

215. Boyle and Sheen, *Freedom of Religion*, 294.

216. Decherf, "French Views of Religious."

professes that it protects religious freedom.[217] On the other hand, as laws relating to religious symbols demonstrate, the State also fulfills the role of policing religious practice.

The French stance of attributing equality to each religion also routinely contributes to the State confronting religious challenges. To some, the French posture appears questionable when the State adopts the role of policing religious practices.[218] Most of the increasing clashes between the French government and religion are deeply rooted in the State's assertion of advancing secularism in the public square.

In France, when the State polices religious practices in the name of "radical neutrality,"[219] this inevitably fuels even more conflict within a specific religion and among different religions. For example, conflicts in France in relation to the wearing of religious symbols intensified amid State policing. A 2004 French law prohibits Muslims from covering their faces in public places, a religious practice of Muslim women.[220] Another law, which the French parliament approved in 2010, prohibits individuals in France from wearing headscarves and other religious symbols in public schools.[221] In Paris, during July 2013, rioters destroyed dozens of cars and police arrested at least ten individuals after officers completed an identity check on a Muslim woman wearing a symbol of her religion, a *niqab*, or full-face veil.[222] Approximately 250 protesters hurled stones at police who fired teargas into crowds, attempting to disperse them. Four hundred other individuals protested in Paris, torching cars, bins, and bus shelters. The day after the protests, rioters burned twenty more vehicles in the surrounding area. This kind of culturally based rioting, motivated by religion, confirms that even in a liberal, democratic, republic society, the French agenda of State secularism can neither ensure true harmony nor guarantee religious freedom for all as it claims.

217. Vaïsse, "Veiled Meaning."

218. Kern, "Islamization of France."

219. Foblets, *Religion in Public Spaces*, 9. Foblets asserts: "One would need to go much further in the practice of state neutrality. An illustration of this latter position, strictly linked to the French context, is the opinion issued in early September 2011 by the "Haut Conseil l 'Intgration' in France, which calls for a radicalization of the concept of neutrality in the workplace."

220. Kramer, "Taking the Veil."

221. Sciolino, "French Assembly Votes."

222. Chrisafis, "Paris riots sparked."

3.4.3 The United Kingdom

Unlike the United States and France, the United Kingdom has not adopted a single constitutional document encompassing freedom of religion. Nevertheless, its government legislated the 1998 Human Rights Act, which according to information Chang et al. present, suggests that the State employs a secular liberal constitutional model.[223] The United Kingdom's principal legislation, however, "guarantees"[224] freedom of thought, conscience, and religion and prohibits discrimination on the basis of religion. Restrictions regarding religion in the United Kingdom[225] must align with democratic principles and the law as well as be necessary to ensure public order and safety. Regarding an individual's freedom of thought, conscience and religion, Article 9 of the United Kingdom's Human Rights Act (1998) states:

> Everyone has the right to freedom of thought, conscience and religion; this right includes freedom to change his religion or belief and freedom, either alone or in community with others and in public or private, to manifest his religion or belief, in worship, teaching, practice and observance.

> Freedom to manifest one's religion or beliefs shall be subject only to such limitations as are prescribed by law and are necessary in a democratic society in the interests of public safety, for the protection of public order, health or morals, or for the protection of the rights and freedoms of others.[226]

223. Chang et al., *Constitutionalism in Asia*, 859. A secular liberal constitutional order typically assents that maximizing individual choice through individual rights constitutes the ultimate good for the State. In regard to the ideals for the relationship between the State and religion, Chang et al. note that although all branches of liberalism and constitutionalism share the four common pillars, the State–religion relationship varies due to a "wide diversity of state–religion constitutional arrangements."

224. Foreign & Commonwealth Office, *Freedom of Religion or Belief*, 1, 24. "Freedom of religion or belief is a key human right. The right to adopt a religion, to practice it without hindrance, to share your faith and to change your religion are all key freedoms that everyone should be able to enjoy. Promoting and protecting the right to freedom of religion or belief is an integral part of our human rights work, making a particular contribution to strengthening the rules-based international order, projecting our democratic values and supporting universal human rights, good governance and contributing to conflict prevention. Moreover, its enjoyment plays an important part in achieving the UK's vision of a more secure and prosperous United Kingdom."

225. *Human Rights Act 1998*. Article 9 of Section 1 provides for restrictions on the freedom to express religious beliefs.

226. "Article 9," *Human Rights Act*.

Although the State and religion are deemed distinct entities in the United Kingdom, with their relationship reportedly indicative of bounds regarding State involvement in religion, the State performs some theological interventions, although subtly, in religious matters. For example, twenty-six bishops of the Church of England sit in the House of Lords.[227] At the beginning of each daily meeting, bishops, known as the Lords Spiritual, read prayers. In addition, they actively engage in the life and work of the upper house. Despite the United Kingdom's stance, tensions have arisen in relation to religious extremists and, at times, threaten both the United Kingdom's national security as well as community cohesion. Consequently, along with the question as to whether religious faith can continue to be treated as a purely private matter,[228] the State has had to confront debates and conflicts[229] regarding the integration of U.K. Muslims who, at times, look to Sharia law rather than British law.[230]

Religious education illustrates another area of contention between the State and religion in the United Kingdom. On the one hand, the United Kingdom projects the stance of religious freedom for all. On the other, the State does not as a matter of course allocate equal benefits to other religions as it does to the Church of England. The United Kingdom's State-recognized[231] church, the Church of England, enjoys more privileges than other religions.

In England, the Church of England connects to the State in numerous ways: For example, part of the national curriculum in State-run schools includes "Christian" education, though this does not mean that they are obliged to follow instructions from the Church of England.[232] Conflicts in

227. "Church of England," para. 1. The Lords Spiritual also address matters other than religious.

228. Holden, *Religious Cohesion*, viii.

229. Berkley Center for Religion, "Religious Freedom in the United Kingdom."

230. Berkley Center for Religion, "Religious Freedom in the United Kingdom."

231. Ahdar and Leigh, Religious Freedom. Ahdar and Leigh argue that in a strict sense, the Church of England is not a real established church. They acknowledge, nevertheless, that it does receive preferential treatment.

232. Ahdar and Leigh, *Religious Freedom*, 102. The Queen, the Supreme Governor of England, appoints bishops for the Church of England. Twenty-six bishops are entitled to sit in the House of Lords: The Archbishops of Canterbury and York; the Bishops of London, Durham, and Winchester; and twenty-one other diocesan bishops according to seniority. This amounts to approximately 4 percent membership of the House of Lords. The church's mission is distinct from the secular mission of government because the church fulfills a religious role. Links to the State do not include government funding. "Nevertheless, citizens have a number of legal entitlements against the Church of England by virtue of its role as a national church which they do not have against other religious bodies." By law, the church must minister to all parishioners, not only church

relation to the State selectively financing only certain religious schools surface within the various religious communities. This unequal treatment of specific religions, the Muslim faith, for example, appears to indicate a State bias favoring Christian religions. During the 1990s, although State-funded Christian schools operated, the State repeatedly denied funding for independent Islamic schools. By 2004, Muslim communities protested, charging the State with religious prejudice. Consequently, the State initiated funding for four Islamic schools. The Department for Education and Skills now routinely allocates funds to help Islamic schools, provided they move to the State sector.[233] The ongoing controversy regarding this practice provides yet another example of the potential inherent tension in the relationship between the State and religion in a liberal constitutional model.

3.5 Political Liberalism Contrasted with Principled Pluralism

3.5.1 Regarding the State–Religion Relationship

As one among numerous spheres in society, according to principled pluralism, the State does not hold sovereignty and supremacy over the other spheres. Part of the role of the State includes maintaining equality between the various societal spheres, including its own. According to Schmidt, the State "has an obligation to enforce mutual respect for the boundary lines separating the different spheres of authority whenever a conflict arises between areas or when one sphere steps over its boundary of authority into the domain of another."[234] Schmidt points out that another responsibility of the State involves preventing authorities within a specific sphere from using their power to act unjustly toward relatively powerless individuals within that sphere. To regulate the State and ensure it remains within its rightful realm, citizens utilize means of both constitutional law and representative government.

Carl H. Esbeck's thoughts align with principled pluralism as he exposes the essence of the differences between political liberalism and principled pluralism regarding the reported neutral stance of the State regarding religion. According to Wolterstorff, the dominant interpretation of the State's neutrality which he terms the separation interpretation (of the First Amendment in regard to the religion-State relationship), widely adopted by liberals, asserts that the government should not in any way advance or hinder any

---

members. These duties include baptism, marriage, and burial of the dead.

233. Soper and Fetzerl, "Religious institutions." Unlike France, in England, school authorities permit females to wear religious head coverings in colors that conform to their school uniforms.

234. Schmidt, "*Principled Pluralist*," 136.

religion.[235] Instead of this type "neutrality" role of the State, Wolterstorff proposes a nuanced concept of government's affirmative impartiality. Regarding the religion or irreligion of various groups, this impartiality interpretation contends that nothing a State says or does demonstrates an absence of its impartiality. Impartiality does not require that the government carry out polices which align with the convictions of all citizens, however, the governmental requirement mandates that the State does not resolve to render support to any religion or irreligion.[236]

Whenever the State can attain one of its lawful purposes without breaching the beliefs of a religion or irreligion, it must do so. Affirmative impartiality entails a positive, forward State role as it requires the State to plainly stand for something deemed valuable, and to also support common good for both religion and irreligion. The State is not to side with the secular worldview, feigning neutrality. Wolterstorff illustrates his point by pointing out different results around the controversy of government's aid to schools based on religious orientation. The impartiality position states that "if the state aids any schools, it must aid all schools, and aid them all equitably—no matter what their religious orientation, if any." However, the separation position based on the State's neutrality claim says the state's public funding is "to aid no school whose orientation is religious."[237] Furthermore, Esbeck argues that political liberal variances are theologically rooted in a secular worldview and that despite contrary claims, the State's neutrality claim proves invalid.

> A person's religious presuppositions travel with him wherever he is whatever he is doing in life. This total unity, it is said, exists not only within each individual but also at corporate levels, including government institutions. Government cannot be dualistic, for it too holds a Weltanschauung or worldview. The deduction follows that state neutrality is not only impossible and thus a myth, but worse, it is a ploy calculated to use the state as an instrument for advancing philosophies that are antithetical to Christianity. In short, the argument concludes, either the state favors Christianity or it favors an opposing philosophy. There is no neutral ground.[238]

In such instances exemplifying tensions between religion and the State, one observation may safely be made. Esbeck stresses that: "The oft-lamented

---

235. Audi and Wolterstorff, *Religion in the Public Square*, 76.

236. Audi and Wolterstorff, *Religion in the Public*, 149.

237. Audi and Wolterstorff, *Religion in the Public*, 76.

238. Esbeck, "Religion and a Neutral State."

tensions between church (religion) and State are not all bad. Rather, the presence of tension is symptomatic of something healthy."[239] While working through the conflicts, each power, church (religion), and State, sharpens and offsets the other. This tension helps confirm that the church, although a relevant part of the world, yet not being so worldly, does not align with the aims of State.

As Rawls downplays the importance of the role of religion in societal institutions, he makes his goal of achieving the liberal ideal of social harmony and peace unsustainable. Institutions such as the family, schools, church (religion), and businesses merit as much significance as the State, simultaneously serving as instruments for the individual development of freedom and justice. Although the goals of Rawls's political liberalism may conflict with principled pluralism, as Esbeck notes, the tension between the two spheres portrays rather a healthy relationship, even according to this liberal concept of the separation of church (religion) and State.

Regarding Rawls's reasoning in relation to intolerance, which transmutes to religious freedom, he admits concern relating to what he terms a practical dilemma:

> Even if an intolerant sect should arise, provided that it is not so strong initially that it can impose its will straight away [. . .] it will tend to lose its intolerance and accept liberty of conscience. [. . .] Of course, the intolerant sect may be so strong initially or growing so fast that the forces making for stability cannot convert it to liberty. This situation presents a practical dilemma which philosophy alone cannot resolve.[240]

While Rawls stresses the importance of justice as fairness in political liberalism, he admits that an injustice may be acceptable, even if unfair, under one condition: when a perceived danger exists that a greater injustice could occur; "an injustice is tolerable only when it is necessary to avoid an even greater injustice."[241] Rawls does not specify what conditions would merit an acceptable injustice. This may include some religions or religious groups deemed as unreasonable or intolerant. Rawls appears to indicate it to be permissible to entrench the religious liberty of perceived dangerous groups that appear potentially disruptive in the existential, institutional stability if they are unable to be transformed to become tolerant. This, according to Rawls, would be to avoid whatever greater injustice may threaten the tolerant groups. Rawls would reason that it would not constitute

239. Esbeck, "Religion and a Neutral State," 88.
240. Rawls, *Theory of Justice*, 219.
241. Rawls, *Theory of Justice*, 4.

a problem to tolerate this lesser injustice to the perceived dangerous and potentially disruptive groups.

This logic leads to the conclusion that for Rawls's public reason under political liberalism, maintaining social stability surpasses the concern for religious freedom. Rawls also contends that "generally speaking, the errors in religion are dangerous; those in philosophy only ridiculous."[242] Rawls does not specifically identify such errors. He appears to suggest that intolerant religions reflect errors in religion and, in turn, pose much more of a potential danger to society than any error or absurdity that a part of any philosophical theory might mirror. The massive terror and atrocities which tens of millions experienced in the twentieth century, including religious individuals, because of adopting Karl Marx's philosophy, proves Rawls's comparison to be both empirically wrong and theoretically invalid.

Although the Rawlsian theory includes the concept of toleration as part of justice and accordingly, "the principles of justice give reasons for tolerance," this question remains unanswered: What attitude should society demonstrate toward the intolerant? In his discussion on whether to tolerate the intolerant, Rawls proposes a principle of conversion to liberty of conscience, for the sake of institutional stability.[243] Based on this concept, if an intolerant sect appears in a well-ordered society through the conversion to liberty process, once that intolerant religious group or sect loses its momentum of growth and influence in society, it will be transformed into a tolerant group.

Instead of discussing ethical principles on constraint or limitations of the principle of tolerance, Rawls shifts the discussion to the practical consideration of the level of the threat. Raphael Cohen-Almagor points out that rather than an argument contingent on the level of the danger, the issue of tolerance constitutes a matter of moral principle, noted not as practical, but ethical.[244] Rawls pursues a line of argument that avoids the philosophical issue: What to do when an intolerant religious sect has taken a solid stronghold in certain society or if a group grows too influential to covert to liberty of tolerance? The essence of this question may be considered a constraint on tolerance and liberty. Instead of specifically addressing this challenging concern, however, Rawls remains vague. He fails to offer a clear-cut solution and instead stresses that this situation presents a practical dilemma that philosophy needs help to resolve.

---

242. Rawls, *Lectures*, 13.

243. Cohen-Almagor, *Boundaries of Liberty*, 76.

244. Cohen-Almagor, *Boundaries of Liberty*.

On a positive note for Rawls, Joseph Grcic stresses that his utilization of the veil of ignorance to exclude information on religion does not minimize the significance of one basic idea that principled pluralism acknowledges that the State does not have the right to determine what constitutes true religion. "Excluding information about a certain subject matter such as religion does not mean Rawls thinks this subject is unimportant but only that it is not relevant at this level for determining justice."[245] According to Grcic, the exclusion of information regarding a citizen's religion mirrors Rawls's way for protecting freedom of religion because this promotes a better understanding of how religion fits into a just society.

As I noted in Chapter 2, Kuyper initially championed principled pluralism's basic ideas, the concepts that Cornelis Van Dam as well as the Center for Public Justice in Washington support. Unlike political liberalism, which contends that although excluded from the public political forum, religion can be the basis of individual political conviction, principled pluralism welcomes religion into the public political environment with few restrictions. As Van Dam stresses, I agree that: "Within certain limits, such as the need to restrain evil, all religions must be treated alike and be given the same freedom and opportunities."[246] Also, contrary to political liberalism, which promotes secularism over religion, principled pluralism reasons that the government cannot favor one religion over another or enforce, for example, the religion of secularism in society.

Principled pluralists contend that all of God's creation including the political sphere not only needs but awaits redemption. The political realm, according to the Reformed tradition, needs to be redeemed "neither no more nor no less than any other sphere of human activity."[247] Principled pluralists believe God continues to work His redemption in this present-day world and argue that Christians should engage in political activity.

3.5.2 Disorder in Rawls's Well-Ordered Society

Rawls's portrayal of a well-ordered society reveals the arbitrary nature of his stated goal for political liberalism, which is to achieve a utopian society, as far as is feasible. Rawls argues that within a well-ordered, reasonable pluralistic democratic society, through the filter of public reason based on "justice as fairness," reasonable citizens with reasonable comprehensive doctrines and ideas reach overlapping consensuses. In the semi-utopian,

245. Grcic, *Free and Equal,* 34.

246. Van Dam, *God and Government,* 65.

247. Sider, "Principled Pluralist Response," 208.

fictional setting, arbitrators further demand that reasonable religious adherents conduct their political discourse by passing through the proviso process. The well-ordered society that Rawls envisages promotes the good of its members. In this made-up society, I maintain that contributions to the public square mandate that any public communication aligns with secular argument and do not contain any input that might be deemed unreasonable, irrational, or religious. Rawls admits the well-ordered society does not and has never existed, saying that "existing societies are of course seldom well-ordered in this sense."[248] Samuel Scheffler notes that, according to Rawls, a public conception of justice effectively regulates a well-ordered society, that is, a society in which:

1. each person accepts and understands that others agree to the same principles of justice; and

2. the fundamental social institutions usually satisfy and are normally known to meet these principles.[249]

In the hypothetical well-ordered society, Rawls states that conditions of moderate scarcity exist. These include "reasonable beliefs (on which to ground the public conception of justice), generally accepted methods of inquiry, fundamental and divergent individual aims and interests supporting claims on the design of social institutions, various opposing and incompatible basic beliefs, and so on."[250] Rawls stresses that he incorporated all the features defining a well-ordered society into the description of the original position,[251] conditions he perceives as recognizably reasonable. Citizens arrive at these conditions through the course of questioning themselves to ascertain what kind of society they might prefer to live in.

Rawls concedes that even though conditions he developed for a well-ordered society may appear reasonable to him and other political liberals, they may appear less than clearly reasonable to makers of constitutions. He additionally concludes that existing societies cannot satisfy the entire set of conditions that a well-ordered society needs.[252] Grcic agrees with Rawls that some (including himself) will disagree with the basis on which Rawls draws for implementing his ideas for developing a society into a well-ordered system of social cooperation.[253] Rawls presupposes that in

248. Rawls, *Political Liberalism*, 5.

249. Scheffler, "Appeal of Political Liberalism."

250. Rawls, *Principles of Justice*, 323.

251. Rawls, *Political Liberalism, Expanded*, 23.

252. Kukathas, *Principles of Justice*, 5.

253. Blunden, *"Rawls' Political Liberalism."*

the well-ordered society of political liberalism, illiberal and intolerant religions will ultimately cease to exist.[254] This summation appears to indicate that a society cannot be well ordered unless religions, such as those that mandate the suppression of other religions, as well as those "religions that insist on religious establishment, or that demand the adoption of a certain comprehensive conception of the good by the whole society,"[255] figuratively speaking, have died out.[256] Rawls does not address the issue regarding what should be done with such religions in a well-ordered society but argues that a well-ordered society will also be a stable one.

Rawls's unrealistic concept of a well-ordered society, particularly as published in *A Theory of Justice*, constitutes a serious problem. Even though Rawls revised his 1971 theory of justice in 1975 and again in 1999, he does not abandon it. As his work in *Political Liberalism* (1993) reveals, Rawls starts to stress that in contemporary constitutional democracies like the United States, disagreements regarding rudimentary issues, such as abortion and morals, can threaten a society's stability. Rawls fails to show that negative consequences will transpire if a society does not stabilize in the sense he proposes.[257]

Rawls's notion of a well-ordered society constitutes part of what he classifies as full compliance.[258] He fails to identify how society arrives at this destination,[259] however. For example, in regard to intolerant religions not highlighted in a well-ordered society, the question of their demise arises. Rawls presumes these religions have died out and states that the rudimentary institutions of a just society "inevitably encourage some ways of life and discourage others, or even exclude them altogether."[260] More questions ensue, including: (1) What does "discourage" mean in this context? (2) "[W]hat does it mean to exclude certain ways of life altogether?"[261] Rawls does not answer these two questions. He points out that even in a well-ordered society, the State may need to utilize its coercive powers to help ensure the stability of social cooperation.

254. Rawls, *Political Liberalism, Expanded*.

255. Rawls, *Political Liberalism*, 197.

256. Waldron, "Lecture 2: What Does," 7–8.

257. Gordon, "John Rawls."

258. Bell, *Ethics and World Politics*, 397. Full compliance theory: "A theory that discusses the norms that justice or morality requires, on the assumption that those norms would be respected by all agents subject to them."

259. Waligore, "Race, Rawls, Self-Respect," 7.

260. Waligore, "Race, Rawls, Self-Respect," 8.

261. Waligore, "Race, Rawls, Self-Respect."

Andy Blunden challenges the validity of Rawls's claim that in a well-ordered society, most citizens not only accept but know that most other citizens accept the identical principles of justice.[262] Rawls asks how can a society "which is made up of all kinds of people, with all kinds of beliefs and all kinds of interests, agree with and support governing principles?"[263] In that a person must explain him/herself in a way that will seem reasonable to people who may not share his/her beliefs, the explanation must also be acceptable to those who share the same beliefs. Here, Rawls's reasoning appears flawed. Hill also stresses that in "this optimal society the principles would generally be the same throughout the society and would be enforced by the State."[264] Rawls's ideal well-ordered society would putatively exemplify a government at its best, with every citizen supposedly agreeing with and supporting the governing principles. The State would also, in principle, effectively institute only those principles.

André Van de Putte suggests that Rawls's proposed ideal of a political community, one with the same comprehensive doctrine uniting all, does not exist, even in a society devoid of violent and unreasonable people.[265] In any society, including Rawls's hypothetical "well-ordered" one, comprehensive doctrines prove too diverse to function as public frames of reference. The resolutions which principled pluralism offers, particularly the level-up approach to allow diverse comprehensive doctrines, including religious ones, in the public square,[266] can ultimately work to advance the common good and justice for all in actual constitutional, democratic societies.

While Rawls may disagree with principled pluralism, he utilizes an elaborate way to serve as the foundation for public good and the equal distribution of justice with filters for reason and rationality. Shaun P. Young notes that Rawls's filters include terms such as "reasonable persons," "reasonable doctrines," "reasonable citizens," and a host of other "reasonable" entities.[267] Blunden argues that Rawls does not aim to pursue social good but instead seeks to discover a marginal overlapping consensus on principles of justice, a quest some consider admirable. Blunden questions whether reasonable pluralism proves sufficient for laying the basis of a stable and well-ordered system of social cooperation in which people could pursue their own ideas of the good within their own associations and communities.

---

262. Blunden, "Rawls' Political Liberalism."
263. Blunden, "Rawls' Political Liberalism," *para. 3 in Introduction.*
264. Hill, "Government, Justice, and Human Rights," para. 1.
265. Van de Putte, "Rawls' Political Liberalism."
266. Wolterstorff and Audi, *Religion in the Public Square,* 112.
267. Young, "Rawlsian Reasonableness," 159–80.

Although a political liberal, Rawls agrees with principled pluralist proponents regarding democracy that it aligns with the concept of a
limited, public-interest State. Similarly, regardless of principled pluralism's
differences to political liberalism, this theory concurs with Rawls's fundamental ideas that "in the public political culture of a democratic society,
citizens are free and equal, and that society should be a fair system of
cooperation."[268] Despite diverse religious and philosophical commitments,
political liberalism can formulate an overlapping consensus on fundamental political matters among religious and other groups holding comprehensive doctrines. As numerous reasonable interpretations of equal, free,
and fair coexist with a myriad of other associated words and concepts,
interpretations of fundamental ideas conflict at times.

Like Cornelis Van Dam, I challenge Rawls's disagreements with principled pluralism and point out that this theory embraces the following
distinctive basic principles:[269] (1) No morally neutral ground exists; (2) all
of life is religious in nature and both Christians and non-Christians have
religious presuppositions they bring into the public square; (3) secularism
and the denial of God's relevance for public life is a religious system; (4)
therefore, it proves impossible to restrict religion to the private personal
sphere of home and church (religion) and to insist that the public square be
without religious convictions; (5) principled pluralism opposes a secularized public square which bans religious voices and practices other than its
own and Christians have the obligation to influence the public discourse in
a biblical direction; principles derived from the Scriptures need to be part of
the debate in the public square so that arguments can be made for a public
policy according to the overriding norms of God's Word.[270]

3.6 Conclusion

My examination of public reason under Rawls's political liberalism in the
light of religious freedom demonstrates that, to a large degree, political
liberalism fails to adequately and fully protect religious freedom for all.
I found this illustrated in the experiences of several Western democratic
countries, where major elements of political liberalism under public reason have significantly impacted the treatment of religions in the public
square. Contrary to political liberalism, which routinely restrains the

---

268. Wenar, *Stanford Encyclopedia of Philosophy*, para. 3 in "Political Conceptions"
section.

269. Van Dam, *God and Government*.

270. Van Dam, *God and Government*, 64.

expression of certain religious and comprehensive views regarding political issues, research confirms that principled pluralism welcomes all groups to equally participate in the public square. In contrast to political liberalism, under a democratic constitutional framework, principled pluralism not only pledges to protect religious freedom but also resolves to foster political environments favorable to citizens' personal and public freedoms, contextually, associationally, and directionally.

Principled pluralism, born and initiated in a cultural backdrop of predominantly Judeo-Christian societies, may also successfully fit into a more mature, pluralistic democratic civil society. In considering the historical, cultural, religious, and social complexities in countries like China, I maintain that a contextualized version of principled pluralism presents the best available option to ensure the protection of religious freedom for all. While Rawls's political liberalism restricts certain religious voices and the views of citizens who do not meet its biased criteria of public reason, principled pluralism argues for the indispensability of the role of religion with governmental impartiality toward all religions as well as anti- or non-religions.

In addition to presenting and expounding on Rawls's political liberalism in the light of religious freedom, I specifically focused my critique of public reason under political liberalism and found that research confirms Rawls's theory repeatedly fails to fully protect religious freedom for all due to: (1) inconsistencies in the PRSR, the proviso, and self-respect; (2) its prescription of containment through the filter of public reason toward comprehensive doctrines deemed unreasonable or irrational; (3) the further manifestation of the deficiency cited in (2) in that it implies the potential infringement of parents' religious freedom through limitations relating to children's religious education, including a mandate for parents to ensure their children's education nurtures their development of the capacity for a sense of justice.

In one sense, Rawls's reasons for proposing political liberalism for developing a normative principle appropriate for producing the constitutional foundations of a democratic society appear admirable. As he seeks an appropriate conception of justice to specify fair terms of social cooperation amid free and equal and reportedly fully cooperating citizens of society, Rawls argues that political liberalism fosters a well-ordered system of social cooperation. Although political secular liberalists claim they try to avoid being arbitrary and exclusive, and despite Rawls's potentially admirable intent, they exclude doctrines that they perceive as unreasonable. In turn, the proponents of political liberalism fail to provide solid, reasonable grounds for their rationale.

Amid a barrage of negative repercussions relating to Rawls's political liberalism, his embrace of pluralism merits respect. Compared to some of his traditional liberal colleagues and predecessors, Rawls's concern for social stability, particularly his progressive view regarding tolerating religious-based arguments in public debate, although delimited by the proviso process, also deserves recognition.

Political liberalism not only holds a covert anti-religious bias, it impedes religious freedom for all. If systematically implemented, political liberalism will, in a sense, create further discrimination against religions. When the State systematically employs Rawls's political liberalism, this society will unlikely reach its goal of being well ordered, the goal that Rawls envisages. Unless public justice is equally and impartially guaranteed and distributed by a fair, democratic, constitutional State, increasing clashes, as demonstrated in contemporary democratic countries, such as the United States, France, and the United Kingdom, will occur among citizens with diverse, sometimes conflicting worldviews.

As it offers fewer restrictions regarding religion in the public square, the application of principled pluralism demonstrates the potential to serve as a reasonable alternative to political liberalism to help stabilize society as well as help maintain and protect religious freedom. Nevertheless, despite the numerous advantages a society may experience under principled pluralism, at this present time, the political situation and State in China do not match the paradigm that Western, culturally based, Christianity-oriented, principled pluralism offers. Principled pluralism does not fit the traditional standard of either a mature pluralistic democratic society or a compete theocracy.

As the principled pluralism theory emphasizes Christianity and supports governmental impartiality toward religions, it offers the potential to stimulate tension between new historical, cultural, and social complexities in countries like China. Although Rawls's political liberalism may have some appeal to a limited number of Chinese intellectuals and scholars, especially within the dissident circle, his theory of legitimization of government authority based on justice and freedom does not theoretically fit the overall needs of countries such as contemporary Communist China.[271] According to Samuli Seppänen, "In contrast to Rawls, Chinese mainstream scholars do not argue that personal freedom, autonomy and equality ought to inform conceptions about governmental legitimacy."[272]

---

271. I indicate this further in Chapter 6 when I relate more about *Baorong Duoyuan's* model for China.

272. Seppänen, "Rawls rejected, ignored," 9.

Nevertheless, as political liberalism has not consistently fully protected religious freedom in the liberal Western world, it would not adequately work to promote the same in China.

Although principled pluralism offers more potential to help stabilize China's pluralistic society, it cannot be mechanically imposed on this "Country of Concern."[273] A contextualized, customized version of principled pluralism could best serve China as a means to help alleviate religion-based tensions and, simultaneously, encourage religious freedom for all. While keeping its authoritative political ruling, China's contemporary stance, arguably with limited but increasing pluralism in economic, cultural, and religious sectors, confirms that a new paradigm should be developed. The proposed model could best serve the need to protect religious freedom for all by contextualizing the traditional model of principled pluralism without falling into the inconsistencies and conflicts of political liberalism. In my next chapter, I explore ways in which religious freedom is exemplified in the field of education and how a modified version of principled pluralism applies to religious freedom in religious education.

273. Berkley Center for Religion, Peace, "Religious Freedom and Restriction in China."

Chapter 4

Political Liberalism and Principled Pluralism Related to Religious Freedom in Public Education

Article 26 proclaims not merely the right to an education, but to an education directed to the full development of the human personality and to the strengthening of respect for human rights and fundamental freedoms . . . [to] promote understanding, tolerance and friendship among all nations, racial or religious groups . . . .[1]

4.1 Introduction

A MYRIAD OF CONCERNS regarding religious freedom include the use or display of religious symbols in public space being policed or handled, as well as the degree of permission the State allocates to different institutions based on religious affiliation. For example, a church can discriminate in its hiring practices if the rationale is based on religious conviction. A dilemma arises, however, regarding how much regulation a State may impose on an institution or a business. For example, based on religious convictions, how much can a business be permitted to discriminate in its hiring policy or employment practices without violating liberal constitutional essentials such as equality and free choice? An even more prominent issue routinely surfaces in contemporary society, concerning the inclusion of religious education in the field of government-funded education. As the arena of education, especially

1. Reinbold, *Seeing the Myth*, 78.

taxpayer-funded education, serves as a vital thermometer for measuring the degree of religious freedom for parents and their child/children, I have chosen this issue as a case example of the State–religion relationship vis-a-vis political liberalism and principled pluralism.

In the previous chapter, I examined public reason under Rawls's political liberalism in light of religious freedom and claimed that political liberalism repeatedly fails to fully protect religious freedom for all. In contrast to political liberalism, principled pluralism nurtures political environments favorable to religious freedom for citizens. In this chapter, I initially define public (State) and private (non-State) schools as well variations in between and explain differences among them, evidenced in funding, curriculum, management and religious education. I then examine the five approaches that diverse states have adopted for implementing religious education. I compare these education models and note ensuing tensions and conflicts within four selected countries and their corresponding stances regarding RE in public-funded schools. Peter L. Berger disagrees with those who project that the secularization of the world would increase from the nineteenth century.[2] Thomas G. Walsh notes that numerous intellectuals and social scientists, who have assumed secularization theory,[3] conclude religion will naturally and progressively wither away as humans develop over time. If this projection proves to be true, then the public demand for religious education would understandably be further diminished. However, as Berger found, from the latter part of the nineteenth-century to contemporary times, a broader resurgence of religion also suggests a process of desecularization.[4] Berger argues, "The world today, with some exceptions [. . .], is as furiously religious as it ever was, and in some places more so than ever. This [. . . indicates] that a whole body of literature by historians and social scientists

---

2. Walsh, "Religion, Peace," para. 3. Walsh asserts that even though religion has frequently contributed to conflict and violence, more substantially it has "served to advance the cause of peace in many profound and substantial ways, including its calls for practices such as non-violence, restraint of acquisitiveness, forgiveness, reconciliation, and just-war theory." Walsh proclaims: "If we attribute the discounting of religion's role in public affairs to the European Enlightenment, and that intellectual and social movement's legacy, as expressed in Marxism, Darwinism, scientific reductionism, positivism, methodological atheism and secularization theory, it may be said that the widespread denial of religion's significance is a fairly recent phenomenon, dating back only a few hundred years." Walsh explains that secularization depicts that as "rationality, science, modernization and the exposure to pluralism unfold, religious worldviews will become recessive," para. 15, Introduction section.

3. Walsh, "Religion, Peace," para. 8, Introduction section. Secularization theory originated in the nineteenth and early twentieth centuries.

4. Padmore, *History of the Pan-African*, 130–34.

loosely labeled "secularization theory" is essentially mistaken."[5] Amidst contemporary conflicting contentions regarding religion and its status in the world, in the context of more pluralistic religious and cultural societies, the demand for the inclusion of religious education in the public education system has, in fact, dramatically increased.

The diverse reasoning regarding the State's aim for education, particularly religious education, as well as conflicting perceptions of its application, contribute to engendering conflicts between the State and religion. On the one hand, as I concluded in Chapter 3, political liberalism's approach to education overemphasizes the role of the State in the name of creation of future citizens with a capacity for justice. Although in itself an honorable goal as agreed by BD, nevertheless, this tactic potentially infringes on parents' religious freedom by justifying State intervention, even as far as non-public education is concerned. On the other hand, adherents of principled pluralism defend the legitimacy of educational choice so that diverse education models, including a certain degree of religious education, may be made available to even State-funded, private-sector managed schools. Most principled pluralist adherents also acknowledge that the state has a duty to provide, as well, a "secular" public system[6] alongside others. Although concerns from both adherents of political liberalism and principled pluralism, seemingly opposing sides, appear legitimate, I assert that the resolutions to diverse conflicting perceptions cannot be obtained by a secularized public education system for the former (political liberalism) nor can the traditional sectarian education model be restored as a viable solution. I assert that principled pluralism provides a better option, though not without flaws. As I conclude in Chapter 3, principled pluralism could provide a more consistent, sufficient foundation for religious freedom than political liberalism when it comes to addressing conflicting views about religious education in government-funded schools.[7]

---

5. Berger, *Desecularization of the World*, 2.

6. Berner, *Pluralism and American*, 37.

7. This refers to basic education for children before they attend college.

4.2 Religious Education in State-funded Public Schools

Just as the word "education"[8] defies a universal, concrete definition, methods for implementing the educational process vary. Johann Friedrich Herbart[9] (1776–1841)[10] and Friedrich Wilhelm August Froebel[11] (1783–1852),[12] prominent philosophers of education, promoted diverse methods in their approaches to education. Nevertheless, they agreed regarding the definitive goal or purpose of all education—developing moral character. Herbart believed that teaching methods should be designed to match the way minds work.[13] Froebel utilized the metaphorical approach and considered kindergarten to depict a garden where children develop, grow, and bloom.

Teaching methods as well as the types of education systems for children also vary. I am focusing on the public education system, considering implications of both political liberalism and principled pluralism for government-funded schools relating to public education. I address the pedagogical question: How can religious education best be implemented in government-funded, increasingly secularized schools without violating the State's impartiality to any religion while simultaneously protecting religious freedom for all?

4.2.1 Schools in Four Liberal States

Internationally, depending on the designs of educational institutions in different countries, the classification of schools varies sharply. For instance, in the United States, private and public schools differ in multiple ways; however, their sources of funding portray the primary difference between them. The U.S. Department of Education reports that the U.S. government

8. Bhattacharya, *Foundations of Education*, 5. Bhattacharya notes that education evolves from the Latin term "educare" which means to "bring up[,] to foster, to lead." Leading or bringing up a child in the way he should go also alludes to Proverbs 22:6, which encourages those who educate or train a child, with the intent to instill the right values in him/her (ESV).

9. Noddings, *Philosophy of Education*, 20. "An early advocate of scientific methods in education, [. . .] Teachers must prepare students for new material by bringing to consciousness relevant experiences students have stored in the apperceptive mass. Then teachers and students can go on to shape the new material so that it is deposited accurately and is accessible for future use. [Herbart's] method is highly cognitive and emphasizes the activity of the teacher more than that of the student."

10. Hilgenheger, "Johann Friedrich Herbart," 649.

11. Noddings, *Philosophy of Education*, 21.

12. Taneja, *Educational Thought*, 122.

13. Noddings, *Philosophy of Education*, 20.

provides funding per student for public schools. As private schools do not receive government funding in the United States, and rely solely on tuition cost to support their school, they typically charge tuition for each student.[14] However, as I will demonstrate in the following sections, this kind of classification and application totally differs from the Dutch school system because most private schools in Netherlands, like the American public schools, receive government funding. Moreover, various funding sources under different classifications of schools will determine if the administration of the school with be on a national or local level, as well as whether the government or a non-government agency designs and controls the school's curriculum. Furthermore, in contrast to the consensus of accepting religious education in purely privately funded schools, including homeschools, the degree of allowance or tolerance of religious education under various countries' school systems can differ dramatically. In turn, the differences regarding children's access to religious education could serve as a major indicator of religious freedom in a State.

In the following sections, I outline the school classifications of each of the four selected countries, the United States, the United Kingdom, France, and the Netherlands. I then point to different funding sources, the role of government and non-government sectors in curriculum design, and school management under different school systems. I also present an account of how each type of school in each country deals with religious education.

4.2.1.1 Schools in the United States

The general educational system in the United States includes, public, charter, non-public (includes parochial and private schools), and home schools. American and international law attribute the primary responsibility for the education of children to their parents—not the State. Nevertheless, since the inception of the U.S. Republic, its cities and States have primarily provided public schooling, which has led to various levels of contemporary governments functioning as primary educators for U.S. citizens. In the United States, though the federal government contributes almost 10 percent to the national education budget, education is primarily the responsibility of state and local governments. Subsequently, its curriculum and management are primarily designed and controlled by government through local school districts. Thus, every state has great control over what is taught in its schools and over the requirements that a student must meet, and it is also responsible for the funding of schooling. In most states, the public education system

14. U.S. Department of Education, *State Regulation of Private Schools.*

is further divided into local school districts, which are managed by a school board representing the local community.[15]

Charter schools, in contrast to public schools, receive funding from both government and non-government sources, including individuals. While charter schools follow public schools' curriculum, they are managed though an independent, individual board of directors, rather than a local school district board. The private and parochial schools obtain funding from individuals, religious institutions, and grants from charitable organizations but do not receive any government funding. The management of non-public and home schools, including school administration and curriculum design, are totally autonomous, and therefore free of interference from both federal and local governments.

Religious education in public-funded schools has been controversial for decades. Currently, religious education is not permitted in public or charter schools but may be taught in non-public and home schools. In the United States, most elementary and secondary private schools are religiously- oriented, with religious education permitted in their curriculum. In home schools, instead of sending their children to a school facility for their education, parents teach their child/children at home. Many parents who send their children to private schools primarily do so to preserve their religious values.

Since the U.S. Supreme Court's landmark ruling in the case of *Abington School District v. Schempp* in 1963 that banned religious exercises, prayers and Bible readings in public schools, the controversy over the rights and freedom for religious education in public school has continued. One major concern regarding that ruling—forbidding these religious exercises in public schools in the name of anti-establishment of religion—the State, in essence, confines the free exercise of religion into private spheres, and promotes secularism to fill the vacuum in the public square. As Supreme Court Justice Potter Stewart noted in his dissent of that case:

> If religious exercises are held to be an impermissible activity in schools, religion is placed in an artificial and state-created disadvantage[. . .]. And a refusal to permit religious exercises thus is seen, not as the realization of state neutrality, but rather as the establishment of a religion of secularism, or at least, as governmental support of the beliefs of those who think that religious exercises should be conducted only in private.[16]

15. Corsi-Bunker, "Guide to the Education System."
16. Eastland, *Religious Liberty*, 59.

While I share the concern expressed by the "Majority Opinion" regarding the protection of religious pluralism for all citizens, that ruling may have gone too far. I reason that some religious education is warranted in public schools. Even though Justice Tom Clark, author of "Majority Opinion" in that case, appeared to insist that public education should be secular-orientated, he acknowledged the fundamental value of learning about religion for students' pedagogical and civility building purposes. Bruce Grelle argues that "the Supreme Court sought to make it clear that learning and teaching about religion in the public schools is perfectly consistent with constitutional principles.[17] According to Justice Clark:

> it might well be said that one's education is not complete without a study of comparative religion or the history of religion and its relationship to the advancement of civilization. It certainly may be said that the Bible is worthy of study of its literary and historic qualities. Nothing we have said here indicates that such study of the Bible and of religion, when presented objectively as part of a secular program of education, may not be affected consistently with the First Amendment.[18]

In the United States, two concerns exist in relation to religious education and their associated responses. Religious groups who desire to maintain the integrity of their faith primarily align with the first concern, traditionally recognized as "free exercise." As they strive to avoid State endorsement of any religion, adherents of both classical liberalism and political liberalism align with the second concern, known as "non-establishment." Scott A. Merriman explains that two clauses exist in the First Amendment: (1) the free exercise clause, which protects the free exercise of religion; and (2) the establishment clause, which refers to protection from any government-established religion.

As numerous courts and leaders have argued that if the State and religion were to oppose, or to exhibit indifference to each other, they will be promoting one blatant, massive misunderstanding regarding the doctrine of State–religion separation. This kind of overt application of separation between religion and state in the education field has positioned parents with strong religious affiliations in jeopardy. It disadvantages these parents economically by unfairly coercing them into paying an excessive amount of tuition. Even though these parents previously contributed to public education expenses through tax payments for their children's private school education, they are penalized if they choose to engage their children's

---

17. Grelle, *Religious Education in Schools*, 81.

18. Abington v. Schempp, *Digital History ID 4087*, para. 3 in Section III.

education in alignment with their own religion or religious tradition. Moreover, I would argue, as stated in Chapter 2, that by banning religious education in public and charter schools, the U.S. educational system could be found violating, to a certain extent, the international norms regarding parents' religious freedom. According to these standards, the State has an obligation to facilitate parents' choice for their children's education according to their religious preference.

Therefore, to best protect religious freedom for all, and increase dialogues and civility, as well as economic equality among all faiths and adherents in the public education system, I propose that religious education proves both necessary and needed in the public education environment. Table 3 portrays four types of schools in the United States, as well as their funding source, curriculum, management, and attitude toward religious education.

Table 3: Four Types of US Schools and Their Attributes[19]

School Classification	Funding Source	Curriculum	Management	Religious Education
Public	Government	Government	Government	Not permitted
Charter	Government and non-Government	Government	Non-government	Not permitted
Non-public, including parochial and private	Non-government	Non-government	Non-government	Permitted
Home school	Non-government	Non-government	Non-government	Permitted

4.2.1.2 Schools in the United Kingdom

The first type of school I note in this section, the most usual form of school in the United Kingdom, are community schools or State schools. Other schools include faith schools, free schools, academies and faith academies, and private schools.[20] State schools, controlled by the local council, and funded by

---

19. Author's original table.
20. *Types of Schools.*

the government, must follow the U.K. national curriculum. In State schools, religious education is integral to the curriculum.

Faith schools, the second type of school I single out, must also adhere to and follow the national curriculum. Religious education is also fundamental to the curriculum in faith schools; however, these schools can choose the material they teach in religious studies. Faith schools may have different admissions criteria and staffing policies than State schools;[21] nevertheless, anyone can apply for a place in them.

The United Kingdom funds "free schools," the third type of school that I examine but the local council does not manage them, nor does the State require these schools to follow the national curriculum. Free schools run on a not-for-profit basis, retain more control over finances, conditions for staff and their pay, the school schedule, and school terms. "They're "all-ability" schools, so can't use academic selection processes like a grammar school."[22] Religious education is permitted in these schools. The following groups can set up Free schools:

- charities,
- universities,
- independent schools,
- community and faith groups,
- teachers,
- parents and businesses.[23]

A governing body, independent from the local council, manages academies, the fourth type of school that I observe in the United Kingdom. These schools can follow a different curriculum than the U.K.'s national curriculum. These government-funded independent schools, managed by an academy trust which employs the school's staff, can also establish their own terms and times. However, they must adhere to the same rules as other State schools regarding admissions, special educational needs, and exclusions. "Some academies have sponsors such as businesses, universities, other schools, faith groups or voluntary groups. Sponsors are responsible for improving the performance of their schools."[24] Faith academies have their own admissions process, and may be partially government

21. *Types of Schools.*
22. *Types of Schools.*
23. *Types of Schools.*
24. *Types of Schools.*

funded, and are also exempt from teaching the national curriculum and differ from non-faith academies as they implement their own admissions processes.[25] Religious education is permitted in non-faith academies and integral in faith academies.

Private schools, the fifth type of school noted in this section, also known as "independent schools," are not funded by the government. Private schools charge fees for students to attend, but the pupils do not have to follow the national curriculum. These schools must register with the government. Some private schools specialize in educating children with special educational needs. The Office for Standards in Education, Children's Services and Skills (Ofsted), the Independent Schools Inspectorate, and the School Inspection Service, government agencies, inspect private schools regularly.[26]

Suzanne Newcombe asserts that English law, applicable in two UK nations, England and Wales, does not mandate the separation of State and religion. Nor, even with the establishment of the Church of England, does the legislation of these nations offer any distinct provision for the State to recognize a group as a religion. In each of the four nations of the United Kingdom, although the law requires that every child receives full-time education, parents may opt to educate their children in church/faith schools, in independent schools, or at home.[27] Newcombe explains that parents of most five- to sixteen-year-olds in the United Kingdom register their children with a "maintained school," supported by public funding. The local education authority oversees and reports the schools' standards to Ofsted to ensure that schools comply with legislation.

Newcombe notes that some religious schools in the United Kingdom hesitate to include teachings about faiths that differ from their own. In many U.K. schools, as teachers often report feeling insecure in sharing information about this critical, frequently controversial subject, religious education does not merit a high rating. An Islamic school incident in 2011 reflects that the United Kingdom appears to promote religious freedom in the State's education system.[28] The incident began with Ofsted carrying out an inspection at the Institute of Islamic Education in Dewsbury in 2011. This gave rise for concerns, however, when, despite the school's practice of isolating students from outside influences and threatening to reprimand any students interacting with children other than Muslims, Ofsted rated the school as "good." Such

25. *Types of Schools.*

26 *Types of Schools.*

27. Newcombe, "Religious Education."

28. Lewis, "Between Lord Ahmed."

a school ethos led to students who reportedly excelled in understanding their own beliefs not being able to understand or empathize with individuals from faiths and backgrounds that differed from their own.

The concern for potentially teaching or indoctrinating students for religious extremism, as well as the lack of understanding of other religions, particularly in Islamic homogeneous schools, prompted some citizens to call for governmental intervention on privately funded school curriculum and management. Jack Straw, a former Home Secretary, warned that just as Hindus, Sikhs, Jews, or Christians must respect U.K. values, schools with many Muslim students must also do likewise.[29] While I believe the U.K. government and the public have a legitimate interest in combating religious extremism and promoting citizenry virtues for national security protection, I assert that the proposed solution is neither sufficient nor necessary.

The proposal will be insufficient in solving the controversy because of the difficulty in defining "British values." While some British officials list values such as "democracy, the rule of law, individual liberty, and mutual respect and tolerance of those with different faiths and beliefs,"[30] no historical unified national consensus seems to exist. David Shariatmadari asserts that "British values are necessarily a work in progress. Defining them is in fact about setting out how we want to be now, or what we could achieve if we put our minds to it. They're [. . .] subject to change, very much part of politics."[31] Moreover, Linda Colley alleges, even if assuming British values were known, that knowledge would not be enough to prevent some radical violent extremists and terrorists from at times threatening to kill their neighbors on God's behalf.[32] Therefore, instead of imposing any new government curriculum into the privately funded religious school, I believe that the U.K. government should increase religious education on diverse religions and beliefs in public-funded schools. Doing this would likely decrease controversy or discontent among some religious faithful who could perceive any new imposed syllabus as government intrusion into religious freedom for them. It could also encourage those faith-based schools, especially homogeneous religious-based ones, to voluntarily engage in civil dialogues with different faiths or religious traditions for developing common good and citizenship. Table 4 reflects differences between five different school types in the United Kingdom and identifies sources by which they

29. Clark, "Muslim Schools Must."
30. "Guidance on Promoting British."
31. Shariatmadari, "What Are British values?"
32. Colley, "British Values, Whatever."

are funded, the curriculum for the type of school, the management source, and the attitude the school holds toward religious education.

Table 4: Five Types of UK Schools and Their Attributes[33]

School Classification	Funding Source	Curriculum	Management	Religious Education
Community or 'State' schools	Government	Government	Government	Integral
Faith schools	Government	Government	Government	Integral
Free schools	Government	Non-government	Non-government	Permitted
Academies and Faith academies	Government and Non-government	Government and Non-government	Academy Trust	Permitted and Integral
Private schools	Non-government	Non-government	Non-government	Permitted

4.2.1.3 Schools in France

Three types of schools in France, which I note in this section, include State or public schools, State-funded and controlled private schools, and privately funded schools. State schools, which the government funds and runs must follow the government curriculum. The center or government strongly controls the first kind of school I introduce, the highly centralized State schools. The government manages these schools in the areas of curricula, financing, and organization, as well as in standards, teacher recruitment, and training. The government determines the structure of schools in the different regions and controls the overall rules that are used to direct these schools. Religious education is not taught in public schools in France. No subject is specifically devoted to the study of religion in public schools, and any teaching covering religion in subjects such as history, French or philosophy must be purely informational.[34]

Two types of private schools exist in France: (1) those contracted to the French government, State-funded and controlled private schools; and (2) those that are non-contracted to the French government, privately funded schools. State-funded and controlled private schools, the second

33. Author's original table.
34. Jackson, "Is Diversity Changing," 20.

type of school I explore in this section, "adhere to the terms and conditions of their contract with the government. In exchange, the State pays their teaching staff. Local authorities fund these establishments to the same extent as state schools."[35]

Privately funded schools, the third type of school I examine in this section, are not funded or managed by the State but must register with the Ministry of Education.[36] Privately funded schools are subject to government inspections not only of their teaching but their management. All staff in these schools must possess the required qualifications. The teaching provided must comply with French education law and meet minimum standards of knowledge."[37] Although a recognized secular State, which characterizes faith schools as private establishments, France typically allocates financial support for certain religious institutions. The State provides government funding to counterbalance the cost of private schooling. Regarding funding and management, non-public schools have the following options:

1. to continue completely independent of government intervention, subject to employing qualified teachers.

2. to be absorbed into the national public education system.

3. to accept government requirements as to curriculum and testing in exchange for staff salaries (*contrat simple*); and

4. to accept, in addition, some government control over pedagogy and the selection of teachers, in exchange for operating expenses as well as salaries (*contrat d'association*).[38]

Some private (faith) schools, for example Catholic schools and most elementary schools, which have limited funding needs, choose the *contrat simple*, number 3 above. Many secondary schools which have higher operating costs choose the *contrat d'association*, number 4 above. "Schools receiving funds from the contrat d'association must demonstrate that they have a distinctive character or philosophy not catered to in the public system."[39] Private schools not religiously orientated usually decide to remain independent of government intervention; nevertheless, they receive a stipulated amount of public funding under an alternate law.

---

35. "Education," *Welcome to France.*
36. "Schools in France."
37. "Education," *Welcome to France.*
38. "Indicator 45: Source."
39. "Indicator 45: Source."

Myriam Hunter-Henin warns that even though the French government recognizes certain rights for schools under the right to religious freedom, the understanding as well as legal standing of these rights may vary
as different individuals routinely subject them to diverse interpretations.
Because of the French law on the Separation of the Church and State,
France created the Department of Religions (Bureau Central des Cultes)
to oversee religious organizations. This body controls the finances and
"oversees the maintenance and the use of religious public assets."[40] This
bureau registers "religious organizations" and grants certain benefits and
legal privileges like tax exemption and the right to receive donations and
legacies.[41] The French Republic reports that as it guarantees freedom of
religion, it does not recognize or support any specific religion. France not
only represents the solitary State in Europe that does not claim an official
religion, it does not provide funding for its churches, nor does it provide
religious education in its schools.[42]

Since attacks by radical Islamists in January 2015, which killed 241
people, France's education minister introduced the secular teaching of
religious facts to emphasize moral and civic education in schools as well
as to promote respect for freedom of speech and opinion.[43] As France has
highlighted the problems that the growing ignorance of young people
regarding religion has posed, in 2002, Régis Debray wrote to the French
minister of education:

> [T]he teaching of "religious facts" (fait religieux) clearly estab-
> lishes the fact that the disappearance among many young people
> of any reference to religious culture prevents them from under-
> standing an essential part of their own heritage, as well as the
> contemporary world.
>   Ignorance and a lack of cultural reference cut young people
> off from their own roots and create problems for them in ac-
> quiring certain fields of knowledge. More importantly, it lays the
> foundation for intolerance and prejudice. Teaching about reli-
> gions and other convictions, together with the broader objec-
> tive of intercultural and citizenship education for young people,
> should play a very important role in reversing this trend.[44]

In the past, rather than providing religious education for students attending State schools, the French appear intent on inoculating citizens from

40. Altglas, "French Cult Controversy," 61.

41. Altglas, "French Cult Controversy," 61.

42. Palmer, *New Heretics of France.*

43. AFP, "France Treads Fine Line."

44. Pépin, *Teaching about Religions,* 10.

the threat to freedom that new religious movements or cults may wield. As France considers pupils to be public beings once inside the school setting and that religion should be confined to the private realm,[45] the State's method for "teaching" (emphasis mine) religious education, I contend, portrays a mixture of the separatist and secularist approaches. I agree with Debray regarding the value of religious education being adopted in State schools, not only in France but in all States. Confronting ignorance of religion with facts through religious education can help the State strengthen religious freedom for all, no matter the type of school.

Registration fees for parents of students attending private schools may be considered expensive. Nevertheless, funding for private schools has become increasingly public and under the association contract, totals approximately the same as fees in the public sector. Xavier Pons, Agnès Van Zanten, and Sylvie Da Costa point out that "the State subsidises teachers, curriculum, organization of diplomas, etc. and [. . . local authorities have charge of] the school premises, classroom equipment and school meals. The funding by local authorities often allows private schools to pay the salaries of non-teaching members of staff."[46] In addition, although principal municipalities are not obliged to fund private primary schools under the simple contract, they increasingly do so. In primary education, municipalities also pay fees for students who study in private schools outside the city.

Table 5 portrays differences between schools in France, relates sources of the schools' funding as well as the kinds of curriculum for each type of school. It also lists the management source, and the attitude the school holds toward religious education.

Table 5: Four Types of French Schools and Their Attributes[47]

School Classification	Funding Source	Curriculum	Management	Religious Education
State or public	Government	Government	Government	Not Permitted
State-funded private Schools	Government	Government	Government	Not Permitted
Privately funded schools	Non-Government	Non-Government	Non-Government	Permitted

45. Ahdar and Leigh, *Religious Freedom*.

46. Pons et al., "National Management of Public," 61.

47. Author's original table.

4.2.1.3 Schools in the Netherlands

In this section, I present four types of schools in the Dutch education system. These include public, private, international, and home schools. The Netherlands fund public schools, the first type of school I examine. The Dutch government also finances private schools, the second type of schools I explore. These schools rank on an equal basis with public schools. Nevertheless, given the central government's direct financing of private schools' expenditure on the same basis as schools governed by municipalities, they are not as independent as private schools in most other countries.[48] Because state grants assist private schools, their number surpasses public schools.[49] As the State's funding also encompasses religious schools,[50] this contributes to decreasing differences in student characteristics.[51] Conversely, the number of Dutch children who attend private schools remains high. All state-subsidized schools in the Netherlands must follow government rules, which includes using the State's mandated curriculum. For both public and private schools, the State directly pays the salaries of teachers, funds schools' educational buildings, and absorbs other school costs. The State also covers all expenses for management and administration of the schools. The primary difference between public and private schools is that, under certain prescribed conditions, only the latter may deny enrolling any prospective pupils. Moreover, private schools, unlike public schools, may charge fees for extracurricular activities.

The 2016 report published by the Centre for Civil Society summarized the following details about schools in the Netherlands:

> A central provision of the Dutch Constitution is that all schools, public and independent, are funded on an equal basis if they observe statutory regulations. These include having a minimum of 260 students, licensed teachers, and a school plan with attainment targets approved by the government-appointed school inspector. The Dutch education system is made up of three major types of schools: public schools, Catholic or Protestant independent schools and non-denominational independent schools. Each of these groups of schools

48. Vermeer, "Religious Indifference," 79.

49. Pépin, *Teaching about Religions*, 15.

50. Crabtree, "Faith Schools, Sectarian Education," last para. in Section 9. The British understanding of a religious-orientated private school correlates to perceiving the school to reflect a religious-orientated environment, like that of a seminary. Crabtree appears to suggest that religious-orientated private schools in the United Kingdom may encompass the potential for religious extremism and indoctrination.

51. Belfield and D'Entremont, "Catholic Schooling."

has national organizations for parents. This produces a large degree of school choice in the Netherlands, one of the education system's primary strengths. Independent schools are very popular, and two-thirds of government-funded schools are independent. Teachers in both public and independent schools are paid according to the same salary scales.[52]

Religious education in public and private schools in the Netherlands is described as both self-evident and controversial.[53] Paul Vermeer notes that: On the one hand, religious education portrays an integral part of the curriculum in most schools in the Netherlands, while on the other hand, some students consider religion to increasingly be out of date and irrelevant.[54] This negative situation reportedly evolved from the tension between the following two "facts" regarding the position of religious education in Dutch schools:

1. Dutch society is becoming a secular society, while religious education is confessional. As a result, the aim of religious education increasingly conflicts with the religious background of students.

2. Separate religious education classes form part of the curriculum only in religiously affiliated schools and are permitted as a legitimate expression of the school's religious identity. The state, therefore, imposes no general educational aims [. . . regarding] religious education.[55]

No national syllabus, nor curriculum, nor any general, nor any professional or educational requirements exist for teachers of religious education classes. Neither has the school inspectorate assessed nor evaluated the quality of religious education classes. Basically, the status of religious education dramatically differs from any other public or private schools' classes. Except for funding teachers' salaries, the Dutch State does not appear to actively involve itself in any related, religious education rapport.

Dutch private faith schools enjoy full liberty on religious education to students. The Dutch State allows religious schools to create their own curriculum and implement teaching aids that complement their religious principles. Each primary school curricula includes the subject "teaching world religion and worldviews (teaching about religion),"[56] This subject, introduced in 1985, aims to increase tolerance in Dutch society.

52. Centre for Civil Society, "Best Practices," 11.

53. Pépin, *Teaching about Religions*, 19.

54. Vermeer, "Religious Indifference," 87.

55. Vermeer, "Religious Indifference," 79.

56. Pol, "Religious education," 1.

The Ministry of Education funds Dutch International Schools, the third type of school that I note in this section. These schools align with the structure of the Dutch educational system; however, the Dutch government does not cover fees that International Schools charge for students. International Schools use English as the medium to teach their international curricula and are subject to inspections by the Dutch authorities. Because the Dutch International schools are allied with regular Dutch schools, to qualify for admittance, a student must comply with one of the following three stipulations:

1. The student has a non-Dutch nationality and has a parent who is working in the Netherlands (or in a Dutch border region) for a temporary period;

2. The student has Dutch nationality and has lived and gone to school abroad for at least two years because a parent was stationed abroad;

3. The student has Dutch nationality and has a parent (with whom the student will be living) who will be stationed abroad within two years and for at least two years. This must be certified by a written statement from the parent's employer.[57]

As in Dutch public and private schools, "confessional religious education"[58] in international schools is optional. Confessional religious education, a form of religious education, primarily aims to cultivate religious commitment to one particular faith,[59] or, in other words, "to strengthen a 'student's belief in a particular religious tradition.'"[60]

The Dutch government does not recognize homeschooling, the fourth type of school I examine. Furthermore, as the "Compulsory Education Act (Article 2, Paragraph 1) states, school attendance is mandatory"[61] for children from the age of five until the age of sixteen, and parents as well as others who homeschool children face challenges those who homeschool in other countries may not encounter. The State may issue a religious exemption, however, for compulsory education. Home schools do not use government curriculum, nor do they receive any government funds. Teaching religious education in home schools is contingent on the educator's discretion.

---

57. Westlake and Ruitenbeek, *Dutch International Schools*, 4.

58. Pépin, *Teaching about Religions*, 19.

59. Kodelja, "Religious Education," 253.

60. Hobson and Edwards, *Religious Education*, 17–18.

61. Ploeger, "Homeschooling in Europe."

The subtle restriction on homeschooling in the name of the State's compulsory education raises concerns as it potentially poses a religious freedom issue. Michael S. Merry and Sjoerd Karsten examined Dutch homeschooling and whether it restricts liberty. They present "[the following] three prominent concerns that might be brought against homeschooling":

1. It aggravates social inequality.

2. It worsens societal conflict.

3. It works against the best interests of children.[62]

Merry and Karsten argue that per the definition of homeschooling, this type of school does not constitute infringement. Instead of basing homeschooling cases on conjectures about hypothetical privatizing effects that reportedly threaten to consume social cohesion, good citizenship or autonomy, they should be based on evidence. Unless unmistakable evidence arises that a child's wellbeing is being breached, restricting a legitimate liberty to choose homeschooling from an array of reasonable educational options depicts an injustice.[63] Merry and Karsten stress that unless the government's concerns are sufficient to substantiate an intervention to ensure the fundamental, as well as the best interests of children, or by State oversight on safety, deciding to homeschool seems congruent with any significant analysis of the liberty for one to follow his/her conscience.

In terms of government funding for religious education in both public and private faith schools, the Dutch education policy displays more consistency to international religious freedom standards than the other three countries I surveyed in this section. However, I agree with Merry and Karsten regarding their concern relating to the potential infringement of religious liberty for students and parents who choose homeschooling. I recommend that instead of passively issuing exemptions for compulsory education to homeschoolers, the Dutch government should follow the model which the U.S., French, and U.K. governments have adopted. This would be acknowledging the full legitimacy of the homeschooling system with minimal State interference, unless otherwise enshrined under international norms on religious freedom. I assert that the State should protect the freedom of parents to choose the type of education they deem will best benefit their children in accord with their religious convictions or preference.

62. Merry and Karsten, "Restricted Liberty," 497.
63. Merry and Karsten, "Restricted Liberty," 511.

Table 6 lists the classifications of schools in the Netherlands, funding sources, curriculums, managements, and determinations toward religious education.

Table 6: Four Types of Dutch Schools and Their Attributes[64]

School Classification	Funding Source	Curriculum	Management	Religious Education
Public	Government	Government	Government	Not permitted
Private	Most are government funded, but some are subsidized	Government funded and contracted to the State; use government curriculum. Non-government funded and not contracted to the State; may use non-Government curriculum.	Government funded and contracted to the State; managed by the government. Non-government funded and not contracted to the State; managed by a non-government body.	Not permitted in government-funded schools and those contracted to the State. Permitted in non-government funded schools and those not contracted to the State.
Bilingual, international, and foreign	Most are government funded, but some are non-government funded	Government funded and contracted to the State; use government curriculum. Non-government funded and not contracted to the State; use non-government curriculum.	Government funded and contracted to the State; managed by the government. Non-government funded and not contracted to the State; managed by a non-government body	Not permitted in government-funded schools and those contracted to the State. Permitted in non-Government funded schools and those not contracted to the State.
Home schools	Non-government	Non-government	Non-government	Permitted

64. Author's original table.

4.2.1.4 *Reflections on the Dutch Education Model*

As shown in the previous section, no other State noted equates with the less rigid separation yet more organic partnership of Church and State than that which characterizes the Dutch model. Unlike the United States and France, the Netherlands provides for the exhibition of religious symbols, identities, and expressions in public, including school settings. In the Netherlands, no wall-of-separation doctrine exists as in the United States, nor is there any semblance of the French secular political nature in the Dutch Constitution. Maussen also notes that in the Netherlands:

> Religious free exercise rights are also guaranteed by other legal regulations. These include not only constitutional articles, such as the articles on freedom of education and freedoms of association, but also general laws, such as the Public Manifestations Act of 1988 (protecting the right to the church bell ringing, the call to prayer, and Catholic processions for example).[65]

Although the Dutch education system initially evolved as a system in which Christianity was dominant, over time[66] it has expanded to become more inclusive of other religions. In the contemporary Dutch education system, it appears that the State now establishes and oversees criteria for religious education.[67] The State does not discriminate regarding funding for schools as it supports both State and religious schools. Consequently, this contributes to all students being able to achieve equally and the fact that the Netherlands funds all schools no matter what their ethos supports a more balanced educational environment. This, in turn, permits the Netherlands to provide a setting in which diverse religions can operate. Such a situation better addresses issues that could likely stagnate in a State with less religious freedom.

In addition to gleaning edifying practices from the Dutch, education systems can replicate positive concepts from the Toledo Guiding Principles.[68] The Advisory Council of the Office for Democratic Institutions and Human Rights (ODIHR) Panel of Experts on Freedom of Religion or Belief, with other experts and scholars, developed approaches to teaching about religions and beliefs in public schools in the participating states of the Organization for Security and Co-operation in Europe (OSCE). These principles help students develop an understanding of the diverse roles that religions hold in the contemporary, pluralistic world and are intended to offer:

65. Maussen, "Religious Governance," para. 13.

66. Arnold, *Popular Education*, 204.

67. Belfield and D'Entremont, "Catholic Schooling."

68. ODIHR Advisory Council, *Toledo Guiding Principles*.

practical guidance for preparing curricula for teaching about religions and beliefs and preferred procedures for assuring fairness in the development of curricula. The starting point is the understanding that teaching about religions and beliefs is not devotionally and denominationally oriented. It strives for student awareness of religions and beliefs, but does not press for student acceptance of any of them; it sponsors study about religions and beliefs, not their practice; it may expose students to a diversity of religious and non-religious views, but does not impose any particular view; it educates about religions and beliefs without promoting or denigrating any of them; it informs students about various religions and beliefs, it does not seek to conform or convert students to any particular religion or belief.[69]

The Toledo Guiding Principles reiterate the value of religious education as one critical component to help protect religious freedom for all. Ideally, the religious education these principles encourage, like that which principled pluralism promotes, will establish positive boundaries for the State without sacrificing boundaries between the State and religion.

4.2.2 Sanctioned Methods for Teaching Religious Education

The trend to include religious education in public schools gives rise to a question which resounds across international headlines: Should RE be allocated a more prominent position in contemporary education, especially public education?[70] If so, how can this demand best be met without risking the erosion of the boundary between the State and religion? In response to this query, I stress that to safeguard religious freedom for all, a goal that both political liberals and principled pluralists agree on, religious education should constitute an essential part of any education system, particularly in contemporary public education. In this subsection, I turn to examine five approaches to teaching religious education. The term "religious education," like the word "education," cannot be specifically and precisely defined. Peter Schreiner considers religious education to constitute "any kind of religious teaching in public or private school, not in families or in the organisations of the faith communities."[71] Peter Tait, headmaster of Sherborne Preparatory School, stresses the need to implement teaching to

---

69 Ahdar and Leigh, *Religious Freedom*.

70. Marshall, "Religion and Education," 239–42.

71. Schreiner, "Religious Education in Europe," 3.

cultivate morality[72] and help young people learn to consider behaviors and issues not merely according to typical contemporary measures of success but, instead, according to moral measures.

If the education of youth does not include proper ethical considerations, Tait stresses, as self-interest surpasses the quest for public good, the State faces the risk of society becoming increasingly fragmented, disjointed, and unstable. According to Tait, for young people to transition into adults who respect the rule of law, educators need to teach them about how to make moral choices. Educators need to help children obtain a value system as a base for their decision-making. This will help counter the prevalent negative mindset in many individuals who see breaking the law as acceptable if they do not get caught.

Teachings relating to morality are also needed to help achieve the "common good." The concept of common good, as I note in Chapter 2, complements Kuyper's considerations of sphere sovereignty. The term also evolves from both religious and secular roots and dates back not only to Catholicism, Islam, Judaism, and Protestantism, but even the U.S. constitution, which proclaims that government should promote "the general welfare." Karen Chan describes common good as:

> the mutual and communal flourishing of many persons who live and act virtuously together in a community. The common good of a group or community will vary according to the members of the community, their needs, their goals, etc. Since there is no concrete definition of the common good, there is no set formula for reaching the common good.[73]

In the pursuit of cultivating morality and common good, Byrne reports that internationally, states typically implement one of the following three sanctioned approaches to implementing religious education. He identifies these classical methods as "learning into [also known as religious instruction]," "learning about," and "learning from" religion.[74] Each teaching style possesses unique traits, yet they also simultaneously manifest overlapping characteristics. The "approaches tend to have different emphases on the role of the learner, the function of education, and the potential of dissent."[75] Ahdar and Leigh identify two additional kinds of approaches to RE that characterize attitudes which different states may implement toward religious

---

72. Tait, "We Should be Teaching."
73. Chan, "The Common Good," 14.
74. Byrne, *Religion in Secular Education.*
75. Byrne, *Religion in Secular Education,* 16.

education: the separatist approach and the extreme secularist approach.[76] I consider these two approaches as well. In the first of the three approaches to religious education which Byrne identifies, the process of learning into religion or religious instruction, students receive instruction in a single formative religious tradition. This approach seeks "to grow a member of a faith into that particular religious tradition by developing beliefs and practices that create membership."[77] Sometimes identified as "indoctrinatory," learning into models are also referred to as "confessional" as Ahdar and Leigh allude to them,[78] or "enfaithing."[79] According to Ahdar and Leigh, religious instruction proposes to instill or develop religious beliefs in the learner. "The confessional approach was often associated with a formal link between an established religion and the State or at least with societies with a clear majority religion."[80] A minority of European countries, including the United Kingdom, continue to implement this partisan approach.

In addition to sending their children to a school using the religious instruction approach for faith-based reasons, some parents may also send their children to such a school due to concerns regarding safety. Joseph G. Kosciw et al. report that research regarding U.S. students found that approximately 16.3 percent of students surveyed "reported feeling unsafe at school because of their religion, and students who identified their religion as something other than a Christian denomination (e.g., Jewish, Muslim, Hindu) or who said they did not have a religion were more likely to feel unsafe at school for this reason."[81] However, the question arises as to whether religious schools, including those using the religious instruction approach, prove better for students in regard to safety and academic quality than public schools.[82]

At times, the learning into religion approach to religious education, delivered by State-recognized religious providers, may routinely exclude non-religious perspectives,[83] and perhaps exclude other religions. Political liberals usually acknowledge religious instruction as an acceptable approach for private schools, but not permissible for public ones. Principled pluralists agree with political liberals as they perceive the learning into approach to be appropriate for private schools.

76. Ahdar and Leigh, *Religious Freedom*, 267.

77. Byrne, *Religion in Secular Education*, 16.

78. Ahdar and Leigh, *Religious Freedom*.

79. Byrne, *Religion in Secular Education*, 16.

80. Ahdar and Leigh, *Religious Freedom*, 267.

81. Kosciw et al., *2011 National School*, 20.

82. Robers et al., *Indicators of School Crime*, iii–ix.

83. Byrne, *Religion in Secular Education*.

Adherents of political liberalism express concern that the religious instruction approach to religious education may stimulate tensions in the private school setting if the instruction becomes coercive. Regarding public school settings, they insist that religious instruction contradicts the principle of neutrality regarding conceptions of what constitutes the common good. Real dangers exist in the religious instruction route, as evidenced in Northern Ireland, where religious schooling has reinforced sectarian divides.[84] Principled pluralists support the right for religious or non-religious groups to utilize the religious instruction approach to religious education. However, they recognize the concerns of political liberals about coercion in both private and public schools, particularly if it has negative repercussions.

In a second approach to religious education, learning about religion, a stance which Adhar and Leigh distinguish as reported State neutrality, the school aims to present the major religions to students without indicating any preference for one over another and without instilling belief in any religion. Ahdar and Leigh stress that when educators confine religious education in schools to facts about religions—for example, the content of a religion's primary beliefs and doctrines, and information about noteworthy figures, events, and practices—objections to religious education in schools prove invalid.[85] Nevertheless, as noted previously, some religious groups may question "whether true neutrality is possible or object to the implicit pluralism towards religions or to specific non-confessional pedagogical approaches towards religious education."[86] Robert Jackson argues that with regard to religious issues, as every State's history conditions its religion, in a sense, the State cannot be entirely neutral.[87]

On the opposite end of the spectrum but still supporting religious freedom, Annie Laurie Gaylor (1955–2015), founder of the Freedom from Religion Foundation (FFRF), acknowledges that devotional instruction and religious exercises dramatically differ from academic instruction or learning about religion.[88] The following stance, which Gaylor published replicates that which principled pluralism supports regarding religious education—that even atheists should have a voice:

> Most social studies and geography classes already study the religious affiliations of an area, and some of their identifying tenets. US students should not grow up in ignorance of the world

84. Curtis, *Human Rights as War.*
85. Ahdar and Leigh, *Religious Freedom.*
86. Ahdar and Leigh, *Religious Freedom,* 267.
87. Jackson, *Rethinking Religious Education,* 14.
88. Gaylor, "Dangers of Religious Instruction."

religions. But by the same token, nor should they grow up in ignorance of the world's dead religions, or the fact that the non-religious and nonadherents are among the largest segments of the world, when it comes to religious identification. Today in the United States fully one in five adults and one in three young persons identifies as "non-religious"[89]

> If we're going to teach religion in the public schools, we must "teach atheism" as well.[90]

The FFRF reports that it works as a voice for atheism, agnosticism, and skepticism as well as acting as a watchdog for the State church to challenge incidents it considers infringements of what it perceives as the constitutional principle of State and church. The FFRF reports as one of its successes the fact that the Bienville Parish Schools in Arcadia, Louisiana, will no longer permit Gideons to distribute Bibles to students. After members of the Gideons physically placed a Bible on each student's desk in a particular grade, the FFRF reported this as a constitutional violation. In a letter to Superintendent William Britt, Staff Attorney Sam Grover wrote: "When a school distributes religious literature to its students, or permits evangelists to distribute religious literature to its students, it entangles itself with that religious message."[91]

Even though I empathize with Gaylor's legitimate concerns, nevertheless, I disagree with her approach to stop the supply of Bibles to students. If the FFRF truly subscribes to international religious freedom norms as listed in chapter 1, I assert that it would avoid that kind of approach (level down). Instead of removing the access to these Christian literatures for all students, likely because of their "offensive" nature to Gaylor's constituents, namely atheist, agnostic, and skeptics, the FFRF should ask the school district to provide opportunities to make diverse represented belief literatures and other faith traditions accessible to students. Therefore, a better approach would be "let-a-hundred-flower-blossom" approach (bottom-up); supporting teachings about *all* religions in public schools, including those worldviews that Gaylor represents.

---

89. Green, "American Religion: Complicated." Green cites statistics that contradict those Gaylor presents. The Pew Research Center finds that the number of Americans not participating in any religion totals approximately 23 percent of the population. Only a small number of this group profess to be atheists (3 percent) or agnostics (4 percent).

90. Gaylor, "Dangers of Religious Instruction," para. 7.

91. Freedom from Religion Foundation, "Students Spared More."

Byrne notes that the learning about religion approach as a stance of State neutrality primarily aims to educate students with regard to religion and diverse religious beliefs.[92] This knowledge-focused, student-driven, "bottom-up" approach perceives education to be a tool for the student to use, employing questions, interpretation, and reflection to augment his/her understanding of religion. According to most political liberalists, if religious education must be integrated into the public school, the learning about religion approach proves ideal.

Principled pluralists differ from political liberals regarding the exclusion of religious education in the public-school environment as they consider religious education as necessary not only in private but also in public schools. They agree with political liberals, nevertheless, that the learning about religion approach proves best in both school environments because learning about other religions may help enhance an individual's understanding of the beliefs of those practicing a religion that differs from his/her own.[93] In addition, the individual who understands the facts and facets of the religious beliefs of divergent religious groups will more likely be open to communicating with them. In turn, this can promote community camaraderie and help decrease tensions between religious and non-religious groups.

In a third alternative approach to religious education, which Byrne describes as learning from religion,[94] teachers typically implement a phenomenological approach. The concept of learning from religion initially linked with the domain of affective "feeling." Although the aim for this method includes facilitating an empathetic approach to different religions by enhancing the students' understanding of diverse religions, Ahdar and Leigh stress that this method does not attempt to instill religious beliefs in the students nor, contrary to learning about religion, does it simply share information about diverse religions. In this approach, students experience traditions and practices of other religious groups as they reflect upon and may even replicate some of these by enacting them. During the experiential exchanges, particularly when different religious practices seem offensive, religious as well as humanist students or their families may find this approach difficult.[95]

Learning from religion differs from religious instruction in that it engages the students as they reflect on their analyses of religions and then relate their understanding to their subjective experiences and interests.

92. Byrne, *Religion in Secular Education*, 17.

93. Gaylor, "Dangers of Religious Instruction."

94. Byrne, "Religion in Secular," 18.

95. Ahdar and Leigh, *Religious Freedom in Liberal*.

Instead of simply relating facts to students about a certain religion, educators will engage students in an experiential activity. For example, one assignment could involve the students drawing a picture of Jesus in the Garden of Gethsemane when darkness falls with directives to portray features to reflect how they perceive Jesus to be feeling. It is interesting to note that the label some school systems assign for this unit of work, *Being Human*, could be considered negative to a student not choosing to participate due to religious beliefs or prejudices.[96]

Byrne suggests that the possibility exists for some educators to use this approach to validate adherence to a specific religious tradition. Nevertheless, as this method aims to enable students, not control them, students may amass numerous opportunities to learn from the religions which instructors introduce. In time, this approach has evolved into "an existential and an applied ethical emphasis which is evaluative. [. . . It] asks: What are the ethical and moral bases of religions and belief systems? And how might they be useful in social action?"[97] The combination of the learning about and learning from religion approaches may best answer the latter question as time reveals not only how the learner engages in society but even more significantly, his/her perception regarding religious freedom for all religions.

The rationale for the separatist approach, the fourth approach which Ahdar and Leigh relate, maintains that the State should strictly separate itself from religious education and delegate this responsibility to the parent.

The absence of State engagement from religious education could contribute to some children who are not part of a religious group—as well as those who have parents not concerned about religious edification–not receiving any religious education. "[O]thers, at best will only learn about their own religious tradition or, at worst, may be uncritically indoctrinated in misperceptions or stereotypes of other religions."[98] The separatist approach, segregating religious education from the school syllabus does not automatically denote religious neutrality. Some may argue that contrariwise, the deliberate omission of religious education, in contrast to other subjects in the curriculum, sends a powerful message that religion does not significantly matter.

Some religious groups may challenge this concept as well as disagree with explicit pluralism in religious education and perceive both as hostile, considering these methods to undermine religious education within the child's family or their religious group. "A separatist approach attempts to avoid these pitfalls by maintaining a strict separation between the state and

---

96. "Level 1 Examples," *RE: Online*.

97. Byrne, *Religion in Secular Education*, 18.

98. Ahdar and Leigh, *Religious Freedom*, 268.

religious groups–leaving religious education to the latter and to parents, outside state schools."[99] In the sense that religious groups are equidistant from the classroom, all religious groups receive equal treatment. Separatism may reinforce segregation in societies divided on religious lines.

A secularist approach to teaching religious education, the fifth method of religious education which Ahdar and Leigh note, strives to dynamically endorse what those adhering to this stance perceive as negative consequences of religious conviction.[100] Some secularists may even deliberately strive to disparage the influence religions may exert on children.

Although secularism generally endorses the separation of the State from religion, not all secularists disparage every aspect of religion. Some scholars contend that based on the degree of separation between the State and religion, two factions of secularism exist: (1) ideological or radical secularism; and (2) moderate secularism. Tariq Modood contends, "Two modes of activity are separate when they have no connection with each other (absolute separation); but activities can still be distinct from each other even though there may be points of overlap (relative separation)."[101] According to Modood:

> it is possible to distinguish between radical or ideological secularism, which argues for an absolute separation between state and religion, and the moderate forms that exist where secularism has become the order of the day, particularly Western Europe, with the partial exception of France.[102]

As Modood points out, the approaches of secularism are not uniform. The distinction between the stance of radical or ideological secularism and moderate secularism toward religious education appears contingent on the attitude regarding the preferred degree of separation between the State and religion. Radical secularism reflects an anti-religion position as it basically advocates for the absolute separation of any religion from State affairs and supports the concept of total dominance of secularism in any public space. Part of the agenda for ideological secularism also seems to be policing religion in the public square.

Moderate secularism, based on the view of relative separation of religion and the State, differs from ideological secularism as it allows room for the State and religion to interact while the ideological approach does not.

---

99. Ahdar and Leigh, *Religious Freedom*.

100. Ahdar and Leigh, *Religious Freedom*, 269.

101. Modood, "Moderate Secularism, Religion," 4–13.

102. Modood, "Moderate Secularism, Religion," 5.

In the field of education, moderate secularism would tolerate some teaching about religion in public schools while radical secularism would advocate for the total ban of any religious education.

Superficially, the position that radical secularism assumes appears similar to Gaylor's stance and may appear to be fair. The promotion of absolute or radical secularism, nonetheless, as Gaylor's FFRF movement seeks to promote, fails to protect religious freedom for all. Radical secularism's extreme approach, like that of theonomy, which I rejected in Chapter 2, advocates the very narrow route of adopting only one religion. While ideological secularists advocate for secularism with no relationship between the State and religion, theonomy as I point out in Chapter 2, proposes that only one religion should reign in the public square. Both ideological secularism and theonomy mirror a similar scenario and stimulate the same adverse effect: failure to protect religious freedom for all.

In a sense, I empathize with the position of moderate secularism because, like principled pluralism, it promotes a relative separation of the State and religion. This approach reflects Kuyper's theory, which I also introduced in Chapter 2. Even though Kuyper contends that each sphere is to maintain sovereignty, nevertheless the diverse spheres, with dynamic interactions, particularly between the church [religion] and the State, organically interrelate. Likewise, as overlap occurs between the State and religion in the moderate secularist approach, I concur with some aspects of moderate secularism, particularly when it acknowledges the benefits of religious education. I absolutely disagree with extreme ideological, "militaristic" secularism being the only ideology in the public square. This approach not only prohibits religious education in public schools, it represents no freedom for other religions.

Even though secularism has increased in power and scope throughout various parts of the world, Modood points out that in most of Western Europe, symbolic links between the State and facets of Christianity remain. Modood stresses that this indicates that "a historically evolved and evolving compromise with religion are the defining features of Western European secularism, rather than the absolute separation of religion and politics."[103] According to Ahdar and Leigh, in any part of the world where the State promotes "a form of official secular humanism in State education [. . . , this] represents a non-neutral and comprehensive ideology which is actively hostile to religion."[104] When the State implements other types of control of religious liberty, as have a number of former Communist countries including

---

103. Modood, "Moderate Secularism, Religion," 5.

104. Ahdar and Leigh, *Religious Freedom in Liberal*, 269.

Central Asian republics and China, this reflects secularism as hostile. Table 7 depicts the responses of political liberalism as compared with principled pluralism to the five approaches to religious education.

Table 7: Five Approaches to Religious Education[105]

Political Liberalism		Principled Pluralism	
Public Schools[106]	**Private Schools**[107]	**Public Schools**	**Private Schools**
Learning into Religion — No, not permissible	Yes, acceptable	*Learning into Religion* — No, not permissible	Yes, appropriate
Learning from Religion — No, because some religious practices offend	Yes, acceptable	*Learning from Religion* — Yes, conditionally acceptable	Yes, appropriate
Learning about Religion — Yes, conditionally	Yes, appropriate	*Learning about Religion* — Yes, conditionally acceptable	Yes, appropriate
Separatist Approach — Yes, preferred	Yes, preferred	*Separatist Approach* — No, not appropriate, fails to protect religious freedom	No, not appropriate or acceptable
Secularist Approach — Yes, conditionally, re. moderate secularists — No, not acceptable regarding ideological or radical secularists	Yes, appropriate re. moderate secularists; permissible regarding ideological or radical secularists	*Secularist Approach* — Yes, conditionally, if aligned with moderate secularism — No, if aligned with radical secularism	No, not appropriate or acceptable

4.2.3 Legal Framework for Religious Education

The attitudes and policies of the State, as well as its legal framework for, and associated regulations concerning education, particularly the role of

105. Author's original table.

106. The term "public school" encompasses any State-sponsored educational institution.

107. The term "private school" encompasses any privately funded educational institution.

religious education in both public and private education systems, reflect the nature of the State–religion model.[108] In this chapter, as I am presenting an overview of the education systems[109] implemented in the United States, France, the United Kingdom, and the Netherlands, I establish the international legal framework for religious education in this subsection. Also, in addition to giving a description of the general education system in each of the four States I examine in Chapter 4, I point out the extent that the State permits religious education in them.

First, rights relating to religious freedom and religious education are enshrined in the European Convention on Human Rights (ECHR) and have been incorporated into UK law. Marion Maddox reports that the ECHR[110] (Article 2 of Protocol No. 1)[111] specifically protects the exercise of religious freedom in compulsory education as it states: "No person shall be denied the right to education. In the exercise of any functions which it assumes in relation to education and to teaching, the State shall respect the rights of parents to ensure such education."[112] The ECHR also stipulates that the State's teaching conform with the parents' religious and philosophical convictions.

Second, rights, which the ECHR acclaims, align with those in the International Bill of Human Rights as well as with ensuing resolutions that propose to protect religious freedom. In addition to the internationally proclaimed, guaranteed protections for the practice of a person's religion or belief, the United Nations ideally aims to establish standards for human rights.[113] Nevertheless, since international as well as State legal mechanisms attempt to enshrine and safeguard religious education for children, the criteria for the implementation of these standards remain open to each State's interpretation.

The interpretation of State and international legal guidelines which occur in the State–religion relationship frequently correlates with the State controlling education to advance its political goals. Peter G. Danchin submits that a "strong negative identification of church and State (for example, in States that are hostile to or persecute religious groups) correlates

---

108. Ahdar and Leigh, *Religious Freedom*.

109. Some terms, such as "charter school," are not universally defined and subject for interpretation in different countries.

110. Council of Europe, "Details of Treaty."

111. Maddox, *Taking God to School*.

112. Danchin and Forman, "Evolving Jurisprudence," 96.

113. United Nations, "Protect Human Rights."

with low levels of religious freedom."[114] Peter Danchin and Lisa Forman note that the ECHR decrees guidelines for the State when it describes how education and teaching should be carried out.[115] To help ensure that education and teaching conform to parents' religious preference, the ECHR states, "the state shall respect the rights of parents to ensure such education and teaching in conformity with their own religious and philosophical convictions."[116] At times, despite international guidelines, such as those the ECHR presents, domestic laws of various states as well as the bodies enforcing them may not consider that the concept of teaching religious education in public schools portrays a positive practice. Applying the philosophy of principled pluralism to the field of education best equips the State with regard to facilitating the most effective State–religion relationship model for meeting citizens' educational needs.

In the following section, I examine the education models implemented by four liberal states and compare them with the international legal framework. I note several tensions and conflicts within these countries' education systems and how they contribute to these states failing to adequately protect religious freedom for all.

4.3 Education Models Implemented by Four Liberal States

Philip Lewis reports that in the European Union, every constitution includes principles of freedom and nondiscrimination. The specific approaches European countries implement to interpret and apply to these ideologies primarily depend on historical traditions regarding the State–religion relationship.[117] As interpretations of the constitution with regard to religious freedom contribute to components determining the implementation of religious education and as such interpretations may, in all probability, differ from one country to another, similarly, the treatment of religions, manifested in State–religion relationships, may also vary. In presenting a sample of the education systems in the United States, the United Kingdom, France, and the Netherlands to illustrate numerous diversities in this field, I examine whether the education systems these states have implemented appear to accommodate or complement religious freedom or have proved hostile toward it.

114. Danchin, "Religion, Religious Minorities," 3.
115. Danchin and Forman, "The Evolving Jurisprudence," 196.
116. Council of Europe, "Details of Treaty."
117. Lewis, "Between Lord Ahmed and Ali G," 129–44.

4.3.1 The Education System in the United States

As part of teaching Christian values,[118] church-controlled schools in early townships in America during the 1720s stressed morality.[119] J. E. Tiles points out that now, as in times past, measures for morality[120] may differ not only within a State but also between individuals and over time. Similarly, teachings in education vary; nevertheless, they appear to mirror the direction that leaders aim for a State to travel or navigate, as well as reflect certain societal goals.[121] Consequently, decisions that State leaders make as well as the ensuing consequences from resolutions regarding education, in particular religious education, not only inadvertently affect the social health of a country, its current position in the international scene, and future generations, they diametrically impact religious freedom.

J. M. Powis Smith points out that in 1924, because the church initially dominated education in the Western world,[122] religion maintained a primary position in the educational realm. Although education of young people in the United States began to progressively transition from the church to the State during the 1820s and 1830s, during this time, the public elementary and secondary schools as well as State colleges and universities basically endorsed Christian education. Harold J. Berman notes that the Presbyterian minister who served as president of the University of North Carolina, founded in 1795, "insisted on regular attendance by students at religious worship and on orthodox religious instruction."[123] Berman notes that even the seventeen State institutions of the 246 colleges and universities established in the US prior to 1860 required students to regularly attend religious services.

According to Francesco Cordasco, the significance of religious education started to decline with the inception of public education and State-sponsored educational institutions in the United States, coupled with the trend of increasing secularization.[124] Carl L. Bankston and Stephen J. Caldas,[125] as well as John A. Ether,[126] point out that the focus for religious

118. Miller, *American Education and Religion.*

119. Walker et al., *Morality in Everyday Life,* 371–405. Walker et al. explain that the fact morality relates to a person's basic way of life and values, it constitutes a fundamental and pervasive component of human functioning.

120. Tiles, *Moral Measures,* 2.

121. Bhattacharya, *Foundations of Education.*

122. Smith, "Church and Education," 46–59.

123. Berman, *Articles of Faith,* 45.

124. Cordasco, *Brief History of Education,* 50.

125. Bankston and Caldas. *Public Education.*

126. Ether, "Cultural Pluralism," 233–34.

education transitioned from the old social order with its religious intonations to a new social order that addressed cultural diversity and cultural pluralism. Religious education changed from emphasizing a community's religious convictions to passing on information to not only develop students' intellectual skills but also cultivate their identities.

John M. Hull reports that historically, in line with principled pluralism, the U.S. Constitution, a founding American document, aims to promote religious freedom for all, limit the State's control over religion, and designate the separation of State and religion.[127] The separation of State and religion, the principle which the Supreme Court surreptitiously imposed, contradicts the design America's Founders desired for the United States as it simultaneously positions the State in a formidable stance against religion.[128] The commonly accepted myth that religion should be totally separated from education erroneously relates to the role of religion in education as well as to the State–religion relationship.[129]

The court first applied the First Amendment's religious liberty clauses to the states during the 1940s. At this time, the separation of church and State became a principle of constitutional law. Michael J. Sandel reports that, "In Cantwell v. Connecticut (1940), the Court held that the Fourteenth Amendment incorporated both the establishment and free exercise clauses of the Bill of Rights, and "rendered the legislatures of the states as incompetent as Congress to enact such laws."[130] Sandel further notes:

> In Everson v. Board of Education of Ewing Township (1947), the Court gave the establishment clause a broad interpretation and emphasized, for the first time, Jefferson's "wall of separation between church and state."[131]

Although controversy encompasses the principle regarding the "wall" between the State and religion, designating that government must remain neutral toward religion, Sandel reports that this ruling is seldom challenged. In early townships in America during the 1720s, prior to the "erection" of the Jeffersonian "wall of separation," as the church formed the central core of the community, religion constituted an integral element in the lives of frontier people. Princeton in New Jersey reflects one example of a prestigious university that emerged from the Log College, an early American school

127. Hull, *Religious Education in Schools*, 4–11.

128. Boston, "Myths Debunked."

129. Yousef, "Role of Religion in Education."

130. Sandel, *Articles of Faith*, 80.

131. Sandel, *Articles of Faith*, 81.

with Christian roots. Christian preachers and church affiliations founded the majority of America's oldest universities, including Brown, Dartmouth, Harvard, King's College (now Columbia University), Rutgers, and Yale.[132] When the Puritans established Harvard University in 1636, the universities adopted "Rules and Precepts" which assert:

> Let every student be plainly instructed, and earnestly pressed to consider well,the main end of his life and studies is, to know God and Jesus Christ which is eternal life and therefore lay Christ at the bottom, as the only foundation of all sound knowledge and learning.[133]

Similarly, the stated goal for Yale College, founded 1701, concurs with that of Harvard. Both universities stress that the critical objective of the student's study encompasses them knowing God in Jesus Christ. One of Princeton's founding statements boldly proclaims allegiance to the Christian faith, "Cursed is all learning that is contrary to the Cross of Christ."[134] In 1954, the United States, under the leadership of President Dwight D. Eisenhower, confirmed its belief in the principles by which America's Founding Fathers established its educational system. At this time, the words, "Under God," reflecting the goals establishing Harvard, Yale, and Princeton, were added to America's Pledge of Allegiance. However, during this time, court decisions began to challenge America's religious freedom, particularly in the field of education.

Despite the religious foundation of the United States, the education system in America no longer reflected the Christian principles and character which founded it. At best, Panichas surmises, the status of education in the United States appears problematic.[135] At worst, as indicated by Gaylor, the U.S. education system had shifted from "freedom of religion" to "freedom from religion." The attitude of those implementing policies for education appeared to reflect the state of contemporary chaos and confusion corrupting the education system.[136] Charles H. Wesley explains that one misunderstanding, the doctrine of State–religion separation, does not indicate that the State and religion are to oppose or exhibit indifference to each other.[137] Haynes argues that another contemporary fallacy posits that the U.S. Constitution mandates

---

132. Stevens, *One Nation under God*.

133. Stevens, *One Nation under God*, 122.

134. Stevens, *One Nation under God*, 122.

135. Panichas, "Remedying the Ills."

136. Panichas, "Remedying the Ills."

137. Miller, *American Education and Religion*, 105.

that public schools must maintain "neutrality" on religion. Neutrality, as I argued in Chapter 3, proves elusive. Nevertheless, religious impartiality by the State, in the sense that it does not demonstrate preference for one religion over another or permit secularism to reign over religion, portrays the best promise for religious freedom for all.[138]

Stephen Macedo recounts a court ruling regarding a complaint filed against U.S. public schools in 1983, *Mozert v. Hawkins*, which illustrates an example of the State's bias. In his verdict regarding the Mozert case, Chief Judge Lively defends the public school's authority to teach values "essential to a democratic society," including toleration.[139] According to Lively, schools may "acquaint students with a multitude of ideas and concepts," if they avoid direct "religious or anti-religious messages."[140] During the *Mozert* case, "born again" Christian families against the local school board in Hawkins County, Tennessee,[141] objected to their children being exposed to readings which reportedly included mental telepathy, futuristic supernaturalism, occultist references, and sources teaching man as God. Ultimately, Chief Judge Lively ruled in favor of the authority of the public school. If public schools do not specifically promote religions or anti-religious information, Judge Lively decreed:

> The lesson is clear: governmental actions that merely offend or cast doubt on religious beliefs do not on that account violate free exercise. An actual burden on the profession or exercise of religion is required.
>
> In short, distinctions must be drawn between those governmental actions that actually interfere with the exercise of religion, and those that merely require or result in exposure to attitudes and outlooks at odds with perspectives prompted by religion.[142]

---

138. Chelini-Pont, "Religion in the Public Sphere," 614–15.

139. Macedo, *Diversity and Distrust*.

140. Macedo, *Diversity and Distrust*, 168.

141. Macedo, *Diversity and Distrust*, 470–71. In *Mozert v. Hawkins*, the "families charged a primary school reading program with denigrating their religious views, both in its lack of religious 'balance' and in the uncommitted, evenhanded nature of the presentations. The complaint was, in part at least, not so much that a particular religious claim was directly advanced by the readings but that the program taken as a whole exposed the children to a variety of points of view and that this very exposure to diversity interfered with the free exercise of the families' religious beliefs by denigrating the truth of their particular religious views. Parent Vicki Frost said that "the word of God as found in the Christian Bible 'is the totality of my beliefs.'"

142. *Mozert v. Hawkins*, "Bob and Alice Mozer."

Macedo reportedly argues for a political liberalism with backbone.[143] He maintains that political liberalism coincides with a type of civic liberalism he perceives in several facets concerning education. He defends a type of civic liberalism that would be based on a limited range of public principles and reasons but with broader and deeper implications than those inherent in political liberalism. This type of civic liberalism would encompass characteristics and capacities common to citizens in general without constraining their religious viewpoints.

Based on the needed teaching on civic and religious tolerance in public schools, both principled pluralism and *Baorong Duoyuan* would align with the decree in Chief Judge Lively's case, as well as with Macedo's viewpoint. However, if the school will help accommodate the concerns of parents with evangelical faith; allowing children to equally access related teachings about their religion in that same school, principled pluralism and *Baorong Duoyuan* would more sensibly line up with the international religious freedom standard to children's rights for religious education.

This type of civic liberalism approach, Macedo emphasizes, often replicates the approach John Rawls suggests in *Political Liberalism*. He notes that although public schools must not only refrain from teaching antireligious or religious messages, they can teach toleration and other values necessary for living in a democratic society. Schools "may teach 'civil tolerance,'" which illustrates the notion that "in a pluralistic society we must 'live and let live.'"[144] According to Macedo, essentially, public schools can teach that every religion is "the same in the eyes of the State, not that they are all the same in the eyes of God."[145] I assert that religious education as included in compulsory education should encourage the exchange of ideas relating to religion, including diverse conceptions of truth.

Bruce Grelle stresses that in the United States, because State and local governments fund and administer the operation of public schools, the schools must maintain "impartiality" toward religion. Grelle notes that although private and parochial schools may endorse religious beliefs and practices, public schools cannot do so due to the "no establishment clause."[146] The school prayer cases, noted in Chapter 3, illustrate the U.S. Supreme Court stance on this prohibition of school-sponsored religious exercises, including devotional Bible reading and organized group prayer.

143. Macedo, "Liberal Civic Education," 473.

144. Macedo, "Liberal Civic Education," 473.

145. Macedo, "Liberal Civic Education," 473–74.

146. Grelle, *Religious Education in Schools*, 48–54.

The Center for Public Justice maintains that the government should focus on maintaining provisions for public equity to guarantee that every child can fairly access a quality education; first, the government needs to treat citizens equitably, then apply the same principle to their rights in relation to religious freedom. At this point in history, as Panichas warns, indoctrinators, reformers, and social engineers often perceive education as a social science. Many visualize learning and teaching goals as prospects for translating into programs of social expediency. In turn, they thwart remedies for restoring educational norms and balance.[147]

Even though the U.S. Constitution has not historically been hostile toward religion, contemporary court decisions regularly increase State control over education. The ensuing decreases in religious freedom promote an even greater separation of State and religion. Observers of the current educational method of teaching in U.S. public schools would likely perceive this contemporary tactic to reflect the secularist stance, what Ahdar and Leigh describe as a model actively antagonistic to religious faith.[148] Consequently, I contend that as the education system in the United States aligns more with the secularist than the separatist method, it does appear hostile to religious freedom. I maintain that the method of religious education that the United States currently adopts, which the Mozert case reflects, depicts the secularist approach.

4.3.2.1 The Education System in the United Kingdom

A myriad of religious schools exists in the United Kingdom. Even though this State does not have recorded a Bill of Rights to ensure rights relating to religious education, nevertheless, freedom of religion and of religious expression are well protected.[149] Prior to the nineteenth century, to the extent of education's availability, the Church of England predominantly controlled schools in England, one of the four countries in the United Kingdom. Since WWII,[150] a substantial multi-religious presence has existed. Robert Jackson notes that until the late 1950s, civic, moral, and religious education in England appeared interrelated. In the atmosphere "of moral and social renewal following the Second World War, [. . . the UK even] saw religious education interpreted as 'non-denominational.'" In education, Christian instruction

---

147. Panichas, "Remedying the Ills."
148. Ahdar and Leigh, *Religious Freedom.*
149. Russo, *International Perspectives on Education,* 209.
150. Hull, *Religious Education in Schools.*

became the basis of morality and citizenship, as well as a principle routinely incorporated for most education.[151]

Hunter-Henin reasons that stipulations regarding religious worship mirror the prevalence of religion in the United Kingdom. The State mandates that schools in England and Wales, even if not religiously characterized, must host an act of worship each day.[152] In addition, in both England and Wales, the law prescribes a broadly Christian character, "for the act of daily worship and for the content of religious education classes."[153] If the State did not offer the premise of freedom of choice for students to opt out of daily worship or religious education classes, this could conversely give rise to charges from religious minorities that the State violates their freedom of or from religion. Consequently, in many legal contexts, the State regards religious organizations as identical to secular organizations and, therefore, subjects both to identical civil laws and tax assessments (e.g., in terms of charitable status).[154]

In the past, as the United Kingdom aligned with the State Church's Erastian system, the State deemed religious education to constitute its responsibility. As the secularization of State institutions increased, the State's approach to the teaching of religion progressively turned into one of condoning nondenominational religious education.[155] Although the State collaborates with the religious community in the United Kingdom at times regarding some activities relating to religious education, the State continues to control, organize, and manage religious education. In State schools only, State institutions not only control the selection, appointment, training, and discharge of teachers, they also determine the remuneration teachers receive.

Robert Long and Paul Bolton explain that the State requires that students receive nondenominational religious education.

> Religious Education (RE) is compulsory for all pupils in local authority maintained schools aged 5 to 16 years unless they are withdrawn from these lessons by their parents. They are not obliged to give a reason, and the school is expected to comply with the request.[156]

---

151. Jackson, *Rethinking Religious Education*, 5.

152. Newcombe, "Religious Education," 376.

153. Hunter-Henin, *Religious Freedoms in European Schools*, 15.

154. Newcombe, "Religious Education," 376.

155. Hull, *Religious Education in Schools*, 11.

156. Long and Bolton, "Faith Schools in England," 6.

In addition to schools in England and Wales hosting an act of worship in ed-ucation, they must introduce citizenship education into their national cur-riculums, including those of faith-based schools. Jackson notes that these two states require pupils to examine Britain's nature as a multi-ethnic and multi-religious society. For example, "students must 'study' the origins and implications of the diverse national, regional, religious and ethnic identities in the United Kingdom and the need for mutual respect and understanding [. . .]."[157] The following portrays ways that the European Parliament seeks to promote education about religion:

1. Schools will step up the teaching about religions as sets of values to-wards which young people must develop a discerning approach, with-in the framework of education on ethics and democratic citizenship.

2. Parliament will promote the teaching of the comparative history of different religions, stressing their origins, the similarities in some of their values and the diversity of their customs, traditions, festivals, [. . . etc.] in schools.

3. Parliament will encourage the study of the history and philosophy of religions and research into those subjects at university, in parallel with theological studies.

4. Schools will cooperate with religious educational institutions to intro-duce or reinforce, in their curricula, aspects relating to human rights, history, philosophy and science.

5. In the case of children, educators will avoid any conflict between the State-promoted education about religion and the religious faith of the families, to respect the free decision of the families in this very sensi-tive matter.[158]

In the United Kingdom, more than 20 percent of pupils in the maintained sector attend State-funded faith schools, while the private sector includes many prestigious Christian foundations. Lewis notes that the "private sector–'public schools'" include many prestigious Christian foundations.[159] Also, ac-cording to Lewis, as all State schools "must teach religious education,"[160] this discipline extends to influence other parts of society. Consequently, religious education can potentially not only counter or slow irrational, expressions of

157. Jackson, *Rethinking Religious Education,* 56.
158. Council of Europe, *Parliamentary Assembly Documents,* 2.
159. Lewis, "Between Lord Ahmed."
160. Lewis, "Between Lord Ahmed."

intolerance toward diverse religions but may also complement religious freedom after students complete their formal education.

4.3.3 The Education System in France

Following the hostility that the 1789 French Revolution demonstrated toward religion, the trend in France has been toward refraining from teaching religion in State schools.[161] Although the French Revolution shaped the
Declaration of the Rights of Man,[162] which "guaranteed unlimited freedom
of 'opinion' ([. . .] and 'belief,' [. . .] it included the proviso [. . . that would]
become highly problematic for France's so-called *sectes* two centuries later.
This proviso in Article X was, '*ne trouble pas l'ordre publique*' (they should
not disturb the peace)."[163] Although this dubious, frequently discussed
article did not define which specific individual rights could share in the
cooperative expression of religiosity, it basically annihilated the absolutist
model of ultimately converting Catholicism into an instrument of the State
as France's national religion that Louis XIV had envisaged. Had this plan
materialized, the education system in France at that time would have been
under the control of the Catholic Church.

Rather than Catholicism becoming France's national religion and in
control of French education, revolutionaries guillotined numerous clerics
and confiscated properties the Catholic Church owned. Susan J. Palmer
recounts that after the insurgents pillaged the French cathedrals, they set
them on fire. Later, they "tried to establish a cult of the 'Goddess of Reason' or the 'Goddess of Liberty.' '*La France modern*' which evolved from
the revolutionaries' conflict with Catholicism" Palmer describes this as "the
philosophy of secularism [. . . which varied] in tone from anticlericalism to
antitheism,"[164] [and] continues to define the French State. It also strongly
affects France's secular stance regarding compulsory education.

Prior to France transitioning into a radical secular State, Matthew Arnold recounts that in 1861, France permitted the display of one significant
religious symbol in public schools: the crucifix. He states, "Conspicuous
were the crucifix and the bust of the Emperor—the indispensable orna-
ments of French public schoolrooms."[165] Arnold further describes the public schools during this time in history as decidedly religious:

---

161. Hull, *Religious Education in Schools*.

162. Passed by France's National Constituent Assembly 26 August 1789.

163. Palmer, *New Heretics of France*, 180.

164. Palmer, *New Heretics of France*, 180.

165. Arnold, *Popular Education*, 98.

First, then, with respect to a question which meets every system of education upon the threshold—the great question, shall it be secular, or shall it be religious? The French system is religious; not in the sense in which all systems profess to be more or less religious, in inculcating the precepts of a certain universal and indisputable morality: it inculcates the doctrines of morality in the only way in which the masses of mankind ever admit them, in their connection with the doctrines of religion. I believe that the French system is right.[166]

Contrary to the existing French system, which Arnold commends, during 1902, Émile Combes, then premier of France, passed a law which prohibited any person from any type of religious order from teaching students in State schools.[167] Palmer reports that on 9 December 1905, after Combes no longer held a State position:

the Law on the separation of church and state made provisions for France to ensure freedom of conscience, to guarantee the free practice of religion, and to prevent any interference of religions in state matters (or vice versa).[168]

The French Constitution of 1958 proclaims two principles which found the State's education system, (1) secularism (laïcité), and (2) educational freedom which leads to the protection of alternative forms of education.[169] According to these principles:

1. Secularism (laïcité), also mentioned in the article L.141-1 of the French code of education [states]: "the Nation guarantees equal access of children and adults to instruction, training and culture: the organisation of a free and secular education at every level is a State duty." This principle implies the secular nature of teaching, curriculum, staff and school premises and the optional character of religious teaching in private schools. But it also requires that the State is neutral towards religion and that public education must not be developed at the expense of religious instruction; hence for instance the obligation for the State to keep one day free during the week for parents who would like to provide their children with religious instruction.

2. The second principle is educational freedom leading to the protection of alternative forms of education such as private education but

166. Arnold, *Popular Education*, 145.
167. Palmer, *New Heretics of France*.
168. Palmer, *New Heretics of France*.
169. Pons et al., "National Management," 59.

also home schooling. Article L.1513 of the French code of education therefore states that primary and secondary schools can be public or private, the former being financed by the State and local political authorities, whereas some actors or associations support the latter.[170]

Following the 1959 Debré Act, which provides funding for most of the private schools that contract with the French government, a significant segment of the student population in France attends private schools.[171] Religious education is not permitted in State-funded and controlled private schools.

Despite numerous attempts to reform the Debré Act of 1959, it remains the legal reference for French education, and attempts to reconcile the above two somewhat contradictory principles in three ways:

1. The act (re)asserts the original principles, however to some degree reformulates them: "The State must provide an education to all children according to their aptitudes 'with equal respect for all beliefs.'"[172] Likewise, the State must defend the educational freedom of private schools that adhere to official norms.

2. Private schools may conceivably enter a contract with the State. Two kinds of potential contracts consist of the "simple contract" and the "association contract." These contracts dictate that private schools must comply with specific State requirements and that schools must maintain their "specific character." The private schools' activities must not impinge on the transmission of the State's national and secular curriculum.

3. The State only accepts a certain type of private school (not private education) which supports activities by specific agreements and official texts.[173]

Except for Alsace-Lorraine, France presents a leading example of a country which does not offer any form of religious teaching. Nevertheless, even though French public schools do not offer any specific courses pertaining to religions, teachers can reference religions in certain disciplines, including the arts, geography, history, language, and philosophy. "In secondary schools, parents or students can ask for the creation of a chaplaincy and, with the authorization of the school authorities, the chaplain can teach religion on the

170. Pons et al., "National Management," 59.
171. Bertola, "France's Almost Public," 3.
172. Pons et al., "National Management," 59.
173. Pons et al., "National Management," 60.

school premises to the students who want to receive this teaching."[174] The State explicitly forbids the designated chaplains from teaching extracurricular classes on religion during designated school hours.

Although a recognized secular State which characterizes faith schools as private establishments, France typically provides financial support for certain religious institutions.[175] In France, religious freedom may appear blurred due to distinctions in a school context that contrast freedom of conscience and freedom of thought. Hunter-Henin explains that freedom of thought ensures the right to independently reexamine beliefs received from family, as well as social groups.

> Freedom of conscience along with its constituent's freedom of religion and freedom of belief guarantees diversity of belief in society and the freedom to express those beliefs.
>
> This way a person can freely adhere to these beliefs, adapt them or turn away from them to something else. Naturally, this is a conceptual distinction and clearly daily life produces constant disharmony between these two freedoms.
>
> But the perspective is not the same and the French view school as the perfect institution to teach future citizens to exploit their faculties of reason and to help them exercise freedom of thought.[176]

The French government decided to highlight the distinction between freedom of conscience and freedom of thought as illustrated in the previous paragraph and support individual freedom by banning conspicuous displays of religious symbols[177] in State schools. As noted in Chapter 3 of this study, France took a calculated risk regarding the question of religious symbols when it passed a law prohibiting students and teachers from wearing conspicuous ones at school, particularly the burqa. Ferrari points out that a correlating link exists between the contemporary prevalent secular conception of France's national identity and certain legal and political choices. The attitude of educating students "to the values of *laïcité* and shielding them from the competing values upheld by religions [. . .] explains the exclusion of the teaching of religion from the school curriculum, [and also] the prohibition of of wearing religious symbols in school."[178] Hunter-Henin argues that some Western countries could

---

174. Ferrari, "Religious Education," 103.

175. Ahdar and Leigh, *Religious Freedom.*

176. Hunter-Henin, *Religious Freedoms in European Schools,* 5.

177. Kramer, "Taking the Veil."

178. Ferrari, "Religious Freedoms," 211.

construe the French law forbidding individuals from wearing the burqa in school settings as a State endeavor to indoctrinate citizens and could perceive this ban as contrary to France's professed support of freedom of conscience[179]—both in and away from compulsory education.

Chelini-Pont regards the dispute concerning the wearing of the burqa in public as reflecting France's inclination to equate the State's neutrality with containment of religious expression in the public sphere. According to Chelini-Pont:

> The dispute revolves around a fundamental ideal of the French republic: laïcité. Although the concept of laïcité defies a precise definition, it embodies the constitutional principle of the state's neutrality. As President Jacques Chirac stated, laïcité "is at the heart of (the French) republican identity." Laïcité strictly calls for a state that is free from an official or exclusive religion; however, this freedom is commonly understood in France as an absence of religious expression in the public sphere. The constitutional principle of laïcité, which permits state neutrality (comparable to the American separation of church and state), differs greatly from its perceived meaning among citizens and the government officials who use the idea to instinctively oppose one's right to manifest religious conviction in the public sphere. It is often said by Frenchmen that laïcité allows religion only in the private sphere.[180]

The French education system, which appears to mirror the need to protect citizens from the threat to freedom that many new religious movements have posed, I surmise, qualifies France as obstinately hostile to religious freedom.

4.3.4 The Education System in the Netherlands

Even though education in the Holland of 1861 remained Christian, the term "Christian" could have more appropriately been identified as "moral." Arnold argues that:

> [T]hose who gave it the name of Christian were careful to announce that by Christianity they meant all those ideas which purify the soul by elevating it, and which prepare the union of citizens in a common sentiment of mutual good will; not 'those theological subtleties which stifle the natural affections, and perpetuate divisions among members of one commonwealth.

179. Hunter-Henin, *Religious Freedoms in European Schools*, 5–6.
180. Chelini-Pont, "Religion in the Public Sphere," para. 2 in "Introduction."

> They announced that the Christianity of the law and of the state was a social or lay Christianity, gradual transforming society after the model of ideal justice not a dogmatic Christianity, the affair of the individual and the Church.

During the late nineteenth and early twentieth centuries, the Dutch educational system confronted political challenges relating to public and private schooling. To try to resolve these concerns, in 1917 a constitutional provision inaugurated the principle of "freedom of education," and stipulated that the State would fund all schools. The State does not discriminate between public and private, religious and secular, but provides funding equally, on a per pupil basis.[181] To complement family values, the freedom of education constitutional clause endows parents with the constitutional right to enroll their children in a State-funded school.[182] This funding extends to parents uniting to establish a new school. In addition, schools enjoy considerable operational autonomy—despite the State funding of most school costs. Parental choice conjoined with school autonomy has been the basis of the Dutch education system for almost a century.

Parental choice continues in the Netherlands[183] as, irrespective of geographic location, State law permits Dutch parents to choose the school they prefer for their children. Nevertheless, education choice for children closely coincides with their parents' voting patterns, as well as connects with the parents' social activities, and their club and union memberships. Belfield and D'Entremont explain that this is to the detriment of school quality being considered in educational choice. This, in turn, could have influenced the introduction of the Dutch regulation to try to ensure quality for all that states that all State-funded schools in the Netherlands "must adhere to curriculum goals, which include attainment targets and instructional hours specified by law, as well as published performance outcomes."[184] Belfield and D'Entremont also point out that, additionally, the Netherlands exerts more control over its private schools than the United States.

At times during the twentieth century, the Netherlands has been criticized for its role as one of the most tolerant states in the world.[185] During the twenty-first century, the clear pragmatism this State demonstrates in

181. Fiske and Ladd, "Dutch Experience," 49–53.

182. Belfield and D'Entremont, "Catholic Schooling."

183. Fiske and Ladd, "Dutch Experience," para. 1 in "Dutch School Funding" section.

184. Belfield and D'Entremont, "Catholic Schooling," para. 6 in "Schools in the Netherlands" section.

185. Roney, *Culture and Customs.*

religious matters and the Dutch method for teaching religious education merits consideration by other countries. "Dutch students outperform students in many other developed countries on such international tests as the Program for International Student Assessment and the Trends in International Mathematics and Science Survey."[186] In addition, the education system which the Netherlands implements contributes to this country ranking among the highest in the United Nations International Children's Emergency Fund scale of children's wellbeing.

In constitutional terms, the Netherlands melds into the classification as a system of "non-establishment" or "separation"; nevertheless, this does not imply that the State adheres to or supports a strict separation model regarding its State–religion relationship.[187] Although the Netherlands should be classified as a system of "non-establishment" or "separation" in constitutional terms, "the State does not have or implement a strict separation model. No equivalent of the 'wall of separation' doctrine as in the US exists in the Netherlands, nor does the State demonstrate France's 'secular nature.'"[188] The Dutch employ a less rigorous model as they permit religious expressions, symbols, and identities in the public realm. Public authorities demonstrate the acceptance of religions in the way they relate to diverse faith-based activities and organizations. The State also guarantees the right to free exercise of religion through diverse legal regulations.

4.4 Religious Education in the U.S., the U.K., France and the Netherlands

Macedo questions whether exposure to diverse religions might in part interfere with religious freedom or if a liberal State can legally make public schooling conditional on parents' consenting that the State can expose their children to diversity that conflicts with familial beliefs.[189] As noted earlier in the Mozert case, Chief Judge Lively denied that this practice constitutes a legitimate threat and argued, "Exposure to something does not constitute

---

186. Fiske and Ladd, "Dutch Experience," para. 4 of 5 in "Introduction."

187. Belfield and D'Entremont, "Catholic Schooling."

188. Maussen, "Religious Governance in the Netherlands," paras. 7–8 in "In Search of the 'Dutch Model'" section.

189. Macedo, "Liberal Civic Education," 468–96. *Mozert v. Hawkins* involved a 1983 complaint by "born again" Christian families against the local school board in Hawkins County, Tennessee. The families charged a primary school reading program with denigrating their religious views, both in its lack of religious "balance" and in the uncommitted, evenhanded nature of the presentations (470).

teaching, indoctrination, opposition or promotion of the things exposed."[190] In this section, I present a critique of religious education in the four different states I have examined.

4.4.1 Religious Education

As it amounts to privileging one religion (Christianity in a nondenominational manner) over others in public institutions, the United Kingdom's law making Christian religious worship compulsory in State schools does not appear compatible with the core of principled pluralism. This practice, as a principle of the U.K.'s State-religious education, not only constitutes a violation of religious freedom and civic equality, but also potentially compromises the State's impartiality. Nevertheless, as I previously noted, in practice, the U.K. schools allocate freedom for parents to withdraw from the mandated worship services. Also, in some areas, schools with predominantly different faiths than Christianity, like Islam, also have the liberty to observe their own religious worship services. The U.K. demonstrates the tendency to include rather than exclude diverse religions in considerations of religious education. This contrasts with both France and the United States, as both these countries construct a wall of separation to distance the State–religion relationship. The French base their model for the State–religion relationship on the presumption that for a country to maintain social cohesion, the majority of its citizens must share a homogeneous set of either religious or secular values.[191] The belief that this type of uniformity constitutes an outdated past legacy, not compatible with a contemporary multicultural and multi-religious society, inspires the pattern for the model of the State–religion relationship.

In part, this perception conveys the idea that the U.K. pattern evolves from the State's recognition that it cannot succeed in forging its citizens' identities. "Consequently, it gives up this claim, limiting itself to providing the legal framework necessary for the peaceful coexistence of different individuals and groups in a plural society."[192] Ferrari asserts that, therefore, the primary task for the United Kingdom's State–religion relationship includes stimulating and maintaining elements in society that create and nurture citizen engagement, solidarity of the State, and personal responsibility.

Educators in the United Kingdom primarily present religious education through a stance of reported State impartiality—the religious education

---

190. Macedo, "Liberal Civic Education," 472.

191. Ferrari, "Teaching Religion," 210

192. Ferrari, "Teaching Religion."

approach. This differs from "the French teaching of no religion."[193] In the United Kingdom, the State focuses primarily on religious plurality. Teachers educate students about ways they can know and understand the diverse religions practiced there.

By contrast with the British approach, a recent example of the French attitude can be found in the incident in August 2016 when French police officers forced a Muslim woman on a beach in Nice to remove some of her clothing as part of the French city's controversial ban on the burkini, causing international protests. Ruwan Rujouleh reports, "there's a danger that France no longer looks any different from Iran or any other theocratic State, where religious police patrol the streets, monitoring women in public places, and checking whether or not they are following the rules."[194] Currently, the United Kingdom accepts new religious movements more readily than does France.[195]

Lewis reports that all E.U. countries include principles of freedom and non-discrimination in their respective constitutions. The specific approaches these countries follow to interpret and apply these ideologies primarily depends on historical traditions regarding the State–religion relationship.[196] As the interpretations may differ from one country to another, similarly, the treatment of diverse religions as well as the implementation of religious education may also vary.

The concern of how best to balance religious freedom for all regarding compulsory education at the same time incorporating the liberal ideal of equality and nondiscrimination presents a common challenge that the United States, the United Kingdom, France, and the Netherlands have all appeared to encounter. Perhaps the various international mechanisms which enshrine the two ideals of religious freedom and equality intrinsically contradict each other in the context of a contemporary, increasingly pluralistic society. For example, when a religion, denomination, or other type of worldview manages a school, an impasse arises.[197] As administrators maintain equality for those students and teachers who adhere to different or perhaps even oppositional religious and worldviews, they must simultaneously preserve the school's freedom to demonstrate its religious faith.

The perception confirming the need for the State to designate room for religion in education evolves from two basic freedoms: (1) the freedom

---

193. Ferrari, "Teaching Religion."

194. Rujouleh, "Burkini Bans."

195. Ferrari, "Teaching Religion," 210.

196. Lewis, "Between Lord Ahmed."

197. Nichols, *Priorities in Religious Education*, 113–23.

of religion; and (2) the freedom of education. The freedom of religion entails, among other things, the right to manifest one's religion "in public and in private" and "in worship, teaching, practice and observance."[198] Schools may be perceived as the institutional environment in which the freedom to communicate and transmit religious views to the religious expression and freedom of conscience needs to be respected.

The State cannot directly inculcate only certain religious views or require that students participate in specific acts that their religious convictions forbid, nor can it mandate that they affirm or profess beliefs contrary to their own. Freedom of education entails the right of groups and individuals to found and manage State or independent primary and secondary schools aligned to their peculiar religious, philosophical, or pedagogical principles. This freedom also includes the freedom of parents to select the school they prefer for their children.[199] According to Haynes, even though discrepancies exist in the implementation of religious education, empowering students to learn about different faiths and diverse ways to understand the world enhances their education and equips future generations to better appreciate the need for religious freedom for all.

4.4.2 Principled Pluralism and Education

Research by Ahdar and Leigh as well as my subjective experiences and communications strikingly confirm that the most intractable disputes between believers and non-believers concern the education and upbringing of children.[200] Diverse perceptions exist not only concerning how and by whom children should be raised but also extend into concepts regarding what students should be taught in school regarding the origin of the world, about religions, and customs intrinsic to dissimilar religions within various States.

Ensuing issues relating to religious education include but may not be limited to the appropriateness of teachings as to whether the bodies of religious adherents may be mutilated and whether males and females should be segregated in educational settings, as conservative Islam mandates. Arguments regarding teachings to be included in religious education may also include contemporary debates regarding concepts defining life: for example, at what point in the biological development of an embryo can one speak of a life which cannot morally be terminated.[201] According to Rawls's political

---

198. Council of Europe, "Details of Treaty."
199. Vermeule, "Veil of Ignorance," 399.
200. Ahdar and Leigh, *Religious Freedom*, 271.
201. Devettere, *Practical Decision Making*.

liberalism, these formidable issues require and should be primarily limited to the guidance of reasonable persons. On the other hand, principled pluralism contends that challenging issues in religious education demand considered contributions from those subscribing to a variety of religious beliefs.

Vivian T. Thayer argues the study of religion in compulsory education can be dangerous. In her discourse against religious education, Thayer poses the question: "Is study about religion really education at all?"[202] She concludes that because "the distinction between the structure and the function of religion, in its application to education," does not prove satisfactory, religious education can cause more harm than good.[203] Additionally, Thayer argues, as discussions regarding religion demonstrate the potential to transition into explosive subjects, students cannot examine these matters critically or objectively as they can other themes. Rawls's political liberalism appears to support this unsatisfactory stance, while principled pluralism, contrariwise, encourages the examination of information that may challenge students to confirm the validity of their personal beliefs.

Some political liberals, like Thayer, argue that religion belongs in the private domain along with other biased theoretical preferences and not in rational public life.[204] From examining several dilemmas confronting education, particularly religious education, I propose that one approach to religious education, specifically principled pluralism, would encourage religious education in any education system. Through the study of religions, students can, as they should, freely examine and choose the religion they prefer on its merits, provided they can make their choice without the imposition of any compulsory measures.

Liam Gearo argues against Thayer's stance of firmly opposing any religious education. Gearo's observation that religion is politically prioritized in education demonstrates a key difference of understandings between the two, regarding both the goal of education and the role that religion demonstrates during the education process, positive in the case of Gearo.[205] These two different perceptions also reflect dissimilar concerns regarding the potential impact of religion.

The different stances which Gearo and Thayer present regarding religious education stimulate a question: Does Rawlsian political liberalism agree with Thayer and deny that any value evolves from religion in the education system? I reason that Rawls would instead more likely agree with Gearo.

---

202. Thayer, *American Education and Religion*.

203. Thayer, *American Education and Religion*, 28.

204. Ahdar and Leigh, *Religious Freedom*, 51.

205. Gearon, *Masterclass in Religious Education*.

In general, political liberalism appears suspicious of religion's role in public affairs and, therefore, may not favor using religion as a direct, dominating, comprehensive doctrine for public policy making. However, if an overlapping consensus under a constitutional framework allows for the practice, political liberalism may not necessarily oppose an educational curriculum which includes students studying about religions as subjects. The concepts founding principled pluralism do, in fact, support offering opportunities for students to obtain knowledge regarding diverse religions. In turn, the mutual understandings that students gain of those practicing religions different from their own will likely, in time, serve to help them better ensure their own religious freedom in the world's increasingly plural milieu.

Two extreme views have frequently been evidenced in the increasingly plural context in which religious education exists. One viewpoint, fundamentalism, may be construed as the attempt to withdraw from cultural and religious obscurities by copiously recognizing only one position and truth. With this approach, teachings in religious education reinforce one solitary, designated religious truth.[206] As I maintained in previous chapters, when individuals endorsing theonomy and other fundamentalist religious approaches adopt this tactic, they consequently discard the value of other religions.

The second extreme view, relativism, adheres to the approach of political liberalism. This viewpoint deems religious education as either unnecessary or argues that it rather belongs to pedagogical, comparative religious studies; devoid of any inherent truth value.[207] Inevitably, as fundamentalism and relativism disavow religious identities and thwart discourse capabilities, both approaches will impede religious freedom for all.

In its opposing stance to fundamentalism and relativism, principled pluralism encourages dialogue among as well as between diverse religious identities. From the principled pluralism perspective, religious education not only serves as a conduit for purification of religious truth from one religious identity, it also creates opportunities for students to enhance their abilities to evaluate religious truths.[208] Following their exposure to religious education that capsulizes diverse religions, students can more freely make sound judgments in choosing or rejecting partial or whole religious truths.

The solution for resolving tensions among the diverse truth claims should not arbitrarily embrace and employ fundamentalist approaches such as theonomy. Nor should the solution abruptly reject the existence of the

---

206. Schweitzer, *On the Edge*, 170.

207. Schweitzer, *On the Edge*.

208. Schweitzer, *On the Edge*.

truth in an agnostic, relativistic claim such as political liberalism. To best protect religious freedom for all, no matter how extreme one may perceive a religion, if the religious adherents operate and manifest their religion under legal norms, their religion merits protection.

In contrast to the dangers of both the religious fundamentalists' exclusivism and the ideological secularists' relativism, I propose that principled pluralism provides the best, most consistent and most coherent political philosophy in securing religious freedom for all. I also stress that for the State to maintain freedom of religion for all, it must match its method for implementing religious education to align with principled pluralism. Otherwise, this misapplication of or failure to apply methods to educate young people regarding diverse religions will ultimately break freedom. Unless the State implements principled pluralism, education will inevitably run into conflict. This will routinely occur primarily due to favoritism, or inconsistencies in practices regarding religious diversity and religious education.[209]

Principled pluralism also advocates for boundaries; not, however, the same restricting constraints that political liberalism proposes. Political liberalism, as per Rawls's directives noted in Chapter 3, will certainly refuse to welcome any form of education about certain religions if any of them may be deemed as "irrational and mad."[210] As a consequence, Rawls's perceptions regarding constraining certain religions from appearing in the public square contradict principled pluralism's commitment to religious freedom.

Principled pluralism, unlike political liberalism, will welcome religious education in both public and private settings. Principled pluralism recognizes religion as an inherent component of human beings and an inalienable part of the fabric of any organic pluralistic society as principles of religious freedom for all. Therefore, religious education proves vital for inclusion in compulsory education to contribute to a future generation who will know how to better help ensure religious freedom for all.

4.5 Conclusion

As noted at the start of this chapter, religion in education is a contemporary global political priority.[211] In this chapter, I have examined how religious education complements a State, its educational system, and the potential for its future generation to maintain religious freedom. Additionally, I surveyed the

---

209. Maussen, "Religious Governance in the Netherlands."

210. Rawls, *Political Liberalism*, 8.

211. Gearon, *Masterclass in Religious Education*.

schools and educational systems in four liberal states,[212] the United States, the United Kingdom, France, and the Netherlands. I also noted whether the methods these states use complement or constrain religious freedom. In addition, my examination of State policies not only contributes to the illustration of principled pluralism as applied to education regarding religious freedom, it simultaneously alludes to the significance of my evolving, modified version of principled pluralism, *Baorong Duoyuan*.

In Chapter 5, as I progress toward contextualizing a model of principled pluralism to address China's need for full religious freedom, I examine historical and contemporary trends and challenges to religious freedom in China. Ultimately, I introduce *Baorong Duoyuan* as a contextualized model of principled pluralism in China and present a demonstration of its application to China as it relates to religious freedom.

---

212. Ahdar and Leigh, *Religious Freedom*, 296.

Chapter 5

Principled Pluralism Contextualized: Toward *Baorong Duoyuan*

Let a hundred flowers blossom and a hundred
schools of thought [resonate . . .].[1]

5.1 Introduction

IN CHAPTER 4, I reasoned that to safeguard religious freedom for all, a goal that both political liberalism and principled pluralism endorse, religious education[2] should constitute an inseparable part of any education system, particularly contemporary public education. After I examined the five approaches that diverse countries have adopted to implement religious education, I compared the education models within public schools in four Western countries and discussed several ensuing controversies and conflicts thereof. I also noted the corresponding stance that each State holds regarding religious education. Initially, in Chapter 5, I review several constraints on religious freedom in China under the traditional State–religion model and examine contemporary challenges to religious freedom under the CCP's State–religion model. I then relate the inherent

1. *Chinese Philosophy, Encyclopedia Britannica,* paras. 2–3. "The Contention of a Hundred Schools of Thought (Baijia Zhengming) [. . .] known as the Golden Age of Chinese philosophy" because a broad range of thoughts were discussed freely.

2. The umbrella of religious education encompasses several approaches for its implementation, five which I discuss later in this chapter. According to Cathy Byrne and to Ahdar and Leigh, these include: (1) learning into religion (also known as religious instruction); (2) learning about religion (also known as reported state neutrality); (3) learning from religion; (4) the separatist approach; and (5) the secularist approach.

unjustifiability of the CCP's current religious policy in principle as well as its unsustainability in practice. In this chapter I also point out that if, as several scholars predict, China becomes "Christian(ized)" in the future and the State transitions into a democracy, *Baorong Duoyuan* could prove to best suit the projected new China.

As the political, economic, cultural, and religious conditions in China are not yet as they would be under a democracy, I consider whether, and if so, under what conditions *Baorong Duoyuan* could help promote, protect, and preserve religious freedom for all. As I noted in Chapter 1, the Chinese term, which translates to "inclusive pluralism" in English also correlates with the theme that the introductory quotation for this chapter reflects—to let each religion (flower/school of thought) resonate or speak freely in the public square.

After explaining the general conditions for *Baorong Duoyuan* in China—pluralization and democratization—I rule out the inclusion in my study of numerous components relating to political liberalism and principled pluralism. I then draw several positive considerations from both these rival theories to design and develop *Baorong Duoyuan* for consideration in China's projected pluralistic, Christianized, democratic environment.

Ultimately, even though my research reveals that principled pluralism rather than political liberalism more closely depicts the intent of *Baorong Duoyuan* to protect religious freedom for all, nevertheless, as I will demonstrate in this chapter, neither principled pluralism nor political liberalism can adequately and sufficiently ensure citizens' religious freedom in the way that international standards stipulate. Consequently, I present *BD* as a proposed foundation for religious freedom in a post-communist, democratic China. At the end of this chapter, I assert that *Baorong Duoyuan*'s theoretical foundation not only counters challenges to religious freedom, it also encompasses the potential to help harmonize interrelations between different worldview orientations, some which I note in the following sections.

5.2 Challenges for China Regarding Religious Freedom

In Chapter 1, I note that the pattern of State supremacy and official orthodoxy has continued in China under a Communist State which dictates that religions must operate under the religious policies of the CCP. Although China's constitution declares that citizens of China shall enjoy "freedom of religious belief,"[3] and despite its guarantee of this proclaimed *freedom*,

---

3. Article 36 of the Constitution of the PRC states: "Citizens of the People's Republic of China enjoy freedom of religious belief."

the State still regards any religious activities conducted outside the CCP's policies as not only heterodox in ideology but also as implying abnormal and, in turn, illegal activities.[4] Any religious groups outside the CCP's approved and sanctioned list[5] therefore become subject to persecution[6] and potential legal prosecution.[7]

Throughout China's history of diverse dynasties, the political structure of imperial authoritarianism has routinely challenged religious freedom for Chinese citizens. Ensuing conflicts and clashes between ruling authorities and religion in China have persisted throughout most of the imperial era and extend into contemporary times.[8] Currently, amid ongoing reports of prosecution and persecution of certain religions and in attempts to justify its renunciation of religious freedom, the CCP regularly claims that hostile foreign forces use religions to permeate Chinese society to win over the population.

5.2.1 Religious Freedom under China's Traditional State–Religion Model

Jonathan Chao, a renowned modern Chinese church historian, confirms that the relationship between the State and religion in China has traditionally been one of supremacy of the State over religion.[9] Since the first group of Nestorian[10] Christian missionaries arrived in China in AD 635, challenges to

4. Bays, *New History of Christianity in China*, 191.

5. Bays, *God and Caesar in China*, 24. World religions like Christianity, Catholicism, Buddhism, Taoism, and Islam are considered "heterodox" in relation to Marxist "orthodoxy," but may conduct their religious activities so long as such activities are under the supervision and control of the State.

6. Bays, *God and Caesar in China*. Even those religions on the approved list, however, were persecuted during the Cultural Revolution (1966–76).

7. Bays, *God and Caesar in China*. All groups outside the CCP's list are declared illegal; nevertheless, some are tolerated while those designated as "evil cult" groups are subject to legal prosecution.

8. Chao, *Chinese Intellectuals*, 10–17. In the history of Christianity in China, three brief periods transpired when church and State enjoyed relative harmony. The Nestorians experienced broad acceptance in China for 210 years until annihilated in AD 845 after heavy persecution against Buddhism by the Confucians in political power during the Tang Dynasty (618–907). The second peaceful period occurred when the Jesuit missionary Matteo Ricci (1552–1600) moved into China in the late sixteenth century, after which Catholicism flourished for nearly a hundred years. The last period of harmony was between 1911 and 1949, from Sun Yat-sen's revolutionaries establishing the Republic of China to the CCP taking power in mainland China.

9. Chao, *Church and State in Socialist China*, 8.

10. Ross, *A Vision Betrayed*. The Nestorian Christians, merchants and missionaries

religious freedom in China have repeatedly erupted in the form of conflicts and clashes between dynasties and religions.[11] After the first Protestant missionary, Robert Morrison (from the London Missionary Society), reached Canton, China in 1807, however, the conflicts between the Christian church and the State escalated. Similarly, until China accepted Catholicism in 1844,[12] Catholics suffered nearly 150 years of suppression as China determined to portray this religious group as a foreign heterodox sect.

Some Chinese have alleged that the gospel came into China with the forces of Western colonial pressure.[13] This impression intensified in 1858 when China lost the Second Opium War. The signing of the resulting imbalanced Treaty of Tianjin, however, included a "toleration clause" that granted foreign missionaries the right to share the Christian faith in the State.[14] This significantly contributed to the Chinese regarding Christianity as a foreign religion (*yang jiao*) that had invaded the territory of traditional Chinese religions.[15]

In traditional China, prior to the rule of the CCP, from the seventeenth century until the collapse of the Qing Dynasty in 1911,[16] most dynasties esteemed Confucianism[17] as the imperial orthodoxy. After Dr. Sun Yat-Sen,

---

from the Nestorian Church of Mesopotamia, arrived in China in 635 during the Tang Dynasty (AD 589–845). In 845, the Emperor Wu Zong, a strict Confucian, ferociously attacked all monastery-based religious organizations. The Nestorians did not survive the imperial purge.

11. Chao, *Chinese Intellectuals and the Gospel*, 9–24.

12. Bates, "Church and State in Traditional China," 13.

13. Zhong, "Between God and Caesar," 36–48.

14. Yip, "China and Christianity," 135.

15. Fuk-tsang, *Christianities in Asia*, 149–72.

16. Bays, *A New History of Christianity*. "The 'Common Program' approved by the CPPCC was in effect China's constitution until 1954, when the NPC approved the first formal constitution. The Common Program, which was the foundation enabling establishment of the PRC on October 1, 1949, contained provision for the "freedom of religious belief for all religious believers," 161.

17. Yao, *An Introduction to Confucianism*, 32–83. Confucius taught that although meticulously observing ancient rituals proves critical, having a sincere heart and a devoted spirit proves to be even more significant: "For if a person lacks humaneness (*ren*) within, then what is the value of performing rituals?" Confucius also held a holistic perception of a person and stressed that if one observed ways a person acted, scrutinized his motives and his tastes, then the person could not conceal his/her real character from others. Later, Dong Zhongshu assumed a primary role in developing a comprehensive Confucian doctrine (based on the concept of mutual responsiveness between Heaven and humans), adapting Confucianism to the new culture of the Han. Confucianism transitioned from a moralistic system to "a universalistic and holistic view providing inescapable sanctions for the deeds of men and the ordering of society, and a place in the cosmos for the imperial system."

a professing Christian, founded the Republic of China in October of 1911, ending the imperial system of China, however, Chinese citizens enjoyed a short-term period of real religious freedom for the first time in the country's history.[18] Wu Zongci confirms that in 1912, the Provisional Constitution of the Republic of China's guarantee of freedom for each citizen's religious belief proved to be a precedent for rulings relating to the State–religion relationship.[19] Zhang Hua similarly notes that, "Throughout Chinese history, multiple religions co-existed, but the policy of religious freedom was proposed for the first time in history in 1912. Therefore, the stipulation on religious freedom in the Provisional Constitution of the Republic of China had landmark significance."[20] Due to the total submission to imperial rule by numerous groups outside the imperial orthodoxy, including Buddhists and the traditional Chinese folk religions,[21] most dynasties typically tolerated them. Some dynasties deemed certain religious groups as disloyal and rebellious to the imperial power, however, and persecuted or eradicated groups like White Lotus,[22] the Taiping Heavenly Kingdom,[23] and Catholics who refused to practice Chinese ancestor worship.[24]

Chao reports that prior to 1911, the dynasty transmitted and enforced Confucian orthodoxy through the education system and the civil service examination system.[25] Although the State tolerated other systems of belief

18. US Department of State, "The Chinese Revolution of 1911."

19. Zongci, *Provisional Constitution of the Republic,* 29.

20. Hua, "Beginning of the Religious Freedom," para. 1 in "Part I: Freedom to Believe" section.

21. DuBois, *Religion and the Making.* Chinese folk religions combine a mixture of ancient ancestor worship with elements of Buddhism, Confucianism, Taoism, and the worship of certain deities.

22. Ching, *Chinese Religions,* 214–15. In the mid-twelfth century, the White Lotus society began as an association of clergy and laymen, who sought to attain rebirth in the Pure Land. These individuals were "committed to vegetarianism, abstinence from wine and killing."

23. Cousineau, *Religion in a Changing World,* 155. In the 1850s, Christian missionary writings in southern China contributed to the "Taiping Heavenly Kingdom," which not only included bits of Judeo-Christian theology but also claimed divine revelation, egalitarian ideals, and communal sharing of property. In the 1840s, after followers armed themselves for protection, they defeated a series of armies the State sent to oppose them. In 1864, several million individuals died when the CCP ultimately exterminated this religious group, which they considered as revolutionary "proto-socialists" deluded by their religion.

24. Sullivan, *Historical Dictionary of the People's.*

25. Cohen, *China and Christianity,* 3–60. See also Wright, *Buddhism in Chinese History,* 65–85.

considered "heterodox."[26] Nevertheless, with this affirmation of Confucian orthodoxy, the CCP implemented codes of law and increased government controls to reduce the influence of religious groups to a level of socio-political insignificance. In turn, the constant propaganda of Communism stimulated an anti-Christian movement in 1922, with the State regularly criticizing Christianity and implicating Christians as the imperial arm of the West.

To counter this religious oppression, numerous Chinese church leaders established Chinese indigenous churches. Nevertheless, Christian Meyer reports that after the robust anti-religious and anti-Christian movement (generally dated 1922–27) gradually subsided, "local popular religion and popular redemptive societies remained subject to persecution [. . . , while the] issue of national identity, which had played a role in the anti-imperialistic attacks against Christianity [. . .] was of continued significance in the 1930s as part of nation-building."[27] From 1921 to 1934, many early CCP leaders perceived religion as a barrier to science and thought that it would eventually dissipate as technology advanced. Vincent Goossaert and David A. Palmer report that some CCP leaders even argued that humans created gods and that Christianity constituted[28] an imperialistic tool. On the other hand, several State leaders admitted that religions such as Buddhism, Confucianism, Judaism, Islam, and Christianity positively impacted humanity.

In their efforts to control certain religions, despite sporadic positive admissions about religion in general, CCP officials would regularly infiltrate religious groups and try to manipulate members. Prior to 1949, as Chao observed, the State developed yet another system of control to contain religious expansion, utilizing religious leaders who worked for the Board of Rites to strictly monitor the activities of religious groups.[29] The State also outlawed other sectarian groups, considering them to be dissenters and potential rebels and, hence, often suppressed these individuals by force. During the Dynastic period, the current emperor determined which religions to promote as well as the religions that the State would tolerate, control, or suppress. Figure 6 depicts the State–religion relationship throughout the Dynastic period.

26. Yang, *Religion in Chinese Society*, 180–217.

27. Meyer, "How the 'Science of Religion,'" 319–20.

28. Goossaert and Palmer, *Religious Question*.

29. Chao, "History of Christianity," 22.

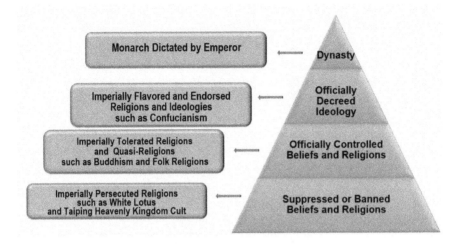

State–Religion Relationship in Dynastic China

On 4 January 1949, ten months prior to the establishing of the PRC, the People's Government of North China used two categories of the CCP's ideologies to ban religions, accusing them of being sects and secret societies and claiming that they economically exploited and psychologically manipulated Chinese citizens. The Chinese government summoned religious leaders and advised them "to turn themselves in to the authorities and to repent if they wanted to avoid a harsh punishment. Meanwhile, the ordinary followers, who had been "fooled" by the reactionary societies, were ordered to withdraw from these associations and to cease any activity if they wanted to avoid being prosecuted."[30] The State promised rewards to these individuals if they provided information regarding groups with plans to sabotage government procedures. This period reflects increasing challenges to religious freedom under the CCP's State–religion model in China, which I note in the next section.

5.2.2 Challenges to Religious Freedom under the CCP State–Religion Model

On 1 October 1949, when the CCP established the PRC, the Party designated atheism as the State's primary, official ideology.[31] Despite reasons for challenging the concept that atheism could legitimately be regarded as a type of

30. Goossaert and Palmer, *Religious Question*, 148.
31. Chao, *Church and State*.

religion,[32] Communism and atheism both aim to weaken the influence of traditional religion.[33] Yang argues that throughout CCP schools inside China, as well as via internal circulars and intermittent propaganda campaigns, CCP theoreticians have reinforced atheism as a Marxist orthodoxy.

After the Communist Party gained power over China in 1949,[34] the State banned religion between 1966–79.[35] Daniel H. Bays stresses that Chinese religious history after 1950 basically appears as "tightly intertwined with the theme of State and Communist Party control, interference, and repression."[36] During the periods of land reform (1950–54) and collectivization (1954–79), popular religions reinforced traditional social concepts which aligned with community solidarity and autonomy. Mickey Spiegel reports that as Communists wanted to integrate collectivized communities into a socialist economy and polity, this contributed to the CCP intensifying attacks on religions.[37]

Document No. 6, issued by the State Council in February 1991, reinforces the major document outlining China's religious policy, Document No. 19, which the Party Central issued in March 1982.[38] Despite China's proclamation of religious freedom, which basically translates to being "free to believe and free not to believe, free to believe in this religion or that religion; within a religion one is free to choose his sectarian differences and is free to move from unbelief to belief and vice-versa,"[39] this freedom does not extend to Chinese citizens. The CCP's concept of freedom of religion, for example, does not include freedom of propagation outside approved places designated for religious activities, nor does it include the right to establish churches according to a person's religious convictions.[40]

---

32. Weiler-Harwell, *Discrimination against Atheists*, 110.

33. Yang, *Religion in Chinese Society*, 58.

34. Pepper, *Civil War in China*.

35. Neubert, "Prof: Religious Trends in China."

36. Bays, *God and Caesar in China*, 34.

37. Spiegel, *China: State Control*, 17–36.

38. Spiegel, *China: State Control*.

39. Leung, and Liu, *Chinese Catholic Church in Conflict*, 21. In his detailed interpretation of Article 36, Li Weihan, former Minister of the CCP's United Front Working Department, the CCP's chief religious policy-making body, states, "Every citizen has the freedom to believe in religion, and also the freedom not to believe in religion. Within a religion, every citizen has the freedom to believe in this or that sect." This basically means that as long as they supported the CCP, monks, Taoists, priests or pastors would be considered friends of the State. The CCP's policy of religious freedom appears to be only a political ploy.

40. Spiegel, *China: State Control*.

In January 1994, the State Council issued Decrees No. 144 and Decree No. 145 governing religious activities among foreigners in China (No. 144)[41] and the requirement which subjects religious groups (No. 145)[42] to State registration. In time, the State implemented numerous other legal ordinances enforcing the State requirement for registration. Since April 1996, for instance, the State intensified its campaign effort to "make religion compatible with socialism," to enforce registration, and to terminate all religious activities not approved by registration.[43] Jinghao Zhou notes that the CCP carried out the policy of "monitoring and regulating all religions,"[44] with the intent of ostracizing Chinese religious organizations from foreign influence. This effort contributed to China's contemporary State–religion relationship, which I examine in the next section.

5.2.3 State–Religion Relationship under Communist China

As noted earlier, China considers religious activities practiced outside of State control or outside patriotic organizations to depict heterodoxy in ideology and to constitute "illegal religious activities," subject to prosecution, or a form of legalized persecution. Although the CCP considers the Three-Self Movement to serve as a distinct tool for the State to control Chinese Christianity,[45] Philip Yuen-sang Leung reports that missionaries planted the roots of the concept prior to Communist control, hoping to

---

41. *Provisions on the Administration of Religious Activities.*

42. Zhou, *Chinese vs. Western Perspectives*, 141.

43. The policy initiatives were set forth by Jiang Zemin, China's president and Chinese Communist Party secretary-general in November 1993 at a national conference on United Front work. At the 1996 Fourth Plenum of the Eighth National People's Congress, Premier Li Peng echoed the same themes. He cited Document No. 19 of 1982, *The Basic Viewpoint and Policy on the Religious Question during Our Country's Socialist Period*, which offered a corrective to the Cultural Revolution policy of severe repression by advocating the cooptation of believers that they might serve socialist construction, and Document No. 6 of 1991, *Circular from Party Central and the State Council Concerning Certain Problems in Further Improving Religious Work.* The latter was the first to mention adaptation, the first to espouse registration as a key supervisory mechanism, and the first to address the practical realities of implementing policy. Li Peng also referred to two 1994 sets of government regulations, No. 144, *Regulations on the Supervision of the Religious Activities of Foreigners in China*, and No. 145, *Regulations Regarding the Management of Places of Religious Activity.* On 1 March 1997, at the opening of the National People's Congress, Li Peng again made reference to the need for religious groups to adapt to socialist society.

44. Zhou, *China's Peaceful Rise*, 173.

45. Zhou, *China's Peaceful Rise.*

unite Chinese Christians. The movement also intended to arouse nationalism and patriotism among this group.[46]

Currently, the Chinese government requires that the Three-Self Movement not only must accept the CCP's leadership but that each church must register with the State. Those conducting individual religious activities must report these to the Three-Self Movement's local committee. Religious leaders must also report all religious activity locations to the provincial Bureau of Religious Affairs. In addition, every six months, each religious group must submit a written report of events to a special committee of the State. The State categorizes activities of house churches that refuse to register with the State as well as the practices of those religions conducting their activities outside the Three-Self Movement, as "illegitimate religious activities."[47] As China regularly labels numerous organized house churches that actively engage in evangelistic expansion as "cultic groups," these consequently become the State's primary targets.[48]

Under the CCP's rule in China, the pattern of State supremacy and official orthodoxy persists. Any religion must adhere to legal State ordinances and operate within CCP religious policies. As the State seeks to propagate its own official orthodoxies, namely Marxism, Leninism, and the Thought of Mao, it only endorses these religions.[49] The CCP considers all other ideologies and beliefs to be heterodox. According to Jason Kindopp:

> The apparatuses of control include the United Front Work Department of the Party, the Religious Affairs Bureau of the state, and "patriotic religious organizations." Church activities that are conducted within this sphere of control are called "normal religious activities" and are given legal status. Only eight major patriotic religious organizations are allowed to operate legally under the CCP's control.[50]

46. Leung, *Christianity Reborn*, 87–107.

47. Sharpe, *Chinese Law and Government*, 5.

48. Numerous reports confirm religious persecution in the PRC, including: Amnesty International, Human Rights Watch, Bush Jr., *Religion in Communist China*; and Kai-lin, *Laogaiying zhong* [Children of God].

49. After the Fifteenth National Congress of the CCP, the CCP added the Thought of Deng Xiaoping.

50. Xiaowen, *Zhongguo Zhongjiao*, 4–9. These comprise: China Taoist Association, the Buddhist Association of China, the Three-Self Patriotic Movement Committee of the Protestant Churches of China, the National Christian Council of China, the Chinese Patriotic Catholic Association, the Chinese Catholic Bishops College, the National Administrative Commission of the Chinese Catholic Church, and the Islamic Association of China. Also, see Leung, *China's Religious Freedom Policy*, 11. The other two initiatives include: (1) wholly and correctly implementing religious freedom policy; (2)

At times, State leaders assert that alien religions plan to subvert the Party's rule.[51] The following, for example, depicts China's explanation for banning the Falun Gong movement:

> Li Hongzhi fabricated the so-called Falun Gong by copying some *qi gong*[52] practices and adding a lot of superstitious beliefs and ravings. Li propagated the explosion of the earth and the doomsday fallacy to fool the public. These concepts have already resulted in physical and mental injuries and even death of people, undermining social stability. Falun Gong bears strong resemblance to heterodox groups like Branch Davidian in the United States and Japanese Aum Doomsday Cult [. . .]. Falun Gong organization, advocating malicious fallacies, has put people's life at risk and wreaked havoc on society.[53]

Yang reports that in 1999, after China banned Falun Gong as an "evil cult" (*xie jiao*), the State jailed the religion's core leaders. In October 1999, following the primary crackdown on Falun Gong, the National People's Congress Standing Committee adopted the Legislative Resolution on Banning Heretic Cults. This offered a sense of legitimacy to the clampdown on Falun Gong and other qigong or cultic groups. Yang further notes, "In the following years provincial governments issued numerous temporary or draft ordinances and administrative orders aimed at controlling religious groups. Eventually these administrative orders were consolidated into the State Council's Regulations of Religious Affairs that took effect on 1 March 2005."[54] In many reported cases of false allegations by the Chinese government to try to validate attacks on certain religions, the evidence produced fails to support the charges.[55]

Elizabeth H. Prodromoummai maintains that it appears at times, as with Falun Gong, that the focus of the State does not necessarily confirm that it recognizes a reported religion as legitimate. Instead, the focus of the State could mean that the attitude the State assumes toward the targeted reported religion encompasses unsubstantiated charges against the group.[56]

---

using legal means to strengthen administration of religious affairs.

51. "President Xi urges China's Religions."

52. Her, *Taking Charge of Your Wellbeing*. Qigong, also spelled Chi-Kung, depicts the study and practice of cultivating vital life force through numerous techniques which include breathing, posture, meditation, and guided imagery.

53. "Definition of 'Religion,'" 199.

54. Yang, *Future of Religious Freedom*, 137.

55. Embassy of the People's Republic.

56. Prodromou, "Protecting Religious Freedom," para. 3 in introductory section.

I maintain that the attitude and understanding which China's contemporary ruling powers adopt towards religious freedom continue to contribute to challenges to religious freedom, just as in the past under China's traditional State–religion regime. Nevertheless, Chinese national religious affairs leaders maintain that their requirement that any religion must adapt to CCP religious policies does not necessitate the changing of fundamental beliefs.[57] Since the 1990s, when President Jiang Zemin launched his campaign on managing religions, one of the three basic strategies regarding religion includes the goal to "make religion adaptable with socialism."[58] One could question, however, how religion can adapt to a philosophy that, at its core, holds that Marxism will lead to the eventual demise of all religions; a philosophy which asserts that "Marxism is incompatible with any theistic worldview"?[59] Regarding the goal of the CCP's campaign to conform religions to communist protocol, CCP scholar Luo Shuze states:

> by religion adapting itself to the socialist society, we mean that with the establishment of the socialist society, religion must adjust itself with corresponding changes in theology, conception, and organization. We require religious believers politically to love the motherland, support the leadership of the Chinese Communist Party, adhere to the socialist path, and act within the constitution and laws of the land [. . .]. It is necessary, through the patriotic religious groups and personages, to expound and interpret the religious doctrine and canon in such a way as to be in the interests of socialism, and inspire and guide the religious believers gradually to modify their negative ways detrimental to national development and social progress.[60]

Yoshiko Ashiwa and David L. Wank point out that in its efforts to convince diverse religions to adapt and modify their ways to match the interests of the CCP,[61] China holds a long tradition of regulating organized religion. One Human Rights Watch representative pointedly summarizes

57. Prodromou, "Protecting Religious Freedom." Also, see: "Legal Protection of the Freedom," para 6. "Religion should be adapted to the society in which it is prevalent. This is a universal law for the existence and development of religion. Now the Chinese people are building China into a modern socialist country with Chinese characteristics. The Chinese government advocates that religion should adapt to this reality."

58. Xiaowen, "Shiji Zhijiao zhongjiao," 4–9. The other two initiatives are: (1) wholly and correctly implementing religious freedom policy; (2) using legal means to strengthen administration of religious affairs.

59. Hunter and Chan, *Protestantism in Contemporary China*, 49.

60. Weihong, *Christianity in China*, 1.

61. Ashiwa and Wank, "*Modern China*," 22–42.

the nature of the CCP's crusade: "the government defines what adaptation is required and by what religion, to the point that religions sometimes have to change or modify their teachings and practices to suit the political objectives of the CCP."[62] In early 1990, CCP elder statesman Chen Yun expressed concerns relating to the control of religion in a letter he wrote to former PRC President, Jiang Zemin:

> Recently I have looked at some materials concerning the increasingly serious problem of religious infiltration, especially the increasingly rampant practice of using religion as a cloak to carry out counterrevolutionary activities. I feel deeply disturbed. Using religion to win over the masses—especially young people—has always been a favourite trick of both our domestic and foreign class-enemies. This is the bitter lesson of several of the communist-led countries that recently lost power. Now is the time for Party Centre to deal vigorously with this matter. We must ensure that it cannot become a destabilising factor.[63]

Luo Weihong stresses that the CCP requires Chinese religions to reconstruct their theological views. Attempts to reach this goal involve government officials aiming at "expounding the basic belief of Christianity in light of China's situation and culture."[64] In 1998, the CCP advised Chinese Christians to renounce "conservative and negative factors,"[65] which Communist officials deemed "cynical, illiberal, irrational, and anti-humanity theological ideologies."[66] Bishop Ding Guangxun promotes one fundamental element of conflict between the independent church and the government, the State's use of the Three-Self Movement [67] and Chinese Christian counselors[68] in its quest for control.[69] Government officials specifically praised Bishop Ding for his contribution of combining "Christian belief with [the CCP's version

62. Spiegel, *China: State Control*, 8.

63. Lambert, "Present Religious Policy," 124.

64. Weihong, *Christianity in China*, 133.

65. Weihong, *Christianity in China*, 133.

66. Weihong, *Christianity in China*, 133.

67. National Committee of Three-Self. Note: the CCP established its rule in 1949, and the government positioned the Three-Self Patriotic Movement to oversee Protestant churches in China. The idea of a "three-self" church included it becoming self-supporting, self-governing, and self-propagating, analogous to church finances, administration, and evangelism, respectively.

68. Wickeri, *Reconstructing Christianity in China*. The CCC purposed to unite (Protestant) Christians and promote a self-governing, self-supporting and self-propagating church in China.

69. Lambert, *Resurrection of the Chinese Church*, 281.

of] reality to form a theory that is both rational and transcendent."[70] Ding's distinctive theology encompassed "justification by love," however, instead of "justification by faith." Bishop Ding also incorporated the Chinese "human nature is good" ideology in his thinking as well as the suggestion of God's acceptance of some CCP martyrs into heaven.

Weihong reports that the CCP considered Bishop Ding's concessions in religion to constitute part of an encouraging constructive theology.[71] This scenario reflects the way that the unofficial house church believers view most "official," seminary-trained clergy (those not a part of the genuine believing community)—as a highly politicized product of the program of adaptation.[72] The position of Xi Jinping, China's current president, further reveals the ideology of the CCP that its work should be to align the hearts and minds of citizens to the CCP. In 2015, the Associated Press reported President Xi to state, "We must manage religious affairs in accordance with the law and adhere to the principle of independence to run religious groups on our own accord. [. . .] Active efforts should be made to incorporate religions into socialist society."[73] This attempt to more completely control religion mirrors one critical point of my argument regarding the dearth of challenges to religious freedom in China.

In addition to the CCP's attempts to restructure and eliminate religion, Zhou chronicles the fact that China utilizes criminal laws to minimize religious influences on society and restrict religious freedom. For example, on 1 July 1979, the Fifth National People's Congress adopted the Criminal Law regarding religions. Article 99 of this ruling states: "Those organizing and utilizing feudal superstitious and secret societies to carry out counter-revolutionary activities will be sentenced to fixed-term imprisonment of not less than five years."[74] Document No. 19, issued on 31 March 1982, provides another illustration. In this statement of religious policy, the CCP's central committee conveyed the warning that religion must not interfere with education, marriage and family life, or politics. Figure 7 depicts the State–religion

70. Weihong, *Christianity in China*, 136–37. Accordingly, Ding's book, *Collected Works of Ding Guangxun* was distributed within the Three-Self Movement churches and seminaries as the textbook for this theological adaptation construction movement. In one article, Ding uses a rhetorical question, asking how our loving God could be so narrow-minded and intolerant such that CCP's martyred heroes, comrades Lei Feng and Zhang Side, for example, who have done so many good deeds for the people, ended up in Hell. See also Ting, *God Is Love*, 621.

71. Weihong, *Christianity in China*, 135.

72. Xinyuan, *Yi Ge Bu Xin Pai*.

73. "President Xi Jinping Warns," paras. 3–4.

74. Zhou, *Routledge International Handbook*, 78.

relationship in contemporary China which contributes to the continuing conflicts and challenges relating to religious freedom for all.[75]

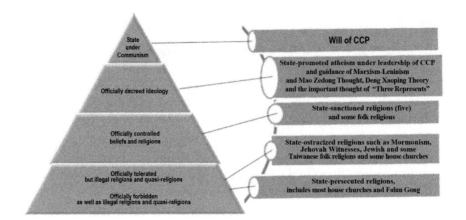

State–Religion Relationship in Contemporary Communist China

The Constitution of the People's Republic of China embraces the State's aim to focus efforts on socialist modernization by adhering to Chinese-style socialism.[76] Ultimately, the State hopes to transition China into an affluent and dominant socialist country with significant culture and democracy. Conversely, China's contemporary State–religion relationship, which aligns with CCP practices, proves counterproductive to the State's reported intents. As the CCP imposes constraints on genuine religious believers, this approach will inevitably lead to further worldview clashes. In the next section, I point out that restrictions the State imposes on religious freedom, restrictions bound by the religious policy the CCP implements, vividly affirm that policy to be unjustifiable and unsustainable.

75. Author's original figure developed and designed from research.

76. Translated in *The Constitution of the People's Republic*, Article 5: "The state upholds the uniformity and dignity of the socialist legal system. No law or administrative or local rules and regulations shall contravene the constitution. All state organs, the armed forces, all political parties and public organizations and all enterprises and undertakings must abide by the Constitution and the law. All acts in violation of the Constitution and the law must be investigated. No organization or individual may enjoy the privilege of being above the Constitution and the law."

5.3 CCP Religious Policy—Unjustifiable and Unsustainable

In Chapter 1, I noted that the CCP promotes atheism as China's dominant ideology. In addition, as noted earlier, in promoting atheism, the State's current CCP policy, which guarantees "freedom of religion" for its citizens, however, ultimately proves unjustifiable in principle. Instead of adhering to its own or international "guidelines"[77] regarding the protection of religious freedom, China consistently exerts pressure on numerous religions. During a national conference on religious affairs held 4 June 1958, Li Weihan clearly articulated the true intention of the CCP's religious policy:

> The freedom of religious belief policy is a revolutionary motto. We have adopted this motto and must enlarge its revolutionary content to end feudalism, and prevent exploiting classes from forcing others to believe in religion. If we thoroughly implement this motto, believers will gradually change from believing in religion toward non-believing. In short, the freedom of religious belief policy is our Party's basic policy towards religion. We can adopt only this policy, not any other policy.[78]

Although this source dates back almost fifty years, Yang reports that the intent of the CCP appears to be to prevent the spread of religion. In the early 1990s, in addition to attempts to decrease the influence of foreign political entities utilizing religion for their own ends, Chinese authorities increased their efforts to stop the infiltration of foreign religious organizations. Yang points out that in recent years the CCP has increasingly invested more resources into controlling religions and intensifying atheist propaganda.[79]

According to Human Rights in China (HRIC), a Chinese non-governmental organization, as of mid-2014, in direct contrast to the true intention of the CCP's religious policy as attested by Li, China has aligned with the following six UN human rights treaties, listed by order of ratification:

1. Convention on the Elimination of All Forms of Discrimination against Women.

2. International Convention on the Elimination of All Forms of Racial Discrimination;

3. Convention against Torture and Other Cruel, Inhuman or Degrading Treatment or Punishment.

---

77. Leung and Liu, *Chinese Catholic Church*, 22.
78. Weihan, "Guangyu minju gongzhuo," 520–81.
79. Yang, "Oligopoly Dynamics."

4. Convention on the Rights of the Child.

5. International Covenant on Economic, Social, and Cultural Rights.

6. Convention on the Rights of Persons with Disabilities.[80]

As of February 2016, no change of status has transpired regarding these treaties in relation to China. In addition to China's façade of allocating support for the above six UN human rights treaties, other reasons for my conviction that the CCP's religious policy model is unjustifiable in principle regarding protection of religious freedom include the following:

1. The State fails to adhere to its own or international guidelines regarding freedom of religious belief.

2. A contradiction exists between the principles of China's constitution and religious regulations, including Party- or State-issued secret documents.

3. A contradiction exists between China's signed pledges and those signed though unratified international obligations regarding human rights and religious freedom protections.

A major contradiction exists within China's constitution between the State's constitutional guarantee of freedoms and the CCP's autocracy rule, embedded in the preamble of the constitution in the rule of law or rule by law. Another contradiction is that the CCP designated certain groups as exempt from religious freedom, including members of the CCP, Communist League, and Young Pioneers, and military service personnel and civil servants. An additional contradiction is that the CCP also legitimized religious discrimination in employment by excluding nonatheistic citizens.[81]

Considering these contradictions, I question how the State's philosophy can be justifiable when it routinely and robotically contradicts itself. My rationale for arguing that the CCP's religious policy model proves unsustainable in practice regarding China protecting religious freedom includes the following reasons:

1. China currently experiences a critical dilemma regarding its inability to enforce specific laws. Although unregistered religious organizations are considered illegal in status, the State must tolerate most of these

---

80. *Human Rights in China.* "Although China signed on to the International Covenant on Civil and Political Rights (ICCPR) on October 5, 1998, it has yet to ratify it. As such, China is not yet bound to the specific provisions of the ICCPR."

81. *Human Rights Watch.*

groups because the CCP cannot jail the millions of dissidents belonging to them.

2. Conflicts of interest exist between central and local government due to tension between the central government's goal for political control and local government's desire to maintain economic development and social stability.

3. Controls on religion, such as suppressing the religious freedom of minorities, will neither protect national security nor fight religious extremism or terrorism. Instead, these efforts have proved counterproductive by further fueling and aggravating more tensions and conflict: for example, crackdowns on Tibetan faithful and Uighur Muslims,[82] accusing some of inciting rebellion and charging them on counts of separatism and terrorism. The banned Falun Gong's international fight,[83] despite a bloody crackdown by the CCP, is another counterproductive example in relation to religious freedom in China.

Considering the myriad of blatant conflicts in relation to the CCP's attempts to control religion, I question how the State's practices can be sustainable when the interpretations and enforcement of laws prove unstable as they are subject to diverse understandings by numerous officials, which in turn nullifies attempts to sustain them. I concur with Leonard Leo and Don Argue and argue that "China's policies fly in the face of abundant evidence suggesting that the way to create more peaceful, prosperous, and stable societies is not by repression, but through freedom."[84] Instead of the CCP strengthening its control of religion, I foresee the likelihood that the State will weaken its quest as it continues to deny religious freedom for its citizens. In the following sections, I further argue against the justifiability in principle and sustainability in practice of the CCP's current religious policy. The research noted earlier in this study indicates that neither the CCP's current religious model nor the designs of political liberalism or of theonomy protect religious freedom for all in China.

---

82. Wee, "U.N. Official calls China's Crackdown."

83. "China's Policies toward Spiritual."

84. Leo and Argue, *United States Commission on International Religious*, para. 8.

5.3.1 Unjustifiability in Principle of the CCP's
Religious Policy Philosophy

Communist conceptions of religions have ranged from "the opium of the people"[85] to "feudal superstition,"[86] to anti-progressive,[87] to their being the foremost obstacles to the party achieving its goal of radical reorganization. In Document No. 19[88] under the heading, "Religion as a Historical Phenomenon in The People's Republic of China,"[89] the CCP defines religion as follows:

> Religion is a historical phenomenon pertaining to a definite period in the development of human society. It has its own cycle of emergence, development, and demise. Religious faith and religious sentiment, along with religious ceremonies and organizations consonant with this faith and sentiment, are all products of the history of society. The earliest emergence of the religious mentality reflected the low level of production and the sense of awe toward natural phenomena of primitive peoples.[90]

CCP officials routinely renounce charges which condemn or challenge the CCP's religious policy and argue that the State protects religious freedom for Chinese citizens. As I recounted earlier, however, despite China's repeated claims of the State's reported policy of "freedom of religion" for its citizens, the CCP promotes atheism as China's dominant ideology while it persecutes certain religions. In addition, as the State simultaneously breaches the ICCPR, the philosophy of its religious policy proves unjustifiable. The adjective, "justifiable," indicates the condition of being "valid, legitimate, warranted, well-founded, [. . .] just, reasonable; defensible, tenable, [or] supportable."[91] I find that in the CCP's attempts to *crack down* on certain religious beliefs or groups, like Protestant house churches, Falun Gong, and Vatican-associated Catholics suspected as non-loyal to China's authoritarian control, the State's policy fails to protect religious freedom for all.[92]

85. Marx and Engels, *On Religion*, 42.

86. Ashiwa, *Modern China*, 40.

87. Larres, *Companion to Europe*.

88. State still subscribes to Document No. 19 philosophy to manage religious affairs in China.

89. Asia Watch Committee, *Freedom of Religion in China*, 44.

90. Asia Watch Committee, *Freedom of Religion in China*.

91. Lindberg, *Oxford American*, 501.

92. Armato, "Ratifying without Resolve." Although China presents itself as a benevolent State that desires to propagate human rights throughout the world, the State does not apply a number of its international human rights commitments to its domestic realm. Under President Xi Jinping, the Chinese administration abolished the

This inherent contradiction in the CCP's religious policy philosophy in that it fails to defend religious freedom implies that said policy is not justifiable, hence its unjustifiability in principle. In addition to the reasoning I present supporting the unjustifiability in principle of the CCPs religious policy, contrary to its own proclamations regarding religious freedom, the policy bans foreign missionary work. The government also refuses to recognize any religious entities that foreign administrators appoint, including the Vatican. As the State routinely declares any unregistered religious groups as illegal,[93] I contend that these practices provide even more grounds to support my argument that the CCP's religious policy philosophy proves to be inherently unjustifiable.

Eric Hyer explains that the fact that Communist Party members cannot choose a theist belief also contradicts the CCP's proclamation of freedom of religious belief. Hyer stresses that "while the constitution of the People's Republic of China recognizes the right to believe or not believe in religion, there is no provision protecting the 'free exercise of religion.'"[94] Hyer further explains that religious practice in China is governed by the 'three-self' (sanzi) regulations:

> Self-governance (no external leadership or authority is recognized), self-support (no foreign financial support is allowed) and self-propagation (proselytizing by foreigners is forbidden).

> These regulations impose restriction on Chinese religious organizations that are counter to the UN Declaration [Article 6] that calls for the freedom to "solicit and receive voluntary financial and other contribution from individuals and institutions," to "train, appoint, elect or designate [. . .] leaders called for by the requirements and standards of any religion or belief," and to "establish and maintain communications with individuals and communities in matters of religion and belief at the national and international levels."

> The "three-self" regulations are restrictions on the "free exercise of religion" and limit the interaction of China's religious communities with their co-religionists around the world.[95]

"reeducation through labor camps," where the State used inhumane and indefinite detention to punish political and religious dissidents. Basically, China has failed to honor its international commitments.

93. "President Xi urges China's religions."

94. Hyer, "Establishment and Free Exercise of Religion," 2.

95. Hyer, "The Establishment and Free Exercise of Religion," 2.

Even though the "three-self" regulations reveal the opposite to be true, Chinese authorities continue to argue that the State protects religious activity, provided the State regulates that activity and it remains within what officials decree as normal religious activity. As Stephen Uhalley Jr. points out, when the State deems an event or activity as outside the official's perceived normal range, Chinese law will fail to provide full guarantees of religious freedom.[96] I assert that the State's record of regularly persecuting persons practicing "illegal" religions, which consequently invalidates CCP claims that it defends religious freedom, reveals a fourth confirmation of the unjustifiability in principle of the philosophy sustaining the CCP's religious policy.

5.3.2 Unsustainability in Practice of the CCP's Religious Policy Philosophy

Currently, the CCP routinely utilizes authoritarian, coercive, and militaristic measures to enforce the State's religious policy. Yongnian Zheng argues that China cannot effectively sustain these types of tactics long term. This lends support to my first point regarding the unsustainability in practice of the CCP's religious policy model. According to Zheng, "With growing foreign interests, global capitalism has an increasingly great incentive to push the transformation of the CCP and to lead the CCP in a 'right direction.' A new system which can guarantee the rule of law and protect human rights will be more sustainable and effective."[97] John P. Synott explains that something being sustained embraces the understanding that the entity can be upheld, kept alive, kept from falling apart, and that it will hold because of having a sound base.[98] Despite not being sustainable, some of the CCP's public statements regarding freedom of religious belief appear promising, such as the following, recorded in Document No. 19:[99]

> What do we mean by freedom of religious belief? We mean that every citizen has the freedom to believe in religion and also the freedom not to believe in religion. S/he has also the freedom to believe in this religion or that religion. Within a particular religion, s/he has the freedom to believe in this sect[—]or that sect. A person who was previously a non-believer has the freedom to

---

96. Uhalley Jr., *China and Christianity Burdened Past*, 3–10.

97. Zheng, *Power and Sustainability*, 206.

98. Synott, *Global and International Studies*, 34.

99. Yang, "Research Agenda on Religious," 6–17.

become a religious believer, and one who has been a religious believer has the freedom to become a non-believer.[100]

Even though the words in Document No. 19 appear to align with the international norms recorded in UN treaties, they do not clearly specify religious practice and organization. David Little points out that some suggest discrimination is not a particularly serious form of "religious persecution."[101] Nevertheless, an abundance of evidence confirms that certain discriminatory practices, particularly those that affect a person's right to support him/herself and his/her family adversely affect an individual. Yang contends that contrary to freedom of religious beliefs, "the CCP members must be atheists and unremittingly propagate atheism. In other words, the CCP members are excluded from holding this constitutional right of PRC citizens and must be committed to atheism."[102] Throughout China, citizens who aspire to gain a position in leadership or hold a position in public service have to denounce religion and profess atheism.[103] Although this stipulation proves impossible for the State to enforce,[104] I contend that the fact that the CCP mandates atheism for Chinese citizens who serve in particular positions shows its base to be unsound and reflects my second point, which argues that the CCP's stated religious policy proves unsustainable in practice.

Vivienne Shue's argument mirrors the third reason I offer for the unsustainability of the CCP's religious policy model in practice, that the CCP perceives diverse religious practices and demonstrations of religious beliefs as serious threats to the Chinese regime. The CCP's perceptions evoke State repression of certain religions as well as persecution of individuals charged with illegal practices.[105] The logic of the State's legitimation routinely transforms most popular religions into a challenge to the CCP's authority. In turn, this continues to perpetuate a cycle of religions challenging the State and the State in turn repressing them. Shue points out that despite religions challenging the State's repression, only a negligible number of protests relating to CCP practices have occurred. There have been "no major social movements, no sustained movement of popular opposition from workers, migrants, poor farmers, women, students,

---

100. Yang, "Research Agenda on Religious," 7.

101. Little, *Protecting the Human Rights*, 33–57.

102. Yang, "Research Agenda on Religious," 7.

103. "Religion Ban for China Communist Party Ex-officials."

104. Yang notes that the Chinese Spiritual Life Survey in 2007 reveals that approximately 84 percent of CCP members and 85 percent of the public reported they hold some religious beliefs and/or participate in some religious practices.

105. Shue, "Legitimacy Crisis," 24–49.

intellectuals, ethnic minorities, or environmentalists. No opposition movement, that is, until [. . .] Falun Gong."[106]

Although individuals and religious groups with grievances against the Party remain voiceless and subject not only to prosecution but persecution by the State, "the mutual religious stimulation that results from congregational worship, using the particular rites and practices of each religion"[107] stimulates empathetic feelings that unite diverse religious individuals with each other. As religious followers meet regularly, they strengthen each other's faith and, in time, will likely gain a stronger voice to support my fourth stance regarding the unsustainability in practice of the CCP's religious policy method—the CCP cannot physically control millions of religious adherents.

Li claims that in the midst of China's dilemmas relating to religious freedom that have contributed to international concerns, the State would do well to consider permitting more freedom of religious beliefs.[108] Li also contends that authorities should consider practices that Freedom House, an international human rights organization, has suggested.[109] These include opening conduits such as public hearings and town meetings that would permit Buddhists, Catholics, Muslims, Protestants, and other religious adherents to express their concerns and offer suggestions. I agree with Li that this State effort could help ease some of the tension and contribute to cultivating a sense of harmony between the State and religious groups. I also agree with Yang as he argues that contemporary globalizing works to counter the CCP's quest to eradicate religions in China and asserts that heavy State regulation cannot exterminate religion.[110] I contend that the efficacy of State power in the types of tactics which the CCP currently implements to fight against religious freedom will ultimately fail as religious groups and believers continue to challenge the CCP's contemporary religious policy, ultimately realizing its unsustainability in practice.Many CCP officials reportedly believe that international subversive forces employ religion to "Westernize" and "divide" China. As Beatrice Leung explains, "The CCP believe that through the pluralization of religious questions, 'dark forces' could be trying to politically pluralize China as a means of subversion."[111] This erroneous perception leads to convictions contrary to research that

---

106. Shue, "Legitimacy Crisis," 25.

107. *Religion under Socialism*, 107.

108. Li, *Civil Liberties*.

109. Li, *Civil Liberties*.

110. Yang, *Religion in Chinese Society*.

111. Leung, *China and Christianity: Burdened*, 307.

supports the premise that religious freedom promotes more positive relationships between the State and citizens.[112]

Chris Seiple and Dennis R. Hoover argue that religious freedom significantly contributes to positive social outcomes. Seiple and Hoover stress that this human freedom energizes religious groups to increase their participation in civil society. Religious freedom may also help reduce conflicts in society, may lessen grievances that religious groups hold toward governments and other citizens, and may ultimately enhance State security.[113] Despite the CCP's misguided concerns and ensuing efforts relating to religions and religious freedom, statistics reveal a revival of diverse religions in China. In turn, this trend complements religious pluralism, one critical condition for my *Baorong Duoyuan* model. Nevertheless, the tyrannical rule of one party, the CCP, clearly controverts another general condition for *BD*, democracy with government rule determined by free elections. In the next section, I assert that the potential for *BD* as a viable option to protect religious freedom for all in China will likely emerge during the foreseeable future.

5.4 Pluralism and Constitutional Democracy: Potential for *BD*

In addition to arguing against the justifiability and sustainability of the CCP's current religious policy, research noted in this study indicates that neither the CCP's current religious model, nor that of political liberalism or theonomy can protect religious freedom for all in China. The following summarizes five defects in the Chinese current system relating to the principles of religious freedom that principled pluralism endorses and enshrined by international norms as noted in Chapter 2.

1. China permits only a limited freedom for its citizens to exercise "the freedom of religious belief" and only a limited number of these individuals may gather and worship in government-approved religions. Members of the CCP, Communist League, and Young Pioneers, and military service personnel and civil servants are forbidden to have freedom of religious belief or to change their belief. These citizens are permitted to believe only in atheism. Moreover, as I mentioned in the previous sections in this chapter, certain religions, quasi-religions, and folk religions or beliefs, which are designated as "evil cults" as I noted earlier, including Falun Gong's spiritual movement and

---

112. Seiple and Hoover, *Future of Religious Freedom*, 315–30.

113. Seiple and Hoover, *Future of Religious Freedom*, 325.

other groups, are totally banned and no citizen may legally believe in them.[114] Members of these groups are subject to severe legal prosecution and persecution.

2. No Chinese citizen has the true freedom to manifest his/her religious belief in any public setting, either as an individual or in a community setting with others. Only certain aspects of government-approved patriotic religions are allowed to be practiced in government-designated venues and they must be administered by government-certified clergy in government-designated areas at State-designated times.

3. Government-approved patriotic religious organizations are fully controlled and partially managed by the Communist Party and its government agencies. Approved religious personnel are also strictly controlled by the relevant agencies of the atheistic CCP and the government.

4. Religious citizens do not have the freedom to participate in political affairs, such as essential public policy making. Neither can they actively engage in some public services, nor can they act freely according to their religious convictions.

5. Some religious education may be tolerated locally and practiced privately but, in general, no religious education is allowed in any public or private education system. As prescribed by law, in the name of the non-interference of China's education sector, the CCP enforces the ban of religious education.

These five major defects demonstrate either a great violation of or major contradiction to religious freedom and further confirm the need for *Baorong Duoyuan* for a pluralistic, Christianized, democratized future China. In lieu of the development of *BD*, however, I contend that principled pluralism currently constitutes the best option for protecting religious freedom in Western democratic societies. As I expounded in Chapter 2, principled pluralism grew out of a historically Christian-orientated culture in the Netherlands, where a social and cultural pluralist society under a democratic, constitutional government had evolved. Therefore, as I mentioned in previous chapters, principled pluralism, due to its inherent Christian heritage that is explicitly noted in the constitution of the Netherlands, China, both currently and in its foreseeable future,[115] would likely reject principled

---

114. Fullerton, "China Bans Religion for Communists," para. 1 in Introduction. "China's estimated 85 million members of the Communist Party have been warned that they are not allowed to have religious beliefs, and that those who do will be punished."

115. Hertzke, "*Future of Religious Freedom: Global*," 3–30.

pluralism in its basic format as an option for the State's constitutional foundation. Furthermore, due to this theory's inherent Christian heritage, explicitly noted in the constitution of the Netherlands, China would likely reject principled pluralism in its basic format as an option for the State's constitutional foundation. If my proposition that principled pluralism in its generic format will fail to meet Chinese acceptance proves true even with China's increasing Christianization, then the ensuing dilemma arises to determine what theory could best potentially meet China's demonstrated need for remediation of the CCP's philosophy and practices regarding religious freedom. Consequently, this deficiency gives me the opportunity to present the potential for my contextualized model of principled pluralism for China, *Baorong Duoyuan*. In an increasing pluralistic society in China, with hundreds of worldviews and religions flourishing and competing, I propose that *Baorong Duoyuan* would prove to be the best option for protecting religious freedom for all in China. The concept of religious freedom, which I allude to throughout this study, does not only refer to freedom for the numerous recognized religions, it also includes protection for atheists, secularists, agnostics, and even non-religious people, as well as anti-religious individuals and groups. The scope of religious freedom under *Baorong Duoyuan* applies to citizens both in their individual roles and in the community with others,[116] not only to ensure the freedom of religious belief in private but to also extend that freedom to include the practice and manifestation of a person's belief publicly.

In developing the name for the theory which this study presents, *Baorong Duoyuan*, I considered a line from a Chinese poem.[117] This line— "Let a hundred flowers blossom and a hundred schools of thought [resonate . . .]"[118]—reflects the ancient adage of "contending of a hundred schools of philosophy" in the Warring States period (ca. 476–221 BC).[119] Each word in this line carries a rich meaning. Hang-li Zeng maintains that Chinese poetry encompasses "beauty in three aspects," and that in translating Chinese poetry into English, translators should attempt to retain the original beauty of the poem in meaning, sound and form.[120] Translating *Baihua Qifang*

---

116. Redekop, *Enlightenment and Community*, 223. This contrasts with the Enlightenment.

117. Wu, "Chinese Poetry." Although poetry does not merit a serious status in the West, particularly in the last two hundred years, in China, as Chinese ancient poetry holds a prominent place of respect, citizens honor ancient Chinese poets and still read poetry regularly.

118. "Roots of Chinese," paras. 2–3.

119. Yu, "Politics and Theatre in the PRC," 90–121.

120. Zeng, "Brief Analysis of the Classical Poetry," 52–58. Zeng stresses that of the

(百花齐放), the word Bai translates to "one hundred," Hua to "flower," and Fang to "bloom." In this context, based on equality, one hundred flowers blossom simultaneously. The Chinese poem with the first line, "Let a hundred schools of thought contend" marked the start of the Hundred Flowers Movement, a brief political campaign in which Mao Zedong deceived citizens with reassurances that they could freely speak to prompt them to verbalize their thoughts. This ploy concluded, however, with Mao betraying the principle of equal voices in the public realm.[121] Contrary to Mao, "All of the Hundred Schools arose in response to practical conditions [sixth–third century BCE]. Their philosophers were either government officials or scholars, traveling from one feudal state to another and offering ideas for social reform."[122] My rationale for the reasoning of one hundred flowers blossoming diametrically opposes Mao's devious intent. *Baorong Duoyuan* advocates for the principle of equal voices in the public square. In the next section, as I examine the basic conditions necessary for *Baorong Duoyuan* pluralism and democracy—I note signs appearing to indicate that in the future, China may be transitioning toward being open to *Baorong Duoyuan*.

5.4.1 The General Conditions for *Baorong Duoyuan*

The CCP's existing practices conflict with two critical components necessary for *Baorong Duoyuan*: (1) the protection of normative directional pluralism; and (2) participatory democracy. Until these dual elements materialize in China, the CCP's practices will continue to sabotage religious freedom for all and prohibit full liberty of individual opinions and voices. As China does not profess either directional pluralism or participatory democracy at this point, and as *Baorong Duoyuan* requires intangible yet critical entities, the control of the CCP mirrors the reality that the Party's leaders would currently negate any consideration of *Baorong Duoyuan*. Nevertheless, the next section reveals that even though the Chinese government continues to reject free elections, which is a requirement for democracy,[123] and despite

---

three aspects regarding Chinese poetry, beauty in meaning, beauty in sound, and beauty in form, beauty in meaning proves most significant. Beauty in sound retains second place in terms of significance, with beauty in form in the third position. Zeng maintains that translators should attempt to reproduce the three beauties simultaneously. In addition to meaning and sound, translators should consider the original rhythm of the poem.

121. King, "Silence that Preceded China's."

122. "Roots of Chinese," paras 2–3.

123. Zhou, "Role of Chinese Christianity, 117–36.

China not yet displaying sufficient pluralization,[124] the citizenry landscape of China appears to reflect some signs of transforming to match the likely conditions for this criterion. The rapid associational and directional religious pluralism along with the projected process of Christianization which potentially leads to Chinese democratization will provide a solid foundation for *Baorong Duoyuan* to be implemented. China, like many countries, has never experienced true diversity of religions, or pluralism, but has sustained religious oligopoly. "In religious oligopoly, the State allows more than one religion to operate legally, but other religions are banned and subject to repression."[125] Yang reports that approximately 20 percent [126] of the 195 independent states[127] in the world qualify as pluralistic, with a few more countries ranking as monopolistic. "The majority of the countries, almost 58 percent, such as China are more or less oligopolistic. [. . .] This global fact of religious oligopoly makes it necessary to rethink and reconstruct theories of church-State [State–religion] relations and religious change within society."[128] Amid ongoing debates about religious pluralism, Yang identifies a group of three words related with the same root (plur-)—*plurality*, *pluralization*, and *pluralism*—to expand on the concept of pluralism which I introduced in Chapter 2 of this study:

- Plurality (diversity) describes the *status* or *degree* of religious heterogeneity within a society.

- Pluralization is the *process* of increasing plurality within a society.

- Pluralism refers to the *social arrangements* favorable to a high or increased level of plurality.[129]

Even though the CCP permits multiple religions to operate, as noted earlier, the State maintains rigid, restrictive regulations on religions and suppresses unorthodox or factional religious movements. Albert points out that even amid reports of some progress related to freedom for Chinese citizens, the CCP increasingly appears to promote Chinese faiths and ideologies, like Confucianism and Buddhism, while State officials also pressure unregistered Christian believers and organizations to convert to the beliefs and practices

---

124. Zhou, "Role of Chinese Christianity."

125. Yang, *Religion in Chinese Society*, 168.

126. Yang, *Religion in Chinese Society*, 166.

127. "Independent States in World."

128. Yang, *Religion in Chinese Society*, 166.

129. Yang, *Religion in Chinese Society*, 168.

of officially recognized religious bodies.[130] According to Yang, the CCP not only promotes the beliefs and practices of China's preferred religions and pressures citizens to conform to them, the State also employs marketization of some of the religions it controls. For example, this State ploy, such as initiated in Beijing, experiences success evolving from the leader's personal skills in marketing his "brand" of Buddhism.[131] Nevertheless, this promotional practice does not constitute pluralization.

Yang notes that a State's legal structure or the absence of it appears to constitute a critical component of whether a State is pluralistic. To implement and maintain a successful pluralistic legal structure that legitimizes religious freedom and complements plurality, the following two considerations must be met:

1. intellectual understanding and a level of social consensus that legitimizes and justifies both an individual freedom of religion and group equality of religions;

2. civic organizations in the civil society that keep in check and balance the State agencies and religious organizations.[132]

Richard Weitz points out that even though the Chinese political system has undergone progress in becoming more democratic, the State still imposes severe restrictions to minimize political pluralism.[133] Pluralism,[134] which I examined in Chapter 2, differs from political pluralism as the latter promotes liberty as the most vital political value. Citizens best attain political pluralism when the State's power is not concentrated at one point as in China but dispersed and distributed. Chinese citizens do not have political pluralism, yet in the sense that they can sometimes verbalize their discontent, although infrequently, with local policies without being punished, they have reportedly experienced some minimal improvements in their rights. Weitz reports, however, that the Chinese government "continues to deny Chinese citizens basic civil and political rights such as the ability to vote in free and fair elections or avoid arbitrary and excessive punishment at the

130. Albert, "Christianity in China," para. 2 in "Chinese Buddhism and Folk Religions" section.

131. Beckford and Demerath, *SAGE Handbook of the Sociology*, 631–34. Government leaders recognize that marketing State-controlled brands of religion that have the support of wealthy overseas supporters as well as, critically, the backing of political authorities, enhances a community's potential to generate economic wealth from tourism and the "heritage" business.

132. Yang, *Religion in Chinese Society*, 68.

133. Wissenburg, *Political Pluralism and the State*, 38.

134. Wattles, "What is Pluralism?" para. 1 in introduction.

hands of abusive public officials."[135] In turn, this prevents China from moving into the democratic mainstream.[136]

In a society qualifying as a part of the democratic mainstream, one that has diverse cultures and groups, that society will less likely show preference for one group over another. Regarding a society's development, Han Zhu contends pluralism symbolizes the fact that considerable progress has occurred and argues, "On the surface, a pluralistic society appears noisy and restless and without consensus. However, such a society will reach a final dynamic balance through its contradictions and in the end, a society full of different views and opinions."[137] I agree with Zhu's summarization that a pluralistic society proves to be healthier and safer than an oligopolistic State like China, intent on leaning only toward and recognizing one side—atheism.

Albert notes that, in some ways, the development of pluralism, particularly directional pluralism, one critical condition for religious freedom, a stipulation that I perceive as mandatory for *Baorong Duoyuan*, appears promising in China. Despite its dictatorship during the past thirty-plus years, since China has started to cautiously open up to the outside world, the State is reportedly transitioning into a more pluralistic society.[138] While some in China strive for pluralism, however, others try to resist or sabotage it.[139] The separation of church and State, an innovation which the United States initially experimented with, mirrors one significant trigger for pluralization. Nevertheless, Yang's study of the development of pluralism in the United States as an example confirms that if pluralization proves to constitute the general trend of development in China, over time, it will win over the resistance. For the general conditions in China to be suitable for the potential of *Baorong Duoyuan* to be apparent, however, China must not only be in the process of becoming but *be* pluralistic. In the next section, as I examine religious pluralization in China, I note how the State's strict regulations regarding religion created the black, red, and gray markets in religion.

Part of directional pluralism encompasses the flourishing of diverse religious worldviews. Yang contends that, ironically, the CCP desires to suppress religion, and the State's strategies to impose strict regulations regarding religious freedom have contributed to unique classifications in

---

135. Weitz, *Global Security Watch*, 6.

136. Weitz, *Global Security Watch*, 6.

137. Zhu, "China's Pluralistic Revolution," para. 4 in "Resolving *revolutionary ire*," section.

138. Albert, "Christianity in China."

139. Yang, *Religion in Chinese Society*.

China's religious market. The restrictions have unexpectedly created three different colored markets in the State's religious system: black, red, and gray. Yang explains:

- A red market of religion includes the five legal religions which the CCP approves: Buddhism, Catholicism, Taoism (also Daoism), Islam, and Protestantism under the label of patriotic associations. The red market also consists of religious activities, believers, and organizations. Yang notes, "Alternatively, this may be called the "open market," because the religious exchanges are carried out openly."[140]

- Certain religions that the State banned created a black market and these operate in secret or underground. Although illegal, the black market of religion, which the State officially banned, includes religious activities, believers, and religious organizations.[141]

- The gray market consists of legally ambiguous groups and activities. Yang explains that "A gray market of religion consists of all religious and spiritual organizations, practitioners, and activities with ambiguous legal status. They can be perceived as both legal and illegal or neither legal nor illegal."[142]

Yang stresses that the gray market, which proves difficult to identify, includes:

1. illegal religious activities which legal religious groups practice; and

2. religious or spiritual practices that individuals or groups do not manifest in religion but in culture or science.[143]

Ironically, according to Yang, when the State's regulations regarding religion become more restrictive and suppressive, the gray market grows larger. "When religious needs cannot be met in the open, red market, and the risks are too high in the illegal, black market, many people would seek what they need in the gray market."[144]

Amy Patterson Neubert notes that two examples of the gray market include: (1) when a State-approved religion distributes pamphlets outside a church or temple, or (2) when individuals practice spiritual beliefs that originate from non-religious sources. "For example, *qigong*, which is a series of

140. Yang, *Religion in Chinese Society*, 86.

141. Yang, *Religion in Chinese Society*.

142. Yang, *Religion in Chinese Society*, 87.

143. Yang, *Religion in Chinese Society*.

144. Yang, *Religion in Chinese Society*, 89.

breathing techniques and exercises rooted in health, has followers that connect it to Buddhism and Taoism and, therefore, add a religious dimension. Another example is a Christian church offering Sunday school to children."[145] Historically, even if the religion merits legal status, the CCP regards teaching religion to children as constituting an illegal practice.

In 2007, regardless of the CCP's constraints on religions, China reports that several tens of millions of individuals profess Buddhism, five million citizens profess Catholicism, approximately 10 million people claim Taoism, 21 million individuals profess Islam, and 23 million people profess Protestantism.[146] Yang contends that these numbers prove to be greater and notes that one recent survey reveals that approximately 85 percent of Chinese admit to either practicing certain religious rituals or have some supernatural beliefs.[147] The CCP's efforts to regulate religions will not reduce religion or religious practices, he stresses but ,instead, will create the triple religious market. According to Yang, "If 85 percent of the Chinese population is at least open toward supernatural beliefs or participating in religious practices, but only small minorities have been recruited into either the government-approved religions or the underground ones, there exists a huge gray market with hundreds of millions of potential religious consumers."[148] Chinese citizens may not formally participate in religious organizations so openly when the State imposes militaristic regulations; nevertheless, they will engage in other forms of religiosity which will not only persist but likely increase.

Yang agrees that the ambiguous nature of a gray market in a severely regulated society like China will potentially contribute to a section of that society whose members will increase in number. These characteristics counter the intent of the CCP and make their goal to regulate religions impossible to achieve.[149] Amid the CCP's losing battle to annihilate religions, I note that although religious adherents regularly experience persecution, their increasing number will further religious pluralism in Chinese society. As I consider this possibility in the next section, I also examine David Aikman's prediction that as China progresses in becoming Christianized, in time, it will become known more as a Christian than an atheistic State.[150]

145. Neubert, "Prof: Religious trends in China," para. 8.

146. Neubert, "Prof: Religious trends in China."

147. Yang, *Religion in Chinese Society*.

148. Yang, *Religion in Chinese Society*, 120.

149. Yang, *Religion in Chinese Society*, 92.

150. Aikman, *Jesus in Beijing*.

5.4.2 China Projected to Become a "Christian(ized)" Democracy

He Guanghu suggests that some of the CCP's negative attitudes toward religion may be slowly yielding to more positive ones as the Party has recognized the trend of religious pluralism occurring in China. In his speech to the Party's Seventeenth National Congress, CCP General Secretary Hu Jintao similarly indicated this potential when he stated: "We should draw upon the positive contributions of religious believers and leaders in the development of the economy and society as a whole."[151] Although some contend that Jintao's statement generally reflects a manifestation of a shift in the Party's policy toward religion, I agree with Guanghu that it simultaneously further validates the intricate relationship between religious studies and China's social development.[152]

Although research has only recently begun to measure and report the impact that Christianity has exerted on China and projects for future decades, Yang foresees the Christianization of China as inevitable. According to Nora Berend, the meaning for the "Christianization" of a State[153] can range from the acceptance of Christianity to the practice of the religion to a myriad of implications, interpretations, and inferences. For the purposes of this study, Christianization relates to Aikman's prediction that Christians will eventually total at least 20 percent of China's population.[154] In the China that Aikman envisions, the State emerges with Christianity as a primary worldview, depicting an international superpower. As it achieves Christianization, Aikman foresees China investing efforts to provide an environment that supports rather than seeks to eradicate religious freedom for its citizens.[155]

Contrary to reports noted earlier in this study regarding the rise of secular humanism and the demise of religions, two major religions, Islam and Christianity, are the fastest-growing contemporary worldviews.[156] Both Yang and Aikman foresee this transformation and point out that:

- between 1950 and 2010, the number of Christians in China increased from 4 million to 67 million;

- by 2030, China is projected to have some 225 million Protestant Christians, a figure similar to the entire Christian population today in the United States;

151. Jintao, "Full Text of Hu Jintao's Report."
152. Guanghu, *Social Scientific Studies of Religion*, 23–46.
153. Berend, *Christianization and the Rise*, 1–46.
154. Aikman, *Jesus in Beijing*, front matter.
155. Jintao, "Full text of Hu Jintao's report."
156. Volf, *Democracy and the New*, 271–82.

- the experience of Christians in South Korea and the United States indicates that it is reasonable to expect the growth will continue at least until it reaches 30 percent of a population projected to reach 1.4 billion in the next 15 years.[157]

Figure 8 reflects the increasing number of Christians in China from 1900.

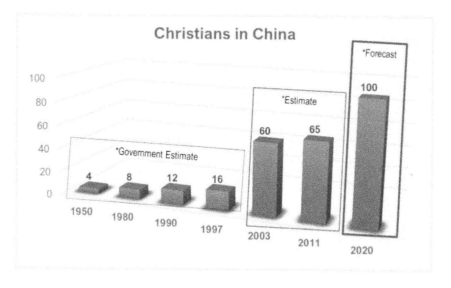

Increasing Number of Christians in China

In agreement with Yang and Aikman, Bryne contends that in the future, China will become Christianized in the sense that its base of Christians will dramatically increase. Likewise, Yang and Volf project that future conditions appear encouraging for the continuing development of a social background in China that is favorable for the State to increase its Christian base, I surmise, as Aikman, that if the Christian worldview does dominate China's political and cultural realms, then the democratization process will conceivably occur. A democratic China with a prevalent Christian base will more likely embrace the potential for the application of *Baorong Duoyuan*, a contextualization of principled pluralism. In the next section, as I examine the potential for China to become a democracy amid and despite ongoing religious persecution, we shall see that a close correlation exists between Christianization and the democratization of a State.

Several authoritarian and totalitarian governments, including the CCP in China, have routinely opposed Protestantism and the prospect of

157. Yang, "Other Chinese Miracle," para. 7 in introductory section.

democracy for the State. Contrary to the contention of Zeng Chuanhui who perceives Protestantism to only constitute a noticeably irrelevant religion in China,[158] G. Wright Doyle argues that Protestantism's "history; indigenous leadership; contextualized literature; rapid growth; geographical distribution; numerical strength; social impact; self-propagation; and official status"[159] confirm that Protestantism constitutes a primary Chinese religion. Doyle also stresses that China's formal recognition by the government of Protestantism as one of five State-approved religions affirms its status.

Yang reports that according to the 2007 Chinese Spiritual Life Survey, 85 percent of China's population were affiliated with some type of religious practice and belief. Many of these individuals practice various folk religions while the survey identified approximately 18 percent as Buddhists. Although it is difficult to determine definite numbers due to CCP penalties for religious membership, research confirms estimates that reveal each year since 1980 Christians have experienced more than 10 percent compounded growth. With Christians currently experiencing the most significant growth, they currently comprise between 5–10 percent of the population.[160]

The Christian Institute reports that Christianity may even be spreading and infiltrating the CCP.[161] As Christians engage more actively in society, instead of hiding, government officials reveal concerns that the increased visible presence of Christianity will affect loyalty to the State. Rodney Stark concludes that in addition to the significant contemporary and predicted increases in Christianity, research reveals an extensive awakening for numerous other religions. Stark asserts, "Buddhism and folk temples seem to be thriving. As for Christianity, even if we ignore the plethora of wildly exaggerated membership claims, the conversion of between 36 to 72 million Chinese is truly remarkable in so short a time."[162] The growth of Christianity has not only included the deprived Chinese, many of the affluent members of Chinese society, including key members of the CCP,[163] have professed Christianity.

Albert notes that China has experienced a significant growth in Christianity since the 1980s and reports:

> There are three state-regulated Christian organizations and many underground house churches which range in size from

158. Chuanhui, "Coalition and Hegemony," 759–82.

159. Doyle, "Culture and Religion," para. 5 in introductory section.

160. Yang, "The other Chinese miracle."

161. China Bans Religious Beliefs," para. 5.

162. Stark "Religious Awakening in China," 282–89.

163 Aikman, *Jesus in Beijing*, front matter.

small to large ceremonies in unidentified churches. In 2010, the Pew Research Center estimated that there were sixty-seven million Christians in China, roughly five percent of the total population. Of these, Pew estimated that fifty-eight million were Protestant, including both state-sanctioned and independent churches. The Beijing-based Chinese Academy of Social Science's estimate is far smaller, tallying twenty-nine million Christian believers.[164]

Consequently, the growth and condition of contemporary Chinese Christianity leads Aikman to contend that Christianity may successfully permeate national life and culture within future decades in China. Yang reports that Aikman qualifies his prediction regarding China being in the process of becoming Christianized, explaining that he [Aikman] does not foresee all Chinese, or even the majority becoming Christians. According to Aikman, "with the present rate of growth in the number of Christians in the countryside, in the cities, and especially within China's social and cultural circles, it is possible that Christians will constitute 20 to 30 percent of China's population within three decades."[165]

Philip Jenkins further confirms that Christians hold a pivotal role in China and that combined results from the Templeton and Pew materials support the concept of the Christianization of China. In 2011, Jenkins reports that the number of Chinese Christians in China totaled approximately 65 to 70 million, nearly 5 percent of the State's population. Despite the unassuming number, "Those 65 or 70 million Christians outnumber the population of major nations like France, Britain, or Italy and the level of Christian commitment is awe-inspiring."[166] Jenkins foresees Christianity experiencing a phenomenal worldwide boom in the future.[167] The Christian Institute similarly reports that "Chinese officials say that there are between 23 and 40 million Christians in the country. However, other estimates indicate that there are between 60 and 120 million believers."[168] Despite State oppression and persecution, the increasing number of Christians may exceed the number of CCP members.[169]

Albert argues that with the number of Christian believers significantly increasing, the religious revival that has appeared to be in progress in China

---

164. Albert, *Christianity in China*, para. 1 in "Christian State-Sanctioned," section.
165. Aikman, *Jesus in Beijing*, front matter.
166. Jenkins, *Next Christendom*, 88.
167. Jenkins, "Believing in the Gospel."
168. "China: Christians more public." para. 3 in introductory section.
169. Jenkins, *Next Christendom*.

over the past four decades[170] confirms that a Christianized China seems inevitable. Some estimate that by 2030, China may have the world's largest population of Christians.[171] I anticipate that, ultimately, as the number of Chinese Christians increases, lives changed for the better will confirm the difference religion makes. The Christianization of China will help transform the country into a civil society which embraces associational, contextual, and directional pluralisms and which fosters respect for the rule of law and the cherishing of fundamental freedoms, including religious freedom, essentially advancing democratic values. In turn, this transition, the democratization of China, as the next section further reveals, will provide fertile ground for China to implement *Baorong Duoyuan*.

Although the relationship between religion and democracy appears ambiguous,[172] nevertheless, the intimate relationship between Christianity, particularly Protestantism, and modern democracy proves less disputable among scholars. Steve Bruce concludes: "Protestantism has been causally implicated in the development of democratic polities and civil liberties and in many particulars the causal connection is the unintended consequence."[173] Samuel P. Huntington also notes the existence of a continuing relationship between democracy and Protestantism in which the latter offers a certain doctrinal and institutional foundation to oppose political repression.[174]

Protestant Reformers, such as John Calvin, Martin Luther, and John Knox, as well as the Puritans in England, and their views on the nature of the State–church relationship during the Reformation and afterward, have been credited with the establishment of the beginning of constitutional democracies in both Western Europe and the American colonies. Calvin as well as others held the "view that both church and state are directly ordained by God with neither subordinate to the other and neither entitled to control the other."[175] Because both State and church are ultimately responsible to the authority of God's transcendent law, the Reformers leave room for citizens to resist tyranny when a civil government violates God's law. After surveying five governments, Calvin's Geneva, Huguenot France, Knox's Scotland, Puritan England and Colonial America, from

170. Albert, "Christianity in China."

171. Albert, "Christianity in China."

172 Anderson, "Introduction: Religion, Democracy," 1–2.

173. Bruce, "Did Protestantism Create Democracy," 3–20. Anthony Gill asserts that although this premise tends to positively link to Europe and the U.S., it did not prove universally true in a study involving Latin American Protestants. See Gill "Weber in Latin America," 42–65.

174. Huntington, *Third Wave: Democratization.*

175. Kelly, *Emergence of Liberty*, 139.

the sixteenth through the eighteenth centuries, regarding the emergence of liberty in the modern world, Douglas K. Kelly notes the influence of Calvin and Calvinism. Kelly credits Protestantism, particularly the Calvinist branch, with playing an instrumental role in the establishment of constitutional democratic governments:

> The American system drew from [. . . the Protestant Calvinist] view [which] contributed much to the American establishment of consent of the governed, covenant or constitutional limitations of all civil power and all institutions, being seen in terms of God's transcendent law, checks and balances of power in the political and legal structure, liberty of conscience, and the inalienable right to resist tyranny, no matter how powerful or legal its pretensions.[176]

The question arises regarding the relationship between Christianization and democratization in China's context. To what extent could the increasing Christianization of China, even under the current Communist regime, accelerate its democratization? Huntington quotes "a 1960s study which suggested that in 91 countries [. . .], the greater the proportion of Protestants the higher the level of democracy."[177] Due to the relatively small percentage of the Christian population in China and the Chinese government's restrictions on Christians public participation, however, some scholars, including Chuanhui, appear to dismiss the possibility that a relationship between Protestant Christianity and democracy exists. Others, like Bruce, argue, however, that Protestantism proves pertinent to democracy in China. From both theological and historical points of views, at a minimum, there is a correlation between the two. This suggests that the Christianization of China might well lead to a process of democratization. Christianization can help lead China to become a democracy. Alec Ryrie asserts that as the current minority of Chinese Protestantism increases in number, they will become more visible and contribute to China transitioning into a democracy. According to Ryrie:

> Post-Mao Chinese Protestantism, for all its growth, [has] remained remarkably invisible. Before 1949, a far smaller Protestant population had a much higher profile. Until recently, religious communities were entirely excluded from the public square, and even TSPM churches were discreet or entirely unseen. Yet growing numbers and confidence have made the invisibility trick harder and less urgent. Since 2000, the old

176. Kelly, *Emergence of Liberty*, 141.

177. Anderson, *Religion, Democracy and Democratization*, 192–218.

dream of "Back to Jerusalem" has resurfaced, and unregistered churches have begun trying to carry the Gospel into China's western provinces. The change became unmistakable after an earthquake struck Sichuan province on May 12, 2008, killing more than eighty thousand people. In the chaotic aftermath, many of the first responders came from churches and made no secret of the fact. Since then, Chinese Protestants have become increasingly prominent in human rights campaigning. Rumor has it that a third or more of China's embattled human rights lawyers are now Protestants.[178]

Aikman contends that China is currently "in the process of becoming Christianized"[179] and stresses that Chinese democratization will not occur without Chinese Christianization. He insists that the Christian movement constitutes part of political liberalization,[180] just as Albert points out, even under the current oppressive environment. With the increase in the number of Christian human rights advocates and lawyers, some party members have expressed concerns that Christianity could serve as a tool to influence China and constitute a unifying force to challenge the CCP's authority.

Yuan Zhiming, an atheist for thirty-six years who became a Chinese filmmaker and Christian activist, explains that the democratization of a State depicts a movement with the principal goal of attaining majority rule with popular free and fair elections.[181] In an interview with Ian Johnson, Zhiming said, "If just 25 percent of Chinese became Christians, then China would be really different. The spirit of communism would be broken."[182] Zhiming additionally contends that a State cannot have human rights or democracy without Christianity[183] and that democracy "is not merely an institution nor simply a concept, but a profound structure of faith. [. . .] The root of democracy is the spirit of Christ."[184] Although Zhiming concurs with Aikman's prediction for the Christianization of China, Aikman ponders the potential for China to implement a viable democracy if the State continues to experience massive corruption, a major concern regarding the CCP.

---

178. Ryrie, *Protestants: Faith*, 423.

179. Aikman, *Jesus in Beijing*, 286.

180. Aikman, *Jesus in Beijing*, front matter.

181. Mok, *Intellectuals and the State*, 190.

182. Johnson, "Jesus vs. Mao?"

183. Aikman, *Jesus in Beijing*.

184. Aikman, *Jesus in Beijing*, 246–47.

Nevertheless, Aikman agrees with Zhiming that for its basic health, China must ultimately become democratic.[185]

Cheng Li asserts that under the communist regime China's transition to democracy (not Western but universal) is likely to be incremental.[186] According to Catharin E. Dalpino, the process of liberalization, which can occur in the context of a long-standing political system, constitutes "a loosening of control by an authoritarian regime without the intention to move immediately toward a democratic transition."[187] While modern history shows that not all democracies nor democratization processes relate to Christianity or Christianization, nevertheless, to a certain degree, an active Christian movement provides an integral component of political liberalization. At a minimum, Christianization offers much-needed moral social conditions, as well as institutional support against tyranny and dictatorship for a State transitioning to democratization. Therefore, a plausible correlation appears to exist between Christianization and the political liberalization process. Zhou concludes that no Chinese democratization can emerge without cooperation from and coordination by the Chinese Christian community. According to Zhou, religious freedom and democracy constitute two critical criteria for founding contemporary democratic societies.[188] I agree with Zhou that Chinese Christianity can serve to help build both a pluralistic and moral society as part of an overall healthy civil society that a democratic China needs.[189] For example, in contrast to the rigid constraints the CCP enforces, Christianity can reflect an optimistic lifestyle example for the Chinese people. The Christianization process can also contribute to common good for all. Zhou lists three preconditions necessary for Christianity to engage in a more robust role in the process of democratization for China. I assert that the following three prerequisites that Zhou notes are necessary for the State to transition to democracy:

1. the separation of the government from the CCP and of religion from the government/CCP;

2. religious believers holding the right to assume public office;

3. the establishment of a pluralistic culture.[190]

---

185. Aikman, *Jesus in Beijing.*

186. Li, *Democratization in China*, 87–109.

187. Dalpino, *Deferring Democracy*, 3.

188. Zhou, *China's Peaceful Rise*, 165.

189. Zhou "Role of Chinese Christianity."

190. Zhou, *China's Peaceful Rise.*

If the government/CCP interferes with religious affairs, Chinese religion cannot become an independent force to influence Chinese society and politics. Currently, Communist Party members fill every important post in China. The CCP's constitution stipulates that all Party members must be atheists. As religious believers do not qualify for central positions in the public square, religions in China are unable to directly influence Chinese politics at the policy-making level. Jayoti Das and Cassandra E. DiRienzo emphasize that evidence confirms greater press freedom, which influences politics, contributes to a more peaceful nation.[191] China's restrictions regarding freedom of press and media, however, counter this consideration as, in turn, they constrain religious freedom and the influence of religion. The Chinese government strictly controls reporting, which affects even the popular media as well as television, radio, and newspapers.[192] Like Zhou, I also argue that Chinese religious believers should be allowed to freely express their beliefs through public media, including television, radio, art, literature, film, journalism, and other public forums.

Wing Thye Woo reports that the State recently admitted the need to improve its governance and that some CCP officials agreed, particularly regarding religion. The State declared that its most important task is to build a harmonious society (designated a democratic society under the rule of law).[193] Albert reports that Jiang Zemin and Hu Jintao, former Chinese leaders, believed Buddhism helped bolster the image of China's peaceful rise and, in turn, supported its growth. This effort contributed to the "CCP's goal of creating a 'harmonious society.'"[194] I suggest that China's changing political and religious climate, which evolves from a dearth of positive CCP ideology and a faith vacuum in the State, could serve as a conduit for democracy, to complement religious freedom for all in China.

Bijian Zheng, reportedly one of China's leading thinkers on ideological questions, recognizes that China needs help from the rest of world, a world which, in a sense, the State alienated itself from.[195] Zheng also acknowledges that the CCP needs to make some adjustments in its quest for "a peaceful rise." I find it particularly pertinent that despite China appearing to be open to change in some areas, research supports Zheng's admission that the relationship between the CCP and organized religion remains volatile and

---

191. Das and DiRienzo, "Conflict and the Freedom," 91–112.

192. Lee, *Chinese Media, Global*, 100.

193. Woo, *Challenges of Governance*.

194. Albert, "Christianity in China," para. 2 "Chinese Buddhism and Folk," section.

195. Zheng, *China's Peaceful Rise*.

conflicted.[196] I agree with Merle Goldman, who proposes that the democratization of China may eventually transpire not merely because of changes that force the State to change but also, perhaps, because of the necessity to change.[197] Goldman further contends that:

> with a much larger, more pluralistic society, and with a more entrenched Leninist structure, [it] may take much longer for China to democratize than the several decades it took Taiwan and South Korea. Nevertheless, the possibility of the emergence of some form of democracy in China in the first half of the next century is not unrealistic.[198]

Yang additionally connects the democratization of China with religious freedom as he argues that until more Chinese elites better understand and appreciate the true concept of religious freedom, further democratization in China will not likely occur and may even prove to be impossible. He also asserts that the organized design of State–religion relations, the comprehension of the religious freedom concept, and a civil society that maintains the dynamic balance prove vital to religious freedom.[199] Yang stresses that religious freedom arguably constitutes "the first freedom in a constitutional democracy, that is, it comes first before the other freedoms and may serve as the basis or wellspring for other freedoms."[200] When aligned with the philosophical intent of international agreements, the positive results that follow the implementation of religious freedom complement a country's economic development and social order.

In previous sections of this chapter, I described the CCP's repressive religious policy as neither justifiable in principle nor sustainable in practice. Despite the number of defects under the current CCP system against religious freedom, confirmed in news reports and scholarly research, I found increasing pluralism in China, including religious pluralization. Simultaneously, as the projection of Christianization in China likely leads to accelerated democratization and pluralism, especially directional pluralism, the progress of democratization also provides the necessary conditions to implement a contextualized version of principled pluralism, namely *Baorong Duoyuan*.

---

196. Albert, "Christianity in China."
197. Goldman, *China: Contemporary Political*, 137–46.
198. Goldman, *China: Contemporary Political*, 146.
199. Yang, "Research Agenda on Religious," 6–17.
200. Yang, *Religion in Chinese Society*, 6.

In this section, I argued from both statistics and scholarly research that the projected rapid expansion of Christianity in China will plausibly lead to China's Christianization. If this projection materializes, based on both the extensive studies about the relationship between Christianization and subsequent democratization, especially the role of Protestantism in Europe and America,[201] and similar experiences in Asia, such as South Korea, most scholars conclude that even if marginally, Christianization serves a significant role in democratization. In the next section, as I establish my *Baorong Duoyuan* model for China with the purpose of protecting religious freedom for all, I stress that in addition to democracy, although with different orientations, as I pointed out in previous chapters, political liberalism and principled pluralism share another essential element, liberal constitutionalism.

According to what I noted in previous chapters, a democratic society with an extensive degree of pluralism is a precondition for both political liberalism and principled pluralism to operate. Steven Michels contends that for a State to be considered a democracy, it only has to meet two criteria, "universal suffrage and competitive elections."[202] In Abraham Lincoln's formulation, "Democracy is the government of the people, by the people, and for the people."[203] In a simpler demarcation, Tibor R. Machan explains that in many parts of the world, democracy similarly reflects the concept of majority rule put into practice after citizens make their preferences known through the procedure of voting.[204]

Machan's point stimulates the following question: How would the fundamental rights and freedoms, particularly religious freedom, of all citizens, especially for those minorities and seemingly insignificant religious groups, be adequately protected without risking a majoritarian dictatorship if democracy merely functioned with majority rule under free elections? In other words, under what kinds of principles would citizens in a democratic society exercise their votes as justifiable and legitimate, especially on coercive matters related to minorities? Furthermore, how could potential damages to the rights and freedoms of minorities and other marginalized groups be remedied or reversed if damaging legislative items are voted on and passed by a majority vote? The answer: when democracy conjoins with constitutionalism, under which both fundamental rights and freedoms are enshrined with guaranteed mechanisms of constitutional reviews and other judicial due processes when any rights and

---

201. Kelly, *Emergence of Liberty*, 141.

202. Michels, *Case against Democracy*, 2.

203. Michels, *Case against Democracy*, 2.

204. Machan, "Reflections on Modern," 63–95.

freedoms are violated. As Rawls points out, a citizen's "exercise of political power [by his/her vote] is proper and hence justifiable only when it is exercised in accordance with a constitution."[205]

The constitution of a State serves as the definitive source of legal and political order for a nation-state system and, basically, establishes the rules for that State as it constitutes the government, organizes the State, and structures the basis for representation of and participation by the people. Other than in the United States, constitutional failure depicts the norm for most States. Despite numerous, diverse crises that the United States has survived, particularly the Civil War, the U.S. Constitution has endured for more than two centuries. In contrast, according to Tonja Jacobi, Sonia Mittal, and Barry R. Weingast, most national constitutions do not even last two decades.[206] As the "median country faces violent political change about once every eight years, [. . .] these changes are often accompanied by changes in constitutional arrangements."[207] According to Abdurrahman Bapir, the basic rights of a constitution encompass two distinct categories:

1. civil rights, which ensure public influence over political decision making, and;

2. civil liberties, which protect individuals against the illegitimate use of coercion. The fact that these rights are today mostly codified and recognized by states does not mean there are no challenges surrounding them.[208]

Contemporary states typically adhere to one of the three following constitutional forms:

1. absolutist constitution;

2. legislative supremacy constitution;

3. liberal constitution.

With an absolutist constitution, rulers are considered the law. They can change and produce the meta-laws. This type of constitution does not prove significant as those in power weaken it. In the legislative supremacy constitution, the legislature can adjust and modify the constitution.[209] Liberal constitutionalism, also known as "new constitutionalism," which

---

205. Rawls, *Political Liberalism, Expanded*, 216.

206. Jacobi et al., "Creating a Self-Stabilizing," 609–38.

207. Jacobi et al., "Creating a Self-Stabilizing," para. 1 in Introduction.

208. Bapir, "Understanding Liberal Constitutionalism," 5.

209. Bapir, "Understanding Liberal Constitutionalism."

I introduced in Chapter 3, refers to written constitutions that contain a charter of rights and mechanisms to protect those rights. Bapir notes that a liberal constitution seeks to institute mechanisms to separate powers and to position checks and balances on governmental powers to protect fundamental human rights.[210]

In some countries, including China, where no constitutional tool such as "judicial review" exists, rights which the constitution stipulates may not wield any power.[211] In addition, abuses of constitutions as well as misinterpretations of their meanings may veto the power of the constitution and negate rights of citizens.

China's written constitution occupies a position somewhere between the absolutist constitution and the legislative supremacy constitution. It may have rights charted within it, but, nonetheless, this constitution lacks a mechanism to protect those rights. Contrary to the basic liberal constitutionalist principle where a mechanism of checks and balance exists among the diverse functions of government to restrain and limit the State's power among its executive, legislative, and judiciary branches, China reflects a "Party-State" ruling system where the constitution remains subject to constant change according to the Party's wishes. No mechanism exists to either enforce the constitutional rights or to remedy the damages to those rights when violated.

When the PRC gained control of China, officials made a point of inserting the freedom of religious belief clause into the Chinese constitution. Yang explains that in 1949 the CCP's temporary constitution of the "'Common Program of the Chinese People's Political Consultative Conference' states that the citizens of the PRC have the freedom of religious belief. This was also adopted in the 1954 Constitution by the First National People's Congress."[212] In 1975, however, during the Cultural Revolution, even though the CCP retained the clause stating freedom of religious belief, the party affixed the phrase "freedom of atheist propaganda" to the constitution. Nevertheless, under Communist rule, China has not appropriated its constitution as the foundation of law regarding religious freedom for its citizens. Although government officials propagate China's constitution as the State's fundamental basic law, due to the nature of China's one-party State system, the will of the CCP supersedes the constitution's authority.

Accordingly, amidst frequent political turmoil in mainland China, the CCP continues to retain the freedom of religious belief clause in

210. Bapir, "Understanding Liberal Constitutionalism."
211. Bapir, "Understanding Liberal Constitutionalism."
212. Yang, *Religion in Chinese Society*, 74.

the constitution. Eric R. Carlson, like Yang, points out that as the CCP utilizes an intricate system of legal procedures and enforcement actions to meticulously supervise religion and religious activities, the State routinely subjects specific religions to repression and tries to eradicate them. Even though China enacted its latest constitution in 1982 to provide for "freedom of religious belief" and protect "normal religious activities," the party does not define either phrase.[213] Yang contends that one concern regarding the adoption of religious freedom in the constitution or basic law may relate to the need for most of China's citizens as well as the elites to mutually understand the principle of religious freedom. The underdeveloped civil society, however, does not offer the essential cultural and social support to uphold this principle.

The United States ratified the First Amendment to the Constitution in 1791 regarding religion. This amendment states that Congress shall make no law respecting an establishment of religion nor any prohibiting the free exercise thereof. This legal arrangement of religious freedom includes disestablishment (no State religion) and deregulation (no prohibition of any religion). This constitutional amendment provides both the fundamental foundation for religious freedom protection and possible legal remedy at the highest judicial level if that freedom is violated.

Neither the "free exercise" nor the "non-establishment" clause is clearly enshrined in China's current constitution because of the CCP's imposed dominant atheistic ideology. Though not without limitations as I have shown in previous sections, Yang argues that due to the fact the principle of separation of State and religion is clearly stated in the constitution, this as a minimum, provides spaces for diverse CCP-tolerated religions or religiously based groups to grow and flourish. Consequently, this trend is likely to increase for more associational, contextual, and religious pluralization. Similarly, China's increasing levels of social, economic, cultural, and religious diversity, which partially evolved from the State's active role in globalization, appear to be ongoing as well.

As I demonstrated in the previous sections, with the increasing level and degree of pluralism and democratization in today's China, the question lies in whether China can evolve into a more progressive form of constitutionalism that, essentially, not only guarantees citizens' basic rights and freedoms, especially true religious freedom in the letter of the law but also enforces it with a robust judicial review process.

Carlson maintains that China's courts have not significantly contributed to protecting religious freedom and even though religious believers,

---

213. Carlson, "China's New Regulations," 747–97.

theoretically, possess a constitutional right to "freedom of religious belief," until the State upholds its constitution, citizens do not have any judicial means to enforce their religious rights.[214] According to Carlson, two diverse perceptions address the understanding of religion in a Chinese context. One opinion interprets religion from a positive and active perspective and argues that religion can readily adapt to the socialist society of contemporary China and meaningfully contribute to the society's conformity and harmony. On 10 May 2011, seventeen Chinese church leaders who appealed to the Chinese Congress exemplified the positive perception Carlsen notes as they utilized China's constitution and universal standards to appeal for remedial measures on behalf of a major persecuted church. The details of the event include: in light of a major crackdown on and forced closure of one of the largest Chinese Protestant house churches in Beijing, the 1,000 plus members of the Beijing Shouwang house church and the seventeen Christian pastors, representing a nationwide house church movement from various Chinese cities, signed and submitted an unprecedented citizens' petition to the National People's Congress, a first since the founding of the Chinese Communist Party.

At their own peril, these seventeen persecuted church leaders called upon the CCP regime to stop the persecution of peaceful church gatherings like that in the Shouwang house church. They also appealed for a constitutional review of government-issued regulations concerning religious affairs, and compliance with the international human rights standards and norms on religious freedom. Furthermore, in a historically significant move, the seventeen church leaders continued to demand that the Chinese Congress enact formal legislation to protect religious freedom for all Chinese citizens as part of inalienable "political rights" and abolish all "regulations" that they deemed incompatible with the spirit of China's constitution and universal standards. The following relates an excerpt from the petition, entitled, "We Stand up for Our Faith: A Citizens' Petition to the National People's Congress on the Church–State Conflicts":

> It is our belief that religious freedom is the paramount freedom of the human society and is a part of the universal values of the international community. In the meantime, it is also the cornerstone of other political rights and property rights. Without the just and universal freedom of religious belief, there will be no way for a multi-ethnic and multi-religious country to build

214. Carlson, "China's New Regulations."

a peaceful civil society and there will be no way to bring forth social stability, ethnic unity and the prosperity of our country.[215]

The second opinion suggests that the existing differences between the religious consciousness value system and the socialist consciousness world outlook and value system inevitably contribute to conflicts between the two. Even though there may appear to be a basic social united front between religion and socialism, on an ideological level, this unity cannot exist.[216] This attitude may persist before the full Christianization and democratization of China materializes. Nevertheless, essentially under *Baorong Duoyuan*, the Communist ideology must either yield its dominance or adapt to a democratized Chinese society.

The impact of the Christianization currently occurring in China emboldens many Chinese church leaders, who despite persecution by the CCP publicly call for basic constitutional, democratic, universal values such as true religious freedom, due process under rule of law, and democratic governance accountable to both God and people. In November 2017, after Chinese government officials blocked Reverend Wang Yi,[217] a Reformed church leader, from attending a major international convention commemorating the five-hundredth anniversary of the Reformation (1517–2017) in Jakarta, Indonesia, four renowned Chinese Reformed Protestant church leaders issued the Jakarta Declaration.[218] In this declaration, the church leaders wrote:

> We hereby sincerely and solemnly call upon the Chinese authorities to confess and repent of their sins before God, the Creator of heaven and earth; and to return the power to the people, governing the country by the rule of law, guaranteeing the basic human rights of all the citizens living in mainland China, Hong Kong and Macau. All people, including Christians and adherents of other faith, human rights defenders, even Communist party members, suspects of corrupt officials and other criminals, were endowed with universal rights by God, and all should be protected by due process, because every person is made in the image and likeness of God. Any government has authority to neither control the Christian church nor restrict any citizen's

215. Min, "No Response to Pastors' Joint," paras. 1–2 in "The Petition Says" section.

216. Xinping, "Religion and Rule of Law," 519–27.

217. Reverend Wang Yi, a friend, is an internationally known constitutional law scholar.

218. "Chinese Pastors Call," para. 3 in "Here We Stand" section.

freedom of religion, belief, thoughts and speech, and their expressions in the public square accordingly.[219]

The Jakarta Declaration projects the call for democratic accountability
of the government in light of the Christianization of China as it *demands*
that Chinese authorities adhere to international human rights standards
and norms for people of all faiths, or of no faith, including CCP party members, with the spirit of liberal constitutionalism:

> The present Constitution of mainland China and the Universal
> Declaration of Human Rights, which the China government
> subscribes to, and other international human rights treaties all
> clearly guarantee the basic rights of every citizen in the matter
> of the freedom of religion and belief. This includes the freedom
> to assemble, the freedom to proselytize and also the freedom to
> travel aboard to participate in religious activities.[220]

Zhuo Xinping explains that in China, two different interpretations of religious freedom exist:

> One interpretation claims that religious freedom includes the
> "absolute freedom" not just to have religious faith, thoughts,
> and ideas, but also engage in religious action and organiza-
> tion. The other interpretation claims that religious freedom
> includes "absolute freedom" only as to religious faith, thoughts,
> and ideas, because such matters are within the area of privacy.
> But as to religious organizations and their activities, religion
> has here only "relative freedom"; since a religious organization
> is a social organization, it must be under legal control like all
> social organizations. [. . . W]hen religion is no more merely
> a private, individual matter, but manifests itself instead as a
> religious organization engaging in activities with others in so-
> ciety, it necessarily must be transparent in its social existence
> and activities, which means it must obey social laws and accept
> social supervision.[221]

Xinping argues that two diverse proposed purposes for legislation on religion exist in China. One proposed purpose encompasses the protection of
religious freedom. Legislation on religion enacted for this purpose express-
es respect for religious belief and other faiths in human society. The other

---

219. "Chinese Pastors Call."

220. "Chinese Pastors Call."

221. Xinping, "Religion and Rule of Law."

proposed purpose includes the intent to control religion or, minimally, to control religious organizations and activities.

According to Xinping, the differences between citizens' and the CCP's understanding of the purposes for religious legislation as well as their comprehension of the social significance and value of religion in Chinese society contrast considerably. The preamble of China's 1982 Constitution, for example, asserts that the expression of freedoms or rights, including those relating to the freedom of religion, will prove unlawful if it violates any of the following four basic principles:

1. keeping the country on the socialist road;

2. upholding the people's democratic dictatorship;

3. promoting the leadership of the CCP;

4. following Marxism–Leninism and the Thought of Mao.[222]

Therefore, when a citizen exercises rights and freedoms, the determination of whether these actions conflict with the state's interests, which include the above four basic principles, may be interpreted in numerous ways. These overarching political principles may have posed the most serious challenges for China to evolve into a modern liberal constitutional State. Nevertheless, as I explore the *Baorong Duoyuan* model for China as a contextualized version of principled pluralism, given the seemingly unstoppable trend of pluralism and democratization that accelerated due to rapid Christianization, a kind of constitutionalism with Chinese characteristics could be gradually emerging. As I researched and stated in Chapter 3, this type of constitutionalism may neither follow the model under political liberalism, because of its failure to protect religious freedom for all, nor completely adopt the model after principled pluralism due to its overtly Christian orientation, reflected in both its historical context in the Netherlands and its constitutional text. Rather, the constitutionalism under *Baorong Duoyuan* will guarantee all Chinese citizens' fundamental rights and freedoms, including religious freedom for all with true State impartiality and a set of constitutional mechanisms which any citizen or group may utilize for appeals and reviews when rights and freedoms are violated. In the next section, to begin the contextualization of principled pluralism, I illustrate differences between the three theoretical models examined in this study—political liberalism, principled pluralism and *Baorong Duoyuan*—in light of religious freedom.

222. Li, *Civil Liberties*, 37.

5.4.3 Contextualization of Principled Pluralism
to Develop *Baorong Duoyuan*

Xu Huang and Michael Harris Bond explain that in the process of contextualization of a theory, the researcher identifies and incorporates relevant and meaningful elements within their context when analyzing empirical phenomena. Huang and Bond emphasize that "researchers must consider contextualization if they are to apply existing theories in new contexts."[223] Even if the researcher should borrow or draw from a theory applied in dramatically different contexts, contextualization can ensure that the researcher generates valid knowledge about phenomena in further novel contexts. Contextualization possesses the potential to:

- enhance existing theories;
- improve their precision, and;
- refine their predictions.[224]

As Huang and Bond note, in the process of contextualization, the researcher generates practical knowledge about phenomena in novel contexts. As I argued earlier, neither principled pluralism nor political liberalism prove to be "baorong"[225] enough to include everyone. Nevertheless, as I presupposed at the start of this study, *Baorong Duoyuan*, which primarily evolves from the contextualization of principled pluralism with considerations gleaned from political liberalism, encompasses religious freedom for all.

In the context of *Baorong Duoyuan*, the Chinese word, "duoyuan" denotes pluralism. Initially, at the start of contextualizing principled pluralism, I considered *Baijia Zhengming* as the term for the title of my study's ensuing theory. *Baijia Zhengming* relates to the quotation at the start of this chapter[226] and would also correlate with the intent of *Baorong Duoyuan*. Similar to the term, "duoyuan," *Baijia Zhengming* basically provides a poetic Chinese way to say "pluralism," to "let a hundred schools of thought contend."[227] The overall phrase, *Baijia Zhengming*, means: free airing of views; air one's views freely; argue things out thoroughly; or freedom of expression.[228] In addition, *Baijia*

---

223. Huang, and Bond, *Handbook of Chinese Organizational*, 37.

224. Huang and Bond, *Handbook of Chinese Organizational*.

225. In Chinese, this means tolerant.

226. "Letting a hundred flowers blossom and a hundred schools of thought resonate" serves to promote the idea that the State should permit each voice or religion have say in the public realm.

227. "Roots of Chinese," paras. 2–3.

228. Encyclopedia Britannica editors, "Chinese Philosophy."

Zhengming, similar to *Baorong Duoyuan*, harmonizes with the Golden Rule, the founding worldview for this thesis.

While recognizing that the inborn value of human dignity resides in the heart of universal human rights, *Baorong Duoyuan* encompasses considerations from both Christian and secular worldviews. John Brian Paprock contends that at the heart of democracy, "every human being possesses an inherent and inviolable worth that transcends the authority of the state," that "flows from the conviction that every person, of whatever social, economic, or political status, of whatever race, creed, or location, has a value that does not rise or fall [. . .] with income or productivity, with a status or position, with power or weakness."[229] In addition, *Baorong Duoyuan* refines codifications of political liberalism and principled pluralism to afford more concrete opportunities for maintaining religious freedom for all in China.

To develop *Baorong Duoyuan*, I considered components from both political liberalism and principled pluralism. As I stated previously, *Baorong Duoyuan* shares the same commitment to liberal constitutionalism as political liberalism and principled pluralism, though without explicitly adopting either a secular worldview like political liberalism or a theistic worldview like principled pluralism. However, *Baorong Duoyuan* more closely replicates principled pluralism as this theory better matches the intent of *Baorong Duoyuan* in protecting religious freedom for all. I argue that *Baorong Duoyuan* will surpass the capacities of principled pluralism as it appeals to a broader base of citizens for the common good of all faith or non-faith adherents. Designed for a liberal constitutional framework in a democratic, pluralistic State, as some predict China will become in the next two decades, *Baorong Duoyuan* emulates the message that the Golden Rule encourages—treat others the way one would want to be treated. Found in all cultures, religions, and worldviews, versions of the Golden Rule range from "those of ancient Egyptian religions to those of West Asia (Judaism, Christianity, Islam), South Asia (Hinduism and Buddhism) and East Asia (Confucianism). Non-religious worldviews such as those of the Council for Secular Humanism and the British Humanist Association"[230] also sanction variations of the Golden Rule. Table 8 compares essential elements of political liberalism, principled pluralism, and *Baorong Duoyuan*.

---

229. Paprock, *Workbook for Interfaith*, 18.
230. Van Der Ven, *Religion: Immediate*, 105.

Table 8: Comparison of Political Liberalism, Principled Pluralism and Baorong Duoyuan[231]

	Political Liberalism	Principled Pluralism	Baorong Duoyuan
Historical origin	Post-Reformation	Late nineteenth century	Early twenty-first century
Social context	Conflicts with irreconcilable yet reasonable worldviews	State demand for conformity and uniformity under pluralism	A projected democratic, Christianized, pluralistic post-Communist China
Worldview orientation	Secular worldview	Judeo-Christian (theist) worldview	More inclusive, impartial, directional, pluralistic worldview
Constitutional perspective	Liberal constitutionalism favoring secular establishment	Liberal constitutionalism with a modest Christian establishment	Liberal constitutionalism with neither secular nor religious establishment
Protection of religious freedom	May protect religious freedom for all religions in private while exercising restraints on religious voices in public political discourses and even constraining certain religions	Tolerates freedom of all worldviews in private settings and in the public square, with minor favoritism toward Christianity	Protects freedom for all worldviews in private as well as in public settings; aligns with international norms for religious freedom
Interrelations of spheres	State-directed social order under a politically charged, uniform "overlapping consensus," with potential strife between contained and noncontained worldviews	Sphere autonomy under organic social unity with potential tension between Christian and non-Christian worldviews	State-facilitated, impartial, harmonious interrelations between different spheres with diverse worldviews
Role of religious education in public schools	May permit certain types of religious education to be taught[232]	Allows religious education to be taught[233]	Encourages religious education to be taught[234]

231. Author's original table.

232. France is more resistant to religious education due to State-sanctioned, secular values.

233. Christian religious education is particularly preferred.

234. Favors school choice regarding teaching of religious education and is aligned with international norms to support religious preferences of parents and legal guardians

As noted in Chapter 3, Rawls contends that, historically, political liberalism, a popular approach to diversity, originated after the Reformation. Politically, as the above table depicts, political liberalism draws from liberalism, as it contends that citizens can work together to support an overlapping consensus. Regarding religion, political liberalism proves to be theologically rooted in a secular worldview. In its constitutional perspective, political liberalism utilizes a constitutional democracy. In terms of protection of religious freedom, even though political liberalism *professes* its commitment to religious freedom, it subtly restrains certain religious views from being expressed in the public square.

In Chapter 2, I reported that Kuyper initially presented primary concepts contributing to the concept of principled pluralism which originated during nineteenth-century movements. Also, as I previously pointed out, Skillen coined the term "principled pluralism" in the twentieth century. As Table 8 portrays, politically, principled pluralism draws from Kuyper's sphere sovereignty theory which reasons that civil government, including the State, can claim and implement only limited authority. In the context of religion, principled pluralism proves to be theologically rooted in a Judeo-Christian worldview. In its constitutional perspective, principled pluralism utilizes a constitutional democratic framework. Principled pluralism aligns with Wolterstorff's argument against the reasoning of political liberalism, which proposes that all citizens will agree on public legislation if religious reasons are omitted from public debate.[235] Regarding the protection of religious freedom, principled pluralism protects a citizen's natural rights, which include the right to freely exercise religion both in private and in the public square.

I submit that *Baorong Duoyuan* essentially seeks to protect the freedom of diverse worldviews not only in private but also in the public square. Hendrik M. Vroom contends that in a broad concept, every view of life may be considered a worldview. These worldviews then "are divided into two classes: secular and religious worldviews."[236] As *Baorong Duoyuan* draws from both principled pluralism, with a Christian foundation, and political liberalism, with secular roots, it applies aptly to all individuals.

In contextualizing principled pluralism to develop *Baorong Duoyuan*, the theory I envisaged for religious freedom in China, I extracted several common denominators from principled pluralism and political liberalism. These consist of:

- Both principled pluralism and political liberalism are contingent on a pluralistic society where diversity is manifested.

---

of children.

235. Wolterstorff, "Why Can't We."

236. Vroom, *Spectrum of Worldviews*, 1.

- Principled pluralism and political liberalism both agree on the need for a democratic government system where the elected officials are accountable to those who elect them in free elections, and both subscribe to a constitutional system that guarantees and protects the fundamental rights of citizens, especially minorities and vulnerable individuals.

- Principled pluralism and political liberalism similarly strive to organize society so that citizens will be "equal and free" (Rawls) and more likely coexist without stimulating conflicts and wars. Principled pluralism shares Kuyper's concepts (build organic unity, where different spheres of society have their own sovereignty, and not State-imposed conformity, as I describe in chapters 2 and 3).

- Principled pluralism and political liberalism both perceive the necessity for two essential components regarding the role of the State:

  – formation of a government with a fundamental structure (a constitutional essential) that includes religious freedom, as Rawls described, noted in Chapter 2;

  – guarantee of a mechanism for the execution of fairness in matters of justice.

- Principled pluralism and political liberalism both aim to promote the goal of citizens working together for the common good of all. (Rawls "ascribed" to do this, yet political liberalism manifests some discrepancies as noted in Chapter 2.)

In a practical sense in a projected Chinese context, drawing from both political liberalism and principled pluralism, *BD* will:

- hold elected officials accountable to citizens.

- subscribe to a constitutional system that not only guarantees but protects the fundamental rights of citizens.

- endeavor to advance a civil society so citizens will be "equal and free."

- formulate a government with a central structure that respects the sovereignty of other spheres, impartially protects religious freedom for all and guarantees a mechanism that will execute fairness in matters of public justice.

- promote the goal of citizens working together for the common good of all.

Even though principled pluralism parallels with political liberalism on numerous points, principled pluralism and *Baorong Duoyuan* differ from Rawls's political liberalism in the following matters relating to the State–religion relationship:

- Political liberalism constrains certain comprehensive concepts, including those of certain religions, from participating in the public square. As I note in Chapter 3, Wolterstorff challenges Rawls's assertion that the State can remain neutral while implementing the restrictions liberalism supports. I agree with Wolterstorff that instead of neutrality, the State needs to assume a nuanced concept of "affirmative impartiality."

- Political liberalism utilizes the filter of proviso under public reason which stipulates that a citizen with a religious worldview who presents a rationale to support a position relating to a public issue must translate that justification into the language of public reason. Consequently, this proves more burdensome for the religious person than the secular individual.[237]

- Political liberalism stipulates that only certain "reasonable persons" (determined by political liberals) can propose principles and standards as fair terms of cooperation to help ensure an overlapping consensus among free and equal, reasonable, and rational citizens.[238]

Consequently, as I expounded in Chapter 3, Rawls's design of political liberalism under public reason fails to adequately and sufficiently protect religious freedom for all so the goal to achieve his proclaimed liberal ideal of social harmony and peace remains unsustainable. In this section, examining principled pluralism to determine how it could best be contextualized for *Baorong Duoyuan* to help China protect religious freedom for all its citizens, I compare six critical components of principled pluralism with six of *Baorong Duoyuan*: social context; worldview orientation; constitutional perspective; protection of religious education, spherical interrelations; and the role of religious education in public schools, my focus for Chapter 6. Historically, as I reported in Chapter 2, principled pluralism, which grew out of Kuyper's theory of sphere sovereignty with a predominantly theocentric Christian reformed orientation, originated in the late nineteenth century. My research regarding religious freedom in China stimulated the idea for *Baorong Duoyuan*, my proposed theory, during the early twenty-first century against a historical background of an atheistic State driven

---

237. Rawls, *Political Liberalism, Expanded*, 453–54.

238. Rawls, *Political Liberalism*, 8.

by Communism. The following six points underlie my formulation of the
ways in which *Baorong Duoyuan* could contribute to addressing any potential deficits noted in principled pluralism and construct countermeasures
necessary to help protect religious freedom for all in a Christianized, post-
communist, democratized future China.

1. *Social Context:* The social context for principled pluralism would fail
   to complement China's current system or its projected future one since
   it promotes a Christian faith-based pillarization approach in response
   to the demands of its originating country (the Netherlands) for conformity and uniformity under pluralism. Sharply different from the
   social context in which principled pluralism originated, my design for
   Baorong Duoyuan grew out of more than half a century of militaristic,
   monolithic, Communism-dominant State rule with hundreds of years
   of imperial culture in which Christianity and a Christian worldview
   had been deeply engraved on the Chinese mind as a Western imperialistic tool for humiliating the Chinese nation and culture. Despite the
   projected emergence of a future democratic, pluralistic, post-communist China with Christianity as a political, social, and cultural minority
   influence, the context of contemporary China promoting a worldview
   counter to Christianity necessitates that the *Baorong Duoyuan* model
   be distinctive from principled pluralism.

2. *Plurality of Worldview:* The Christian worldview orientation of principled pluralism would likely factor into China rejecting this theory
   and it being excluded as a feasible option for the future Christianized,
   democratic Chinese government as its orientation derives from the
   Judeo-Christian (theist) worldview. *Baorong Duoyuan*, with its more
   inclusive, affirmative impartial, pluralist worldview supersedes principled pluralism with criteria open to adherents of all religions or beliefs
   as well as to those of non-religions and anti-religions. The worldview
   orientation of *Baorong Duoyuan* is itself intrinsically pluralist and not
   specifically Christian.

3. *Constitutional Impartiality:* Principled pluralism's constitutional perspective of liberal constitutionalism with a modest Christian establishment as explicitly stated in the Dutch Constitution would likely
   repel the projected post-communist China due to those who may
   not lean toward or want to be linked to any Christian concept. As
   Baorong Duoyuan adheres to the constitutional perspective of liberal
   constitutionalism with neither secular nor religious establishment, it
   would not present the same perspectives of principled pluralism but
   those of a more inclusive, impartial, directional pluralist worldview

and, therefore, could provide an attractive, acceptable alternative for China's future.

4. *Equality of Religious Manifestations:* As I conclude in Chapter 2, although principled pluralism tolerates freedom of all worldviews in private settings as well as in the public square, with its minor favoritism toward Christianity in societal and cultural settings, this theory would not likely be readily accepted or successfully mesh with the religious diversity projected for the future China which would embrace all worldviews without favoritism. As *Baorong Duoyuan* aligns with international norms for religious freedom, my proposed theory would meet the need in the projected future China to protect freedom for all worldviews in the private sphere as well as in public settings, individually and communally.

5. *Harmony of Sphere Interrelations:* Regarding the interrelations of spheres, principled pluralism promotes the concept of each sphere being autonomous under an organic social unity. This method increases the potential for tension between the Christian and the non-Christian worldview, however, and, in turn, would negate principled pluralism's compatibility with China's future diversity. *Baorong Duoyuan*'s support for State-facilitated, affirmative impartial, harmonious interrelations between different spheres with diverse worldviews makes it a better match for the future China than principled pluralism.

6. *Religious Education in Public Schools:* In the future Christianized, democratized China, the role of religious education in public schools, which I focus on in Chapter 6, will constitute a critical criterion in education. Even though principled pluralism more closely matches *Baorong Duoyuan* in this area as it allows religious education to be taught, nevertheless, principled pluralism's preference for a Christian-based religious education system would cause this theory to lose its potential as an optimal choice for a post-communist, normative directional pluralistic, democratized China. Overall, *Baorong Duoyuan* exceeds principled pluralism not only because it encourages RE to be taught in public schools but also because it supersedes this theory by encouraging the inclusion of religious education in *all* public schools. *Baorong Duoyuan* further facilitates religious freedom for parents and guardians, as prescribed by the various international norms, by permitting them to ensure that their children's education aligns with their preferred religion.

Baorong Duoyuan surpasses both political liberalism and principled pluralism in its potential to best ensure religious freedom in China's projected future; nevertheless, *Baorong Duoyuan* may not appeal to China's current governing officials because the CCP restricts religious freedom in the State's limited pluralistic society for the sake of protecting its monopoly on political power. In the future, if Chinese citizens choose to reject Communist rule, voluntarily or otherwise, and China, as projected, transitions into a democratic, pluralistic State, then *Baorong Duoyuan* will offer the best option for the State to help ensure religious freedom for all.

5.5 Conclusion

From research for this chapter, after examining challenges for China regarding religious freedom under China's traditional State–religion relationship model and under the current rule of the CCP, I assert that both the historical imperial model and current method under CCP prove unjustifiable and unsustainable. Nevertheless, and despite the CCP failing to uphold "the freedom of religious belief," a phrase which China retains in its current constitution, several scholarly sources project that within the next two decades, China will become a Christianized democracy. I also investigated the dilemma of whether, despite the seemingly eternal mode of political authoritarian rule continuing to operate in China, evidence of pluralism— associational, contextual, and even directional in a descriptive sense—has begun to manifest itself in the State. After comparing political liberalism and principled pluralism, I conclude that *Baorong Duoyuan*, my contextualized model of principled pluralism, encompasses components that make this theory practical, understandable, and culturally accessible.

In Chapter 6, I continue to present the vision sustaining *Baorong Duoyuan* as the most viable option for China's education model given the State's anticipated status. I also consider criteria relevant to the potential implementation of RE under *Baorong Duoyuan* in a post-communist China's education system and discuss numerous challenges confronting China's contemporary education system in relation to including religious education. After I compare political liberalism and principled pluralism as potential alternative theoretical foundations for China's education system, I propose that *Baorong Duoyuan* could stimulate better, more positive progress regarding the State's education system and fill China's moral vacuum, particularly with the inclusion of religious education. I continue to argue that, ultimately, *Baorong Duoyuan* offers the best option for China in its projected Christian, democratized future to enhance religious education to help ensure religious freedom for all.

Chapter 6

Baorong Duoyuan in a Post-Communist China's Education System

[T]he contribution of religious education to religious freedom is highly diverse. On the one hand, a narrow, traditional approach may lead to a kind of mental closure and a failure to make contact with the contemporary world. At its best, however, "learning from religion" is a unique resource for the advancement of human freedom.[1]

〜JOHN M. HULL

6.1 Introduction

RELIGIOUS EDUCATION NOT ONLY reflects an investment in a State's global economic realm,[2] its absence or inclusion in education simultaneously determines the dearth or growth of religious freedom. The inclusion of religious education in compulsory education could also, as the International Association for Religious Freedom (IARF) notes, enhance respect and mutual understanding between individuals, and promote "harmony, or at least tolerance," between communities or individuals of different religions or beliefs.[3] In contemporary China, the exclusion of religious education in its education system helps the CCP further regulate, restrict, and restrain religious freedom.

1. Hull, *Religious Education in Schools*, 10.
2. Stewart, *World-Class Education*.
3. "International Association for Religious," panel 5.

In Chapter 5, leading up to the focus for this chapter, considering religious education under *Baorong Duoyuan* in the education system of a post-communist China, I reviewed numerous constraints the CCP imposes regarding religious freedom in China under the traditional State–religion model. I also examined contemporary challenges to religious freedom under the CCP's State–religion model and presented China's stance regarding RE. Additionally, I examined the unjustifiability of the CCP's contemporary religious policy in principle and scrutinized its unsustainability in practice. I recounted predictions that China will become "Christian(ized)" in the future and that, ultimately, the State will transition into a democracy. I argue that *Baorong Duoyuan* would best suit the projected new China and that assimilating religious education into its future post-communist, Christianized, democratized, education system could stimulate, support, and sustain the prospect of religious freedom for all. Furthermore, RE in China now, as well as in the future, could help students appreciate and develop their own identities.[4]

In Chapter 6, I examine the vision for, the criteria necessary to stimulate, and the development of the design for the implementation of religious education under *Baorong Duoyuan* in post-communist China's education system. I discuss several conflicts and deficiencies of China's contemporary education system, particularly regarding religious education, which inherently contribute to the State's failure to protect religious freedom for all. I concurrently expound an unfulfilled concern from Chapter 4: If education systems under principled pluralism and political liberalism would not effectively contribute to China's ideological goals for education, could *Baorong Duoyuan*, a contextualized model of principled pluralism, stimulate positive progress in the State's pedagogy realm, particularly with the inclusion of religious education?

As I further examine alternative theoretical foundations for China's education system, namely, political liberalism and principled pluralism, to reveal what education under these two concepts could demarcate, I ultimately propose *Baorong Duoyuan* to constitute a viable option for China's education model in its projected democratic, Christianized State.

6.2 Confronting Challenges to Religious Education

Allan Walker, Shuanye Chen, and Haiyan Qian note that most states revere education as the foundation for building a competitive economy with creative, innovative, and knowledgeable workers.[5] According to Vivien

---

4. Taylor, "Responses," 59.
5. Walker et al., "Leader Development," 410–34.

Stewart, China's ideological goals include plans to transition the State from an agricultural and low-wage manufacturing economy to a global leader in various fields. This objective reflects only one of the critical challenges confronting the State's contemporary education system.

China's long-term goal for students to complete twelve years of schooling universally throughout the State by 2020 reflects another challenge for China in the realm of education.[6] Yu Tianlong asserts that additional challenges in China's education system include the need for moral education and that:

> Political emphasis continues to be reflected in most recent governmental policies in moral education. [. . .] Despite new changes in education and society, the politics of moral education remains like a ghost: omnipotent, influencing and controlling educators' thinking and practice.[7]

Accordingly, if China becomes a democratized, Christian State as projected, the implementation of *Baorong Duoyuan* could help the State meet the following three aforementioned educational goals: (1) transitioning from its agricultural and low-wage manufacturing role to leading in other areas, including science, medicine, and technology; (2) students universally completing twelve years of schooling; (3) addressing the need for moral education. If China were to overcome these challenges relating to education, particularly regarding religious education, this would, in turn, simultaneously constitute a practical, positive investment in the State's future.[8] In addition, I suggest that under *Baorong Duoyuan*, the implementation of religious education in China's education system holds potential seeds to stimulate, support, and sustain religious freedom for all in the State.

6.2.1 Challenges in China's Education System

Leslie Grant et al. note that the State's extreme focus on examinations has contributed to China's academic deficiencies. For example, China's citizens experience low averages in completing schooling and discrepancies exist between rural and urban high school attendance. In addition, China's traditional education system bolsters authoritarian teachers, encourages conformity and, in turn, discourages the development of students' creativity. According to Grant et al., the Chinese Ministry of Education (MOE) had tried to correct

---

6. Stewart, *World-Class Education*, 67.

7. Tianlong, *Citizenship Education in China*, 90.

8. Stewart, *World-Class Education*.

some of China's academic failures by starting to implement venues for the expression of creativity and innovation in the State's academic curricula nationwide. Nevertheless, "teacher talk" still dominates the classroom with the teacher perceived as an authoritative model. Students perceive teachers as experts with instant answers for every question.[9]

Despite the central government reportedly starting to relinquish a portion of its control over the curriculum and assessment, the CCP continues to control most critical aspects of education, including the development and selection of textbooks. Due to the test-orientated system in China's education system and the Party's excessive ideological control, achieving a quality-orientated education, which would stimulate innovation and creativity, remains questionable.

Some recent educational reform efforts by the CCP that have not fully materialized may complement *Baorong Duoyuan*'s vision for China's future education system. At times, these efforts have included the CCP permitting teachers at the local and provincial school levels to both develop and select some textbooks. In efforts to improve the State's education system, Chinese education leaders systematically study approaches and strategies that other countries implement. The aim of recent major curricula reforms that the MOE has introduced appears to be to direct China away from its traditional didactic classroom practices which emphasize memorization to the implementation of more Western approaches that integrate inquiry methods into teaching strategies and encourage more student participation in classrooms.[10] In educating pupils regarding values, Caroline Koh reports that some Chinese teachers have begun to favor and implement more informal approaches to teaching certain moral values, the approach *Baorong Duoyuan* will encourage in teaching. These include role-modeling, leading by positive example, and maintaining a positive, harmonious environment to help students learn about the basic virtues of good citizenship, such as loyalty, sacrifice, patriotism, and morality.[11]

The challenge remains that the role models and cited examples reflect CCP ideological political indoctrination without sufficient credibility. Javier C. Hernández reports that, currently, amid concerns that the Party can sustain its hold over Chinese youth, President Xi Jinping has begun to restructure political education in China's more than 283,000 primary and secondary schools.[12] According to Hernández's observation of Xie Hong, a

9. Grant et al., *West Meets East*.

10. Stewart, *World-Class Education*, 67.

11. Koh, "Moral Development, 83–101.

12. Hernández, "To Inspire," para. 5.

teacher of fifty fourth-grade Chinese students at the Workers and Peasants Red Army Elementary School in Yuqing County, China:[13]

> The school's curriculum recounts the experience of Mao's soldiers during the early years of the revolution, who are portrayed as heroically fighting to free China from rapacious warlords and Japanese invaders. As at some Red Army schools, students wear military uniforms around campus; in Ms. Xie's classroom, that is a privilege reserved for the best students.[14]

Another challenge regarding China's education system involves issues relating to diverse cultures in China. James Leibold points out that China does not deliberately use the term "multi-cultural education"; nevertheless, the MOE and the State Ethnic Affairs Commission frequently refer to the significance of "cultural pluralism" (*wenhua duoyanxing*).[15] As in the West, the school level portrays the primary arena where the State may implement cultural pluralism, particularly in developing a curriculum to promote understanding and tolerance of diverse cultural and knowledge systems. However, the success of the ongoing process of curriculum reform for multi-cultural education in China requires a political environment that will allow both structural and directional pluralism. *Baorong Duoyuan* provides these, but the CCP still resists them.

Fan Wang argues that China's elevated level of ethnic diversity constitutes a significant factor contributing to a negative relationship in the State's economic growth across Chinese provinces. According to Wang, "people have a tendency to associate with, socialize with, and be more comfortable with people who appear similar to themselves."[16] I argue that the restrictions and constraints the CCP imposes throughout various spheres in the State, which extend to excluding religious education in China, negatively impact religious freedom and obstruct opportunities to potentially cultivate rich relationships between diverse groups of citizens. Spring suggests that nurturing expectations for student achievement in school may be accomplished by the following three practices:

1. targeted encouragement by parents, counselors, and teachers;

2. campaigns to decrease the dropout rate;

---

13. Hernández, "To Inspire," paras. 1 and 3.
14. Hernández, "To Inspire," para. 24.
15. Leibold, *Minority Education in China,* 2.
16. Dincer and Wang, "Ethnic Diversity and Economic."

3. ensuring students experience freedom of religion in schools.[17]

Contrary to China's Communist foundation, the design for *Baorong Duoyuan* serves to complement the relationship between religion and the State because it offers concise, concrete concepts to address and help eradicate challenges in education, including the State's current denial of the value of religious education. As I contemplate several dilemmas in education under political liberalism and principled pluralism in the following section, I ultimately explain how *Baorong Duoyuan* would supersede these two theories in a post-communist, democratized China. It would also help ensure religious freedom inside and outside of the education setting. Unlike the CCP's control which negatively impacts and stifles religious freedom for all in the State, *Baorong Duoyuan* promotes religious freedom and enhances understanding between diverse religious groups as well as between those professing no religion or proclaiming to be anti-religious.

6.2.2 Ways the Traditional Family and the Community Relate to Education and the State

Chao reports that prior to 1911, in the Dynastic period, the State transmitted and enforced Confucian orthodoxy through the education system.[18] Later, according to Mei-Ju Chou, Yi-Chan Tu, and Kai-Ping Huang, Chinese citizens abandoned the principles of Confucianism for a time, but they revived these ideologies in the twentieth century.[19] Olga Lang stresses that Confucius did not consider the interests of the family and those of society or loyalty between family and community to contradict each other, but that he and his close followers perceived the family as "the root of the State."[20] To Confucius, strengthening the family and kin simultaneously served to bolster the State. In time, when the interests of the family started to contradict those of the community or State, this concept changed, and the family became a means for these entities to accomplish their goals.

Despite the CCP's concentrated tactics to control citizens' lives to further State goals, familial bonds remain strong in China. Chou, Tu, and Huang explain that instead of emphasizing any god or the afterlife, Confucianism, with humanism constituting its primary principle, spotlights the world and the family. "This position is founded on the perception that

17. Spring, *Political Agendas for Education.*

18. Cohen, *China and Christianity,* 3–60. See also Wright, *Buddhism in Chinese,* 65–85.

19. Chou et al., "Confucianism and Character," 59–66.

20. Olga Lang, *Chinese Family and Society,* 55.

humans can be taught and improved with personal and community efforts, especially self-cultivation."[21] Chou, Tu, and Huang note:

> One principle that Confucianism highlights, filial piety, depicts a principle protracted in the Chinese culture. This principle indicates that there must be deference to older individuals, mostly within one's family. This principle is perfectly encapsulated in Confucius' statement "when I walk along with two others, they may serve me as teachers. I will select their good qualities and follow them, their bad qualities and avoid them." Under these conditions, family is not something contrived; it is a major part of one's development.[22]

The Confucian principle of modeling behavior on that of one's elders helps explain why those in the younger generation frequently follow their elders without question and why they rarely, if ever, challenge them or their teachers. Tamara Hamlish explains that family includes immediate family members and encompasses grandparents and married siblings.[23] Joseph C. W. Chan stresses that even though the Confucian perception of human life fundamentally molded the basic configuration of Chinese society and culture throughout the past two thousand years, it has never constituted an established religion. According to Chan: "The interest of Confucianism as a religious humanism lies in its concern for this world, with a clear mission to improve human life and society."[24] Nevertheless, Zinghao Zhou points out that because Confucianism and Chinese traditional religions prove morally centered, the CCP willingly utilizes these vehicles to promote the common good and family values.[25]

Grant et al. assert that certain traits of Chinese culture encourage some overlap between school and family. Similar to the ways that parents assume their children will be submissive, teachers expect students will respect and submit to their teaching and authority. These authors state that "strong interdependence [exists] among family members, and children are raised with the belief that their school performance reflects on their family's honor."[26] Rosemary Foot explains that according to Asian values, the rights of an individual, as well as those of the family, succumb to respect for authority and

---

21. Chou et al., "Confucianism and Character," paras. 1–2 in Section 2.1.

22. Chou et al., "Confucianism and Character," paras. 1–2 in Section 2.1.

23. Hamlish, *China: A Global Studies*, 151–202.

24. Chan, *Religion and Human Rights*, 88.

25. Zhou, "Religious Education in China," 82.

26. Grant et al., *West Meets East*, 26.

the rights of the community.[27] I concur with the point that Confucius presented hundreds of years ago: that the family, an integral component of the community, constitutes an equal and autonomous partner with the State, as well as with other sovereign spheres of society, like businesses and educational institutions. Vincent Goossaert and David A. Palmer report that as the CCP perceives education to constitute a base from which the State may enhance the quality and "cultural level" of citizens, the Party strongly promotes education in both rural and urban communities. Peggy A. Kong observes that parents in rural communities highly value education for the futures of their children.[28] According to Kong:

> Rural residents considered their own quality of life lacking compared to what they believed was the good quality of life of urban residents. They explained [. . .] that rural conditions were less developed and that their work and living conditions were "bitter" (ku).[29]

Parents in the rural community which Kong observed considered that living in cities and obtaining an education not only indicated success but were necessary for survival. In sharing their reasons for supporting their children's education, these parents explained that they believed education represents a necessity for living in contemporary society.[30]

Aligning with the idea that the interests of the family and those of society or loyalties to one or the other are not in opposition to each other, the family instead being the base on which State is founded,[31] Lang stresses the need for members of Chinese communities to support and complement each other.[32] Samuel Ling asserts that parents need to encourage their children[33] to consider careers other than the traditional ones: for example, in the fields of business, science, technology, or medicine. Alternatively, careers in areas of the social sciences and humanities contribute to the development of positive, significant ideas for a society's pluralistic worldview[34] and, ultimately, serve to benefit the community.

27. Foot, *Rights beyond Borders*, 155.

28. Kong, "'To Walk Out,'" 360–73.

29. Kong, "'To Walk Out,'" para. 3 in "To Walk Out" section.

30. Kong, "'To Walk Out.'"

31. Lang, *Chinese Family and Society*, 55.

32. Lang, *Chinese Family and Society*, 55.

33. Ling with Cheuk, *"Chinese" Way of Doing Things*.

34. Ling with Cheuk, *"Chinese" Way of Doing Things*, 78.

In China's contemporary society, as Koh notes regarding democratic societies, states as well as classrooms increasingly reflect their diverse religious populations. Despite numerous controversies and reservations regarding teaching of morality, progressively pluralistic States, including China, generally expect citizens to demonstrate moral behavior. Although venues for the inculcation of moral education may vary from one State to another, as well as from one school to another, RE provides students with the opportunity to better understand a plurality of values and beliefs.[35]

Koh explains that China currently includes moral education within the purview of citizenship education, known as *Deyu* in Chinese. In the past, *Deyu*, which denotes ideological moral political education, utilized indoctrination to emphasize compliance with the CCP's social and political mandates. Currently, moral education involves a focus on moral development through life and learning experiences.[36] As this study reflects, the cultivation of moral values through education, particularly through religious education, comprises a controversial subject. Despite debates, research reveals that the need for moral values to be propagated overwhelmingly exists in contemporary China. I argue that this need will prove to be ongoing not only in the projected future China but throughout the increasingly, religiously pluralistic world and that religious education could best fulfill this need. I propose that if implemented in a post-communist democratized, Christianized China, RE under *Baorong Duoyuan* could contribute to ultimately strengthening citizens' morality. Religious education could also help counter residual effects from China's contemporary "moral vacuum," which I examine in the following section.

6.2.3 China's Contemporary "Moral Vacuum"

Arthur Kleinman admits that a common consensus regarding morality in China concerns him and several of his friends. The claim that "China [. . .] has no moral compass today"[37] correlates with findings from a significant survey conducted in 2014 on "social diseases" in China, as Huaihong He explains: "As many as 88 percent of respondents (60.2 percent fully agreed and 27.8 percent agreed somewhat) believed that China has been beset with a 'social disease of moral decay and the loss of trust.'"[38] Widely occurring phenomena which regularly contribute to the State's ethical and moral

35. Koh, "Moral Development."
36. Koh, "Moral Development."
37. Kleinman et al., *Deep China*, 274.
38. He, *Social Ethics in a Changing*, front matter.

problems include a decline in professional ethics among Buddhist monks, doctors, lawyers, teachers, and particularly government officials. According to He, the level of severity and the scale of moral disruption in the State depict symptoms of China's contemporary moral miasma.

Ma Jian, an author whose books are banned in China, stresses that the CCP's perceptions of procreation and childbirth as political, like most other facets of human life in the State, also contribute to China's moral vacuum. According to Jian, initially, after the CCP gained control of China in 1949, Mao outlawed abortion and the use of contraception, encouraging families to have children. He intended to increase the State's workforce and the ranks of the People's Liberation Army. Mao's strategy backfired, and China's population doubled from approximately 500 million in 1949 to almost a billion thirty years later. After Deng Xiaoping gained power in 1978, the State implemented the one-child policy to align with China's goal to restrict its population to 1.2 billion by the year 2000.[39] Chinese couples could legally give birth to only one child, unless they lived in the countryside and their first child was a girl. Then the family could have two children.

Even though this temporary control to engineer society recently ceased to be enforced, the State continues to intrude into its citizens' intimate lives. Steven Jiang, Paul Armstrong, and Susannah Cullinane report that in October 2015, the CCP issued the following statement, which took effect on 1 January 2016: "To promote a balanced growth of population, China will continue to uphold the basic national policy of population control and improve its strategy on population development. China will fully implement the policy of "one couple, two children" in a proactive response to the issue of an aging population."[40] Like Jian, Jiang, Armstrong, and Cullinanne argue regarding China's previous one-child policy that even its current two-child policy will not erase years of the brutal practices of forced abortions and sterilizations under this plan. I agree with Jiang, Armstrong, and Cullinanne because, under this plan, a child conceived during a third pregnancy would be forcibly aborted without the mother's consent. The killing of millions of babies[41] in the name of State-controlled economic development relativizes the value of life to materialism and contributes to the rapid moral decline in Chinese society.

Kleinman et al. recount that with the advent of China's moral vacuum, the ideology of the CCP no longer proves acceptable to many

39. Jian, "China's Barbaric."

40. Jiang et al., "China unveils," paras. 4 and 5 in introductory section.

41. Huey, "China: Two Child," para. 8. "The one-child policy has been brutally enforced in China over the past 35 years. China's Ministry of Health estimated in 2013 that 336 million babies had been aborted in compliance with this policy."

citizens. Subsequently, a resistance to official atheism as well as a seemingly delegitimatized Communist credo has transpired and contributed to even high-ranking cadres withdrawing support for the State's once-powerful Communist stance.[42] While Communism has undermined traditional Chinese moral values, citizens' corrosive cynicism has similarly tainted Confucian convictions. I contend that the inherent meaning of the quotation, "Schools should also teach students about the different ultimate sources for morality, including religion,"[43] further alludes to the need for a better understanding of morality. It also reiterates the fact that even though the CCP will not currently permit this teaching, the need for religious education in China exists. I argue that fulfilling this critical need in China will more likely be feasible in China's projected democratic, Christianized future under *Baorong Duoyuan*.

6.2.4 Dearth of Freedom Regarding Religious Education

No real freedom for religious education exists in China. Magda Hornemann stresses that the restrictions which China implements regarding RE "reflect the authoritarian State's desire to exercise control over religious groups."[44] Hornemann contends that China's restrictive measures regarding religious education mirror the State's goal to ensure that religious groups do not promote political subversion or become independent of the State. Nevertheless, the CCP's objectives sometimes undermine its projected goals.[45] The control that the State extends to religious education not only contributes to social instability, it may also further pit religious groups against the State.

According to the 2014 *International Religious Freedom Report*, the CCP only permits parents to teach the beliefs of officially recognized religious groups to children under the age of 18. Children may also participate in religious activities; however, Xinjiang officials require that minors complete nine years of compulsory education before they can receive religious education. Adults who *force* minors to participate in religious activities become subject to legal penalties.[46] As I note in Chapter 5, the CCP promotes the teaching of atheism in schools, and mandates that atheism be taught as the guiding ideology at all levels of education in China.

---

42. Kleinman et al., *Deep China*, 274.
43. Tianlong, *Citizenship Education in China*, 6.
44. Hornemann, "China: Tight State Controls," para. 5 in introductory section.
45. Hornemann, "China: Tight State Controls," para. 2.
46. U.S. Department of State, *China*.

Lan Li stresses that even though the CCP has written citizens' rights of religious freedom into every PRC constitution since 1954 and claims to permit freedom of religious belief, in practice, the ideological position of the CCP has been that of atheism.[47] Xiaohuan Su explains that the Confucian imperial orthodox ideology did not promote atheism nor was it atheist. Neither did Confucianism oppose the State religious ritual of ancestor worship or numerous other religious ceremonies, including the worship of heaven and earth, or the worship of *sheji* (State).[48] According to Don Starr, in China "the kindergartens [. . .] begin to train children in the classroom learning skills that characterise Confucian learning environments: respect for the teacher, self-discipline in learning and respect for fellow students."[49] In recent decades, a number of major universities have initiated some teachings about religions by establishing either a department of religion,[50] as at Peking University.[51] Some universities have set up study centers specializing in research about certain religions, such as Christianity, as at Renmin University.[52]

Yik-Fai Tam notes that increased attention to the academic study of religion at a number of Chinese institutions for social science research, including the Central Nationalities University in Beijing, has benefited several minority religious communities.[53] The religious departments and centers do not examine diverse religions and beliefs to better understand them, but either study about religion as a way of comparative world religion studies or conduct research about religion as a way of encouraging a philosophical or cultural point of view. For example, Jinghao Zhou reports that the Department of Philosophy at Beijing University offers the following religious courses:

> Introduction to Religion, Marxism on Religion, Classic Texts of Chinese Buddhism. Classic Texts of Chinese Islam. Introduction to Qur'an. Original Text of Daoism, Introduction to the Bible, Religious Philosophy, History of Christianity, History of Buddhism, and Science and Religion.[54]

47. Li, *Popular Religion.*

48. Su, *Education in China,* 12.

49. Starr, "China and the Confucian."

50. Yang, *Religion in China.*

51. "Department of Philosophy and Religious."

52. "Advanced Institute for Religious."

53. Tam, *Chinese Religious Life,* 39–49.

54. Zhou, "Religious Education in China," 81.

Although the departments of English Language and Literature at a number of other Chinese universities offer various religious courses, including "Reading the Bible," professors cannot teach the Bible from a religious perspective, only from a cultural one.[55] The CCP's purpose for permitting teachings about religions appears to correlate with what Zhou surmises regarding the State's hope for religious schools as well as the goal for the training of professional clergy. The CCP anticipates that those citizens who receive training in religion will ultimately love the socialist motherland and support China's leadership.[56]

Hornemann reports that, currently, certain religious groups cannot teach religious education in China. As I noted in Chapter 4, when the State includes religious education in public education, the approach directly correlates with religious freedom as it reflects the State's stance on religious pluralism. The CCP only permits State-approved religious groups associated with China's five State-backed monopoly faiths to "apply to set up educational institutions for the study of their faith or training of clergy."[57] In addition to the CCP dictating that teachers may only teach subjects within the State's enforced curriculum, State regulations and practices determine the number of institutions as well as the size of each facility.

6.2.5 Confronting Challenges to Religious Education in China

Yang notes that although religious education of children proves to be a common practice in most countries, Chinese authorities routinely prohibit children younger than eighteen from receiving religious education.[58] John Taylor argues that religious education "should be conceived as a tool to transmit knowledge and values pertaining to all religious trends."[59] Taylor stresses that as RE includes the foundations of religious belief, it profoundly differs from catechism or theology and, instead, religious education contributes to the broader framework of diverse education models that international standards define.[60] I agree with Taylor that religious education represents more of pedagogical than theological value.

I argue that restrictions and constraints the CCP imposes throughout various spheres in the State, which extend to excluding religious education

55. Zhou, "Religious Education in China," 81.
56. Zhou, "Religious Education in China."
57. Hornemann, "China: Tight State Controls," para. 2.
58. Yang, *Religion in China*.
59. Taylor, "Responses to United Nation's," 59.
60. Taylor, "Responses to United Nation's," 59.

in China, not only negatively impact religious freedom but also negate opportunities for the teaching of truths in relation to understanding individuals who differ from one another. In turn, the dearth not only in freedom, but also in knowledge, further compounds the negative relationship with the State's economic growth as well as obstructs opportunities to potentially nurture rich relationships between diverse groups of citizens.

When educators teach information about diverse religions in an inclusive, non-biased way, religious education can help individuals better understand those who believe in and practice other religions as well as those professing agnosticism, atheism, or anti-religious beliefs. Conversely, transmitting knowledge about religious education in an exclusive, biased way can stimulate misunderstandings between individuals with diverse beliefs. Norman Richardson stresses that: "[R]eligion in schools is capable of being either very creative or very malign."[61] Religious education can either help students grow personally and become stronger in their faiths or it can stunt their personal growth and contribute to their faith becoming weaker. Creative RE can help students become more knowledgeable and, if they desire to do so, able to credibly transfer their allegiance to that of another belief system. Conversely, negative religious education can hinder students from learning about other religions or beliefs and, even if they desire to do so, block them from investigating the possibility of transferring their commitment to a different ethos.

As noted earlier, China's 1982 Constitution stipulates that its citizens have the right to believe in "normal religion." As the State does not define what constitutes normal, however, the meaning remains unclear, with local authorities determining diverse meanings of the word at their discretion. Taylor argues that although the Chinese constitution specifies that citizens are free to believe in any religion, the CCP limits their religious practice by a plethora of regulations. According to Taylor, individuals in China "can worship in temples, churches, and mosques that are registered with the government, but if they worship in settings other than the ones officially designated for religious practice, they place themselves in a situation of potential illegality."[62] Clergy, imams, monks, priests, and pastors can reportedly lecture, perform religious rituals, and lecture to laypeople; nevertheless, they must not engage in these or other religious activities in any locations other than those CCP officials consider appropriate.

Zhou explains that teaching a moral and social code depicts one distinctive characteristic of Chinese traditional religions. As the CCP remains

---

61. Richardson, *Religious Education in Schools*, 17.
62. Laliberté, *Chinese Religious Life*, 198.

sensitive about any perceived political aspects of religions, particularly Christianity and Islam, the State diligently monitors and controls overt religious activities, including religious education.[63] Due to the incalculable restrictions the CCP imposes on religious education in China, this critical, potentially positive mode for enhancing morality in the State remains undeveloped with limited influence.

Contemporary challenges to RE in China primarily relate to restrictions the CCP regularly imposes. Nevertheless, even in China's projected democratized, Christianized future, with the CCP's control negated, the implementation of religious education will likely require that the MOE overcomes several of the following ongoing, as well as, numerous unfamiliar obstacles:

- textbooks that do not present information to help students understand or discuss diverse religions, or anti- or non-religious beliefs, or their codes for living,

- a situation when teachers are nonspecialists in religious education,

- the need to recognize diversity within each religion and understand that each one, as well as non- or anti-religious beliefs, encompasses variety, with some individuals of the same religion or belief interpreting their faith in diverse ways,

- the need to openly acknowledge controversy and, at times, encourage pupils to critically examine religions, getting them to realize not all of religion constitutes a "good thing,"

- the need to understand the social reality of diverse religions and that of anti- or non-religious beliefs, including perceptions relating to ethical or philosophical matters,

- the need to examine the role of religious education in nurturing community cohesion and in educating for diversity and realize this will empower students to identify their personal attitudes, biases, opinions, feelings, and stereotypes, or

- the need to cultivate respect for the devotion of others to their beliefs yet retain the right to criticize, evaluate, and question viewpoints that differ from one's own;the need to comprehend the power that religion as well as non and anti-religious beliefs possess in the lives of individuals, as well as in their emotions, feelings, and intellect.[64]

63. Zhou, "Religious Education in China."
64. Ofsted, *Making Sense of Religion.*

Despite the CCP's preference for atheism, the State's contemporary goals relating to pluralism could conceivably position religious education as a priority for China to implement in its education system. I argue, however, that this would more likely successfully transpire in China's projected democratic, Christianized future. As the State would incorporate information to support its goal to develop moral, educated citizens, these individuals could, in China's foreseeable future, not only learn about but experience the religious freedom that religious education presupposes. Nevertheless, the system underlying the State's foundation for the implementation of RE, as I discuss in the following section, will confront barriers that *Baorong Duoyuan* can best overcome.

6.3 Barriers to Successfully Implementing Religious Education

In Chapter 5, I listed several fundamental concepts that I drew from both political liberalism and principled pluralism to develop *Baorong Duoyuan* as an alternative for a post-communist, democratized China to help protect religious freedom for all. Although political liberalism and principled pluralism both purportedly aim to empower citizens to conjoin their efforts to pursue the common good for all, as each conditionally supports religious freedom, political liberalism as well as principled pluralism would encounter barriers prohibiting the implementation of religious education in China's projected future State. In some areas of religious education, political liberalism would align with *Baorong Duoyuan*, yet counter this theory in others. Similarly, principled pluralism would correlate with aims of *Baorong Duoyuan* in some respects, yet it would contravene this theory in several others. Despite areas of congruence with my contextualized model of principled pluralism, however, I argue that both political liberalism and principled pluralism would experience more as well as more extreme challenges to implementing religious education than would *Baorong Duoyuan*.

6.3.1 Implementing Religious Education under Political Liberalism

In addition to political liberalism devaluing religious education in compulsory education, I noted in Chapter 3 that political liberalism, an offshoot of liberalism, fails to demonstrate impartiality regarding participation in the public square by preventing specific sects from drawing upon comprehensive doctrines. Although Rawls claims that political liberalism promotes citizens' equal rights, including religious freedom, his reasoning falters as it relates to a pluralism of comprehensive religious, philosophical, and moral doctrines regarding inclusion in the public square. Consequently, due to its constraints regarding reasoning about religion, political liberalism would fail to successfully serve as a foundation for education in China's projected future. As this bias would likewise translate into decisions regarding religious education, I argue that political liberalism would, subsequently, fail to demonstrate impartiality as far as education, thereby constructing one significant barrier to the successful implementation of religious education in China's projected future.

Bryan T. McGraw argues that even though religious individuals may be reasonable and show respect for others and their differing views, one may not reasonably expect that they would, as political liberalism directs, agree to prescind from their religion-based moral convictions when engaging in public discourse in political or educational arenas.[65] I agree with McGraw and with the challenge that George Lazaroiu[66] makes regarding the reasoning Rawls attributes to political liberalism:

> Rawls refers to a view of individuals only to the extent required to attain his aim of typifying persons as free and equal. The identities of people that are incompletely composed by their visions of what is essentially important are individuals' non-public or moral identities (political identity is not partly made up by individuals' views of what is fundamentally valuable). Specific goals and aspirations are indispensable to nonpolitical identity. [. . .] Individuals have a power to constitute and reconsider their views of value, being free to select them: pluralism about visions of value is a vital aspect of a liberal society. Each person has specific rights that cannot be abandoned simply for other individuals to gain more advantages.[67]

Religion seldom proves to constitute a strictly spiritual matter but rather involves moral instructions as to how an individual is to act in daily secular affairs. Although one may reasonably expect religious individuals to act with a certain amount of civility in the public realm, showing respect for others and their different views, it may not be reasonable or even practical expect them to act in the public square without reference "to their deeply held, religiously based moral convictions."[68] So, even if

65. McGraw, *Faith in Politics*.

66. Lazaroiu, "Political Ontology," para. 1 in Conclusion.

67. Lazaroiu, "Political Ontology," para. 1 in Conclusion.

68. Den Hartog, *Public Discourse*, para. 2 in "How to Build a Principled Pluralism" section.

aspects of Rawls's political liberalism appear reasonable to some as a way of encouraging social harmony to a point, I argue that certain principles, particularly regarding the exclusion of religion from the public square, do not equate with fairness or justice.

Another likely insurmountable barrier I foresee for political liberalism in a post-communist, Christianized democracy would be that this theory aligns more with Western than Eastern reasoning. Nevertheless, Mehmet Fevzi Bilgin argues for the prospects of non-Western contexts, such as China, being favorable to adopting Rawls's political liberalism. Although Bilgin recognizes the reality of the religious resurgence in numerous non-Western societies, he contends that political liberalism constitutes a significant theoretical potential resource for States such as China. Bilgin disputes previous research which finds that the socio-political conditions in China and other non-Western societies may fail to satisfy the sociological requirements that political liberalism stipulates. Instead of concluding that countries like China, "will have to wait centuries to live up to the social and moral standards of political liberalism,"[69] Bilgin insists that the conditions for a State to adopt political liberalism do not require the sociological assumptions or the extensive time that Rawls appears to suggest.[70]

The institution of a political liberalism regime would not encourage political liberalism's essential political reasonableness among the diverse religious views anticipated in China's future. When considering political liberalism, Rawls contemplates: "How is it possible there may exist over time a stable and just society of free and equal citizens profoundly divided by reasonable though incompatible religious, philosophical, and moral doctrines?"[71] In the scenario Bilgin notes, the political and social conditions in China primarily prove neither free nor equal.

Bilgin may have a legitimate point by assuming that a non-Western State might not need an extended period to meet at least some of the conditions for political liberalism to be implemented. Nonetheless, to satisfy the political liberalism model in a country like China, as I noted in Chapter 5, under the pattern of State supremacy over religion regarding the State–religion relationship in both its traditional model in the Dynastic period and contemporary patterns under the leadership of the Communists, the short-term transition toward a mature environment where a civil and democratic society can flourish will take much longer than Bilgin states. In fact, Rawls repeatedly

---

69. Bilgin, *Prospects for Political Liberalism*, 359.

70. Bilgin, *The Prospects for Political Liberalism*.

71. Rawls, *Political Liberalism*, xviii.

proclaims that he envisages his structure of the political liberalism model as based on the social-political conditions of the United States.

In addition to political liberalism's unreasonable "reasonableness," Jethro K. Lieberman notes another barrier to implementing religious education under political liberalism. In Rawls's original position, Lieberman recounts that Rawls recreates flesh and blood people into disembodied spirits and shrouds them in a "veil of ignorance." These individuals reportedly do not have any knowledge about their place in society, or about their class or social status and converge into one single individual. Consequently, the need for discussion dissipates while unanimity becomes certain. Rather than considering real constructions of actual individuals, ideological conflicts dissipate under political liberalism.[72] According to Van de Putte, Rawls's theoretical process would prove counterproductive and contribute to even more challenges for religious education in a post-communist China. Putte argues that the political ideas of freedom and equality relate to the will to achieve a fair society despite ideological conflicts.[73]

As I argued in Chapter 5, although Rawls claims that political liberalism promotes citizens' equal rights, including religious freedom, his reasoning falters as it relates to a pluralism of comprehensive religious, philosophical, and moral doctrines.[74] Chinese citizens do not currently, nor will they typically, converge into one single individual to affirm one another's doctrines in the future. Political liberalism's inability to impartially recognize, reiterate, and resolve conflicting perceptions, coupled with its thinly veiled biases toward certain religious and comprehensive doctrines, renders it improbable as a means of successfully implementing religious education in China's projected future. However, for assorted reasons, principled pluralism, similar to political liberalism, as I submit in the following section, would also fail to effectively serve as a theoretical foundation for implementing religious education in a post-communist China's education system.

6.3.2 Barriers to Implementing Religious Education under Principled Pluralism

Following their exposure to information relating to diverse religions when receiving religious education, students can more objectively choose or reject what they discern as partial or whole religious truths. Nevertheless, as I note in Chapter 5, principled pluralism, which primarily originated from

72. Lieberman, *Liberalism Undressed.*

73. Van de Putte, "Rawls" Political Liberalism.

74. Hill Jr., *Respect, Pluralism, and Justice,* 240.

a Dutch culture, depicts a Christian, theologically based theory. Due to principled pluralism's basic Christian foundation, this theory, as political liberalism, would routinely encounter barriers prohibiting the successful implementation of RE in China's projected Christianized, democratized future State. The foundation of principled pluralism will particularly limit its appeal and its acceptance by numerous non-Christian groups, atheists, and non or anti-religious sects. In addition, controversies could emerge periodically as well as challenges to guidelines and content for religious education because principled pluralism could encompass preferences for texts biased toward Christianity. In addition, the probability exists that some secularists, numerous atheists as well as others professing religious faiths other than Christianity would at times object to principled pluralism's prioritization of values.[75]

In Chapter 2, I noted that Schweitzer suggested the principled pluralist perspective for religious education creates opportunities for students to strengthen their abilities to evaluate religious truths.[76] Although principled pluralists would likely consider these prospects as positive, those with allegiances to beliefs other than Christianity would probably challenge its validity. Glenn argues that although many parents appear to prefer that education includes religious education, where the law permits or requires RE, the results have typically proved unsatisfactory. The outcomes have failed to satisfy either non-believers or believers.[77] Similarly, in China's projected Christianized future, non-religious as well as non-Christian adherents could fear that their children may be indoctrinated, while Christians may perceive that the predictable generic focus of religious education could distort and trivialize their faith.

In Chapter 4, I reported that principled pluralism supports dialogue within individual religions as well as between various religious groups, principally Christian ones. Nevertheless, in a sense, as I previously noted by referring to Schmidt, because principled pluralism emphasizes the significance of associations and communities, this prompts principled pluralists to circumvent individualism (particularly in extreme formats).[78] I submit that principled pluralism's emphasis on Christianity and the de-emphasis that it gives to individualism could construct a significant barrier to the implementation of religious education. Charles L. Glenn's argument against the stance that principled pluralism would adopt in religious

75. Jackson, *Rethinking Religious Education.*

76. Schweitzer, *On the Edge.*

77. Glenn, *Equal Treatment of Religion,* 90.

78. Schmidt, "Principled Pluralist."

education, stressing that Christianity supersedes other beliefs, illustrates this expected obstacle. According to Glenn, "In elementary education, an emphasis upon how groups and individuals in society differ in their convictions and loyalties does not seem appropriate."[79]

Principled pluralism's theistic posture, coupled with its historical Christian origin, would likely invite conflict with certain atheists, those with no religious beliefs, and those who are anti-religious. As a result, a significant barrier for the implementation of religious education under principled pluralism could arise.

Proponents of principled pluralism, like those of political liberalism, argue that principled pluralism supports religious freedom. Although a Christian worldview serves as the theological foundation for principled pluralism regarding issues concerning religious freedom, the philosophical stance that principled pluralism basically supports proves inclusive. This position reflects views which most other religions mirror and includes the atheistic worldview, written in Article 36 of China's constitution.

If principled pluralism should arbitrarily employ fundamentalist approaches such as theonomy in the implementation of religious education, tensions among the diverse truth claims of other and non-religious beliefs would arise. If principled pluralism were to demonstrate favoritism for the Christian religion or not give other diverse non-Christian beliefs due exposure, this would devalue religious education as it is taught in public schools, and erect a barrier of suspicion to the potential positive implementation of RE under principled pluralism.

The United Nations Educational, Scientific and Cultural Organization (UNESCO) states the following to emphasize the need for recognizing and affirming the value of diverse religions as far as children are concerned:

> There is no single approach to respecting religious and cultural rights in education systems. Separate schooling systems for different religions or languages can serve to discriminate against and marginalize groups of children if the schools are afforded inequitable funding and status. They can also serve to exclude and marginalize children from educational and employment opportunities. Conversely, the imposition of a uniform schooling system that takes no account of minority cultures and religions can serve to oppress and undermine children from those communities and contribute to educational failure and high drop-out rates.[80]

---

79. Glenn, *Equal Treatment of Religion*, 91.
80. United Nations, *Human Rights-Based Approach*, 78.

Instead of constructing barriers to the implementation of religious education in a post-communist, democratized, Christianized China, UNESCO asserts that the foundation for religious education must respect diverse religions and afford freedom for parents and guardians to ensure that the religious and moral education their children receive conforms with their own convictions.[81] As public schools would likely utilize one of four[82] out of five approaches to implementing religious education under principled pluralism, interpretations with regard to the chosen approach as well as its intensity could conceivably favor Christianity.

Although principled pluralism would comply with legal guidelines within domestic, regional, and international norms, it could subtly or perhaps even overtly support a preference for Christianity in teaching. This would counter UNESCO's recommended guidelines and international norms regarding RE and would likely contribute to one more barrier to religious education succeeding under principled pluralism. Consequently, for this and the other reasons I noted in this section, I conclude that in their approaches both political liberalism and principled pluralism would fail to overcome significant barriers to the implementation of religious education.

6.3.3 Religious Education under Political Liberalism and Principled Pluralism

The numerous inherent barriers which political liberalism and principled pluralism could present regarding religious freedom confirm that neither theory would prove successful for implementing religious education in a post-communist, Christianized democracy. Nevertheless, in this section, I envisage how religious education would be taught under political liberalism as well as under principled pluralism. This further confirms my arguments regarding inadequacies that the two theories would provide for religious freedom and ultimately supports my stance that *Baorong Duoyuan* offers the best option for religious education in China's future.

---

81. United Nations, *Human Rights-Based Approach.*

82. The five approaches to teaching religious education, introduced in Chapter 4, are: (1) learning into religion (LI); (2) learning about religion (LA); (3) learning from religion (LF); (4) separatist approach; (5) secularist approach.

6.3.3.1 Religious Education as Portrayed
under Political Liberalism

Political liberalism would fully support the separatist approach for religious education in China's projected future because this would distance the teaching of religions from public education. In Chapter 4, I noted that Ahdar and Leigh explained that separatists argue the responsibility for religious education belongs to the parents and that the State should firmly separate itself from RE. Without religious education in public schools in China, however, some students would only know about their own family's religion or, at the other extreme, due to misconceptions, become prejudiced against others with beliefs different from their own.[83] Although political liberalism would conditionally support the moderate secularist approach because this method tolerates some teaching of religions, it would still offend some religious individuals.[84] Political liberalism would typically reject religious education aligning with ideological or radical secularists.

In the public-school system in China's projected post-communist future, political liberalism would not permit the teaching of religious education using the religious instruction method. Political liberalism would stipulate, however, that although certain conditions would constrain RE from being taught using the learning about religion approach, this approach would be acceptable. Political liberalism would never, however, permit the teaching of religious education using the learning from religion method. According to the reasoning of political liberalism, learning from religion could offend certain religious adherents or those professing non or anti-religious beliefs. I argue contrariwise that the learning from religion approach in religious education would best equip China's future generation to understand beliefs of others that differ from their own—religious, non-religious, and even anti-religious. The preference of political liberalism for the separatist approach in religious education would prove biased toward the "religious" philosophies of atheists and those with anti-religious beliefs. It would also, ultimately, constrain religious freedom in education for young people.

6.3.3.2 Religious Education as Portrayed
under Principled Pluralism

Contrary to political liberalism adopting the separatist approach as its preference regarding religious education, principled pluralism would negate this

---

83. Ahdar and Leigh, *Religious Freedom*, 268.
84. Modood, "Moderate Secularism."

option as it fails to protect religious freedom for all and, in a sense, appears to demonstrate a preference for non- and anti-religious beliefs. Principled pluralism would concur with political liberalism regarding the secularist approach to religious education. Like political liberalism, principled pluralism would permit the moderate approach in teaching religious education. Principled pluralism would, like political liberalism, determinedly prohibit RE from aligning with ideological or radical secularists. In addition, principled pluralism would conditionally approve the religious instruction approach as the one to be utilized in religious education in the public-school setting in China's projected post-communist future, as long as the teaching of one specific religion did not dominate the process. Similarly, principled pluralism would conditionally approve the learning about religion method for teaching religious education as long as the teachings and practices of one religion were not overemphasized in the learning sessions.

Principled pluralism would also support the learning from religion approach to religious education, provided one religion did not dictate that its beliefs and practices override others in the school. If religious education were implemented under principled pluralism's Christian base, however, it could potentially favor Christianity. In turn, this could negate equal representation of other religions, atheism, and beliefs professing anti-religious views. This could work to counter RE in public schools and sabotage the potential for its success in a post-communist, Christianized, democratic China.

In the next section, I focus on the vision, criteria, and design for the implementation of religious education under *BD*. I propose that as *Baorong Duoyuan* will complement RE, it would best serve as the foundation for religious education in China's future education system.

6.4 Implementing Religious Education under *Baorong Duoyuan*

I argue that the CCP's rationale for promoting Confucianism and Chinese traditional religions, while banning other religions and religious education, does not promote but counters the common good for all and the family values of Chinese citizens. Amitai Etzioni explains that religion fills the vacuum left when values the State previously promoted wane, as with Communism, for example, or when, as in China, citizens experience a moral vacuum and find the State's values unfulfilling. Etzioni emphasizes that, in turn, billions of individuals embrace religion. For example, in politically and economically underdeveloped countries, which would include China, the "avoidance of teaching moral and religious values [. . .] is not the case."[85] Rather than secularization overtaking society and people becoming less religious or abandoning religious beliefs, relegating religion to the private sphere as political liberalism advocates, religion constitutes a critical source of ethical and spiritual guidance for many Chinese individuals.

Contrary to many secular policy makers as well as numerous political liberals who question the value of religion and whether religious education should be implemented in public schools, I argue that religious education possesses the potential to simultaneously enhance a person's understanding of their own belief system and contribute to their gaining an enhanced empathetic understanding of others practicing different beliefs. While political liberalism and principled pluralism could conceivably overcome some of the barriers that I note in the previous sections, they would likely fail to successfully implement religious education in China's future education system. Nevertheless, as I examine basics contributing to the vision, criteria, and development of *Baorong Duoyuan* in the next sections, which confirm my proposition that my theory would best suit religious education in China's projected future as a Christianized democracy.

6.4.1 Vision of Religious Education under *Baorong Duoyuan*

In contrast to political liberalism and principled pluralism erecting barriers to the success of religious education in China's projected Christianized, democratized State, *Baorong Duoyuan*, a contextualized "offshoot" of principled pluralism, promotes the potential for religious education to flourish and bloom. Nevertheless, despite numerous differences with political liberalism and principled pluralism, *Baorong Duoyuan* shares some similarities with these two theories, and a particular one which Robert Jackson notes—growth in understanding one's own beliefs as well as those of other individuals.[86] In the vision that I foresee for religious education in China under *Baorong Duoyuan*, religious education would be equally accessible for all in each educational institution and school and, as a result, this growth would permeate the State.

In considering the implementation and growth of religious education that I foresee for China in its projected future, I agree with Gottfried Adam and Martin Rothgangel that aspirations regarding religious education constitute an ongoing process with continuing reflections on diverse

---

85. Etzioni, "Religion and the State," para. 1 in "Religion is Not "History"" section.
86. Jackson, *Rethinking Religious Education*.

levels.[87] Nevertheless, I envisage that the projected format of RE will be learner-centered with transparent goals and expectations of achievements for students. Jackson relates several other goals and benefits for religious education as follows:

> a key aim for religious education is to develop an understanding of the grammar—the language and wider symbolic patterns—of religions and the interpretive skills necessary to gain that understanding. The achievement of this aim requires the development of critical skills, the application of which opens up issues of representation, interpretation, truth and meaning. Religious education develops self-awareness, since individuals develop through reflecting upon encounters with new ideas and experiences. Religious education is thus a conversational process in which students, whatever their backgrounds, continuously interpret and reinterpret their own views in the light of what they study.[88]

The following three notable pedagogical values may be gained from religious education under *Baorong Duoyuan*'s model:

1. It provides access for all students to learn about different religions, including atheistic and anti-religious beliefs and the diverse cultures affiliated with each religion or belief system.[89] By providing equal access to religious education for all students, regardless of their personal religious affiliation, lack of religion, or anti-religious belief, religious education under *Baorong Duoyuan*'s model equips students for learning about diverse religions and different worldviews. This proves especially important in the Chinese context because traditional Chinese society tends to be homogeneous,[90] utilizing a monolithic system both with regard to religion and ethnically and politically, to organize a designated social order. Under *Baorong Duoyuan*, the promotion of religious education in a more heterogeneous, pluralistic manner will also help neutralize and de-emphasize the negative impact of the Communist, atheistic-oriented educational culture.

---

87. Adam and Rothgangel, *Basics of Religious*, 131–44.

88. Jackson, *Rethinking Religious Education*, 169.

89. Yecheng, *Davidson in China*, para. 3.

90. Raadschelders, and Vigoda-Gadot, *Global Dimensions of Public*, 111. "In truly and sociologically homogeneous societies people share a language, a history, and an ethnicity."

2. It helps students develop and apply critical skills to interpret truth and meaning.[91] Religious education under *Baorong Duoyuan* would foster further directional pluralism, at least in a descriptive way. Learning from and about diverse faiths and belief traditions regarding the way other individuals interpret their personal truth-claims would help students from differing religions develop critical thinking skills and better prepare themselves to defend both their own and other individuals' faith and freedom of expression when challenged and would also be helpful in promoting understanding of other beliefs.

3. It fosters partnerships to promote common good and counter religious extremism. As Jackson additionally notes, another subsequent long-term benefit that I envisage for the implementation of religious education under *Baorong Duoyuan* is that it contributes to "Fostering positive relations between religious groups of different faiths."[92] Consequently, *BD* can also establish partnerships that could help promote the common good of those with diverse belief systems.

As students study different belief systems, religious education will empower them to engage in knowledgeable communication and better understand those from diverse cultures as well as others professing diverse beliefs. This proves especially critical following 9/11 with much of terrorism originating from either homegrown, radicalized terrorists in a homogeneous religious environment or brainwashed by international extremist religious propaganda.

The vision for religious education in compulsory education under *Baorong Duoyuan* will include the full protection of religious freedom and cultural rights of all groups. This will include atheists and agnostics as well as those professing non or anti-religious beliefs. I argue that contrary to stifling freedom of religion as the CCP continues to do, despite claims to the contrary, the implementation of religious education under *Baorong Duoyuan* possesses the seed for religious freedom to subsequently root and grow in China. To prepare the ground for my vision regarding the implementation of religious education under *Baorong Duoyuan* so that it can begin to germinate, I propose that China's future MOE introduces several positive criteria that I present in the next section.

---

91. Jackson, *Rethinking Religious Education*, 169.
92. "Principled Pluralism: Report of the Inclusive," para. 3.

6.4.2 Criteria for Implementing Religious Education
under *Baorong Duoyuan*

To help ensure that the implementation of religious education under *Baorong Duoyuan* in a post-communist China encompasses principles which will nurture RE, it mandates that the MOE clearly identifies necessary principles for RE. Criteria founding the plan for religious education must be clearly constructed and documented with methods to ensure accountability. I propose that the future Chinese education system implements the following benchmarks. Although these standards reflect three crucial areas for education reform to align with *Baorong Duoyuan*, education leaders should not use these as an excuse to penetrate the education system with a secularist worldview in the name of "State neutrality." These benchmarks include:

1. Guidelines for teaching religious education should neither promote nor suppress the teaching of any one legal worldview, religious belief, or non-belief.

2. In teaching religious education, the State should promote freedom of education as being compatible with the principles of religious freedom, aligning with international norms.

3. The State should clearly present criteria to ensure protection of the right for parents to exercise their preference to choose or set up education institutions for their children according to their religious or non-religious affiliation.[93]

These three proposed criteria for implementing *Baorong Duoyuan* prove compatible with the basic principles of religious freedom manifested regarding education and align with various international human rights instruments, including the *Universal Declaration of Human Rights*, the ICCPR, and the ICESCR, as well as the Declaration of the Rights of the Child (Geneva Declaration), the Canadian Children's Rights Council, and the UN Convention on the Rights of the Child.

To develop criteria for implementing religious education in China's future education system, I draw from both the OSCE, specifically the Toledo Guiding Principles on Teaching about Religious Beliefs in Public Schools, and information that Grant et al. published. These authors stress that Chinese scholars found that most teachers do not use evidence which empirical studies generate to guide their teaching but, instead, rely on conventional wisdom. Consequently, the following framework for implementing religious education under *BD* reflects seven major guidelines drawn from

---

93. Maussen, "Religious Governance in the Netherlands."

Chinese "conventional wisdom,"[94] contextualized to be compatible with OSCE principles which stipulate that educators are to:

1. develop and maintain an environment conducive to learning that respects human rights, fundamental freedoms, and civic values,

2. study and understand students' belief systems, demonstrating a commitment to religious freedom,

3. ensure objectivity in teaching about religions and beliefs without favoring one religion over another,

4. establish a spirit of mutual respect and understanding for students that they may replicate as they relate to others,

5. clarify goals and organize learning opportunities, implementing creative and varied vehicles for learning,

6. cultivate the attitude, knowledge, and skills to help students learn in fair and balanced ways about diverse beliefs and religions as well as non- or anti-religious beliefs, and

7. include a focus on key historical and contemporary developments but also reflect local and global concerns relating to religion.

Another critical criterion for the implementation of religious education under *Baorong Duoyuan* would be the stipulation that teachers and other educators receive mandatory initial as well as ongoing training, i.e. continuing educational units (CEUs). Training sessions for teachers could include identifying ways to help students understand diverse beliefs in China's pluralistic population. These educational sessions for teachers would equip them to best facilitate religious education by introducing and reiterating basic concepts which align with *Baorong Duoyuan* and help ensure religious freedom in the school setting.

One distinctive feature of religious education under the *Baorong Duoyuan* model is that its compliance with international norms guarantees the rights of parents and legal guardians and ensures their preferred role in choosing their children's education according to their religious preference. This is critical both to protecting the religious freedom of parents and legal guardians and guaranteeing their choice for their children's religious education. The UN Human Rights Committee reaffirmed these principles during its 48th session:

> The Committee is of the view that article 18.4 permits public
> school instruction in subjects such as the general history of

94. Grant et al., *West Meets East*, 13.

religions and ethics if it is given in a neutral and objective way. The liberty of parents or legal guardians to ensure that their children receive a religious and moral education in conformity with their own convictions, set forth in article 18.4, is related to the guarantees of the freedom to teach a religion or belief stated in article 18.1. The Committee notes that public education that includes instruction in a particular religion or belief is inconsistent with article 18.4 unless provision is made for non-discriminatory exemptions or alternatives that would accommodate the wishes of parents and guardians.[95]

According to Carolyn Evans, the European Court of Human Rights asserts that the duty of the State regarding religious education encompasses more than the content of classes. It also extends to concerns which affect parents and students. Evans further notes that the parents' religion or belief must be respected in religious education. Equipping educators with principles for involving parents in children's religious education depicts one more prominent criterion that could help circumvent misunderstandings regarding religious education, ensuring both that parental rights in this area are honored[96] and that the beliefs of their children are recognized.[97] Cultivating classroom practices to ensure that religious education remains compatible with the principle of religious freedom for all could additionally contribute to parents more favorably consenting to their children participating in RE. In the next section, as I propose a design for the implementation of religious education under *Baorong Duoyuan* in China's projected future, the recommended format must include fair and unbiased examinations of different beliefs as this will help students better understand those practicing different religions, both inside and outside the educational setting.[98] I consider this necessary to ensure that the interests of the majority do not overshadow those of the minority.

6.4.3 Design for Implementing Religious Education under *Baorong Duoyuan*

The design for the implementation of religious education in public education under *Baorong Duoyuan* in China's projected future draws insights from a myriad of sources both inside and outside the education setting.

95. Human Rights Committee, "General Comments and General," point 6.

96. Evans, *Religion and Human Rights*, 188–203.

97. Maussen, "Religious Governance in the Netherlands."

98. Evans, *Religion and Human Rights*.

The scheme would develop and implement "Life Education,"[99] with specific plans for education that include religious education (learning from religion). The design would ensure that employees, teachers, and others officially involved in education were transparent, fair, and accountable to help ensure that students obtain a quality education free from religious persecution. The design would allow for protection of each person's religious freedom. It would also provide guidance and implement strategies to develop and encourage student engagement and excellence not only in academic achievements but also in the areas of arts, health, morality, and other national and global concerns.[100] Curricula would reflect the advocating of multicultural education.[101]

The foundation for the design of religious education would evolve from but not be restricted to international guidelines for religious freedom and relevant research regarding religious education. To enable students to learn correct attitudes about different religions, the design for religious education under *Baorong Duoyuan* would include equipping teachers with certain "tools." These tools would contain the curriculum, textbooks, and strategies to complement both religious education and religious freedom. I assert that implementing religious education using these types of tools would help students learn to overcome barriers in communicating with others not only in their current education setting but also later when they become adults and can contribute to social progress.

As I assert in Chapter 4, under *Baorong Duoyuan*, the constitution for a future post-communist, Christianized, democratic China will explicitly stipulate that the State:

1. will guarantee freedom of religious belief for all citizens as prescribed in international human rights norms;

2. shall treat all religions, beliefs, or non-beliefs impartially and equally;

---

99. Ng and Chan, *Religious Education in Schools*, 40. "'Life Education' consists of a school's planned provision to promote its pupils' personal, social, and spiritual development. This program includes learning from religious education in a multi-faith approach, education about death and life, character education, career education, and physiological health education. These aims correspond with the educational ideas of the Republic of China's Constitution, which emphasizes that education and culture are a means to develop people's national consciousness, autonomous consciousness, moral consciousness, physical health, and social and life intelligence."

100. Concepts adapted from "The Responsibilities of the Ministry."

101. Leibold, *Minority Education in China*.

3. shall not only protect citizens' freedom of religion or freedom of religious belief but also secure and preserve the manifestation of their religion or belief;

4. shall not establish any national religion, belief, or non-belief.

For public schools, the guiding philosophy will be that of structural and directional pluralism under *Baorong Duoyuan*. The guiding philosophy for private schools will be categorized as freedom of school choice, with parental and legal guardian preference. For public schools, the MOE will establish and facilitate multiple religious education curriculums, with a minimum requirement that the content should be in the form of "learning about religion." Content in the form of "learning from" and "learning into" religion may be made available for optional studies. The curriculum in private schools should be designed by the local school board to reflect the school choice of different faith or non-faith traditions. The syllabus will comply with minimum national education standards for liberal arts and science. The minimum national standard should be the promotion of fundamental rights and freedoms as given in the State constitution, aligning with international human rights standards and norms. Public and private schools will be managed with a degree of local and community autonomy as will the employment of teachers. In managing and employing teaching staff under *Baorong Duoyuan*, the MOE will maintain a national resource pool for qualified, registered religious education teachers.

In the implementation of religious education under *Baorong Duoyuan*, the primary goal—to promote religious freedom for all, must constitute a core factor founding all considerations. Public funding should be available for all schools with money allocated impartially, regardless of the school's religion or non-religious belief, including schools organized by adherents of an atheistic worldview. Funding for private schools may be obtained from multiple sources, including the State, businesses, local community organizations, and private citizens. Table 9 illustrates concepts for the implementation of religious education under *Baorong Duoyuan*.

Table 9: Design of Religious Education under Baorong Duoyuan[102]

	Public School	**Private School**
Goal	Promote religious freedom for all	Promote religious freedom for all
Funding source	Public funding available without bias toward religion	Funding obtained from multiple sources, including the State, businesses, local community organizations, and private citizens
Guiding philosophy	Structural and directional pluralism under *Baorong Duoyuan*	Freedom regarding school choice (parental and legal guardian preference)
Religious education curriculum	State-facilitated, multiple curriculums with a minimum requirement of content in the form of "learning about religion" (content in the form of "learning from" and "learning into" religion may be made available for optional studies) Promotion of fundamental rights and freedoms in the State constitution, aligning with international human rights standards and norms (minimum national standard)	Local school board designed to reflect the school choice of different faith or non-faith traditions, with minimum national education standards for liberal arts and science Promotion of fundamental rights and freedoms in the State constitution, aligning with international human rights standards and norms (minimum national standard)
School management *Teacher employment*	Local and community autonomy in both hiring and management. State-facilitated national resource pool for qualified, registered teachers of religious education	Local and community autonomy in both hiring and management. State-facilitated national resource pool for qualified, registered teachers of religious education

To promote the cultural, mental, and physical development of students and nurture their moral and spiritual growth in an anticipated post-communist society with a pluralist worldview under the *Baorong Duoyuan* model, the State operates as a facilitator to develop the curriculum. By working with the

---

102. Author's original table.

local school board to develop multiple diverse curricula, the content will reflect the school choice of diverse faiths or non-faith traditions and align with international human rights standards and norms. In addition, the syllabus for religious education would be structured to help prepare students to effectively embrace experiences, opportunities, and responsibilities later in life.[103] The curriculum would specifically equip instructors to teach students to:

- examine and analyze diverse religious beliefs as well as non- or anti-religious beliefs and practices of religions and worldviews,

- use coherent reasoning in synthesizing their own and other individuals' arguments and ideas regarding sources of wisdom and authority, ensuring accurate references to their historical, cultural, and social contexts,

- evaluate various expressions and ways of life inherent in diverse religions and worldviews in a clear, well-informed way,

- explain varied responses to reflective questions about diversity, the expression of identity, meaning, and value,

- argue for and validate personal positions regarding vital questions about the nature of religion and evaluate the perspectives of others,

- utilize several research methods to study, as well as critically evaluate various approaches to, and perspectives relating to, concerns regarding community cohesion, mutual understanding, and respect for all, locally, nationally, and globally, and

- research and skillfully present several rational, reasonable arguments which profoundly encompass moral, religious, and spiritual concerns.[104]

The successful implementation of the religious education curriculum is aligned with and relies on the choice of textbooks. At times, in public schools, due to concerns about freedom of religion in religious education and concerns about religious and non- or anti-religious beliefs, some parents insist that the school exempt their children from reading specific textbooks. According to Lieberman, both the school exempting a child from reading a specific textbook and the school board having the right to require that a student utilize prescribed textbooks that prove to be morally or politically biased. Although withdrawing offensive textbooks could eradicate some conflicts, if a minority were to control which textbooks could or couldn't

---

103. Religious Education Council.
104. Religious Education Council.

be used, then this would likely diminish learning and undermine religious education. To protect the religious freedom of students who may be offended by certain texts or teachings, perhaps teachers could offer alternative texts.[105] Parents could ask that their children be exempt from these classes or enroll them in a non-public school, which would still be state-funded, where their preferred religion or belief would be taught.

Under *Baorong Duoyuan*, the choice of textbooks would reflect all religions, including minority religions or beliefs. No content containing bias or prejudice of any kind toward any religion or belief should be included. Results from a 2011 study entitled *Connecting the Dots: Education and Religious Discrimination in Pakistan* indicate texts that illustrate this point. The study found certain examples of bias toward certain religions, a practice contrary to that which China should use in its projected future State. For example, passages "portray Pakistani Christians as Westerners or equal to British colonial oppressors, and Pakistani Hindus as Indians, the arch enemy of Pakistan."[106] The textbooks, which reportedly reach more than 41 million children, portray religious minorities in a negative light, depicting them as inferior and untrustworthy. Robert P. George, an American legal scholar and political philosopher, states:

> Pakistan's public-school textbooks contain deeply troubling content that portrays non-Muslim citizens as outsiders, unpatriotic, and inferior; are filled with errors; and present widely disputed historical "facts" as settled history.
>
> Missing from these textbooks are any references to the rights of religious minorities and their positive contributions to Pakistan's development. The set textbooks sadly reflect the alarming state today of religious freedom in Pakistan. A country's education system, including its textbooks, should promote religious tolerance, not close the door to cooperation and coexistence.[107]

The study recommended that Pakistan's MOE should replace current biased texts with revised textbooks to indicate that religious freedom reflects the protection the State's constitution provides to all Pakistanis. Similarly, I propose that the MOE in a projected post-communist, democratic constitutional China ensures that both the design of the curriculum and the content of textbooks mirror religious freedom for all in religious education, especially for minorities.

105. Lieberman, *Liberalism Undressed.*
106. "Pakistan: Public School."
107. "Pakistan: Public School," para. 2.

When working with other educational specialists developing strategies for the implementation of religious education under *Baorong Duoyuan*, China's future MOE needs to assess potential areas of difficulty students may experience[108] to equip teachers to address these concerns. At times, some students may struggle to understand specific concepts of religions that differ from their own. To address this concern, teachers need a variety of teaching strategies for students when they analyze and relate facets of different beliefs. To help students feel less threatened by diverse religions and beliefs, teachers may also need to employ creative approaches when comparing information extracted from other resources to material in textbooks. Under *Baorong Duoyuan*, as teachers utilize strategies to respond to challenges in religious education, they may find that some students interacting with diverse beliefs need empathy, especially when these beliefs diametrically oppose those taught at home. Using the learning from religion approach to religious education, the method I recommend, teachers could implement perspective-taking exercises for considering diverse religions. For this strategy, teachers would orchestrate opportunities for students to perceive themselves in the positions of others with beliefs that differ from their own. Participating in such an assignment would help students to better understand the viewpoints and feelings of others as well as motivate them to consider or predict the impact that their behaviors might have on other individuals.[109]

According to Koh, perspective-taking exercises may not only stimulate empathy and humanitarianism but can also nurture students' moral affect and cognition. Meryl Chertoff recommends several tactics to help young people transferring from one culture to another that could also break down barriers concerning religion when implementing religious education in China's projected future State.[110] Engaging young people in dialogue and uniting them into broader community programs portray generic strategies that the MOE could approve for teachers to utilize in the learning from religion approach. More specific examples of these techniques include but would not be limited to:

- Storytelling. Teachers could utilize narratives portraying different religions as well as clarifying values that individuals with certain religious and non or anti-religious beliefs hold. This could prove particularly effective for humanizing others with diverse beliefs.

---

108. National Council for Curriculum.

109. Koh, "Moral Development."

110. Chertoff, "Principled Pluralism: Report," para. 3.

- "Show and tell." Students could share religious practices and traditions within a designated "show and tell" classroom session. These scenarios could, henceforth, help promote a spirit of respect and tolerance for others and their beliefs.

- Community service. Involving students in community service programs would expose them to diverse populations and beliefs and enable them to contribute to the welfare of others while practicing moral actions[111] and, as Chertoff notes, they would also be working for and contributing to the common good of society.[112]

Numerous elements must exist for a pluralistic society to thrive. These include "religious identity, positive inter-religious relations, increased education, and understanding and dialogue."[113] Chertoff argues that:

> individual families should also work to promote pluralism; young people should be encouraged to engage with and discover new cultures while having the choice to retain their own beliefs. "Safe places," where people from diverse backgrounds can come together and talk about their faith and beliefs should be promoted, especially in formal education settings from a young age. [. . . M]ediation in these initiatives will reassure families that their children will not lose their own faith, but rather gain a basic education that highlights shared values, shared stories and holidays. This type of education serves to break down religious barriers and promotes shared ethical values.[114]

In China's post-communist, democratized State, strategies for implementing religious education under *Baorong Duoyuan* would also need to ensure that legal provisions in religious education comply with international guidelines to:

1. end positive privileges for religion and for religious people, acts (speech, behavior), and organizations,

2. afford equal treatment in all kinds of organizations as well as in diverse domains and spheres of life in relation to religious education, and

3. limit opportunities for voluntary self-separation from religious education based on the religious (or non or anti-religious) views a person holds and/or ethnicity, in an attempt to combat (involuntary) segregation

111. Koh, "Moral Development."
112. Chertoff, "Principled Pluralism: Report," para. 3.
113. Chertoff, "Principled Pluralism: Report," para. 3.
114. Chertoff, "Principled Pluralism: Report," para. 4.

and unequal treatment and unequal opportunities for members of religious as well as non-religious groups and communities.[115]

Amid contemporary globalization, Chinese perceptions can negate or nurture the way citizens understand other cultures and religions. Tam notes that "the growing importance of religion in international affairs, the attention to ethnicity as a global political force, and the rise of China as an economic and political power"[116] all impact minority religious communities in the People's Republic. I submit that these issues likewise affect other communities, families, and education in the State. Tam contends that discussions of religion and public life in China must also include the numerous ways in which minority ethnic communities contribute to understanding how religion will shape the common future of China. I agree but, additionally, argue that understanding diverse cultures and their religious beliefs as well as recognizing contributions of all communities in China and how they impact the State's strengths and weaknesses will help determine the State's future. As I elaborated in the previous section, because Chinese citizens' perceptions of family and community affect the State, understanding these entities will, subsequently, affect the vision, design, and criteria for the implementation of religious education in a post-communist China's education system under *Baorong Duoyuan*.

6.5 Conclusion

As a foundation for implementing religious education in China in a projected post-communist, democratic, Christianized State, *Baorong Duoyuan* would provide a safe, impartial environment for those adhering to diverse religions as well as for those with non-religious beliefs to express their beliefs without fear of persecution or prosecution. *Baorong Duoyuan* will include religious education to equip students to better understand and more effectively communicate with others who adhere to religious beliefs that differ from their own philosophies. As *Baorong Duoyuan* would enhance religious freedom in China's education system, it would simultaneously help stimulate, support, and sustain religious freedom for all as young people learn to live out the understandings that they learn regarding religious pluralism.

In addition to *Baorong Duoyuan* demonstrating more compatibility with international norms than political liberalism or principled pluralism in relation to religious freedom, my theory also proves to be more inclusive

---

115. Maussen, "Religious Governance."

116. Wikeri, and Tam, *Chinese Religious Life*, 53.

of diverse beliefs than either of these theories in terms of religious freedom for all. As *BD* will incorporate impartiality regarding the State's diverse religious groups, implementing religious education under this theory in a post-communist education system in China will prove more effective than either China's current communist foundation, political liberalism, or principled pluralism. As I argued in Chapter 5, *Baorong Duoyuan* draws from both principled pluralism with a Christian foundation, and political liberalism with secular roots. Because it utilizes teaching about religion in religious education, *Baorong Duoyuan* may be acceptable to all groups, those adhering to a specific religion as well as atheists and those professing non- and anti-religious beliefs.

Unlike some of the CCP's unsustainable efforts to improve China's contemporary education system, *BD* specifically targets challenges in the projected future China with sustainable, realistic solutions and goals. If China, as sources in Chapter 5 project, becomes a Christianized democracy under a constitutional design without any national religious or non-religious establishment, with full guarantees of all aspects of religious freedom, then it would impartially facilitate the integration of diverse populations and beliefs/religions into a more harmonious State. In that future China, religious education could enhance the understanding of the value of other religions or beliefs in strengthening the support for religious freedom for all.[117] From implementing the lessons gleaned from religious education under *Baorong Duoyuan*, both individually or collectively from State to family, citizens would learn to listen and speak to one another to reveal common understandings and goals in life, despite their differences.

In the next and concluding chapter of my study, I summarize why neither political liberalism nor principled pluralism would be acceptable to a future post-communist, constitutional democratic China in relation to religious freedom. Thus, I propose my *Baorong Duoyuan* model with its distinctively designed goal of protecting religious freedom for all would be the best choice.

---

117. Tamara, *China: A Global Studies Handbook*, 151–202.

Chapter 7

Baorong Duoyuan for a
Post-Communist China

The human solidarity that I envisage is not a global uniformity
but unity in diversity [another name for integral pluralism].
We must learn to appreciate and tolerate pluralities, multiplicities,
cultural differences.[1]

⌒ HANS-GEORG GADAMER

7.1 Introduction

IN CHAPTER 1, I stated the theme of my thesis in a hypothetical question:
What guiding philosophy could best help procure, provide and protect
religious freedom for all in a post-communist, Christianized, democratic
China? Initially, I chose two alternative philosophies, political liberalism, the most popular model that most Western democracies adopt, and
principled pluralism, originating from the Netherlands. Kuyper pioneered
principled pluralism, which his colleagues further developed. After exploring and expounding both political liberalism and principled pluralism in subsequent chapters, using religious education as my benchmark, I
concluded that neither theory would sufficiently protect religious freedom
for all, nor would the projected future China accept political liberalism
or principled pluralism. Although principled pluralism appeared to be
a better option in protecting religious freedom than political liberalism

1. Dallmayr. *Beyond Orientalism.*

264

in Western democracies, it falls short in several ways to ensure religious freedom for all. Therefore, as the need for a distinctive theory unfolded, I contextualized principled pluralism to develop *Baorong Duoyuan*, which matches its meaning, inclusive pluralism.

7.2 Chapters 2 through 6

7.2.1 Chapter 2

In Chapter 2, I posed the question: Among Christian political theories, could principled pluralism best protect religious freedom for all, and if so, how? In this chapter, I initially explored the history and theoretical foundation of principled pluralism, and then explained various elements contributing to the development of this theory. I examined contemporary implications of principled pluralism, particularly in relation to the State–religion relationship. My research confirmed that under the design of sphere sovereignty and structural pluralism, contrary to theonomy and other Christian, non-pluralistic approaches, principled pluralism's philosophy, with a Christian worldview orientation, would most coherently and consistently provide protection of religious freedom for all.

7.2.2 Chapter 3

In Chapter 3, I considered this question: Among the liberal, secular-orientated political philosophies, could Rawls's political liberalism offer a viable option for protecting religious freedom? From my examination of Rawls's concept of public reason under political liberalism in this chapter, I discovered that although this theory embraces a positive goal of achieving harmony among different reasonable, yet irreconcilable comprehensive religious or moral ideas in a plural democratic society, it would fail to protect religious freedom for all. I concluded that due to its doctrine of PRSR and the proviso, the mechanism to try to achieve an overlapping consensus under political liberalism's design through public reason, it would neither sufficiently nor completely safeguard religious freedom for all citizens. I also determined that with its doctrine of containment regarding certain groups deemed as "unreasonable and irrational," political liberalism could potentially infringe the religious freedom of some citizens.

7.2.3 Chapter 4

The nature of religious education in a State's public-school system constitutes one of the best thermometers to test whether a country protects religious freedom for all its citizens. In Chapter 4, I addressed the question: In what ways could religious education complement a State's education system? When I surveyed how RE had been implemented in the education systems of the United States, the United Kingdom, France, and the Netherlands, I found conflicts and clashes between the State and minority religious groups. Under political liberalism in the United States, the United Kingdom, and France, as well as among religious groups, tensions have often run high. Under principled pluralism, however, although not without instances of conflict with Muslims due to its Christian constitution, society in the Netherlands routinely demonstrated more harmony than the other three states I surveyed. I proposed that to safeguard religious freedom, the State should implement religious education as a vital component of its public education system.

7.2.4 Chapter 5

Three questions contributed to my research in Chapter 5:

1. What kind of theory could potentially enable China to achieve the goal of realizing religious freedom for all citizens?

2. If such a model exists, under what conditions could it be successfully implemented?

3. Are these conditions foreseeable in China's projected future State?

From historical and contemporary research, I concluded that in present-day China, under the CCP's current repressive regime, the claim that China experiences religious freedom would be unjustifiable and unsustainable. Nevertheless, I also concluded from research that a projected, inevitable Christianization of China will accelerate the process of pluralization and constitutional democratization—two general necessary conditions for a *Baorong Duoyuan* system to develop in the future State. I maintained that under both directional pluralism and a constitutional, democratic, socio-political system, *Baorong Duoyuan*, which contextualizes the principled pluralism model, provides the best potential theory for China. With a constitutional design unlike that of either the Netherlands or China, and with no religious or non-religious establishment, *Baorong Duoyuan* could best help facilitate religious freedom for all.

7.2.5 Chapter 6

How would *Baorong Duoyuan* safeguard religious freedom with a design for religious education in a post-communist, democratic China? In answering this question in Chapter 6, I initially pointed out that conflicts and deficiencies in China's contemporary education system, particularly regarding religious education, substantially contribute to China's failure to protect religious freedom for all. I then presented two criteria that contributed to my vision for religious education under *Baorong Duoyuan*: (1) public funding for all schools; and (2) school choice. I ultimately proposed that under a specific constitutional guarantee, *Baorong Duoyuan* would not only prove more compatible with international norms than principled pluralism, it would provide a positive, sustainable option in a projected post-communist education system in China to help ensure religious freedom for all.

7.3 Results of Study

These findings from chapters 2–6 contribute to fulfilling my study's aim: to determine the best guiding philosophy under which religious freedom for all could be protected in a post-communist, Christianized, democratic China. I maintain that if Chinese citizens consent to implementing my theory as a vehicle for protecting religious freedom, they would find that *Baorong Duoyuan*, which aligns closely with international norms under a liberal constitutional framework, offers the most reasonable, consistent, and coherent guiding solution to help ensure their consensus.

Despite much study about religious freedom, my work in developing *Baorong Duoyuan* convinced me that the following tough questions still need to be addressed:

- How the State can best handle the following two extremes relating to religious freedom:

  - those who call for anything but religion in state affairs; and

  - those who espouse the cause of "nothing but religion."

- How can the State protect the freedom of one group, whether religious, non-religious, or anti-religious, without permitting that group's freedom to infringe on another group's rights?

- Can the tolerant tolerate the intolerant, particularly when an extreme secular group in control attempts to advance its agenda but excludes those with religious views? The other side of this potential prejudice may also prove true as some religious extremists may want to enforce their rules regarding religion on all in society.

7.4 Conclusion

Reflecting on the time I invested in conducting my study, I realize that the process presented several common collegiate challenges amid some expected scholastic struggles. Throughout the examination of various works from diverse authors, I learned that, in some ways, I could even agree with those opposing my perceptions. One benefit that resulted from completing the challenging course of research surprised me. Ultimately, this study transformed me from a compassionate, biased activist, ready to take a stance of "us [Christians] against them [political liberalism adherents and CCP officials]" to a more objective, yet compassionate academician. At times, when I became disheartened, I reflected on the message Winston Churchill shared on 29 October 1941, when he addressed the boys of Harrow School. The following words from his speech encouraged me:

> Never give in,
> Never give in,
> never, never, never, never—
> In nothing, great or small,
> large or petty—never give in except to convictions of honour
> and good sense![2]

In the real world, as the CCP perceives differences among diverse religions to threaten its control, Chinese government officials too often abuse their power to try to force others to "give in" to the Party's dictates. As I noted at the start of this study, in attempts to eradicate certain religions, the CCP often employs torture and other cruel methods of force to fabricate evidence against the State. I assert that never giving in to states which like China deny religious freedom to citizens, as well as exerting efforts to eradicate religious persecution of individuals at local and international levels, can help secure religious freedom for others throughout the world.

As Gadamer envisages, in a model world, contrary to government officials persecuting those practicing diverse religions, State representatives would appreciate and tolerate those with different beliefs. In our less than ideal world, no matter what a person's religious, non-religious, or anti-religious beliefs may be, I maintain that citizens who have religious freedom need to tune in to the cries of "Help . . . Help? Help!" from those who do

---

2. Churchill, *Never Give In.*

not. We not only need to listen to cries from those being persecuted for their religious beliefs in China and throughout our global community, we also need to do what we can to help facilitate religious freedom for all. Ideally, I believe that under *Baorong Duoyuan*, all religious, non-religious, and even anti-religious individuals and groups in a post-communist, Christianized, democratic China would realize that freedom.

Bibliography

2014 Report on International Religious Freedom: China (Includes Tibet, Hong Kong, and Macau) (14 October 2015). http://www.state.gov/j/drl/rls/irf/2014/eap/238288. htm.

2017 Annual Report Overview 2017. https://www.uscirf.gov/sites/default/files/2017%20 Annual%20Report%20Overview.pdf.

Abington v. Schempp. *Digital History ID 4087. http://*www.digitalhistory.uh.edu/disp. textbook.cfm?smtID=3&psid=4087.

"Academies." In *Types of Schools.* https://www.gov.uk/types-of-school/academies.

Adam, Gottfried, and Martin Rothgangel. "Reasons for Religious Education in PublicSchools." In *Basics of Religious Education* [Translation of *Religion-spädagogischesKompendium*] edited by Gottfried Adam et al., 131–44. Bristol, CT: V&R,2014.

"Advanced Institute for Religious Studies, Renmin University of China." In Berkley Center for Religion. Peace & World Affairs. https://berkleycenter.georgetown. edu/organizations/advancedinstitute-for-religious-studies-renminuniversity-of-china.

Ahdar, Rex, and Ian Leigh. *Religious Freedom in the Liberal State.* 2nd ed. Oxford: Oxford University Press, 2013.

Aikman, David. *Jesus in Beijing: How Christianity Is Transforming China and Changing the Global Balance of Power.* Lanham, MD: Regnery, 2012.

Albert, Eleanor. "Christianity in China." Council on Foreign Relations (CFR) (07 May 2015). http://www.cfr.org/china/christianity-china/p36503.

Aldridge, Jerry. "The Politics of Education (among the Periodicals)." *Childhood Education* 79.3 (2003). http://www.questia.com/read/1G198467550/thepolitics-of-educationamong-the periodicals.

Al-Hibri, Azizah, Jean Bethke Elshtain, and Charles C. Haynes. *Religion in American Public Life: Living with Our Deepest Differences.* New York: Norton, 2001.

Alon, Ilan, and Gregory Chase. "Religious Freedom and Economic Prosperity." *Cato Journal,* 25.2 (2005) 405. http://www.cato.org/pubs/journal/cj25n2/cj25n2-14. pdf.

Altglas, Véronique. "French Cult Controversy at the Turn of the New Millennium: Escalation, Dissensions and New Forms of Mobilisations across the Battlefield." In *The Centrality of Religion in Social Life: Essays in Honour of James A. Beckford*, edited by Eileen Barker, 55–68. Burlington, VT: Ashgate, 2008.

Amity News Service. "Provisions on the Administration of Religious Activities of Aliens within the Territory of the People's Republic of China." Decree no. 144 of the State Council signed by Premier Li Peng (31 January 1994). http://www.amitynewsservice.org/page.php?page=1143.

Anderson, John. "Does God Matter, and If So Whose God: Religion and Democratization." In *Religion, Democracy and Democratization*, edited by John Anderson, 192–217. London: Routledge, 2013.

———. "Introduction: Religion, Democracy and Democratization." In *Religion, Democracy and Democratization*, edited by John Anderson, 1–2. London: Routledge 2013.

Anthony, Kenneth V., and Susie Burroughs. "Day to Day Operations of Home School Families: Selecting from a Menu of Educational Choices to Meet Students' Individual Instructional Needs." *International Education Studies* 5.1 (2012) 1–17.

Armato, Gabriella. "Ratifying without Resolve." *Berkeley Political Review*, 1 April 2016. http://bpr.berkeley.edu/2015/04/01/ratifying-without-resolve/.

Arnold, Matthew. *The Popular Education of France: With Notices of That of Holland and Switzerland*. London: Longman, Green, Longman, and Roberts, 1861.

"Article." *Human Rights Act, 1998*. http://www.legislation.gov.uk/ukpga/1998/42/schedule/1/part/I/chapter/8.

"Article 18." In *Universal Declaration of Human Rights United Nations* (2014). http://www.un.org/en/documents/udhr/.

Ashiwa, Yoshiko, ed. *Making Religion, Making the State: The Politics of Religion in Modern China*. Stanford, CA: Stanford University, 2009.

Ashiwa, Yoshiko, and David L. Wank. "An Introductory Essay." In *Making Religion, Making the State: The Politics of Religion in Modern China*, edited by Yoshiko Ashiwa and David L. Wank, 1–21. Stanford, CA: Stanford University Press, 2009.

Audi, Robert. *Democratic Authority and the Separation of Church and State*. New York: Oxford University Press, 2011.

———. "The Place of Religious Argument in a Free and Democratic Society." *San Diego LawReview* 30 (1993) 677–92.

———. *Religion in the Public Square: The Place of Religious Convictions in Political Debate*. Lanham, MD: Rowman & Littlefield, 1997.

Audi, Robert, and Nicholas Wolterstorff. *Religion in the Public Square: The Place of Religious Convictions in Political Debate*. Lanham, MD: Rowman & Littlefield, 1997.

Bahnsen, Greg L. "The Theonomic Position." In *God and Politics: Four Views on the Reformation of Civil Government*, edited by Gary Scott Smith, 21–53. Phillipsburg, NJ: Presbyterian and Reformed Company, 1989.

Bailey, Tom, and Valentina Gentile. "Introduction." In *Rawls and Religion*, edited by Tom Bailey and Valentina Gentile, 16–43. New York: Columbia University Press, 2015.

Bankston, Carl L., and Stephen J. Caldas. *Public Education—America's Civil Religion: A Social History*. New York: Teachers College, 2009.

Bapir, Abdurrahman. "Understanding Liberal Constitutionalism: Judicial Review, Protection of Rights and Constitutional Norms During Emergencies." In *Academia*. https://www.academia.edu./9449606/UnderstandingLiberalConstitutionalism_ Judicial_Review_Protection_of_Rights_and_Constitutional_Norms_During_ Emergencies.

Basu-Zharku, Iulia O. "The Influence of Religion on Health." 2011. http://www. inquiriesjournal. com/articles/367/2/the-influence-ofreligion-on-health.

Bates, M. Searle. "Church and State in Traditional China." Unpublished paper, seminar on modern China, Columbia University (November 1967).

Bavinck, Herman. *Our Reasonable Faith*. Grand Rapids: Eerdmans, 1956.

Bays, Daniel H. "A Tradition of State Dominance." In *God and Caesar in China: Policy Implications of Church-State Tensions*, edited by Jason Kindopp and Carol Lee Hamrin, 25–39. Washington, DC: The Brookings Institution, 2004.

———. *A New History of Christianity in China*. Malden, MA: Wiley Blackwell, 2012.

B.C. "The EU and Faith: A Religious Policy by Stealth." *The Economist* (3 July 2013). http://www.economist.com/ blogser/asmus/2013/07/euand-faith.

Beauchamp, Tom L. "The Nature of Applied Ethics." In *A Companion to Applied Ethics*, edited by R. G. Frey and Christopher Heath Wellman. Malden, MA: Wiley & Sons, 2008.

Beckford, James A., and Jay Demerath. "Case Studies from Around the World." In *SAGE Handbook of the Sociology of Religion*, edited by James A Beckford and Jay Demerath. Thousand Oaks, CA: Sage, 2007.

Beiner, Ronald. *Civil Religion: A Dialogue in the History of Political Philosophy*. New York: Cambridge University Press, 2011. https://www.persecution.net/download/ plural.pdf.

Belfield, Clive and Chad D'Entremont. "Catholic Schooling in the Netherlands Offers Lessons for the US School Choice Debate." *Momentum*, 36 (February/March 2005.

Bell, Duncan. "Glossary." In *Ethics and World Politics*, edited by Duncan Bell. New York: Oxford University Press, 2010.

———. "What Is Liberalism?" *Political Theory* (26 June 2014). http://ptx.sagepub.com/ content/ 42/6/682.

Bellamy, Richard, *Liberalism and Pluralism: Towards a Politics of Compromise*. London: Routledge, 2002.

Benedikter, Thomas. "Territorial Autonomy as a Means of Minority Protection and Conflict Solution in the European Experience—An Overview and Schematic Comparison." *Szekler National Council* (2010). http://sznt.sic.hu/en/index.

Berend, Nora. "Introduction." In *Christianization and the Rise of Christian Monarchy: Scandinavia, Central Europe and Rus' c.900–1200*, edited by Nora Berend, 1–46. New York: Cambridge University Press, 2007.

Berger, Peter L. "The Desecularization of the World: A Global Overview." In *The Desecularization of the World: Resurgent Religion and World Politics*, edited by Peter L. Berger, 1–18. Grand Rapids: Eerdmans, 1999.

Berkley Center for Religion, Peace, and World Affairs. "Religious Freedom and Restriction in China." Washington, DC: Georgetown University, Berkley Center for Religion, Peace, and World Affairs, 2015. https://berkleycenter.georgetown. edu/essays/religiousfreedomand-restriction-in-china.

Berkouwer, G. C. *The Providence of God*. Grand Rapids: Eerdmans, 1952.

Berman, Harold J. "Religious Freedom and the Challenge of the Modern State." In *Articles of Faith, Articles of Peace*, edited by James Davison Hunter and O. S. Guinness, 40–53. Washington, DC: Brookings Institution, 1990.

Berner, Ashley Rogers. *Pluralism and American Public Education: No One Way to School*. New York: Palgrave Macmillan, 2017.

Bertola, Giuseppe. "France's Almost Public Private Schools" (2015). https://pdfs. semantic scholar.org/f02f/e282e49435822227642208dfd713d5c6b5f8.pdf.

Bhattacharya, Srinibas. *Foundations of Education*. New Delhi: Atlantic, 1996.

Biggar, Nigel, and Linda Hogan, eds. *Religious Voices in Public Places*. New York: Oxford University Press, 2009.

Bielefeldt, Heiner. *Freedom of Religion or Belief: Thematic Reports of the U.N.'s Special Rapporteur 2010, 2013*, Bonn: Verlag fur Kultur und Wissenschaft, 2014.

Bilgin, Mehmet Fevzi. "The Prospects for Political Liberalism in Non-Western Societies," 359–76. St. Mary's City, MD: St. Mary's College of Maryland, 2007.

Blackford, Russel. *Freedom of Religion and the Secular State*. Hoboken, NJ: Wiley and Sons, 2012.

Blunden, Andy. "Rawls's Political Liberalism." (2003). http://ethicalpolitics.org/ablunden/pdfs/rawls.pdf.

Bogdan, David. "Reconciling Social Cohesion, Religious Law and Secular Rights." *Geopolitics, History and International Relations* 4.2 (2012) 107–12.

Bogue, Carl W. "The Theonomic Response to Principled Pluralism." In *God and Politics: Four Views on the Reformation of Civil Government*, edited by Gary Scott Smith, 100–106. Phillipsburg, NJ: Presbyterian and Reformed Company, 1989.

Boston, Rob. "Myths Debunked: Religious Right Activists Love to Spread False Information about the Separation of Church and State. Here Are Ten Rebuttals." *Church & State* (February 2015). http://churchandstate.org.uk/2015/02/ten-religious-right-mythsaboutchurch-state-separation-and-whythey-arewrong/.

Boyd, Gregory A. *The Myth of a Christian Nation: How the Quest for Political Power Is Destroying the Church*. Grand Rapids: Zondervan, 2005.

Boyle, Kevin, and Juliet Sheen, eds. *Freedom of Religion and Belief: A World Report*. London: Routledge, 1997.

Bratt, James D. *Abraham Kuyper: Modern Calvinist Christian Democrat*. Grand Rapids: Eerdmans, 2013.

———. *A Centennial Reader*. Grand Rapids: Eerdmans, 1998.

Brems, Eva, and Janneke Gerard, eds. *Shaping Rights in the ECHR*. New York: Cambridge University Press, 2013.

British Broadcasting Corporation. [Organizational Department of the Communist Party of China: Retired cadres and members must abide by the rules do not believe in religion] *BBC*, 5 February 2016. http://www.bbc.com/zhongwen/simp/china/2016/02/160205_china_retired_officials_party_rule.

———. "Perspectives: Should Britain become a Secular State?" (22 March 2013). http://www.bbc.co.uk/religion/0/21883918.

Brito, Uri. "An Analysis of Kuyper's Lecture: Calvinism a Life System." *Resurrectio et Vita* (11 December 2007). http://apologus.wordpress.com/2007/12/11/ananalysis-of-kuyper%E2%80%99s-lecture-calvinism-a-life-system-part-2/.

Brook, Timothy. "The Politics of Religion: Late-Imperial Origins of the Regulatory State." In *Making Religion, Making the State: The Politics of Religion in Modern China*, edited by Yoshiko Ashiwa and David L. Wank, 22–42. Stanford, CA: Stanford University, 2009.

Brooks, Thom, and Fabian Freyenhagen, eds. *Legacy of John Rawls*. New York: A&C Black, 2005.

Bruce, Steve. "Protestantism Create Democracy?" *Democratization* 11.4 (2004) 3–20.

Burke, Edmund. *Reflections on the Revolution in France*. Edited by Thomas H. D. Mahoney. Indianapolis: Bobbs-Merrill Educational, 1952.

Bush Jr., Richard. *Religion in Communist China*. Nashville: Abingdon, 1970.

Buss, Doris, and Didi Herman. *Globalizing Family Values: The Christian Right in International Politics*. Minneapolis: University of Minnesota Press, 2003.

Byrne, Cathy. *Religion in Secular Education: What in Heaven's Name Are We Teaching Our Children?* Boston: Brill, 2014.

Calhoun, Craig. "How Does Religion Matter in Britain's Secular Public Sphere?" (10 June 2016). http://blogs.lse.ac.uk/religionpublicsphere/2016/06/how-doesreligion-matter-in-britainssecular-public-sphere/.

Calvin, John. *Institutes of the Christian Religion, vol. IV*, xx.14 and xx.15. "Of Civil Government." https://www.ccel.org/ccel/ calvin/institutes.vi.xxi.html.

Cambridge University. *Home School: The Cambridge Advanced Learner's Dictionary & Thesaurus*. https://dictionary.cambridge.org/dictionary/english/homeschooling.

Carlson, Eric R. "China's New Regulations on Religion: A Small Step, Not a Great Leap, Forward." *Brigham Young University Law Review* 3 (2005) 747–97.

Cavanaugh Sr., William T. *The Myth of Religious Violence: Secular Ideology and the Roots of Modern Conflict*. New York: Oxford University Press, 2009.

Centre for Civil Society. "Best Practices in Regulation of Private Education." http://ccs.in/sites/default/files/research/research-best-practices-in-regulationof-private-education.pdf.

Chan, Joseph C. W. "Confucianism and Human Rights." In *Religion and Human Rights: An Introduction*, edited by John Witte, Jr. and M. Christian Green. New York: Oxford University Press, 2012.

Chan, Karen. "The Common Good and the Virtuous Political Leader." In *Common Good: Chinese and American Perspectives*, edited by David Solomon and P. C. Lo. Notre Dame, IN: Springer, 2014.

Chan, Kim-Kwong. "The Christian Community in China-The Leaven Effect." In *Evangelical Christianity and Democracy in Asia*, edited by David H. Lumsdaine. New York: Oxford University Press, 2009.

Chang, Wen-Chen, et al. *Constitutionalism in Asia: Cases and Materials*. Portland OR: Hart, 2014.

Chao, Jonathan. *Church and State in Socialist China, 1949–1988*. Oxford: The Oxford Center for Mission Studies, 1989.

———. "The Gospel and Culture in Chinese History." In *Chinese Intellectuals and the Gospel*, edited by Samuel Ling and Stacey Bieler, 9–24. Phillipsburg, NJ: P&R, 1999.

Chaplin, Jonathan. "The Bible, the State and Religious Diversity: Theological Foundations for 'Principled Pluralism.'" *Kirby Laing Institute for Christian Ethics* (2009). http://klice.co.uk/uploads/ EST08JC.pdf.

———. "Dooyeweerd's Theory of Public Justice: A Critical Exposition." PhD diss., London School of Economics and Political Science, 1983.

———. "The Full Weight of Our Convictions: The Point of Kuyperian Pluralism." *Cardus* (1 November 2013). https://www.cardus.ca/comment/article/4069/the-point-ofkuyperian-pluralism/.

———. "The Gospel and Culture in Chinese History." In *Chinese Intellectuals and the Gospel*, edited by Samuel Ling and Stacey Bieler, 10–17. Phillipsburg, NJ: P&R, 1999.

———. "Governing Diversity: Public Judgment and Religious Plurality." Seminar Paper, Centre for Theology and Public Issues (CTPI). *University of Edinburgh* (14 November 2011).

———. *Herman Dooyeweerd: Christian Philosopher of State and Civil Society.* Notre Dame, IN: University of Notre Dame Press, 2011.

———. *Talking God: The Legitimacy of Religious Public Reasoning.* London: Theos, 2008.

Chelini-Pont, Blandine. "Religion in the Public Sphere: Challenges and Opportunities." *Brigham Young University Law Review* 2005.3 (2005) 611–28.

Cheng Li. "Christianity in China: A Force for Change?" (3 June 2014) http://www. brookings.edu/events/2014/06/03-christianityas-aforce-for-change-in-china.

Cheng, May M. C. "House Church Movements and Religious *Freedom in China.*" 1.1 (19 March 2003). http://muse.jhu.edu/login?uri=/journals/china/v001/1.1cheng. html.

Chertoff, Meryl. "Principled Pluralism: Report of the Inclusive America Project." *Rural Forum* (2016). http://rumiforum.org/qprincipled-pluralism-reportof-the-inclusiveamerica-projectq-with-meryl-chertoff/.

China Aid, *2014 Annual Report, Religious and Human Rights Persecution in China.* Midland, Texas, China Aid Association, 2015. https://drive.google.com/file/d/0B024UfutRtHodGVzbWhyLUtCdjg/view.

———. *2016 Annual Report, Chinese Government Persecution of Churches and Christiansin Mainland China* (January–December) China Aid Association (2017). https://drive.google.com/file/d/0BwO5hRHaKWdOQWUwYTdDcnZSTnc.

———. China Aid (2016). http://www.chinaaid.org/.

"China Bans Religious Beliefs for 88 Million People." (21 July 2017). http://www. christian.org.uk/news/china-bans-religious-beliefs-88millionpeople/.

"China: Christians More Public as Gospel Spreads Rapidly." (14 December 2014). http://www.christian.org.uk/news/china-christians-morepublic-as-gospel-spreads-rapidly/z.

"China Focus: China Highlights Morality in Class." Edited by Zhu Ningzhu (28 February 2014). http://news.xinhuanet.com/english/china/201402/28/c_133151128.htm.

"China (Includes Tibet, Hong Kong, and Macau)." *Bureau of Democracy, Human Rights and Labor International Religious Freedom Report for 2014.* (2014). http://www. state.gov/j/drl/rls/irf/religiousfreedom/index.htm#wrapper.

"China's Policies Toward Spiritual Movements." *House Hearing, 111 Congress* (18 June 2010). https://www.gpo.gov/fdsys/pkg/CHRG111hhrg57902html/CHRG111 hhrg5902.htm.

"China's Policy on Religion." *About China on People.com* (2007). http://englishpeoplecom.cn/92824/92845/92875/6442436.html.

Ching, Julia, *Chinese Religions,* London: Macmillan, 1993.

Chou, Mei-Ju, Yi-Chan Tu, and Kai-Ping Huang. "Confucianism and Character Education: A Chinese View." *Journal of Social Sciences,* 9.2 (2013). http://www. questia.com/read/1P3-3024867511/confucianism-and-character-education-a-chinese-view.

Choudhry, Suji. *Migration of Constitutional Ideas.* New York: Cambridge University Press, 2007.

Chrisafis, Angelique. "Paris Riots Sparked by Police Identity Check on Veiled Muslim Woman." *The Guardian* (21 July 2013). http://www.theguardian.com/world/2013/jul/21/paris-riots-policeidentitycheckmuslim.

Christian Times. "Pakistan: Public School Textbooks Continue to Teach Intolerance." *ChristianTimes.pk,* 11 April 2016. https://www.christiantimes.pk/683-pakistan publicschool-textbooks-continue-to-teach-intolerance/.

Chuanhui, Zeng. "Coalition and Hegemony: Religion's Role in the Progress of Modernizationin Reformed China." *Brigham Young University Law Review* (2011) 759–82.

"Church of England in Parliament" (2017). https://churchinparliament.org/aboutthe lordsspiritual/.

Churchill, Winston S. *Never Give In! The Best of Winston Churchill's Speeches.* New York: Hyperion, 2003.

Cinotti, D. N. "The Incoherence of Neutrality: A Case for Eliminating Neutrality from Religion Clause Jurisprudence." *Journal of Church and State* 45.3 (2003) 499–533.

Clark, Laura. "Muslim Schools Must Respect British Values, Declares Jack Straw." *Daily Mail* (London), 22 April 2014. https://www.dailymail.co.uk/news/article-2609332/ Islamicschool -hardliners-confiscated-Easter-eggs-pupilshead-Ofsted-takes-charge-inquiryMuslim-Trojan-Horse-plot.html.

Cline, Erin M. *Confucius, Rawls, and the Sense of Justice.* New York: Fordham University Press, 2013.

Cohen-Almagor, Raphael. *The Boundaries of Liberty and Tolerance: The Struggle against Kahanism in Israel.* Gainesville, FL: University of Florida Press, 1994.

Cohen, Paul A. *China and Christianity: The Missionary Movement and the Growth of Chinese Antiforeignism, 1860–1870.* New York: Cambridge University Press, 1963.

Coi, Yong-Joon. "Dooyeweerd's View of Culture." In *The Dooyeweerd Pages* (2000). http://www.dooy.salford.ac.uk/papers/choi/ch1.overview.html.

Condé, Victor. *A Handbook of International Human Rights Terminology.* Lincoln, NE: University of Nebraska Press, 1999.

Congressional Research Service. *Human Rights in China: Trends and Policy Implications.* Washington, DC (2009). https://pdfs.semanticscholar.org/fa3a/534a9a8d122e46a c52e1a91a82a482cdbd2b.pdf.

Constitution of the People's Republic of China. Beijing, PRC: Foreign Language, 1982. http://english.people.com.cn/constitution/constitution.html.

Constitution of the People's Republic of China, Article 36. Religious Freedom section, www.npc.gov.cn/englishnpc/Constitution/node_2825.htm.

Colley, Linda. "British Values, Whatever They Are, Won't Hold Us Together." *Guardian,* 17 May 2006. https://www.theguardian.com/commentisfree/2006/may/18/ comment.britishidentity.

Cooley, Aaron. "Liberalism: Notes on a Concept for Educators and Educational Researchers." *Educational Research Quarterly* 32 (2009). http://www.questia.com/ read/1P3174699986.

Cordasco, Francesco. *A Brief History of Education: A Handbook of Information on Greek, Roman, Medieval, Renaissance, and Modern Educational Practice.* Totowa, NJ: Rowman & Littlefield, 1976.

Cornell University. "Definition of 'Religion.'" *International Law, Legal Information Institute,* 199 (2003) https://www.law.cornell.edu/wex/international_law.

Cornell University Law School. "First Amendment" (2014). http://www.law.cornell.edu/constitution/first_amendment.

———. "Establishment Clause." Legal Institute (n.d.). http://www.law.cornell.edu/wex/establishmentclause.

———. "Free Exercise Clause." *Legal Information Institute* (n.d.). https://www.law.cornell.edu/wex/free_exercise_clause.

Corsi-Bunker, Antonella. "Guide to the Education System in the United States." University of Minnesota, n.d. https://isss.umn.edu/publications/UEducation/2.pdf.

Costa, Danielle. "Rawls: Neutrality, Resources, and Primary Goods." *Tufts University: PHIL193: Rawls Seminar* (3 March 1999). http://www.indyflicks.com/danielle/papers/paper02.htm.

Council of Europe. "Details of Treaty No. 005: Convention for the Protection of Human Rights and Fundamental Freedoms" (2017). https://www.coe.int/en/web/conventions/full-list//conventions/treaty/005.

———. "Details of Treaty" No. 009: Protocol to the Convention for the Protection of Human Rights and Fundamental Freedoms" (2017). http://conventions.coe.int/treaty/en/Treaties/Html/009.htm.

Council of Europe, Parliament. *Parliamentary Assembly Documents 1999 Session (First part, January 1999) I.* Strasbourg: Counsel of Europe, 1999.

Cousineau, Madeleine, ed. *Religion in a Changing World: Comparative Studies in Sociology.* Westport, CT: Praeger, 1998.

Crabtree, Vexen. "Faith Schools, Sectarian Education and Segregation: Divisive Religious Behavior (UK Case Study)" (2010). https://www.humanreligions.info/faithschools.htm.

"Crack: Religion and Education." Belfast: Johnston, 2002. In *New York Times Guide to Essential Knowledge: The A Desk Reference for the Curious Mind,* 2nd ed., edited by John W. Wright et al.. New York: Macmillan, 2007.

Curtis, Jennifer. *Human Rights as War by Other Means: Peace Politics in Northern Ireland.* Philadelphia: University of Pennsylvania Press, 2014.

Dallas Baptist University. "Fact Sheet on Abraham Kuyper" (2014). http://www3.dbu.edu/naugle/pdf/factsheet_abraham.pdf.

Dallmayr, Fred Reinhard, *Beyond Orientalism: Essays on Cross-Cultural Encounter,* Albany, NY: SUNY, 1996.

Dalpino, Catharin E. *Deferring Democracy: Promoting Openness in Authoritarian Regimes.* Washington, DC: Brookings Institution, 2011.

Danchin, Peter G., and Lisa Forman, eds. "The Evolving Jurisprudence of the European Court of Human Rights and the Protection of Religious Minorities." In *Protecting the Human Rights of Religious Minorities in Eastern Europe,* edited by Peter G. Danchin and Elizabeth Cole. New York: Columbia University Press, 2002.

———. "Religion, Religious Minorities and Human Rights: An Introduction." In *Protecting the Human Rights of Religious Minorities in Eastern Europe,* edited by Peter G. Danchin and Elizabeth Cole. New York: Columbia University Press, 2002.

Dankowski, Dariusz. *Public Debate according to John Rawls.* Chicago: Loyola University Press, 2008.

———. "Religious Argumentation." In *Public Debate according to John Rawls*. Chicago: Loyola University Press, 2008.

Das, Jayoti, and Cassandra E. DiRienzo. "Conflict and the Freedom of the Press." *Journal of Economic and Social Studies* 4.1 (2014) 91–112.

De Albornoz, Carrillo A. F. *The Basis of Religious Liberty*. New York: Association, 1963.

"Declaration of Independence." In *Congress, July 4, 1776, The Charters of Freedom a New World is at Hand* (2014). http://www.archives.gov/exhibits/charters/declaration_transcript.html.

De Jasay, Anthony. "Liberalism, Loose or Strict." *Independent Review* 9.3 (2005). http://www.questia.com/read/1G1-128364604.

Del Fattore, Joan. *The Fourth R: Conflicts over Religion in America's Public Schools*. New Haven, CT: Yale University Press, 2004.

Demartino, George. *Global Economy, Global Justice: Theoretical Objections and Policy Alternatives to Neoliberalism*. London: Routledge, 2000.

"Department of Philosophy and Religious Studies, Peking University." *Berkley Center for Religion, Peace & World Affairs*. http://www.isd.pku.edu.cn/index.php?m=content&c=index&a=show&catid=31&id=58/.

Derher, Rod. "The Religion of Secularism." *American Conservative* (18 March 2014). http://www.theamericanconservative.com/dreher/the-religion-ofsecularism/.

De Sousa Santos, Boaventura. "The Heterogeneous State and Legal Pluralism in Mozambique."*Law & Society Review* 40.1 (2006) 39–75.

Devettere, Raymond J. *Practical Decision Making in Health Care Ethics: Cases and Concepts*. 3rd ed. Washington, DC: Georgetown University Press, 2010.

De Wall, Heinrich. "Religious Education in a Religiously Neutral State: The German Model." In *Law, Religious Freedoms and Education in Europe*, edited by Myria Hunter-Henin. Farnham, UK: Ashgate, 2013.

Dincer, Oguzhan C., and Fan Wang. "Ethnic Diversity and Economic Growth in China." *Journal of Economic Policy Reform* 14.1 (March 2011), 110. http://dept.ku.edu/~empirics/Courses/Econ844/papers/ethnic%20and%20econ%20growth%2in%20China.pdf.

Dobbins, Mike. *Atheism as a Religion: An Introduction to the World's Least Understood Faith*. Create Space Independent, 2014.

Donnelly, Michael P. "Homeschooling: Pluralistic Freedom, Not Parallel Society." Home School Legal Defense Association (9 September 2007). http://www.hslda.org/hs/international/Germany/200709190.asp.

———. *Home School Legal Defense Association* (17 September 2007). http://www.hslda.org.

Donohue, Kathleen G. *Freedom from Want: American Liberalism and the Idea of the Consumer*. Baltimore: John Hopkins University, 2003.

Dooyeweerd, Herman. "The Christian Idea of the State" (De Christelijke Staatsidee). Translated by John Kraay, edited by D. F. M. Strauss. Presented at a day for anti-revolutionary youth on 3 October 1936. Apeldoorn, Rotterdam-Utrecht, Libertas-Drukkerijen.

———. *In the Twilight of Western Thought*. Phillipsburg, NJ: P&R, 1999.

———. *A New Critique of Theoretical Thought*. Philadelphia: P&R, 1955.

———. *Roots of Western Culture: Pagan, Secular, and Christian Options*. Edited by Mark Vander Vennen and Bernard Zylstra. Translated by John Kraay. Toronto: Wedge Foundation, 1979.

Doyle, G. Wright. "Culture and Religion: How 'Chinese' Is Protestantism in China?" In *Global China Center: Christianity in China*, 14 March 2009, introductory section. http://www.globalchinacenter.org/analysis/christianity-inchina/culture-andreligion-howchinese-is-protestantism-in-china.php.

Dreben, Burton. "On Rawls and Political Liberalism." In *The Cambridge Companion to Rawls*, edited by Samuel Freeman, 316–46. New York: Cambridge University Press, 2003.

Driver, Tom E. *Liberating Rites: Understanding the Transformative Power of Ritual.* Boulder, CO: Westview, 1998.

DuBois, Thomas David. *Religion and the Making of Modern East Asia.* Cambridge: Cambridge University Press, 2011.

Dunning, William A. "A Century of Politics." *The North American Review* 179 (577) (December 1904). https://ia601609.us.archive.org/33/items/jstor.

Durham, W. Cole, Matthew K. Richards, and Donlu D. Thayer. "The Status of and Threats to International Law on Freedom of Religion or Belief." In *The Future of Religious Freedom: Global Challenges*, edited by Allen D. Hertzke. New York: Oxford University Press, 2013.

Eastland, Terry. *Religious Liberty in the Supreme Court.* Washington, DC: Ethics and Public Policy, 1993.

Eberle, Chris, and Terence Cuneo. "Religion and Political Theory." In *Stanford Encyclopedia of Philosophy* (winter 2017 edition), edited by Edward N. Zalta. https://plato.stanford.edu/archives/win2017/n entries/ religion-politics/.

Eck, Diana L. *A New Religious America: How a 'Christian Country' Has Become the World's Most Religiously Diverse Nation.* New York: HarperCollins, 2002. Harper Collins ebook.

———. "A New Religious America." Religious Freedom as a Human Right, *Issues of Democracy* 6.2 (2001) 14–19.

———. "The Pluralsim Project" (2016). http://www.pluralism.org/pluralism/what_is_pluralism.

Edgar, William. "The National Confessional Position." In *God and politics: Four Views on the Reformation of Civil Government*, edited by Gary Scott Smith, 176–99. Phillipsburg, NJ: P&R, 1989.

Embassy of the People's Republic of China in the United States of America. "Chinese Government Outlaws Falun Gong." http://www.china-embassy.org/eng/zt/ppflg/t263446.htm.

———. "China Refutes U.S. Charges on Religious Freedom" (2016). http://www.chinaembassy.org/eng/zt/zjxy/t36496.htm.

Encyclopedia Britannica. "Chinese Philosophy" (2018). https://www.britannica.com/topic/Chinese-philosophy#ref171469.

Encyclopedia of Religion in American. Edited by Jeffrey D. Schultz et al. Phoenix, AZ: Oryx, 1999.

———. "Roots of Chinese Humanism." In *Chinese Philosophy* (2018). https://www.britannica.com/topic/Chinese-philosophy#ref171469.

Esbeck, Carl H. "Religion and a Neutral State: Imperative or Impossibility?" *University of Missouri School of Law Scholarship Repository* 15 (1984) 67–88.

Ether, John A. "Cultural Pluralism and Self-Identity." *Educational Leadership*, Association for Supervision and Curriculum Development (December 1969) 233–34.

Etzioni, Amitai. "Religion and the State: Why Moderate Religious Teaching Should Be Promoted." *Harvard International Review* 28.1 (2006) 14–17.

European Commission. "Organisation of the Education System in the Netherlands." In *Education, Audiovisual & Culture Executive Agency*, European Commission (2008/09). https://estudandoeducacao.files.wordpress.com/2011/05/holanda.pdf.

European Court of Human Rights. "European Convention on Human Rights." Council of Europe (2010). http://www.conventions.coe.int/Treaty/en/Treaties/Html/005.htm/.

———. "How the EU Works" (2015). http://europa.eu/abouteu/index_en.htm.

Evangelical Fellowship of Canada. "Being Christians in a Pluralistic Society: A Discussion Paper on Pluralism in Canada." *The Social Action Commission of the Evangelical Fellowship of Canada*. Discussion paper, 25 November 1997.

Evans, Carolyn. "Religion and Freedom of Expression." In *Religion and Human Rights: An Introduction*, edited by John Witte, Jr. and M. Christian Green, 188–203. New York: Oxford University Press, 2012.

"Faith Schools." In *Types of Schools*. https://www.gov.uk/types-of-school/faith schools.

Fancourt, Nigel. "Teaching about Christianity in Religious Education: A Review of Research." *Journal of Beliefs & Values, Studies in Religion & Education* 38.1.1 (2017) 121–13.

Farr, Thomas F. "Religious Freedom and International Diplomacy." In *Future of Religious Freedom: Global Challenges*, edited by Allen D. Hertzke, 331–52. New York: Oxford University Press, 2013.

Farrelly, Colin. "Neutrality, Toleration, and Reasonable Agreement." In *Toleration, Neutrality and Democracy*, edited by Dario Castiglione and Catriona McKinnon. Notre Dame, IN: Springer, 2013.

Ferrari, Silvio. "Teaching Religion in the European Union: A Legal Overview." In *Religious Education and the Challenge of Pluralism*, edited by Adam B. Seligman. New York: Oxford University Press, 2014.

Ferry, Leonard, D. G. "Floors without Foundations: Ignatieff and Rorty on Human Rights." *Logos: A Journal of Catholic Thought and Culture* 10 (2007) 80–105.

Fesser, Edward. *Locke*. Oxford: One World, 2007.

Findlaw. "Types of School: Private and Parochial School" (2017). http://education.findlaw.com/education-options/types-of-schools-private and parochial-school.html.

Finer, S. E., Vernon Bogdanor, and Bernard Rudden. *Comparing Constitutions*. Oxford: Oxford University Press, 1995.

Fiske, Edward B., and Helen F. Ladd. "The Dutch Experience with Weighted Student Funding: The Netherlands Centralized School Funding, Long-Term Stability of Education Policies, and Extensive Social Services Contribute to Its Success, Weighted Student Funding Might Not Translate Well into the U.S. System." *Phi Delta Kappan*, 92.1 (2010) 4953.

Fitzgerald, Charles P. "Opposing Cultural Traditions, Barriers to Communication." In *Christian Missions in China: Evangelists of What? Problems in Asian Civilizations*, edited by Jessie G. Lutz. Boston: Heath and Co., 1965.

Fitzgerald, Michael. "Satan, the Great Motivator; The Curious Economic Effects of Religion." *Boston Globe*, 15 November 2009. http://archive.boston.com/bostonglobe/ideas/articles/2009/11/15/the_curious_economic_effects_of_religion/.

Fleming, James E., and Linda C. McClain. *Ordered Liberty: Rights, Responsibilities, and Virtues.* Cambridge, MA: Harvard University Press, 2013.

Flood, Gavin, ed. *The Importance of Religion: Meaning and Action in Our Strange World.* Malden, MA: Wiley-Blackwell, 2012.

Flowers, Ronald Bruce. *That Godless Court? Supreme Court Decisions on Church State Relationships.* Louisville, KY: Westminster John Knox, 2005.

Foblets, Marie-Claire. "Religion and Rethinking the Public–Private Divide." In *Religion in Public Spaces: A European Perspective*, edited by Silvio Ferrari and Sabrina Pastorelli. London: Routledge, 2016.

Foot, Rosemary. *Rights beyond Borders: The Global Community and the Struggle over Human Rights in China.* Oxford: Oxford University Press, 2000.

Forbes, Hugh Donald. *George Grant: A Guide to His Thought.* Toronto: University of Toronto, 2007.

Foreign & Commonwealth Office. *Freedom of Religion or Belie—How the FCO Can Help Promote Respect for this Human Right* (2016). https://www.gov.uk/government/uploads/system/uploads/attachment_data/file/561516/Freedom_ofReligion_or_Belief_Toolkit__2016.pdf.

"France Treads Fine Line Teaching Religion in Secular Schools." *Digital Journal* (20 October 2017). https://www.digitaljournal.com/news/world/france-treadsfineline-teachingreligion-in-secular-schools/article/505522.

"Freedom of Education" (2017). *Expatica.* https://www.government.nl/topics/freedomof-education/anyone-can-set-up-a-new-school.

"Freedoms of Speech, Religion Clash Over Anti-Islam film." *NOLA Media Group* (18 September 2012). http://www.nola.com/ politics/index.

"Freedom of Religion or Belief." *European Union External Action* (2015). http://eeas.europa.eu/human_rights/frb/index_en.htm.

"Free schools." In *Types of Schools.* https://www.gov.uk/types-of-school/free-schools.

Freedom from Religion Foundation. "Students Spared more Bible Distributions." http://ffrf.org/legal/other-legal-successes/item/25093-students-spared-more bibledistributions-october-19-2015.

Freeman, Samuel. "Original Position." In *Stanford Encyclopedia of Philosophy* (2014). http://plato.stanford.edu/entries/original-position/.

Friedman, B. "Neutral Principles: A Retrospective." *Vanderbilt Law Review* 50.2 (1997) 503–36.

Fu, Bob, and Nancy French. *God's Double Agent: The True Story of a Chinese Christian's Fight for Freedom.* Grand Rapids: Baker, 2014.

Fuk-tsang, Ying. "Mainland China." In *Christianities in Asia*, edited by Peter C. Phan. Malden, MA: Wiley Blackwell, 2011.

Fullerton, Jamie. "China Bans Religion for Communists." *The Times*, 20 July 2017. https://www.thetimes.co.uk/article/china-bans-religion-for-communistsbqd8ozhn9.

Gagliarducci, Andrea. "A Quiet Threat: Religious Freedom Dwindling in Europe, US." *Catholic News Agency* (Vatican City, 4 November 2014). http://www.catholicnewsagency.com/news/a-quiet-threat-religious-freedomdwindling-in-europe-us11509/.

Galston, William A. "Defending Liberalism in American." *Political Science Review* 72 (1982) 621–29.

———. *Liberal Pluralism: The Implications of Value Pluralism for Political Theory and Practice.* New York: Cambridge University Press, 2002.

Gaus, Gerald E. "The Place of Autonomy within Liberalism." In *Autonomy and the Challenges to Liberalism: New Essays,* edited by John Christman and Joel Anderson, 272–306. New York: Cambridge University Press, 2005.

Gaus, Gerald, and Kevin Vallier. "The Roles of Religious Conviction in a Publicly Justified Policy." *Philosophy and Social Criticism* 35.5 (2009) 51–76. DOI: 10.1177/0191453708098754.

Gaylor, Annie Laurie. "The Dangers of Religious Instruction in Public School." *Religion & Politics* (2014). https://religionandpolitics.org/2014/01/07/the-dangers-of-religious-instruction-in-public-schools/.

Gearon, Liam. *Masterclass in Religious Education: Transforming Teaching and Learning.* New York: Bloomsbury, 2013.

General Assembly. http://www.un.org/documents/ga/res/47/a47r135.htm.

George, Robert. "Clash of Orthodoxies." In *First Things,* August 1999. https://www.firstthings.com/article/1999/08/a-clash-of-orthodoxies.

George, Robert P., and Christopher Wolfe. *Natural Law and Public Reason.* Washington, DC: Georgetown University, 2000.

Glenn, Charles L. "What Would Equal Treatment Mean for Public Education?" In *Equal Treatment of Religion in a Pluralistic Society,* edited by Stephen V. Monsma and J. Christopher Soper. Grand Rapids: Eerdmans, 1998.

Gill, Anthony. "Religious Pluralism, Political Incentives, and the Origins of Religious Liberty." In *Future of Religious Freedom: Global Challenges,* edited by Allen D. Hertzke, 107–27. New York: Oxford University Press, 2013.

———. "Weber in Latin America: Is Protestant Growth Enabling the Consolidation of Democratic Capitalism?" *Democratization,* 11.4 (2004) 42–65.

"Global Concepts, Knowledge Transfer, and Local Discourses." In *Globalization and the Making of Religious Modernity in China: Transnational Religions, Local Agents, and the Study of Religion, 1800–Present,* edited by Thomas Jansen et al., 297–341. Leiden: Brill, 2014.

Gold, Susan Dudley. *Engel v. Vitale: Prayer in the Schools.* New York: Marshall Cavendish Benchmark, 2006.

Goldman, Merle. "Is Democracy Possible?" In *China: Contemporary Political, Economic, and International Affairs,* edited by David Denoon, 137–46. New York: New York University, 2007.

Goodman, Lenn E. *Religious Pluralism and Values in the Public Sphere.* New York: Cambridge University Press, 2014.

Goossaert Vincent, and David A. Palmer. *The Religious Question in Modern China.* Chicago: University of Chicago Press, 2011.

Gorard, Stephen, Chris Taylor, and John Fitz. *Schools, Markets and Choice Policies.* London: Routledge, 2003.

Gordon, David. "John Rawls." In *American Conservative,* edited by Andy Ross (28 July 2008). http://www.andyross.net/rawls.htm.

Gottlieb, Roger S. *Joining Hands: Religion and Politics Together for Social Change.* Boulder, CO: Westview, 2002.

Grant, Leslie, et al. *West Meets East: Best Practices from Expert Teachers in the U.S. and China.* Alexandria VA: ASCD, 2014.

Grcic, Joseph. *Free and Equal: Rawls's Theory of Justice and Political Reform.* New York: Algora, 2011.

Green, Emma. "American Religion: Complicated, Not Dead." *Atlantic Monthly* (12 May 2015).

Grelle, Bruce. "Learning to Live with Difference: Teaching about Religion in Public Schools in the United States." In *Religious Education in Schools: Ideas and Experiences from around the World*, edited by Zarrin T. Caldwell, 48–54. Oxford: International Association for Religious Freedom (IARF), 2001.

———. "Religion and Public Education in the United States Politics, Ethics, Law, Pedagogy." In *Religion and Public Education in the United States and Germany*, edited by Dagmar Pruin et al., 77–90. New Brunswick, NJ: Transaction, 2007.

Grillo, R. D. *Pluralism and the Politics of Difference: State, Culture, and Ethnicity in Comparative Perspective*. Oxford: Clarendon, 1998.

Grudem, Wayne. "Why Christians Should Influence Government for Good." *Wayne Grydem, Professor of Theology and Biblical Studies* (2016). http://www.waynegrudem.com/.

Guanghu, He. "Chapter One Thirty Years of Religious Studies in China." In *Social Scientific Studies of Religion in China: Methodology, Theories, and Findings*, edited by Fenggang Yang and Graeme Lang, 23–46. Leiden: Brill, 2011.

———. "President Xi Jinping Warns Against Foreign Influence on Religions in China." *Guardian*, 20 May 2015. https://www.theguardian.com/world/2015/may/21/president-xijinping-warnsagainst-foreign-influence-on-religions-inchina.

"Guidance on Promoting British Values in Schools Published." Department for Education and Lord Nash (27 November 2014). https://www.gov.uk/government/news/guidance-on-promotingbritish-values-in-schools-published.

Guo, Sujian. China's *"Peaceful Rise." In the 21st Century: Domestic and International Conditions*. Burlington, VT: Ashgate, 2006.

Habper, Ida Husted. "Why Women Cannot Vote in the United States." *The North American Review*, 179.577 (1904) 484–98.

Hamlish, Tamara. "Chinese Society and Culture." In *China: A Global Studies Handbook*, edited by Robert André LaFleur, 151–202. Denver, CO: ABC CLIO, 2003.

Hananel, Sam, and Mark Sherman. "Supreme Court Rules for Missouri Church in Playground Case." *Fox News U.S.*, 26 June 2017. www.foxnews.com/us/2017/06/26/supreme-courtrules-for-missouri-church-in-playground-case.html.

Hang-li, Zeng. "A Brief Analysis of the Classical Poetry Chinese-English Translation: From the perspective of 'Beauty in Three Aspects.'" ser. 74.7.2, *Sino US English Teaching*, 52–58. ISSN 1539-8072, USA, February 2010.

Hardin, Russell. *Liberalism, Constitutionalism, and Democracy*, Oxford: Oxford University Press, 1999.

Harkov, Lahav. "Israeli Ministers Approve Controversial Jewish State Bill." *Jerusalem Post* (7 May 2017). http://www.jpost.com/Israel-News/Politics-AndDiplomacy/Ministersapprove-controversial-Jewish-State-bill-489972.

Harris, Harriet A. *Fundamentalism and Evangelicals*. Oxford: Clarendon, 1998.

Harsanyi, David. "Rand Paul Is Right: Social Conservatives Should Embrace Libertarianism." *The Examiner* (28 February 2014).

Hartog, Jonathan Den. "The 1950s, Principled Pluralism, and the Future of America." *Public Discourse*. http://www.thepublicdiscourse.com/2014/12/13991/.

Haupt, Claudia E. *Religion–State Relations in the United States and Germany: The Quest for Neutrality*. New York: Cambridge University Press, 2012.

He, Baogang. *The Democratisation of China*. London: Routledge, 2002.

He, Huaihong. *Social Ethics in a Changing China: Moral Decay or Ethical Awakening?* Washington, DC: Brookings Institution, 2015.

Hedges, Chris. *When Atheism Becomes Religion: America's New Fundamentalists.* New York: Simon and Schuster, 2009.

Her, Peng. "Qigong." In *Taking Charge of Your Wellbeing* (7 July 2014), University of Minnesota. http://www.takingcharge.csh.umn.edu/explore-healingpractices/ qigong.

Hernández, Javier C. "To Inspire Young Communists, China Turns to 'Red Army' Schools." *New York Times*, 15 October 2017. https://www.nytimes.com/2017/10/15/ world/asia/china-schools-propaganda-education.html.

Hertzke, Allen D. "Introduction: Advancing the First Freedom in the Twenty-First Century." In *The Future of Religious Freedom: Global Challenges*, edited by Allen D. Hertzke, 330. New York: Oxford University Press, 2013.

Heslam, Peter Somers. *Creating a Christian Worldview: Abraham Kuyper's Lectures on Calvinism.* Grand Rapids: Eerdmans, 1998.

Hilgenheger, Norbert. "Johann Friedrich Herbart." Prospects, Paris: ONESCO International Bureau of Education XXIII 3.4 (2000) 649–64.

Hill, Jr., Thomas E. "The Problem of Stability in Political Liberalism." In *Respect, Pluralism, and Justice: Kantian Perspectives.* New York: Oxford, 2000.

Hill, R. A. "Government, Justice, and Human Rights." Virginia State University (2016). http://www.bu.edu/wcp/Papers/Poli/PoliHill.htm.

Hindman, Douglas Blanks, et al. "Structural Pluralism, Ethnic Pluralism, and Community Newspapers." *Journalism and Mass Communication Quarterly* 76.2 (1999) 250–63.

Hirschl, Ran. *Constitutional Theocracy.* Cambridge, MA: Harvard University Press, 2011.

Hitchcock, James. *The Supreme Court and Religion in American Life*, Vol. 2. Princeton, NJ: Princeton University Press, 2004.

Hobson, P. R., and J. S. Edwards. *Religious Education in a Pluralist Society.* London: Woburn, 1999.

Holden, Andrew. *Religious Cohesion in Times of Conflict: Christian-Muslim Relations in Segregated Towns.* New York: Continuum International, 2009.

Hollenbach, David S. J. *The Common Good and Christian Ethics.* Cambridge: Cambridge University Press, 2002.

Hood, Ralph W., Peter C. Hill, and Bernard Spilka. *The Psychology of Religion: An Empirical Approach.* New York: Guilford, 2009.

Horn, Michael B. "The Rise of Micro-Schools: Combinations of Private, Blended, and at Home Schooling Meet Needs of Individual Students." *Education Next* 15.3, 2015. https://www.questia.com/library/journal/1G1-424457376/the-rise-ofmicro-schoolscombinations-of-private.

Hornemann, Magda. "China: Tight State Controls on Religious Education." *Forum 18 News Service*, 15 May 2013. http://www.forum18.org/archive.php?article_ id=1835.

H.R. 2431 (27 January 1998). http://www.state.gov/documents/organization/2297. pdf.

Huang, Joyce. "Church Crackdown Continues in China." (10 December 2015). http:// www.voanews. com/content/church-crackdown-continues-inchina/3096816.html.

Huang, Xu, and Michael Harris Bond. *Handbook of Chinese Organizational Behavior: Integrating Theory, Research and Practice.* Northampton, MA: Elgar, 2012.

Hua, Zhang. "The Beginning of the Religious Freedom Policy in the Republic of China." http://www.pacilution.org/english/ShowArticle89d7.html?ArticleID=3128.

Huey, Craig. "China: Two Child Policy and Morality." *Election Forum* (5 November 2015). https://www.election forum.org/international/china-two-child-policyand-morality/.

Huffington Post. "China's President Xi Jinping Says "Religions Must Be Free from Foreign Influence." *Huffington Post* (21 May 2015). http://www.huffingtonpost.com/2015/05/20/chinaxi-jinping-religion_n_7342360.html.

Hughes, James L. *Froebel's Educational Laws for All Teachers.* New York: Appleton, 1897.

Hull, John M. "The Contribution of Religious Education to Religious Freedom: A Global Perspective." In *Religious Education in Schools: Ideas and Experiences from Around the World*, 4–11. https://iarf.net/wp-content/uploads/ 2013/02/Religious Education-in Schools.pdf.

Human Rights Committee. *General Comment 22, Article 18 (Forty-Eighth Session, 1993).* Compilation of General Comments and General RecommendationsAdopted by Human Rights Treaty Bodies, UN Doc. HRI/GEN/1/Rev.1 at 35, in *University of Minnesota Human Rights Library.* http://hrlibrary.umn.edu/gencomm/hrcom22.htm.

Human Rights Watch. *Freedom of Religion in China.* Washington, DC: Asia Watch Committee, 1992.

Hunter, Alan, and Kim-Kwong Chan. *Protestantism in Contemporary China.* New York: Cambridge University Press, 2007.

Hunter, James Davison. "Religious Freedom and the Challenge of Modern Pluralism." In *Articles of Faith, Articles of Peace: The Religious Liberty Clauses and the American Public Philosophy*, edited by James Davison Hunter and Os Guinness, 54–73. Washington, DC: Brookings Institution, 1990.

Hunter-Henin, Myriam. "Introduction." In *Religious Freedoms in European Schools: Contrasts and Convergence*, 1–36, Burlington, VT: MPG Book Group, 2011.

Huntington, Samuel P. *The Third Wave: Democratization in the Late 20th Century.* Norman, OK: University of Oklahoma, 2012.

Hushbeck Jr., Elgin L. *Christianity and Secularism.* Gonzalez. FL: Energion, 2007.

Hyer, Eric. "The Establishment and Free Exercise of Religion: Observing the UN Declaration on Religious Tolerance and Non-Discrimination." Provo, UT: Brigham Young University, 2006. http://www.casaasia.es/dialogo/2006/esp/hyer.pdf.

IARF Trifold Pamphlet 2015 (2015). https://iarf.net/wpcontent/uploads/2015/06/IARF-Trifold-Pamphlet-2015.pdf.

"Independent States in the World Fact Sheet." *Department of State.* https://www.state.gov/s/inr/rls/4250.htm.

"Indicator 45: Source of Funds for Education: What is 'Public' and 'Private' Education." National Center for Education Statistics. https://nces.ed.gov/pubs/eiip/eiip45s1.asp/

Indicators of School Crime and Safety: 2013. Bureau of Justice Statistics, National Center for Education Statistics, Executive Summary (2013).

"International Association for Religious Freedom." Information Pamphlet, https://iarf.net/wpcontent/uploads/2015/06/IARF-Trifold-Pamphlet 2015.pdf.

The International Association for Religious Freedom (IARF) is a UK-based charity working for freedom of religion and belief at a global level.

International Covenant on Civil and Political Rights (2015). http://www.ohchr.org/en/professionalinterest/pages/ccpr.aspx/.

Ivison, Duncan. "Locke, Liberalism, and Empire." In *Philosophy of John Locke: New Perspectives*, edited by Peter R. Anstey, 86–105. London: Routledge, 2004.

Jackson, Robert. "Is Diversity Changing Religious Education? Religion, Diversity and Education in Today's Europe" (2009). http://wrap.warwick.ac.uk/2931/1/WRAP_Jackson_Jackson_Nordic_2009_chapter1-2154.pdf/.

———. *Rethinking Religious Education and Plurality: Issues in Diversity and Pedagogy.* New York: Routledge, 2004.

Jacobi, Tonia, Sonia Mittal, and Barry R. Weingast. "Creating a Self-Stabilizing Constitution: The Role of the Takings Clause." *Northwestern University Law Review* 109.3 (2015) 609–38.

Jansen, Thomas, et al., eds. *Globalization and the Making of Religious Modernity in China: Transnational Religions, Local Agents, and the Study of Religion, 1800–Present.* Leiden: Brill, 2014.

Jenkins, Philip. "Believing in the Gospel South." *First Things* (December 2006). http://www.firstthings.com /article/ 2006/12/believing-in-the-global-south.

———. *The Next Christendom: The Coming of Global Christianity.* New York: Oxford University Press, 2011.

Jian, Ma. "China's Barbaric One-Child Policy." *Guardian*, 6 May 2013. http://www.theguardian.com/ books/2013/may/06/chinas-barbaric-one-childpolicy.

Jiang, Steven, Paul Armstrong, and Susannah Cullinane. "China Unveils Two-Child Policy." Cable News Network, Turner Broadcasting System, Inc. (2016). http://www.cnn.com/2015/12/27/asia/china-two-child-policy/.

Jintao, Hu. "Full text of Hu Jintao's Report at 17th Party Congress." Edited by Du Guodong (24 October 2007). http://news.xinhuanet.com/english/200710/24/content_6938749.htm.

Johnson, Ian. "Jesus vs. Mao? 'An Interview with Yuan Zhiming.'" *The New York Review of Books* (4 September 2012). http://www.nybooks.com/daily/2012/09/04/jesus-vs-maointerview-yuan zhiming/.

Johnson, R. "Rawlsian Liberalism." PHIL 213, *Political and Social Philosophy* (n.d.). http://web.missouri. edu/~johnsonrn/rawls.html.

Jung, Patricia Beattie, and Loyle Shannon Jung, eds. "Rights and Wrongs: An Interview with Nicholas Wolterstorff." In *Moral Issues and Christian Responses*. Minneapolis, MN: Fortress, 2012.

"Just What Is a Charter School, Anyway?" Interview by Claudio Sanchez, edited by NPR. *How Learning Happens*, 1 March 2017. https://www.npr.org/sections/ed/2017/03/01/511446388/just-what-is-a-charter-school-anyway.

Ka-che Yip. "China and Christianity: Perspectives on Missions, Nationalism, and the State in the Republican Period, 1912–1949." In *Missions, Nationalism, and the End of Empire*, edited by Brian Stanley and Alaine Low, 132–43. Grand Rapids: Eerdmans, 2004.

Kai-lin, Ho. *Laogaiying zhong de taianju erleu* [Children of God in the labour camp] Taibei: Guangqi, 1990.

Kelly, Douglas F. *Emergence of Liberty in the Modern World: The Influence of Calvin on Five Governments from the 16th through 18th Centuries.* Phillipsburg, NJ: P&R, 1992.

Kern, Soeren. "The Islamization of France in 2013." Gatestone Institute (4 January 2014). http://www.gatestoneinstitute.org/4120/islamization-france.

Kerr, Colin. *A Heaven-Backed Rebellion: Uncovering the Political Vision of Christian Liberals.* Nashville, IN: Unlimited, 2008.

Kickasola, Joseph N. "The Theonomic Response to Christian America." In *God and Politics: Four Views on the Reformation of Civil Government,* edited by Gary Scott, 15057. Phillipsburg, NJ: P&R, 1989.

Kindopp, Jason. "Fragmented Yet Defiant: Protestant Resilience under Chinese Communist Party Rule." In *God and Caesar in China: Policy Implications of Church–State Tensions,* edited by Jason Kindopp and Carol Lee Hamrin, 122–48. Washington, DC: The Brookings Institution, 2004.

King, Gilbert. "The Silence That Preceded China's Great Leap into Famine." Smithstionian. com (26 September 2012). http://www.smithsonianmag.com/history/the-silence-thatpreceded-chinasgreat-leap-into-famine51898077/#yM3RgTSshzWACBQA.9.

Kis, János. *Constitutional Democracy.* Budapest, Hungary: Central European University, 2003.

Kleinman, Arthur, et al. *Deep China: The Moral Life of the Person, What Anthropology and Psychiatry Tell Us about China Today.* Berkeley, CA: University of California Press, 2011.

Kodelja, Zdenko. "Religious Education and the Teaching about Religions." https://www.dlib.si/stream/URN:NBN:SI:DOC-DG7VU9DH/e59ad208-37594776-a5e5e8d2b7bd18e4/PDF.

Koh, Caroline. "Moral Development and Student Motivation in Moral Education: A Singapore Study." *Australian Journal of Education* 56.1 (2012) 83–101.

Kong, Peggy A. "'To Walk Out': Rural Parents' Views on Education." *China: An International Journal* 8.2 (2010). http://www.questia.com/read/1G1240579701/to-walk-out-ruralparents-views-on-education.

Kosciw, Joseph G., et al. *The 2011 National School Climate Survey: The Experiences of Lesbian, Gay, Bisexual and Transgender Youth in Our Nation's Schools.* New York: Gay, Lesbian & Straight Education Network, 2012.

Kozinski, Thaddeus J. *The Political Problem of Religious Pluralism: And Why Philosophers Can't Solve It.* Lanham, MD: Lexington, 2012.

Kramer, Jane. "Taking the Veil." *New Yorker* (22 November 2004). http://www.newyorker.com /magazine/2004/11/22/taking-the-veil.

Kuperus, Tracy. *State, Civil Society and Apartheid in South Africa: An Examination of Dutch Reformed Church–State Relations.* New York: St. Martin's, 1999.

Kuru, Ahmet T. "Assertive and Passive Secularism State Neutrality, Religious Demography, the Muslim Minority in the United States." In *Future of Religious Freedom: Global Challenges,* edited by Allen D. Hertzke. New York: Oxford University Press, 2013.

Kuyper, A. *Soevereiniteit in Eigen Kring* Amsterdam: Kruyt, 1880. http://www.reformationalpublishingproject.com/pdfbooks/Scanned_Books_DF/SouvereniteitinEigenKring.pdf.

Kuyper, A. *Calvinism: Six Stone-lectures.* Princeton, NJ: Biblio Life, 1898.

———. *The Practice of Godliness.* Grand Rapids: Eerdmans, 1948. http://www.calvin.edu/library/database/crcpi/fulltext/ctj/123578.pdf.

Kuyper Center Review: Volume Three: Calvinism and Culture. Edited by Gordon Graham. Grand Rapids: Eerdmans, 2013.

Kuyper Centre for Christian Worldview Studies. https://www.allaboutworldview.org/worldview-teaching-of-abraham-kuyper-faq.htm.

Lalibertém, André. "Contemporary Issues in State–Religion." In *Chinese Religious Life*, edited by David A. Palmer et al., 191–208. New York: Oxford University Press, 2009.

Lambert, Tony. "The Present Religious Policy of the Chinese Communist Party." *Religion, State & Society* 29.2 (2001) 121–29. https://biblicalstudies.org.uk/pdf/rss/29-2_121.pdf.

Lamberts, Emiel. *Christian Democracy in the European Union, 1945/1995: Proceedings of the Leuven Colloquium.* Leuven: Leuven University Press, 1995.

Lang, Olga. *Chinese Family and Society.* New Haven, CT: Yale University Press, 1946.

Larres, Klaus, ed. *A Companion to Europe since 1945.* Hoboken, NJ: John Wiley & Sons, 2014.

Lawrenz, Mel. "How Should We Understand the Law?" *Bible Gateway* (7 January 2015). https://www.biblegateway.com/blog/2015/01/how-should-weunderstand-the-law/.

Lazaroiu, George. "The Political Ontology of Rawls's Work." *Analysis and Metaphysics* 13 (2014). http://www.questia.com/read/1P33554660951/thepolitical-ontology-of-rawlss-work.

Lee, Chin-Chuan. *Chinese Media, Global Contexts.* London: Routledge, 2003.

Lee, Han Young. *From History to Narrative Hermeneutics.* New York: Lang, 2004.

Lee, Morgan. "Pastor of China's Largest Church Jailed for Protesting Removal of 1,500 Crosses." *Christianity Today.* http://www.christianitytoday.com/gleanings/2016/february/pastor- chinalargest-church-jailed-crosses-gu-yuesechongyi.html.

Leibold, James. *Minority Education in China: Balancing Unity and Diversity in an Era of Critical Pluralism.* Hong Kong: Hong Kong University Press, 2014.

Leigh, Ian. "Objective, Critical and Pluralistic? Religious Education and Human Rights in The European Public Sphere." In *Law, State and Religion in the New Europe: Debates and Dilemmas,* edited by Lorenzo Zucca and Camil Ungureanu. New York: Cambridge University Press, 2012.

Leo, Leonard, and Don Argue. "The Huffington Post—Confronting China's Failure on Religious Freedom." United States Commission on Religious Freedom (n.d.). http://www.http://www.uscirf.gov/news-room/op-eds/thehuffingtonpost-confronting chinas-failurereligious-freedom.

Leung, Beatrice. "The Catholic Church in Post-1997 Hong Kong: Dilemma in Church-State Relations." In *China and Christianity: Burdened Past, Hopeful Future,* edited by Stephen Uhalley and Xiaoxin Wu. Armonk, NY: Sharpe, 2001.

Leung, Beatrice. *China's Religious Freedom Policy: The Art of Managing Religious Activity.* Hong Kong: Lingnan University Press, 2005.

Leung, Beatrice, and William T. Liu. *Chinese Catholic Church in Conflict: 1949–2001.* Boca Raton, FL: Florida Universal Press, 2004.

Leung, Philip Yuen-sang. "Conversion, Commitment, and Culture: Christian Experience in China, 1949–99." In *Christianity Reborn: The Global Expansion of Evangelicalism in the Twentieth Century,* edited by Donald M. Lewis, 87–107. Grand Rapids: Eerdmans, 2004.

"Level 1 Examples." RE: Online (2013). http://www.reonline.org.uk/wordpress/wpcontent/uploads/2013/01/Level-Examples-1-and-1-2.pdf/.

Levinson, Natasha. "Contemporary Political Theory and Education." In *Handbook of Educational Theories*, edited by Beverly Irby et al. 67–78. Charlette, NC: Information Age, 2013.

Lewis, Philip. "Between Lord Ahmed and Ali G: Which Future for British Muslims?" In *Religious Freedom and the Neutrality of the State*, edited by W. A. R. and P. Sj. Koningsveld, 129–44. Paris: Peeters, 2002.

Lian, Xi. *Redeemed by Fire: The Rise of Popular Christianity in Modern China*. Cambridge: Yale University Press, 2010.

———. Hanover College. "Cultural Christians" and Political Dissent in Contemporary China, Fairbank Center for Chinese Studies (21 October 2011). http://fairbank. fas.harvard.edu/event/xi-lian-hanover-college-culturalchristians-and-political-dissent-contemporarychina.

Li, Cheng. "The Local Factor in China's Intra-party Democracy." In *Democratization in China, Korea and Southeast Asia? Local and National Perspectives*, edited by Ds. Kate XiaoZhou et al., 87–109. London: Routledge, 2014.

Li, Lan. *Popular Religion in Modern China: The New Role of Nuo*. Burlington, VT: Ashgate, 2015.

Li, Xiaobing. *Civil Liberties in China*. Santa Barbara, CA: ABC-Clio, 2010.

Lieberman, Jethro K. *Liberalism Undressed*. New York: Oxford University Press, 2012.

Lindberg, Christine A. *Oxford American Writer's Thesaurus*. Oxford: Oxford University Press, 2012.

Ling, Samuel, and Stacey Bieler, eds. *Chinese Intellectuals and the Gospel*. Phillipsburg, NJ: P&R, 1999.

Ling, Samuel, with Clarence Cheuk. *"Chinese" Way of Doing Things: Perspectives on American-Born Chinese and the Chinese Church in North America*. Phillipsburg, NJ: P&R, 1999.

Little, David. "Religious Minorities and Religious Freedom: An Overview." In *Protecting the Human Rights of Religious Minorities in Eastern Europe*, edited by Peter G. Danchin and Elizabeth A. Cole, 33–57. New York: Columbia University Press, 2002.

Liu, Guoli. *Politics and Government in China*. Santa Barbara, CA: ABC-Clio, 2011.

Living with Difference, Community, Diversity and the Common Good. Report of the Commission on Religion and Belief in British Public Life, Chair: The Rt Hon Baroness Elizabeth Butler-Sloss GBE, Cambridge: The Woolf Institute, 2015.

Locke, John. *A Letter Concerning Toleration*. Edited by James Tully. Indianapolis, IN: Hackett, 1983.

Lodge, Carey. "Church Wins Land Dispute after Pastor's Wife Bulldozed During Church Demolition Protest." *Christian Today* (20 April 2016). http://www.christiantoday. com/article/church.wins.land.dispute.after.pastors.wife.bulldozed.during.church. demolition.protest/84975.htm.

Long, Robert, and Paul Bolton. "Faith Schools in England: FAQs" (House of Commons Library, 2017). http://www.parliament.uk/commonslibraryintranet.parliament. uk/commonlibrary.

Lum, Thomas, and Hannah Fischer. *Human Rights in China: Trends and Policy Implications*. Washington, DC: Congressional Research Service, 2009. https:// pdfs.semanticscholar.org/fa3a/534a9a8d122e46ac52e1a91a82a482cdbd2b.pdf.

Luo, Renfu, et al. "Behind before They Begin: The Challenge of Early Childhood Education in Rural China." *Australasian Journal of Early Childhood* 37.1 (2012) 55–64.

Ma, Hing-keung. *Moral Development and Moral Education: An Integrated Approach, Educational Research Journal,* 教育研究學報, 24.2. Hong Kong Educational Research Association, Winter 2009.

Macedo, Stephen. *Diversity and Distrust: Civic Education in a Multicultural Democracy.* Cambridge, MA: Harvard University Press, 2009.

———. "Liberal Civic Education and Religious Fundamentalism: The Case of God v. John Rawls?" *Ethics* 105.3 (1995) 468–96. http://links.jstor.org/sici?sici =00141704%28199504%29105%3A3%3C46%ALCEARF%3E2.0CO%3B2-Q.

Machan, Tibor R. "Reflections on Modern Democracy." *Review of Contemporary Philosophy* 14 (2015) 63–95.

Mackey, Bonnie W., et al. "Demographics of Home Schoolers: A Regional Analysis within the National Parameters." *Education* 132.1 (2011) 133–40.

Making Sense of Religion. Ofsted London England: Alexandra House, 2007. https://dera. ioe.ac.uk//11105/1/Making%20sense%20of%20religion%20PDF%20format%29. pdf.

Macmullen, Ian. *Faith in Schools? Autonomy, Citizenship, and Religious Education in the Liberal State.* Princeton, NJ: Princeton University Press, 2007.

Maddox, Marion. *Taking God to School: The End of Australia's Egalitarian Education?* Sydney: Allen & Unwin, 2014.

Maffettone, Sebastiano. *Rawls: An Introduction.* Malden, MA: Polity, 2010.

Mahoney, Jon. "Public Reason and The Moral Foundation of Liberalism." In *Legacy of John Rawls,* edited by Thom Brooks and Fabian Freyenhagen, 85–106. New York: A&C Black, 2005.

Markets and Choice Policies. Types of School. *Gov.UK. https://www.gov.uk/.*

Marquand, David. "We Shouldn't Forget Liberalism's Religious Roots." *New Republic* (2014). http://www.newrepublic.com/article/119511/how liberalismlost-itsway-religious-rootsideology/.

Marshall, Joanne M. "Religion and Education: Walking the Line in Public Schools." *Phi Delta Kappan* 85.3 (2003) 239–42. http://www.questia.com/read/1G1109868286/ religionand-education-walking-the-line-in-public.

Marshall, Paul. *God and the Constitution: Christianity and American Politics.* Lanham, MD: Rowan & Littlefield, 2002.

Marx, Karl, and Friedrich Engels. *On Religion.* Mineola, NY: Dover, 2012.

Massaro, Toni M. "Some Realism about Constitutional Liberalism." *Constitutional Commentary* 28.3 (2013). http://www.questia.com/read/1G1335625865.

Maussen, Marcel. "Religious Governance in the Netherlands: Associative Freedoms and Non-Discrimination after 'Pillarization,' the Example of Faith-Based Schools." *Geopolitics, History and International Relations* 6.2 (2014). http://www.questia. com/read/1P33502772001/religiousgovernanceinthenetherlands-associative.

McGraw, Bryan T. *Faith in Politics: Religion and Liberal Democracy.* New York: Cambridge University Press, 2010.

McIlwain, Charles Howard. *Constitutionalism: Ancient and Modern.* Clark, NJ: The Lawbook Exchange, 2005.

Mels, Sara, and Christiane Timmerman. "General Introduction." In *Religions in Movement: The Local and the Global in Contemporary Faith Traditions*, edited by Robert W. Hefner et al.. London: Routledge, 2013.

Menezes, Isabel, and Bartolo Paiva Campos. "Values in Education: Definitely: 'Your Feet Are Always in the Water.'" In *Moral Education and Pluralism*, edited by Mal Leicester et al.. London: Falmer, 2000.

Merriman, Scott, A. *Religion and the Law in America: An Encyclopedia of Personal Belief and Public Policy*. 2 vols. Santa Barbara, CA: ABC-CLIO, 2007.

Merry, Michael S., and Sjoerd Karsten. "Restricted Liberty, Parental Choice and Home-Schooling." *Journal of Philosophy of Education* 44.4 (2010) 497–514.

Meyer, Christian. "How the 'Science of Religion' (*zongiiaoxue*) as a Discipline Globalized 'Religion' in Late Qing and Republican China, 1890–1949—Global Concepts, Knowledge Transfer, and Local Discourses." In *Globalization and the Making of Religious Modernity in China: Transnational Religions, Local Agents, and the Study of Religion, 1800–Present*, edited by Thomas Jansen et al., 297–341. Leiden: Brill, 2014.

Mill, John Stuart. *On Liberty and Other Essays*. 1859. Reprint, New York: Digireads. com, 2010.

Miller, J. Hillis. "Religion in a State University." In *American Education and Religion: The Problem of Religion in the Schools*, edited by F. Ernest Johnson. New York Institute for Religious and Social Studies, 1952.

Min, Jeong Kii. *Sin and Politics: Issues in Reformed Theoloy*. New York: Lang, 2009.

Min, Zhang. "No Response to Pastors' Joint Petition; Shouwang Church's Situation Becomes More Perilous." *China Aid* (2 June 2011). http://www.chinaaid. org/2011/06/noresponse-to-pastors-joint-petition.html?

Minogue, Kenneth. *The Liberal Mind*. Indianapolis, IN: Liberty Fund, 2001.

Modood, Tariq. "Moderate Secularism, Religion as Identity and Respect for Religion." *Political Quarterly* 81 (2010) 62–80.

Mok, K. *Intellectuals and the State in Post-Mao China*. New York: St. Martin's, 1998.

Monsma, Stephen V. *Positive Neutrality: Letting Religious Freedom Ring*. Westport, CT: Greenwood, 1993.

"Moral Education in the Life of the School." Association for Supervision and Curriculum Development, ASCD Panel on Moral Education, Educational Leadership, Alexandria, VA, May 1988.

Moten, Abdul Rashid. "Religious Pluralism in Democratic Societies: Challenges and Prospects for Southeast Asia, Europe, and the United States in the New Millennium." *Contemporary Southeast Asia* 29.1 (2007). http://www.questia.com/ PM.qst?a=o&d=5020964900.

Mouw, Richard J. *Uncommon Decency: Christian Civility in an Uncivil World*. Downers Grove IL: InterVarsity, 2011.

Mouw, Richard J., and Sander Griffioen. *Pluralisms and Horizons: An Essay in Christian Public Philosophy*. Grand Rapids: Eerdmans, 1993.

Muller, Wim. "China: An Illiberal, Non-Western State in a Western-centric, Liberal Order?" *Baltic Yearbook of International Law*, 2015 Forthcoming, Social Science Research Network (1 December 2014). http://papers.ssrn.com/sol3/papers. cfm?abstract_id=2575643.

Murphy, Karen. *State Security Regimes and the Right to Freedom of Religion and Belief: Changes in Europe Since 2001*. London: Routledge, 2013.

Nathan, K. S. *Religious Pluralism in Democratic Societies: Challenges and Prospects for Southeast Asia, Europe, and the United States in the New Millennium.* Singapore: Kuala Lumpur Malaysians Association for American Studies, 2007.

National Center for Education Statistics. "Table 206.10: Number and Percentage of Homeschooled Students Ages 5 through 17 with a Grade Equivalent of Kindergarten through 12th Grade, by Selected Child, Parent, and Household Characteristics: 2003, 2007 and 2012" (2017).

National Committee of Three-Self Patriotic Movement of the Protestant Churches in China. *Berkley Center for Religion, Peace, and World Affairs* (2017). https://berkleycenter.georgetown.edu/organizations/national-committee-ofthree-self-patriotic-movement-ofthe-protestant-churches-in-china.

National Council for Curriculum and Assessment. *Post-Primary Religious Education Guidelines for Teachers of Students with Mild General Learning Disabilities.* Dublin: NCCA, n.d. https://www.ncca.ie/en/resources/pp_religion.

National Council for Curriculum and Assessment (NCCA). "Religious Education Guidelines for Teachers of Students with Mild General Learning Disabilities" (n.d.). http://www.ncca.ie/uploadedfiles/PP_Religion.pdf.

National Heritage Academies. "Difference between Private and Public Schools" (2017). https://www.nhaschools.com/en/About-Us/Pages/Differencebetween-Private-and-PublicSchools.aspx.

National Secular Society. "What Is Secularism?" (2015). http://www.secularism.org.uk/what-is-secularism.html.

Neubert, Amy Patterson. "Prof: Religious Trends in China Fueled by Government Restrictions." Purdue University News Service (1 December 2011).

Neuhaus, Richard John. *The Naked Public Square: Religion and Democracy in America.* Grand Rapids: Eerdmans, 1986.

Newcombe, Suzanne. "Religious Education in the United Kingdom." In *Routledge International Handbook of Religious Education*, edited by Derek H. Davis and Elena Miroshnikova. London: Routledge, 2013.

Newman, Jay. *On Religious Freedom.* Ottawa, ON: University of Ottawa Press, 1991.

Ng, Shu-Sum, and Wenko Chan. "Introducing 'Life Education' in Taiwan." In *Religious Education in Schools: Ideas and Experiences from around the World*, edited by Zarrin T. Caldwell, 39–42. London: IARF, 2002. https://iarf.net/wpcontent/uploads/2013/02/Religious-Education-in-Schools.pdf.

Nichols, Kevin. "Roots in Religious Education." In *Priorities in Religious Education: A Model for the 1990s and Beyond*, edited by Brenda Watso, 113–23. Bristol, PA: Taylor & Francis, 1992.

Nickel, Kelly. *Pocket Patriot: Quotes from American Heroes.* Cincinnati, OH: Writers Digest, 2005.

Noddings, Nel. *Philosophy of Education.* Boulder, CO: Westview, 1998.

NOLA Media Group. http://www.nola.com/politics/index.ssf/2012/09/freedoms_of_speech_religion_ cl.html/.

Nong, Qiao, [reported in Chinese]. "Church Leader's Wife Dead after Buried Alive during Church Demolition." Translated by Carolyn Song. Written in English by Brynne Lawrence, Chinaaid (18 April 2016). http://www.chinaaid.org/2016/04/church-leaders-wife-deadafter buried.html.

Norton, Michael Barnes. "Religious Pluralism." In *Internet Encyclopedia of Philosophy.* http://www.iep.utm.edu/rel-plur/.

Noveck, Scott M. "The Promise and Problems of Treating Religious Freedom as Freedom of Association." *Gonzaga Law Review* 45.2 (2010) 745–72.

Nussbaum, Martha C. "Perfectionist Liberalism and Political Liberalism." *Philosophy & Public Affairs* 39.1 (2011) 25–30.

ODIHR Advisory Council of Experts on Freedom of Religion or Belief. *Toledo Guiding Principles on Teaching about Religions and Beliefs in Public Schools*. Warsaw, Poland: OSCE Office for Democratic Institutions and Human Rights, 2007.

O'Donovan, Oliver. *Resurrection and Moral Order: An Outline for Evangelical Ethics.* Grand Rapids: Eerdmans, 2001.

O'Hair, Madaíyn Murray. *The Atheist: Madalyn Murray O'Hair*. New York: New York University, 2003.

O'Neill, Shane. *Impartiality in Context: Grounding Justice in a Pluralist World.* Albany, NY: State University of New York, 1997.

"OSCE Guidelines on Teaching about Religion and Beliefs in Public Schools." In *Toledo Guiding Principles on Teaching about Religions and Beliefs in Public Schools.* Vienna: Organization for Security and Co-operation in Europe, 2007.

Palmer, Susan J. *The New Heretics of France: Minority Religions, La République, and the Government-Sponsored "War on Sects.* New York: Oxford University Press, 2011.

Padmore, George. *History of the Pan African Congress.* London: Hammersmith, 1963.

Panichas, George A. "Remedying the Ills of American Education." *Modern Age,* Intercollegiate Studies Institute (2003). https://www.highbeam.com.

Paprock, John Brian. *Workbook for Interfaith Ambassadors.* Raleigh, NC: Lulu, 2011.

Patterson Neubert, Amy. "Prof: Religious Trends in China Fueled by Government Restrictions." Purdue University News Service (1 December 2011).

Patton, Paul. "Foucault and Rawls: Government and Public Reason." In *Government of Life: Foucault, Biopolitics, and Neoliberalism,* edited by Vanessa Lemm and Miguel Vatter, 141–62. New York: Oxford University Press, 2014.

Peerenboom, Randall. *China Modernizes: Threat to the West or Model for the Rest?* New York: Oxford University Press, 2007.

Peng, Liu. *China Security* 4.4 (Autumn 2008). http://mercury.ethz.ch/serviceengine/Files/ISN/94437/ichaptersection_singldocument/92015208-effb-4d80-8f9e16942687c06b/en/4.pdf.

Pennanen, Joonas. "Political Liberalism and the Preventive Containment of Unreasonable Beliefs and Behavior." 25 (2015) 191–208. http://journals.sussex.ac.uk/index.php/sspt/ article/view/34.

Pepper, Suzanne. *Civil War in China: The Political Struggle, 1945–1949.* Lanham, MD: Rowman & Littlefield, 1999.

Pépin, Luce. *Teaching about Religions in European School Systems Policy Issues and Trends.* London: Alliance Trust, 2009.

Perks, Stephen C. *A Defense of the Christian State: The Case against Principled Pluralism and the Christian Alternative.* Taunton, UK: Kuyper Foundation, 1998.

Perlin, Jonah. "Liberal Religious Political Advocates: Religion as a Conversation Starter: What Liberal Religious Political Advocates Add to the Debate about Religion's Place in Legal and Political Discourse." *Georgetown Law Journal* 100.1 (2011) 331–66.

Perry, John. *The Pretenses of Loyalty: Locke, Liberal Theory, and American Political Theology.* New York: Oxford, 2011.

Petrin, Dennis P., and Frans Visscher. "Revisiting Sphere Sovereignty to Interpret Restrictions on Religious Freedom." *Philosophia Reformata* 80 (2015) 99–122. https://platformforsocialtransformation.org/download/religiousfreedom/Petri-Visscher%20-%20Revisiting%20sphere%20sovereignty%20to%20interpret%20restrictions%20on%20religious%20freedom.pdf

Philogène, Gina, *From Black to African American: A New Social Representation.* Westport, CT: Praeger, 1999.

Ploeger, Ruth. "Homeschooling in Europe." https://europe.stripes.com/education/homeschoolingeurope.

Pocock, J. G. A. *Political Thought and History: Essays on Theory and Method.* New York: Cambridge University Press, 2009.

Pol, Henk. "Religious Education in Dutch Schools" (2013). http://mmiweb.org.uk/eftreold/reeurope/netherlands_2013.pdf.

Ponce, Pedro. "The Philosophy of Justice: John Rawls." *Humanities* (November/December 1999). https://www.questia.com.

Pons, Xavier, Agnès Van Zanten, and Sylvie da Costa. "The National Management of Public and Catholic Schools in France: Moving from a Loosely Coupled Towards an Integrated System?" *Comparative Education* 51.1 (2015) 57–70.

Posterski, Donald. "What on Earth Is Evangelism?" In *Part of the Problem, Part of the Solution: Religion Today and Tomorrow*, edited by Arvind Sharma. Westport, CT: Praeger, 2008.

Price, Richard. *Moral Limit and Possibility in World Politics: Political Science.* Content Technologies, Inc.: Phoenix, AZ, 2014. http://www.huffingtonpost.com/2015/05/20/China-Xi Jinping Religion_N_7342360.html.

"Private Schools." In *Types of Schools.* https://www.gov.uk/types-ofschool/private schools.

Prodromou, Elizabeth H. "Protecting Religious Freedom Abroad." *Harvard International Review* (1 July 2011). http://hir.harvard.edu/protecting-religious-freedom-abroad/.

"Protestantism." *Patheos Library* (2016). http://www.patheos.com/Library/Protestantism.

Prusak, Bernard G. "Politics, Religion & The Public Good: An interview with Philosopher John Rawls." *Commonweal*, 25 September 1998, CXXV, 16. http://www98.homepage.villanova.edu/bernard.g.prusak/interviewwithrawls.htm.

Pryor, C. Scott. "Principled Pluralism and Contract Remedies." McGeorge Law Review 40.3 (2009). http://www.regent.edu/acad/schlaw/facultystaff/docs/pryor/principled.pdf.

Putnam, Hilary. "John Rawls." In *Proceedings of the American Philosophical Society* 1 (2005). https://www.questia.com/read/1P3-840756281.

Raadschelders, Jos, and Eran Vigoda-Gadot. *Global Dimensions of Public Administration and Governance: A Comparative Voyage.* Hoboken, NJ: Wiley & Sons, 2015.

Race, G., ed. *Leadership and Change in Human Services: Selected Readings from Wolf Wolfensberger.* London: Routledge, 2003.

Radio Poland. "Ritual Slaughter of Farm Animals 'Unconstitutional' in Poland, Court Rules" (28 November 2012). http://www.thenews.pl/1/9/Artykul/119809Ritual slaughterof-farmanimals unconstitutional-in-Poland-court-rules.

"Ratifying without Resolve." *Berkeley Political Review* (1 April 2015). http://bpr.berkeley.edu/2015/04/01/ratifying-without-resolve/.

Rawls, John. "The Idea of Public Reason Revisited." *University of Chicago Law Review* 643 (Summer 1997). http://www.jstor.org/stable/1600311. Also in J. Rawls, *The Law of Peoples.* Cambridge, MA: Harvard University Press, 1999.

———. "Justice as Fairness: Political Not Metaphysical." *Philosophy and Public Affairs* 4.3 (1985) 251–76.

———. *Justice as Fairness: A Restatement.* Edited by Erin Kelly. Cambridge, MA: Harvard University Press, 2001.

———. "The Law of Peoples." In *On Human Rights: The Oxford Amnesty Lectures,* edited by Stephen Shute and Susan Hurley. New York: Basic, 1993.

———. *Lectures on the History of Moral Philosophy.* Edited by Barbara Herman. Cambridge, MA: Harvard University Press, 2000.

———. *Political Liberalism.* New York: Columbia University Press, 1993.

———. *Political Liberalism: Expanded Edition.* New York: Columbia University Press, 2005.

———. *Political Liberalism: Expanded Edition.* New York: Columbia University Press, 2013.

———. "The Priority of Right and Ideas of the Good." In *Collected Papers,* edited by Samuel Freeman. Cambridge MA: Harvard University Press, 1999. http://www.jstor.org/stable/1600311.

———. *A Theory of Justice.* Rev. ed. Cambridge, MA: Belknap, 1999.

Redekop, Benjamin W. *Enlightenment and Community: Lessing, Abbt, Herder, and the Quest for a German Public.* London: McGill-Queen's, 2000.

Reidy, David A. "Rawls's Wide View of Public Reason: Not Wide Enough." *Res Publica* 6.1 (2000) 4972.

Reinbold, Jenna. *Seeing the Myth in Human Rights.* Pennsylvania Studies in Human Rights. Philadelphia: University of Pennsylvania, 2016.

"Religion in the Constitution of the United Kingdom." Washington, DC: The Berkley Center for Religion, Peace, and World Affairs, 2014. http://berkleycenter.georgetown.edu/essays/religion-inthe-constitution-oftheunited-kingdom.

Religious Education Council of England and Wales. *A Curriculum Framework for Religious Education in England.* London: Religious Education Council of England and Wales, 2013. http://www.medway.gov.uk/pdf/REC%20RE%20curric%20framework%20Oct%202013.pdf.

"Religious Freedom in China." Berkley Center for Religion, Peace & World Affairs, Georgetown University, 2015. http://berkleycenter.georgetown.edu/essays/religiousfreedom-in-china.

"Religious Freedom in the United Kingdom." *Berkley Center for Religion, Peace & World Affairs,* 2015. http://berkleycenter.georgetown.edu/essays/religiousfreedom-in-theunitedkingdom.

"The Responsibilities of the Ministry of Education." *Ministry of Education of the People's Republic of China* (2015). http://en.moe.gov.cn/About_the_Ministry/What_We_Do/201506/t20150602_191288.html.

Rhonheimer, Martin. *The Common Good of Constitutional Democracy: Essays in Political Philosophy and on Catholic Social Teaching.* Washington, DC: Catholic University of America Press, 2013.

Richardson, Norman. "Religious Education in Northern Ireland: Towards New Relationships." In *Religious Education in Schools: Ideas and Experiences from around the World*, edited by Zarrin T. Caldwell. London: IARF, 2002. https://iarf. net/wp-content/uploads/2013/02/ Religious-Education-in-Schools.pdf.

Robers, Simone, et al. *Indicators of School Crime and Safety: 2013*. Washington, DC: National Center for Education Statistics, U.S. Department of Education and Bureau of Justice Statistics, Office of Justice Programs, U.S. Department of Justice, 2013.

Roney, John B. *Culture and Customs of the Netherlands*. Santa Barbara, CA: Greenwood, 2009.

Rosenfeld, Michael, and Andra's Sajo'. "Spreading Liberal Constitutionalism." In *Migration of Constitutional Ideas*, edited by Sujit Choudhry. New York: Cambridge University Press, 2007.

Ross, Andrew C. *A Vision Betrayed: The Jesuits in Japan and China, 1542–1742*. Edinburgh: Edinburgh University Press, 1994.

Rothgangel, Martin. "What Is Religious Education? An Epistemological Guide." In *Basic of Religious Education*, edited by Gottfried Adam et al. Bristol, CT: V&R, 2014.

Rowen, Henry S. "China: Big Changes Coming Soon." *Policy Review* 170 (2011) 35–43.

Rujouleh, Ruwan. "Burkini Bans: Why France Is Giving Iran a Run for Its Money." (25 August 2016), CNN International edition. http://edition.cnn.com/2016/08/25/ opinions/burkini-ban-france.

Russo, Charles J. "Analysis and Recommendation." In C. Russo, *International Perspectives on Education, Religion and Law*. London: Routledge, 2014.

Rumi Forum. Principled Pluralism: Report of the Inclusive America Project, interview with Meryl Chertoff, in *Rumi Forum*. http://rumiforum.org/principledpluralism-report-ofthe-inclusive-america-project-with-merylchertoff/.

Ryan, Alan. "Liberalism." In *A Companion to Contemporary Political Philosophy*, 2nd ed., edited by Robert E. Goodin et al. Malden, MA: Blackwell, 2007.

———. *The Making of Modern Liberalism*. Princeton: Princeton University Press, 2012.

Ryrie, Alec. *Protestants: The Faith That Made the Modern World*. New York: Harper Collins/Penguin, 2017.

Salem, Hajer ben Hadj. "A Golden Opportunity: Religious Pluralism and American Muslims Strategies of Integration in the Us after 9/11, 2001." *Journal for the Study of Religions and Ideologies* 9.27 (2010) 246–60.

Sandel, Michael J. "Freedom of Conscience or Freedom of Choice?" In *Articles of Faith, Articles of Peace: The Religious Liberty Clauses and the American Public Philosophy*, edited by James Davison Hunter and O. S. Guinness. Washington, DC: Brookings Institution, 1990.

Schaefer, David Lewis. *Illiberal Justice: John Rawls vs. the American Political Tradition*. Columbia, MO: University of Missouri Press, 2007.

Schaffer, Jim. "Religious Persecution in China: Woman Dies as Couple Buried Alive in Demolished Church." *Nonprofit Quarterly* (26 April 2016). https:// nonprofitquarterly.org/2016/04/26/religious-persecution-in-chinawoman-dies-as couple-buried-alive-in-demolished-church/.

Scheffler, Samuel. "The Appeal of Political Liberalism." In *John Rawls: Political Liberalism and the Law of Peoples*, edited by Chandran Kukathas. London: Routledge, 2003.

Schmidt, Corwin E. "The Principled Pluralist Perspective." In *A Principled Pluralist Perspective Church, State and Public Justice: Five Views*, edited by P. C. Kemeny. Downers Grove, IL: InterVarsity, 2009.

"Schools in France: State, Private, Bilingual and International Schools" (2017). https://www.expatica.com/fr/education/French-education-schools-inFrance_476645.html.

Schreiner, Peter. "Religious Education in Europe." Oslo University (2005). http://resources.eun.org/etwinning/europa2.pdf/.

Schrotenboer, Paul G. "The Principled Pluralist Response to Theonomy." In *God and Politics: Four Views on the Reformation of Civil Government*, edited by Gary Scott Smith. Phillipsburg, NJ: P&R, 1988.

Schweitzer, Friedrich. "Religious Education. Identity and Faith in (Post-)Modernity: More Than a Biographical Approach? A Personal Attempt at Finding the Red Thread in My Academic Work on Religious Education." In *On the Edge (Auto) biography and Pedagogical Theories on Religious Education*. Notre Dame, IN: Springer, 2013.

Sciolino, Elaine. "French Assembly Votes to Ban Religious Symbols in Schools." *New York Times*, 11 February 2004. http://www.nytimes.com/2004/02/11/international/europe/11FRAN.html.

Seidman, Louis Michael. "Should We Have a Liberal Constitution?" Georgetown Law Faculty 7.39 (2011). http://scholarship.law.georgetown.edu/cgi/viewcontent.cgi?article=1739&cntxt=facpub.

Seiple, Chris, and Dennis R. Hoover. "Religious Freedom and Global Security." In *Future of Religious Freedom: Global Challenges*, edited by Allen D. Hertzke. New York: Oxford University Press, 2013.

Seppänen, Samuli. "Rawls Rejected, Ignored and Radicalised: Debating Procedural Justice in China." The Chinese University of Hong Kong Faculty of Law Research Paper No. 201713 (26 June 2017). https://papers.ssrn.com/sol3/ papers.cfm?abstract_id=2992419.

Seymour, Julia A. "China Denies Accusations of Religious Freedom Violations." World (9 May 2016). https://world.wng.org/2016/05/china_denies_accusations_of_religious_freedom_violations.

Shadid, W. A. R., and P. S. Van Koningsveld. *Religious Freedom and the Neutrality of the State: The Position of Islam in the European Union*. Leuven, Belgium: Peeters, 2002.

Shah, Timothy. *Religious Freedom, Why Now? Defending an Embattled Human Right*. Princeton, NJ: Task Force on International Religious Freedom of the Witherspoon Institute, 2012.

Shariatmadari, David. "What Are British Values? You Asked Google—Here's the Answer." *Guardian*, 3 February 2016. https://www.theguardian.com/commentisfree/2016/feb/03/what-are-british-values-google#comments.

Sharpe, M. E. *Chinese Law and Government*. Abingdon: T & F Informa, 2003.

Shea, Nina. *In the Lion's Den: A Shocking Account of Persecuted and Martyrdom of Christians Today and How We Should Respond*. Nashville: Broadman & Holman, 1997.

Shenzhi, Li. "*Hongyang Beida de ziyou zhuyi chuantong*" (Promoting and developing the liberal tradition of Beijing University). In *Ziyou zhuyi de xiansheng: Beida chuantong yujinxiandai Zhongguo* (The harbinger of liberalism: The tradition of Beijing University and modern China), edited by Liu Junning, 1–5. Beijing: Zhongguo renshi chubanshe, 1998.

Shiffrin, Steven H. *The Religious Left and Church-State Relation*. Princeton, NJ: Princeton University, 2012.

Shklar, Judith. "Liberalism of Fear." In *Political Thought and Political Thinkers*, edited by Stanley Kauffman. Chicago: University of Chicago Press, 1998.

Shue, Vivienne. "Legitimacy Crisis in China?" In *State and Society in 21st Century China: Crisis, Contention, and Legitimation*, edited by Peter Hays Gries and Stanley Rosen. London: Routledge, 2004.

Sider, Ronald J. "Principled Pluralist Response." In *Church, State and Public Justice: Five Views*, edited by P. C. Kennedy. Downers Grove, IL: InterVarsity, 2009.

Siedentop, Larry. *Inventing the Individual: The Origins of Western Liberalism*. London: Penguin, 2015.

Simpson, Rick. "Can a Faithful Christianity Embrace a Pluralistic Theology of Religions?" *ANVIL* 17.2 (2000). https://biblicalstudies.org.uk/pdf/anvil/17-2_109.pdf.

Skillen. James W. *The Good of Politics (Engaging Culture): A Biblical, Historical, and Contemporary Introduction*. Grand Rapids: Baker, 2014.

———. "Justice for Education: Guideline #4 for Government and Citizenship." Public Justice Report, Fourth Quarter, 2006. http://www.cpjustice.org/PJR2006Q4/JusticeforEducation.

———. *Recharging the American Experiment: Principled Pluralism for Genuine Civic Community*. Grand Rapids: Baker, 1984.

———. "Reformed . . . and Always Reforming?" In *Church, State, and Citizen: Christian Approaches to Political Engagement*, edited by Sandra F. Joireman, 53–72. New York: Oxford University Press, 2009.

Slagstad, Rune. "Liberal Constitutionalism and Its Critics: Carl Schmitt and Max Weber." In *Constitutionalism and Democracy*, edited by Jon Elster and Rune Slagstad. New York: Cambridge University Press, 1993.

Smith, Alan. "Executive Summary Education, Conflict and International Development." Department for International Development, February 2003. http://www.gsdrc.org/docs/open/sd29.pdf.

Smith, David T. *Persecution and Political Order in the United States*. New York: Cambridge University Press, 2015.

Smith, Gary Scott. *Faith and the Presidency from George Washington to George W. Bush*. New York: Oxford University Press, 2009.

———. "The Principled Pluralist Response to National Confessionalism." In *God and Politics: Four Views on The Reformation of Civil Government*, edited by Gary Scott Smith. Phillipsburg, NJ: P&R, 1989.

Smith, James K. A. *Introducing Radical Orthodoxy: Mapping a Post-Secular Theology*. Grand Rapids: Baker Academic, 2004.

Smith, J. M. Powis. "The Church and Education." *Journal of Religion* 4.1 (1924) 46–59.

Smith, Steven D. "The Illusion of Religious Neutrality." Online Library of Law and Liberty (3 April 2012). http://www.libertylawsite.org/liberty-forum/theillusion-ofreligious-neutrality/.

Social Action Commission of the Evangelical Fellowship of Canada. "Being Christians in a Pluralistic Society." A Discussion Paper on Pluralism in Canada, *The Evangelical Fellowship of Canada* (25 November 1997). https://www.persecution.net/download/plural.pdf/.

Sohail, Khalid. *Freedom of Religion, Freedom from Religion: A Collection of Essays and Interviews*. Toronto: White Knight, 2007.

Sokol, Sam. "Denmark Outlaws Jewish and Muslim Ritual Slaughter as of Next Week." *Jewish News in The Jerusalem Post* (14 February 2014). http://www.jpost.com/JewishWorld/Jewish-News/Denmark-outlaws-Jewish-and-Muslim-ritual-slaughter-as-of-nextweek-341433.

Song, Robert. *Christianity and Liberal Society*. Oxford: Clarendon, 1997.

Sonntag, Selma K. *The Local Politics of Global English: Case Studies in Linguistic Globalization*. New York: Lexington, 2003.

Soper, J. Christoper, and Joel S. Fetzerl. "Religious Institutions, Church-State History, and Muslim Mobilization in Britain, France, and Germany." *Journal of Ethnic and Migration Studies* 33.6 (2007). http://ces.ufl.edu/files/ReligiousInstitutionsChurchState_030609.pdf.

Spiegel, Mickey. *China: State Control of Religion*. Edited by Sidney Jones and Jeri Labor. New York: Human Rights Watch, 1997.

Spring, Joel. *Political Agendas for Education: From the Religious Right to the Green Party*. 2nd ed. Mahwah NJ: Lawrence Erlbaum Associates, 2002.

Sproul, R. C. "What Is Reformed Theology?" A Teaching Series. (2013). http://www.ligonier.org/learn/series/what_is_reformed_theology.

Spykman, Gordon J. "The Principled Pluralist Position." In *God and Politics: Four Views on The Reformation of Civil Government*, edited by Gary Scott Smith. Phillipsburg, NJ: P&R, 1989.

Stahl, Gerry, and Friedrich Hesse. "Let a Hundred Flowers Bloom; Let a Hundred Schools of Thought Contend." *International Journal of Computer Supported Collaborative Learning* 6.2 (2011) 139–45. DOI:10.1007/s11412-011-9118-8.

Stakelbeck, Erick. "Britain: Sharia Law Expands." Limits to Growth (2012). http://www.limitstogrowth.org/articles/2012/11/15/britain-sharialawexpands/.

Standard Newswire. "Chinese Pastors Call on China's Communist Party to Cease Human Rights Violations—Seek Help from Global Community." "Here We Stand: A Call from Jakarta" section, 17 March 2017. http://www.standardnewswire.com/news/9966113293.html.

Stark, Rodney. "The Religious Awakening in China." *Review of Religious Research* 52.3 (2011) 282–89.

Starr, Don. "China and the Confucian Education." www.universitas21.com/relatedfile/download/343.

Starr, Nichol Jeannette. "Who Asked You? The Appropriateness of U.S. Leadership in Promoting Religious Freedom Worldwide." *Vanderbilt Journal of Transnational Law* 33.4 (2000). http://www.questia.com/read/1G167532880/who-asked-you-the\appropriateness-of-u-s-leadership.

Starr, Paul. "Why Liberalism Works." *The American Prospect* (April 2007). https://www.princeton.edu/~starr/articles/articles07/Starr.WhyLiberalismWorks.pdf.

Status of Ratification Interactive Dashboard. http://indicators.ohchr.org.

Stetson, Ranae. "Common Traits of Successful US Charter Schools." *Childhood Education* 89.2 (2013) 70–75.

Stevens, Leon G. *One Nation Under God*. New York: James, 2013.

Stewart, Vivien. *A World-Model of Excellence and Innovation*. Alexandria, VA: ASCD, 2012.

Stoker, Wessel. *The Religious Ascription of Meaning in Relation to the Secular Ascription of Meaning: A Theological Study*. Translated by Lucy Jansen-Hofland and Henry Jansen. Atlanta, GA: Bodopi B.V., 1996.

Strauss, D. F. M. "The Best Known but Least Understood Part of Dooyeweerd's Philosophy." In *Herman Dooyeweerd Glossary*. Lanham, MD: University of America, 2012.

Strong, Tracy B. *Voice and Silence of Public Space: Popular Societies in the French Revolution*. Public Space and Democracy. Minneapolis, MN: University of Minnesota, 2001.

Su, Xiaohuan. *Education in China: Reforms and Innovations, Beijing Class Education: Learning from International China*. Beijing: China Intercontinental Press, 2002.

Su, Zhenhua, et al. "Is the Poor Quality of Chinese Civic Awareness Preventing Democracy in China? A Case Study of Zeguo Township." *Asian Perspective* 36.1 (2012) 43–69.

Sullivan, Lawrence R. *Historical Dictionary of the People's Republic of China*. Lanham, MD: Scarecrow, 2007.

Sullivan, Meg. "U.S. Civil War Illustrates Costs, Benefits of Diversity, Say UCLA Economists." UCLA Newsroom (13 January 2009). http://newsroom.ucla.edu/releases/us-civil-war-illustrates-costs-77940.

Sullivan, Winnifred F. "The Impossibility of Religious Freedom." *The Immanent Frame* (2014). http://blogs.ssrc.org/tif/2014/07/08/impossibility-ofreligiousfreedom/.

Sultany, Nimer. "The State of Progressive Constitutional Theory: The Paradox of Constitutional Democracy and the Project of Political Justification." *Harvard Civil Rights, Civil Liberties Law Review*. http://harvardcrcl.org/wpcontent/uploads/2012/03/Sultany1.26.12.pdf.

"Summary of Dooyeweerd's Cosmonomic Philosophy." 'Enkaptic Relationships'section. http://kgsvr.net/dooy/summary.html.

Sunder, Madhavi. "Keeping Faith—Reconciling Women's Human Rights and Religion." In *Religion and Human Rights: An Introduction*, edited by John Witte, Jr. and M. Christian Green. New York: Oxford University Press, 2012.

Sunstein, Cass. *Why Societies Need Dissent*. Cambridge, MA: Harvard University Press, 2003.

Supreme Court of the United States. "The Court and Constitutional Interpretation." www.supremecourt.gov/about/constitutional.aspx.

Sutter, Robert G., and William R. Johnson, eds. *Taiwan in World Affairs*. Boulder, CO: Westview, 1994.

Synott, John P. *Global and International Studies: Transdisciplinary Perspectives*. Victoria, AU: Cengage Learning Australia, 2004.

Tait, Peter. "We Should Be Teaching Morals and Ethics in Our Schools." *Telegraph*, 11 March 2015, Education section. http://www.telegraph.co.uk/education/educationopinion/11463380/We-should-be-teaching-morals-andethics-inourschools.html.

Taneja, V. R. *Educational Thought and Practice*. New Delhi, India: Sterling, 1995.

Tarleton, Yvonne. "Church Fights to Keep the Faith in Schools; Ethos: More Than Religious Instruction." *Daily Mail* (10 September 2008). http://www.questia.com/read/1G1-184716156/church-fights-to-keep-thefaithin-schools-ethos.

Tam, Yik-Fai. "The Religious Life of Ethnic Minority Communities." In *Chinese Religious Life*, edited by David A. Palmer et al. New York: Oxford University Press, 2011.

Taylor, G. "Freedom of Religion Scarce in Iran, China." *Washington Times* (20 May 2013). www.washingtontimes.com/news/2013/may/20/freedom-ofreligionscarce-in-iranchina/?page=all.

Taylor, John. "Responses to the United Nation's Study Paper on 'The Role of Religious Education in the Pursuit of Tolerance and Non-Discrimination." In *Religious Education in Schools: Ideas and Experiences from around the World*, edited by Zarrin T. Caldwell. London: IARF, 2002. https://iarf.net/wpcontent/ uploads/2013/02/ReligiousEducation-in-Schools.pdf.

Taylor, Quentin P. "An Original Omission? Property in Rawls's Political Thought." *Independent Review* 8.3 (2004) 387–400.

Taylor, Steve. "Dogmatic and Spiritual Religion." *Psychology Today* (2014) https://www. psychologytoday.com/us/blog/out-the-darkness/201412/dogmatic-and-spiritual-religion.

Tayob, Abdulkader. "Islam and Democracy in South Africa." *Focus 62* (August 2011). http://hsf.org.za/resource-centre.

Temperman, Jeroen. *State-Religion Relationships and Human Rights Law: Towards a Right to Religiously Neutral Governance.* Leiden: Koninklijke Brill, 2010.

Thayer, Vivian T. "An 'Experimentalist' Position." In *American Education and Religion: The Problem of Religion in the Schools,* edited by F. Ernest Johnson. New York: Institute for Religious and Social Studies, 1952.

Thiemann, Ronald F. *Religion in Public Life: A Dilemma for Democracy.* Washington, DC: Georgetown University Press, 1996.

Tianlong, Yu. "Educating for World Citizens in Chinese Schools: Moral Education in the Cosmopolitan Age." In *Citizenship Education in China: Preparing Citizens for the Chinese Century,* edited by Kerry J. Kennedy et al. London: Routledge, 2013.

Tiles, J. E. *Moral Measures: An Introduction to Ethics, West and East.* London: Routledge, 2000.

Ting, K. H. *God Is Love: Collected Writings of Bishop K. H. Ting.* Colorado Springs, CO: Cook Communications Ministries International, 2004.

Tominaga, Shigeki. "Voice and Silence of Public Space: Popular Societies in the French Revolution." In *Public Space and Democracy,* edited by Marcel Hénaff and Tracy B. Strong, 79–94. Minneapolis: University of Minnesota Press, 2001.

Tourkochoriti, Ioanna. "The Burka Ban: Divergent Approaches to Freedom of Religion in France and in the U.S.A." *The William and Mary Bill of Rights Journal* 20.3 (2012) 791–852.

Trigg, Roger. *Religion in Public Life: Must Faith Be Privatized?* New York: Oxford University, 2007.

Tseng, Yen-Lun. "A Judicial Response to the Call of National Reconstruction: Revisiting the Supreme Court of Japan's Adjudication of the Cabinet Order No. 325." *National Taiwan University Law Review* 9.1 (2015). https://ssrn.com/abstract=2591225 orhttp://dx.doi.org/10.2139/ssrn.2591225.

Tubb, Gerald. "Faith School Bans Pupils from Meeting 'Outsiders.'" *Sky News* (25 July 2015). http://news.sky.com/story/1524949/faith-school-bans-pupilsfrom-meeting-outsiders.

UCA News. "President Xi Urges China's Religions to Shun Foreign Influences" (21 May 2015) http://www.ucanews. com/news/president-xi-urges-chinas religions-to-shunforeign-influences/73636. *Types of Schools.* https://www.gov.uk/types-of-school.

Uhalley Jr., Stephen. "Burdened Past, Hopeful Future." In *China and Christianity: Burdened Past, Hopeful Future: Burdened Past, Hopeful Future,* edited by Stephen Uhalley and Xiaoxin Wu. London: Routledge, 2001.

"UN Treaty Bodies and China." In *Human Rights in China.* http://www.hrichina.org/en/untreaty-bodies-and-china.

United Nations. "Protect Human Rights." http://www.un.org/en/sections/what-wedo/protecthuman rights/.

United Nations Educational, Scientific and Cultural Organization/United Nations Children's Fund. *A Human Rights-Based Approach to Education for All.* New York: United Nations Children's Fund/ United Nations Educational, Scientific and Cultural Organization, 2007.

United Nations Human Rights Office of the High Commissioner. "Article 13 International Covenant on Economic, Social and Cultural Rights." In International Standard. http://www.ohchr.org/EN/Issues/Education/SREducation/Pages/International Standards.aspx.

U.S. Department of Education Office of Innovation and Improvement Office of Non Public Education. *State Regulation of Private Schools* (2009). https://www2.ed.gov/ admins/comm /choice/regprivschl/regprivschl.pdf.

U.S. Department of State. "The Chinese Revolution of 1911." *Office of the Historian* (n.d.). https://history.state.gov /milestones/1899-1913/chineserev.

U.S. Department of State. *International Religious Freedom Report for 2014: China (Includes Tibet, Hong Kong, and Macau).* Washington, DC: Bureau of Democracy, Human Rights and Labor, n.d. https://www.state.govj/drl/rls/irf/religiousfreedom/ index.htm#wrapper.

United States Social Security Death Index. "Madalyn M O'hair." http://www. FamilySearch.org.

USCIRF. *Annual Report 2015: China.* Washington, DC: United States Commission on International Religious Freedom, 2016. http://www.uscirf.gov/sites/default/files/ China%202015.pdf.

Vaïsse, Justin. "Veiled Meaning: The French Law Banning Religious Symbols in Public Schools." In *U.S.-France Analysis Series.* Washington, DC: The Brookings Institution, March 2004.

Van Dam, Cornelis. *God and Government: Biblical Principles for Today: An Introduction and Resource.* Eugene, OR: Wipf and Stock, 2011.

Van Der Ven, Johannes A. "Reflective Comparativism in Religious Research: A Cognitive Approach." In *Religion: Immediate Experience and The Mediacy of Research: Interdisciplinary Studies, Concepts and Methodology of Empirical Research in Religion,* edited by Hans-Günter Heimbrock and Christopher P. Scholtz. Frankfort: Vandenhoeck & Ruprecht, 2007.

Van de Putte, André. "Rawls's Political Liberalism, Foundations and Principles." In *Ethical Perspectives* 2.3 (1995) 107–29. http://www.ethicaperspectives.be/viewpic. php?TABLE=EP&ID=832.

Van Til, K. A. "Abraham Kuyper and Michael Walzer: The Justice of the Spheres." *Calvin Theological Journal* 40 (2005) 267–89. http://www.calvin.edu/library/database/ crcpi/fulltext/ctj/123578.pdf.

Vermeer, Paul. "Religious Indifference and Religious Education in the Netherlands: A Tension Unfolds." *Theo-Web: Zeitschrift für Religionspädagogik* 12 (2013) 79–94.

Vermeule, Adrian. "Veil of Ignorance Rules in Constitutional Law." *Yale L.J.* 111.2 (2001) 399. http://www.yalelawjournal.org/essay/veil-ofignorance-rulesinconstitutional-law.

Vincent, Andrew. "Liberalism and Citizenship." In *Edinburgh Companion to Liberalism,* edited by Mark Evan. Chicago: Psychology, 2001.

Vischer, Robert K. *Conscience and the Common Good: Reclaiming the Space between Person and State.* New York: Cambridge University Press, 2010.

Viteritti, Joseph P. *Choosing Equality: School Choice, the Constitution, and Civil Society*. Washington, DC: Brookings Institution, 2012.

———. *The Last Freedom: Religion from the Public School to the Public Square*. Princeton, NJ: Princeton University, 2009.

Voice, Paul. *Rawls Explained: From Fairness to Utopia*. Chicago: Open Court, 2011.

Volf, Miroslav. "A Voice of One's Own—Public Faith in a Pluralistic World." In *Democracy and the New Religious Pluralism*, edited by Thomas Banchoff. New York: Oxford University Press, 2007.

Vroom Hendrik M. *A Spectrum of Worldviews: An Introduction to Philosophy of Religion in a Pluralistic World*. New York: Rodopi, 2006.

Waldron, Jeremy. "Lecture 2: What Does a Well-Ordered Society Look Like?" Holmes Lectures, Harvard Law School, 2009. http://www.law.nyu.edu/sites/default/files/ECM_PRO_063313.pdf.

Waligore, Timothy. "Race, Rawls, Self-Respect, and Assurance: How Past Injustice Changes What Publicly Counts as Justice." https://www.academia.edu/1905110/Race_Raw_Self- Respect_and_Assurance_How_Past_Injustice_Changes_What_Publicly_Counts_as_Justice.

Walker, Allan, Shuanye Chen, and Haiyan Qian. "Leader Development across Three Chinese Societies." In *International Handbook on the Preparation and Development of School Leaders*, edited by Jacky Lumby et al. London: Routledge, 2009.

Walker, Lawrence J., et al. "Reasoning about Morality and Real-Life Moral Problems." In *Morality in Everyday Life: Developmental Perspectives*, edited by Melanie Killen and Daniel Hart. New York: Cambridge University Press, 1999.

Walsh, Thomas G. "Religion, Peace and the Post-Secular Public Sphere." *International Journal on World Peace* 29.2 (2012) https://www.questia.com/library/journal/1P3-2718515531/religion-peace-and-the-post-secular-public-sphere.

Waluchow, Wil. "Constitutionalism." In *Stanford Encyclopedia of Philosophy*, edited by Edward N. Zalta. Stanford, CA: Stanford University, Metaphysics Research Lab, Spring 2014 edition. http://plato.stanford.edu/archives/spr2014/entries/constitutionalism/.

Wang, Fan. "Ethnic Diversity and Economic Growth in China." Oguzhan Dincer, Department of Economics, Illinois State University. http://economics.illinoisstate.edu/odincer/Diversity&GrowthinChina.pdf.

Wattles, Jeffrey. "What Is Pluralism?" Kent, OH: Kent State University, 2002. http://www.wabashcenter.wabash.edu/syllabi/w/wattles/mdiverse.htm.

Wee, Sui-Lee. "U.N. Official Calls China's Crackdown on Uighurs "Disturbing."" *Reuters* (11 March 2015). http://www.reuters.com/article/us-chinaunxinjiangid USKBN0M723520150311.

Wegner, Gerhard. *Political Failure by Agreement: Learning Liberalism and the Welfare State*. Northampton, MA: Elgar, 2008.

Weihan, Li. "Guangyu minju gongzhuo zong jiao wenti." Tongyi zhanxian wenti yu minzuwenti,. Beijing: Renmin, 2004.

Weiler-Harwell, Nina. *Discrimination against Atheists: A New Legal Hierarchy among Religious Beliefs*. The Circuit Court of Appeals for the Eighth Circuit. El Paso TX: LFB Scholarly, 2011.

Weithman, Paul J. "Rawlsian Liberalism and the Privatization of Religion: Three Theological Objections Considered." *Journal of Religious Ethics* 22 (1994) 3–28.

————. *Rawls, Political Liberalism and Reasonable Faith.* New York: Cambridge University, 2010.

————. *Why Political Liberalism? On John Rawls's Political Turn.* New York: Oxford University, 2011.

Weihong, Luo. *Christianity in China.* Translated by Zhu Chengming. Beijing: Intercontinental, 2004.

Weitz, Richard. *Global Security Watch—China.* Santa Barbara, CA: Praeger, 2013.

Welcome to France. "Education." Different Types of Schools section. https://www.welcometofrance.com/en/education.

Wells, David F., ed. *Reformed Theology in America: A History of Its Modern Development.* Grand Rapids: Eerdmans, 1985.

Wenar, Leif. "John Rawls." In *Stanford Encyclopedia of Philosophy*, edited by Edward N. Zalta. "3.4 Political Conceptions of Justice" section. Stanford, CA: Stanford University, Metaphysics Research Lab., 2017. https://plato.stanford.edu/entries/rawls/.

Westlake, Robert, and Kees van Ruitenbeek. *Dutch International Schools Annual Report.* http://www.dutchinternationalschools.nl/wp-content/uploads/2017/03/DutchInternational-Schools-Annual-Report-2016.pdf.

Wickeri, Philip L. "Christianity in China: Secularization, Diversity, and Social Harmony." *Ecumenical Review* 67.1 (2015) http://www.questia.com/read/1G1-417471912/christianity-in-china-secularization-diversity.

————. *Reconstructing Christianity in China: K. H. Ting and the Chinese Church.* Maryknoll, NY: Orbis, 2015.

Wikeri, Philip L., and Yik-Fai Tam. "The Religious Life of Ethnic Minority Communities." In *Chinese Religious Life*, edited by David A. Palmer et al., 50–67. New York: Oxford University Press, 2011.

Williams, Rowan. Rome Lecture: "Secularism, Faith and Freedom" (23 November 2006). http://rowanwilliams.archbishopofcanterbury.org/articles.php/1175/rome-lecturesecularism-faith-and-freedom/.

Wilson, Jamie J. *Civil Rights Movement.* Santa Barbara, CA: Greenwood, 2013.

Wissenburg, Marcel. *Political Pluralism and the State: Beyond Sovereignty.* London: Routledge, 2009.

Wohlrab-Sahr, Monika. "Integrating Different Pasts, Avoiding Different Futures? Recent Conflicts about Islamic Religious Practice and Their Judicial Solutions." *Time Society* 13.1 (March 2004).

Woldring, Henk E. S. "The Quest for Truth and Human Fellowship in a Pluralist Society." *Truth and Human Fellowship* (n.d.). http://maritain.nd.edu/ama/Truth/Truth306.pdf/.

Wolterstorff, Nicholas. "Abraham Kuyper (1837–1920)." In *Teachings of Modern Christianity on Law, Politics, and Human Nature*, Vol. 1, edited by John Witte, Jr. and Frank S. Alexander. New York: Columbia University Press, 2006.

————. "Why Can't We All Just Get Along with Each Other?" In *Religious Voice in Public Places*, edited by Nigel Biggar and Linda Hogan. Cary, NC: Oxford University Press, 2009. DOI:10.1093/acprof:oso/9780199566624.003.0002.

————. *Understanding Liberal Democracy: Essays in Political Philosophy.* Edited by Terence Cuneo. Oxford: Oxford University Press, 2012.

———. "Rights and Wrongs: An Interview with Nicholas Wolterstorff." In *Moral Issues and Christian Responses*, edited by Patricia Beattie Jung and Loyle Shannon Jung. Nashville, TN: Fortress, 2013.

Wolterstorff, Nicholas, and Robert Audi. *Religion in the Public Square: The Place of Religious Convictions in Political Debate*. Lanham, MD: Rowman & Littlefield, 2000.

Woo, Wing Thye. *The Challenges of Governance Structure, Trade Disputes and Natural Environment to China's Growth*. Studies & Analyses No. 349. Warsaw: Center for Social and Economic Research, 2007.

Wood, Kay. *Education: The Basics*. London: Routledge, 2011.

World Report 2014: China Events of 2013. https://www.hrw.org/worldreport/2014/countrychapters/china-and-tibet.

World Watch Monitor. "China: Woman Buried Alive in Church Demolition." (19 April 2016). https://www.worldwatchmonitor.org/coe/4194126/4382787/4419559/.

Wright, Arthur. *Buddhism in Chinese History*. Stanford: Stanford University Press, 1959.

Wu, Annie. "Chinese Poetry." *China Highlights* (25 January 2015). http://www.chinahighlights.com/travelguide/culture/chinese-poetry.htm.

Wu, Harry. "Classicide in Communist China." *Comparative Civilizations Review* 67 (2012) 102–6.

Xiaobing Li. *Civil Liberties in China*. Santa Barbara, CA: ABC-Clio, 2010.

Xiaowen, Ye. "Shiji Zhijiao zhongjiao gongchuo de Sikao" [Reflections on the religious work at the change of millenium] *Zhongguo Zhongjiao* [Religion in China] 20.1 (2000) 4–9.

Xie, Zhibin. *Religious Diversity and Public Religion in China*. Burlington, VT: Ashgate, 2006.

Xinping, Zhuo. "Religion and Rule of Law in China Today." *Brigham Young University Law Review* 3 (2009) 519–27.

Xinyuan, Li. *Yi Ge Bu Xin Pai de Biaoben, Ding Guanxun Jinzuo Pingxi: An Example of Unbelief, Analysis of Ding Guangxun's Latest Works*. Chicago: Christian Life, 1999.

Yang, C. K. *Religion in Chinese Society*. Berkeley, CA: University of California Press, 1961.

Yang, Fenggang. "Miraculous Numbers." In "Cracks in The Atheist Edifice." Safety in numbers section (1 November 2013). https://www.economist.com/news/briefing/21629218-rapidspreadchristianity-forcing-official-rethink-religion-cracks, 2013.

———. "Oligopoly Dynamics and the Triple Religious Markets in China." In *Future of Religious Freedom: Global Challenges*, edited by Allen D. Hertzke. New York: Oxford University Press, 2013.

———. "The Other Chinese Miracle: Great Awakening Shifts Growth of Global Christianity to the East." Global Plus: Religion in China, *The Association of Religion Data Archives* (1 December 2015). http://globalplus.thearda.com/globalplus-religion-n-china/.

———. *Religion in China: Survival and Revival under Communist Rule*. New York: Oxford University Press, 2012.

———. "A Research Agenda on Religious Freedom in China." *Institute for Global Engagement* 11.2 (Summer 2013) 6–17.

Yao, Xinzhong. *An Introduction to Confucianism*. New York: Cambridge University Press, 2000.

Ye Cheng. "A 'Homogeneous' China?" *Davidson in China*, 15 September 2012. http://china.davidson.edu/news/a-homogeneous-china/.

Yip, Ka-che. "China and Christianity: Perspectives on Missions, Nationalism, and the State in the Republican Period, 1912–1949." In *Missions, Nationalism, and the End of Empire*, edited by Brian Stanley and Alaine Low. Grand Rapids: Eerdmans, 2004.

Young, Shaun P. "Rawlsian Reasonableness: A Problematic Presumption?" *Canadian Journal of Political Science / Revue Canadienne De Science Politique* 39.1 (2006) 159–80. http://www.jstor.org/stable/25165924.

Yousef, Asma. "Role of Religion in Education." *Washington Report on Middle East Affairs* (28 February 2001). http://www.questia.com/read/1P3592501221/roleof-religion-ineducation.

Yovel, Yirmiyahu. *Spinoza and Other Heretics: The Adventures of Immanence*. Princeton, NJ: Princeton University, 1989.

Yu, Shiao-ling. "Politics and Theatre in the PRC: Fifty Years of Teahouse on the Chinese Stage." *Asian Theatre Journal* 30.1 (2013) 90–121.

Zemin, Jiang. "Gaodu Zhongshi Minzu Gongzhuo He Zhongjiao Gongzhuo." In Documentation Centre of Party Centraland Policy Section of Religious Affairs Bureau, edited by Xinsichi Zongjiao and Gongzuo Wensin Xuanbiam. Beijing: Zhongjiao Wenhua, 1995.

Zeng, Hang-li. "A Brief Analysis of the Classical Poetry Chinese–English Translation: From the Perspective of 'Beauty in Three Aspects.'" *Sino-US English Teaching* 7.2 (2010) 52–58.

Zhang, Jing. "Cultivating Moral Competence of Chinese Undergraduates with KMDD Sessions." *Ethics in Progress* 4.1 (2013) 48–56.

Zheng, Yongnian. "Can the Communist Party Sustain Its Rule in China?" In *Power and Sustainability of the Chinese State*, edited by Keun Lee et al. London: Routledge, 2009.

Zhihong, Zeng, and Zeng Xiaoying. "Inclusive Development: The Mode of Equalization of Basic Public Cultural Service in Chinese Urban and Rural Areas." *Cross Cultural Communication* 9.5 (2013) 23–29.

Zhong, Yang. "Between God and Caesar: The Religious, Social, and Political Values of Chinese Christians." *Problems of Post-Communism* 60.3 (2013) 36–48. DOI: 10.2753/PPC1075-8216600303.

Zhou, Jinghao. *China's Peaceful Rise in a Global Context: A Domestic Aspect of China's Road Map to Democratization*. Lanham, MD: Lexington, 2010.

———. *Chinese vs. Western Perspectives: Understanding Contemporary China*. Lanham, MD: Lexington, 2013.

———. "Religious Education in China." In *Routledge International Handbook of Religious Education,* edited by Derek Davis and Elena Miroshnikova. London: Routledge, 2013.

———. "The Role of Chinese Christianity in the Process of China, Democratization." *American Journal of Chinese Studies* 13.1 (2006) 117–36. https://www.jstor.org/stable/44288819.

Zhu, Han. "China's Pluralistic Revolution." Translated by Li Jingrong (26 May 2013). http://www.china.org.cn/opinion/2013-05/26/content_28924995.htm.

Zhufeng, Luo, ed. *Religion under Socialism in China*. Translated by Donald E. Macinnis and Zheng Xi'an. Armonk, NY: Sharpe, 1991.

Zieba, Maciej. "The Temple in the Polis." In *A Free Society Reader: Principles for the New Millennium*, edited by Michael Nochavak et al. Lenham, MD: Lexington, 2000.

Zimmerman, Yvonne C. *Other Dreams of Freedom: Religion, Sex, and Human Trafficking.* New York: Oxford University Press, 2013.

Zongci, Wu. *The Provisional Constitution of the Republic of China and Its Origins.* Taipei City, Taiwan: Zhongzheng, 1978.

Zucca, Lorenzo. "RELIGARE: The Central Conflict." In *Belief, Law and Politics: What Future for a Secular Europe?* edited by Katayoun Alidadi et al. Burlington, VT: Ashgate, 2014.

Zuckerman, Phil. "The Secular Life." *Psychology Today* (28 July 2004). https://www.psychologytoday.com/blog/the-secularlife/201407/whatdoes-secular-mean.

———. "What Does 'Secular' Mean? It Means Being Non-Religious. But What Does That Mean?" *The Secular Life, Psychology Today* (28 July 2014). https://ww.psychologytoday.com/blog/the-secular-life/201407/what-doessecular-mean.

Zúñiga, Didier. "What's Wrong with Charles Taylor's Moral Pluralism." *Ithaque* 17 (2015) 21–43.